Arguments

and

Arguing

The Products and Process of
Human Decision Making

D0465383

Arguments

and

Arguing

The Products and Process of Human Decision Making

Thomas A. Hollihan
University of Southern California

Kevin T. Baaske
California State University, Los Angeles

WAVELAND
PRESS, INC.
Prospect Heights, Illinois

For information about this book, write or call:
   Waveland Press, Inc.
   P.O. Box 400
   Prospect Heights, Illinois 60070
   (847) 634-0081

Acknowledgments

"A Model for Systems Analysis," from pages 3–4 of *Public Policy Decision-Making: Systems Analysis and Comparative Advantage Debate* by Bernard L. Brock. Copyright © 1973 by Harper & Row Publishers, Inc. Reprinted by permission of HarperCollins Publishers, Inc.

Bill Clinton's presidential nomination acceptance speech, used with permission, Democratic National Committee.

George Bush's presidential nomination acceptance speech, used with permission, Republican National Committee.

Final round of the Cross Examination Debate Association National Tournament, from *Championship Debates and Speeches*, Vol. 7, 1993, by American Forensic Association.

Preface

Arguments and Arguing: The Products and Process of Human Decision Making is intended to meet the needs of students enrolled in undergraduate courses in argumentation. Because the text also introduces students to rhetorical theory, and to several of the most important theorists, it may also be suitable for courses in rhetoric. The book offers chapters on arguing in specialized fields and contexts, including: academic debate, courts of law, political campaigns, business and organizations, and interpersonal communication. Thus, it may also be of interest to those seeking materials for courses in these areas.

Why This Book at This Time?

This book, probably like many textbooks, was born as much from a sense of frustration as one of inspiration. The frustration developed because the books available to us did not really suit the approach that we took to our classes. We both teach argumentation at the undergraduate and graduate level. There are many very fine undergraduate argumentation texts available. However, there seemed to be a profound gap between the materials available for undergraduate classes and the recent argumentation scholarship being published in our journals, presented at our conferences, and taught in graduate courses. Most undergraduate texts do not discuss the contemporary theoretical developments in argumentation, and if they do discuss them, they seem to do so only by appending a small explanation of these developments to an already completed manuscript. In essence, most books are not written from any particular theoretical perspective. We hope that you will find our book different.

Ours is the first undergraduate text to embrace the narrative or storytelling approach to the study of argumentation. The narrative approach has attracted significant attention from argumentation theorists and critics for several years, but it has not been the organizing focus of an undergraduate text. Most argumentation books emphasize the "formal" aspects of reasoning. They are written as if their audience was composed almost exclusively of debaters, and as if academic debate was the paradigm for how arguments should be conducted. We think this approach misleads students, and makes learning about argumentation seem unimportant or artificial. Many students will never engage in formal debating, and most will not do so once they leave college. Yet all students will argue throughout their lives.

While this book also teaches some of the techniques and principles of debate, it assumes that debate is but one forum for creating and evaluating arguments. This book emphasizes that arguments exist wherever humans interact, and that the process of arguing is therefore as humanly natural as is eating or sleeping. This book refutes the assumption that rhetorical theory, argumentation, interpersonal communication, and persuasion are separate and unconnected subfields. It stresses their relationship and the ways in which their subject matter overlaps. Finally, the book tries to engage students by offering clear, compelling, and current examples of the principles that are discussed.

The Organizational Plan

Arguments and Arguing is organized into two parts. Part I discusses the general principles and theories of argumentation. It introduces the narrative approach to argumentation, and draws heavily on Walter Fisher's narrative paradigm. We also discuss Kenneth Burke's dramatistic theory of communication, especially his discussions of the importance of the symbol as an instrument for communication. To establish the claim that arguments are a naturally occurring dimension of communication, we cite the work of Wayne Brockriede. These early chapters also draw upon Karl Wallace and Milton Rokeach in exploring how values shape arguments, and on Chaim Perelman in discussing the importance of audience. We also introduce Stephen Toulmin's notion of argument fields at this juncture to support our view that arguments should be adapted to particular audiences and contexts. The remaining chapters in Part I look at how arguments are actually developed. We examine alternative techniques for analysis, different types of arguments, and the grounds for establishing arguments. Finally, we offer suggestions both for creating and refuting arguments.

In Part II we introduce the different characteristics and requirements for creating arguments in specialized field contexts. One chapter familiarizes students with academic debate; a second, for students expecting to participate in tournament-type debating, deals with the more complex issues of debate theory. The remaining chapters discuss the unique requirements for arguing in political campaigns, the courtroom, business or organizations, or in interpersonal conversations.

Acknowledgments

This book has been influenced by many people, including those who taught us about arguments, our colleagues (with whom we have argued!), and the many students whom we have taught how to argue. We are reluctant to name people individually, for we will surely omit someone, but there are some people who must be mentioned. We would especially like to thank: Jim Klumpp, Walt Fisher, Stephen O'Leary, and Randy Lake, colleagues who give meaning to the term "collegiality." We are grateful to the following reviewers: Jeffery L. Bineham, St. Cloud State University; Pat Ganer, Cypress College; Steven R. Goldzwig, Marquette University; Dale A. Herbeck, Boston College; Jack Kay, Wayne State University; and Robert Powell, California State University, Fresno. Patti Riley deserves a special thank you for her countless ideas, helpful feedback, and supreme patience. A special thank you also to Nancy Baaske for her support and assistance.

Jane Lambert served as our editor, supervising the preparation of the manuscript in its formative stages. Nancy Lyman assumed responsibility next, and actually made sure that the finished product made it to the presses. We would like to thank both of them for their help.

Finally, and most importantly, we would like to thank Alexandra and Sean Hollihan, and Megan Baaske, who had to defer many weekends of fun until after their Dads got this book finished.

T.A.H.
K.T.B.
Los Angeles, California

Contents

PART II Argumentation in Specialized Fields 141

10 Basic Academic Debate 143

11 Advanced Academic Debate 161

12 Argumentation in Political Campaigns 179

13 Argumentation and the Law 192

Arguments

and

Arguing

The Products and Process of
Human Decision Making

PART I

Principles of Argumentation

Our goal in this book is to demonstrate the important role that arguments play in helping you to understand complex issues, form opinions, shape decisions, and resolve disagreements. We therefore present argumentation as an essential dimension of the human communication process. Part I of the book introduces you to argumentation theory and principles, and Part II considers the unique characteristics of argumentation in specialized fields or contexts.

In Chapter 1 we introduce the notion that humans rely on symbols to create and share meanings. Because humans create different meanings and hold different opinions, the urge to argue is natural. This chapter focuses on the different meanings of the term argument, the importance of argumentation in decision making, and the role that our values play in the arguments we develop. Finally, Chapter 1 discusses the importance of ethics in argumentation.

Chapter 2 examines the stories people use to structure and create their arguments. These stories help people to understand and evaluate arguments, and provide an important means for using arguments to explore complex issues.

Chapter 3 makes the case that because arguments are typically generated to influence someone's opinions or actions and are shaped by human values, arguers should consider the beliefs or values of their audience when creating their claims.

Arguments are, of course, expressed through language. In Chapter 4 we focus on the linguistic dimensions of arguments. Specifically, this chapter looks at our use of linguistic devices in the creation and evaluation of stories.

In Chapter 5 we consider the role that argumentation plays in the development of critical thinking skills. This chapter discusses different strategies used in

1

argumentative analysis, and offers recommendations that will sharpen your analytical skills.

Chapter 6 discusses different types of arguments, focusing on the differences between inductive and deductive claims. This chapter also introduces the syllogism, and offers insight into how arguments can be diagrammed.

In Chapter 7 our attention turns to the grounds for argument. We include here a discussion of how arguments are discovered and how they are evaluated. This chapter considers the different types of grounds available to arguers, and also contains a brief discussion of the unique challenge that the use of statistical support poses.

Chapters 8 and 9 are really companion chapters. In Chapter 8 we focus on the process of building arguments. The chapter discusses the importance of research, offers recommendations for conducting research, suggests strategies for note-taking, and gives advice on how to organize your findings into arguments. Chapter 9 then focuses on refuting arguments, or the process of undermining the argumentative claims advanced by others. This chapter also discusses some very common fallacies (arguments that are logically flawed), and provides advice on how fallacies can be identified.

By the time you have finished Part I of *Arguments and Arguing* you should have a well formed understanding of the component parts and principles of argumentation. This groundwork should prepare you for the discussion of the unique traits of argumentation in specialized settings that is offered in Part II.

1

Argumentation as a Human Symbolic Activity

The feature that most distinguishes humans from other creatures is their capacity for using **symbols.**[1] Symbols might be defined as special types of signs. As the name implies, "signs call attention to *sig*nificances: they relate to what has been perceived; they point to, indicate, or denote something other than themselves."[2] Symbols are the primary building blocks of our language system, and they allow us to name objects, emotions, and actions, and to share our thoughts and feelings with others. The ability to share in a symbol system permits us to build social communities and to jointly solve problems in order to improve the quality of our lives. This symbolic capacity also puts us in touch with the past. Through the sharing of significant symbols, both orally in the form of stories, and through personal journals, books, manuscripts, and even films, we learn of the events, values, and experiences of those who lived before us. Thus, humans have the complex and sophisticated ability to symbolically experience the past and to anticipate the future.

As symbol users we are constantly seeking ways to improve the quality of our lives. No matter how satisfying our current situation, we are apt to imagine ways in which our lives, our society, and our world can be improved. Much of our symbolic "tinkering" is designed to achieve such improvements. We also continually encounter problems that we believe must be resolved. We seek material rewards so that we can live both more comfortably and free from want. We encounter diseases that cut short lives and so we try to find cures. We witness problems in our schools and so we seek ways to improve our educational system. We see the personal and social destruction caused by drug abuse and we look for solutions. We see damage to our environment and we look for ways to conserve and better manage our resources. In all of these activities, we use symbols to name the problems that we face, to develop common understandings, and to propose and evaluate solutions.

Because humans are fundamentally social beings, we derive satisfaction from our interactions with others. Throughout history humans have improved their

3

condition in life by pooling their knowledge and sharing their discoveries with each other. Despite this instinctive pull to interact with other people and to build social communities, we often pursue objectives that seem fundamentally incompatible with those that are pursued by others. In our personal and public lives, in relationships between friends and lovers, and in relationships between nations and cultures, our problems sometimes seem so great as to be insolvable—beyond compromise, beyond accommodation.

Our collective experience, the accumulated understanding of history, demonstrates that when communication fails and people cannot reach accommodations with each other, the potential for misunderstanding, conflict, and even war dramatically increases. The situations that spark conflict will never disappear. Thus, learning how to reach understanding, how to identify, analyze, name, and then solve the problems that we individually and collectively face is essential if we wish to live in harmony.

This book provides the communication skills required for human problem solving and decision making and for the maintenance of effective and harmonious social relations. This book is about **arguments**—the claims that people make when they are asserting their opinions and supporting their beliefs—and **arguing**—the process of resolving differences of opinion through communication.

Senses of the Term *Argument*

Two different, but equally important, senses of the term *argument*[3] correspond to two of argument's most important objectives—effective decision making and the achievement of social harmony. The first, which can be called *Argument1*, refers to the claims that people make. As we have mentioned, when people encounter problems they seek solutions. To find solutions they must consider the causes of the problems, and they must weigh the costs and benefits of different solutions. Advances in all aspects of human intellectual life evidence the creativity and the reasoning capacity of human decision makers. Our intense desire to understand our world and to improve our condition in it, combined with our ability to reason and to argue, prompts us to assert our knowledge claims—in essence, testing them out through this exposure.

We know that people respond to problems in a variety of ways. As a result of differences in their experience, culture, education, values, interests, objectives, and so forth, people will isolate different problems and propose different solutions. These different opinions compete for acceptance within society. We also know that not all opinions are deemed equal. Some ideas seem more credible and compelling than others, and some people are granted more credibility than others. Just as people's differences cause them to respond to problems differently, they will also evaluate arguments differently. The "marketplace of ideas" is thus a marketplace of competing arguments, where the "sellers"—arguers hawking their worldviews—seek to find "buyers" who will accept their claims. Eventually, some arguments win support and perhaps gain wide public agreement, while other arguments fall by the wayside and are eventually forgotten. Why some arguments win support while others fail is among the primary issues discussed in this book.

The second sense of the term argument, which can be called *Argument2*, refers not to the statements and claims that people make, but rather to the type of interactions in which these claims are developed. This sense of the term *argument* refers to an interaction characterized by disagreement. To argue with someone is to have a dispute with them. From this perspective, an argument does not exist until some person perceives what is happening as an argument.[4] Most textbooks in argumentation emphasize the first sense of the term argument and not the second sense. These books primarily want to help people learn how to become better arguers, meaning more insightful or analytical arguers. While this is also one of our primary goals, we believe that the second sense of the term argument is also important. The ability to conduct a civilized and polite argument with someone—the ability to argue and disagree with someone while also managing to protect your relationship with them—is one of the most important things that people must learn.

Often, people are taught that they should avoid arguing with others. In our society, arguments are often seen as unhealthy and destructive. Our language system itself is predisposed toward agreement, and those who choose to argue are often viewed as disagreeable or even unpleasant.[5] These people are often described as argumentative, which is certainly not a flattering term. We believe, however, that arguing can be healthy both for relationships and for societies. People argue to negotiate their social perspective with others and to enhance their understanding of complex problems. Our primary concern is that people learn how to argue constructively. Constructive arguments permit disagreements to surface so that people can examine alternative ways of viewing problems, identify different solutions, and select from the competing positions those that are most compelling.

These two senses of the term argument may be summarized as follows:

Argument1: Claims that people make.
> *Example:* The United States has a moral obligation to send troops to Bosnia to protect the lives of Muslims.

Argument2: Types of interactions in which people engage.
> *Example:* The dispute that would occur when someone disagreed with the above stated claim by, for instance, responding that the United States cannot always play the role of the world's peacekeeper, and that European nations should step in and protect the Muslims.

It is possible to make arguments (argument1) without engaging in disputes or disagreements (argument2). If we agreed on the need to send U.S. troops to Bosnia, for example, there would be no argument2. However, it is not possible to have disputes (argument2) without making knowledge claims (argument1). Disagreements are therefore expressed through argument1.

The distinction offered here between argument1 and argument2 is important because it illustrates that argumentation is not merely a problem-solving capability. Argumentation is a very basic social and communication skill, and it has profound importance for the quality and character of our interactions with others.

Argumentation and Individual Decision Making

We are continually compelled to make decisions in our personal lives. What college should I attend? What should be my major? Should I buy a car? Do I have the money to take the vacation that my friends are planning? For whom should I vote? Should I accept the job offer that will require me to move across the country and away from my friends and family? All of these decisions, and thousands like them that we make every day, test our analytical and argumentative abilities. Whenever we are compelled to carefully consider alternative choices and to make decisions, we make use of arguments. Thus, as a problem-solving activity, argumentation may involve decisions and choices that are distinctly intrapersonal in nature, issues that will never be disclosed to or discussed with others.

Often, however, we are called upon to discuss and account for our decisions. In such discussions we explain our actions to those people whose opinions matter to us. We want them to understand why we made the choices that we made. We make our choices based upon our understanding of the world and of the problems we face. We strive to be rational, and we want others to validate our rationality and to confirm that our choices were, in fact, the right ones. Most of us are accountable to others for many of the choices that we make. Obviously we are accountable to our parents; even after most of us have become adults we are driven by the desire to please them and to make them proud of us. We are also accountable to other family members, to employers, to coworkers, and to our friends. Thus, even intensely personal decisions must be argued out with an assumed audience in mind.

Argumentation and Democratic Decision Making

The ability to argue is a fundamental survival skill for life in a democracy. The ability to argue for the positions that you believe to be true is one important way that citizens are empowered. Our democratic political system assumes that citizens have the knowledge and the ability to decide complex issues for themselves, and the system's continued health and vitality depends upon the respect that citizens have for each other and for the democratic process. Democratic decision making requires an informed, capable, and interested citizenry.

The preservation of democracy also demands that people meet certain accepted standards of civility and decorum in their public lives. It is unseemly when our political candidates level their negative attacks and scurrilous charges at each other. Certainly we would not wish to see all of our argumentative interactions degenerate to such a point that they resemble arguments between umpires and managers in major league baseball.

As citizens of a democratic nation we surrender certain powers to those whom we elect to govern. We acknowledge the right of these officials to set limits on how fast we may drive, to assess taxes that we must pay, to determine what chemicals we may freely ingest, and so forth. The elected officials must, however, convince us that they are acting in our best interests, for if a majority of our citizenry (or even a substantial, well organized and vocal minority) decided not to accept the legitimacy of the established political order, or the correctness, fairness, and justice of the laws, our society would quickly disintegrate.

Given that people do not always agree, and that there are always differences of opinion regarding the course of action that our government policy should take, argumentation is the primary means for shaping the course of public policy. As citizens, we participate in public debates, express our opinions, listen to and evaluate the arguments made by competing politicians. Ultimately, we pledge our support to one candidate or another, and to one political position or another, by the way that we cast our vote. Lively public arguments occur around almost all complex policy issues that shape our daily lives. Issues such as abortion, gun control, or capital punishment, for example, are sure to spark spirited debates. Political candidates seek to create arguments that will attract public support and win elections. They must listen to the public's arguments in order to understand and to best carry out the will of their constituents. The very formation and deliberation of public policy centers around the evaluation of public arguments in legislative hearings and in debates on the floor of Congress, in state legislatures, or in city council chambers.

Argumentation skills are important for our political life because they enable us to express our opinions in a coherent manner, so that we can make ourselves understood, and thus convince others that they should share our beliefs. These skills are also important, however, because we must be consumers and critics of public arguments. People who understand argumentation principles are more careful and critical audiences for arguments. We are exposed to a myriad of different arguments on a daily basis. Advertisers, political leaders, newspaper reporters, and so forth, all attempt to influence our opinions. Knowledge of argumentation theory should make you a more skeptical listener who is better able to analyze the merits of the arguments that you hear. Obviously such knowledge will make for a better informed electorate—one that is less susceptible to the deceptive or exaggerated claims made by political demagogues.

Argumentation and Values

As we have mentioned, people are continually trying to make sense of their worlds by naming and structuring their experiences. Kenneth Burke, a noted rhetorical theorist and literary critic, observed:

One constructs his [sic] notion of the universe or history, and shapes attitudes in keeping. Be he poet or scientist, one defines the "human situation" as amply as his imagination permits; then, with this ample definition in mind, he singles out certain functions or relationships as either friendly or unfriendly. If they are deemed friendly, he prepares himself to welcome them; if they are deemed unfriendly, he weighs objective resistances against his own resources, to decide how far he can effectively go in combating them. . . . Our philosophers, poets and scientists act in the code of names by which they simplify or interpret reality. These names shape our relations with our fellows. They prepare us for some functions and against others, for or against the persons representing these functions. The names go further: they suggest how you shall be for or against. Call a man a villain, and you have the choice of either attacking or cringing. Call him mistaken, and you invite yourself to attempt setting him right.[6]

The very act of naming—the choice of one symbolic referent over another—helps to form our attitudes and **values.** It thus should come as no surprise that all arguments, to some extent, concern human values.

Certainly some arguments concern more important or substantive values than do others. For example, an argument about who makes the best pizza in town may center on the value of thin versus thick crust. Perhaps to the true pizza afficionado this is a value of great significance, but most of us can enjoy both thick- and thin-crusted pizzas. On the other hand, an argument about abortion will involve assessments of such competing values as a woman's right to privacy versus the need to protect the life of the unborn. These are certainly more significant and complex value questions.

The declaration that all arguments concern human values does not, therefore, imply that all values are equally significant. Still, issues of value underlie virtually all concerns that people are inspired to argue about. This also means that some issues will prove especially difficult to resolve, because they reveal differences that are tied to people's very fundamental conceptions of themselves. Milton Rokeach defined values as "abstract ideals, positive or negative, not tied to any specific attitude, object or situation, representing a person's beliefs about ideal modes of conduct and ideal terminal goals."[7]

While persons hold many different attitudes and beliefs, Rokeach argued that they include only a few, perhaps a dozen or so, values.[8] Values are formed very early in our lives, and while they are certainly changed by our education and experiences, they are by and large stable touchstones from which we can draw lessons and create meanings for our experiences.[9] We learn values at the knees of our parents, from our schools, and from religious instruction. But, we also learn them merely by experiencing day-to-day life in our culture. Thus, to grow up in America is to be influenced by the American value system. However, there is not just one American value system, but many different and often competing conceptions of values that exist and even thrive in different communities. Thus, the values that guide daily life in the rural Midwest may be quite unlike those operating in an Eastern city, or in the suburbs of a Western city. There also may be important differences in values that are reflected in particular social economic experiences, ethnic communities, subgroups, or families. As a result, there is no one American value culture; instead there are many competing American cultures influencing public values.[10]

Values dramatically shape the arguments that people make and the arguments that they will find convincing. We argue in accordance with those truths that we accept.[11] These values are also influenced by people's sense of their interests. Because our values are shaped by the situations in which we find ourselves, our objective both in making and evaluating arguments will be to improve our place in the world and to reinforce our conceptions of ourselves. It makes intuitive sense, therefore, that young, single women may be more inclined to favor a pro-choice position on abortion, and that middle-aged and older men may be more inclined to oppose a woman's right to choose an abortion. It is reasonable to assume that poor citizens may be inclined to support increased government spending on social programs to help provide for human needs, while affluent citizens from the suburbs may be motivated to cut such programs in order to keep their taxes as low as they can. People are influenced by values, and their values are in part shaped by the particular problems and needs that they face as they attempt to create a more perfect and satisfying life for themselves and for their loved ones.

Acknowledging the role of human values in argumentation also helps make us aware that while arguments may be designed to reach the "truth," there may be more than one "truth." Our sense of what is true is shaped by our values and experiences. Thus, complex value questions are often complex precisely because there is no single true answer. Reasonable people can and do differ on issues such as abortion, capital punishment, euthanasia, and access to pornography. Any arguer who chooses to participate in the public dialogue on these issues must acknowledge the role of his or her values in shaping his or her arguments, and must also be aware that the persons with whom he or she is arguing may see the world through very different value structures.

The values that people hold also shape what claims they see as worthy of argument. The claim that the government should not concern itself with regulating the safety of food or prescription drugs might not spark much controversy at a convention of the American Libertarian party, but it would probably seem preposterous to most of the delegates at a Democratic party convention. Democratic delegates would probably not take this idea seriously, and thus might not even deem it worth arguing. For another example, Democrats might actively support legislation to increase the tariffs on all imported automobiles from Japan, while Republicans might support reducing the tariffs that are currently in place. The values that people hold function as lenses through which they view their world, and the way in which one views the world largely determines what one accepts as true and what one believes must be contested.

Values also play a dramatic role in determining argumentative sufficiency. It should be easier to convince a farmer that the government should set minimum price supports for agricultural products than to convince the urban consumer who would have to pay the resulting higher prices. The farmer presumably would value most the financial security for producers that the government price supports provide, while the consumer presumably would value most the competitive free market in which products are sold at the lowest possible prices. When people have fundamentally different values there will be more conflict, and it will be far more difficult to reach agreement. Likewise, an arguer facing an audience that holds fundamentally different values from his or her own will find it especially challenging to persuade that audience to support the positions that he or she is defending.

We often hear it claimed that when values come into conflict we might as well forget about arguments; that people cannot, or will not, reason about issues of value. While doing so is not easy, there is no satisfactory alternative to arguing about value differences.[12] We know from experience that value disagreements cannot be ignored, for if the differences are substantial they will eventually lead to conflict. The situation in the Middle East provides an example. The Israelis and their Arab neighbors have been in or near a state of war for almost fifty years as a result of unresolved conflicts concerning religious beliefs, cultural traditions, and historical divisions. Young Arabs and Israelis have been raised in a climate of fear and distrust. The creation and maintenance of an effective argumentative dialogue on such a problem, though enormously difficult, is clearly better than the alternative: a full-scale war that could kill thousands of people.

The fact that all arguments are to some extent shaped by human values suggests that we can reason about issues, even when those issues are characterized by profound differences in values.[13] Learning how to discover and account for those differences, how to accommodate people who hold values different from your own, while preserving a sense of civility and respect for them, will make for a far more hospitable and even safer world.

Ethics and Argumentation

The continuing references that we have made to the importance of maintaining a sense of civility and decorum in arguing reveals how important we believe the issue of **ethics** is for the student of argumentation theory and practice. Examining ethics in argumentation generally means examining the arguer's motives and means. Wayne Brockriede, a distinguished argumentation theorist, suggests that the images that arguers have of each other are particularly important in shaping the nature of argumentative exchanges. Brockriede proposes a metaphor to express this relationship.[14] He declares that some arguers are like rapists. These arguers see those with whom they are arguing as objects or as inferior human beings, and their intent is to manipulate or violate these objects. The rapist seeks to gain or to maintain a position of superiority—whether to make his or her case prevail or to put the other person down.

A second type of arguer is the seducer. Whereas the rapist conquers by force of argument, the seducer operates through charm or deceit. Like the rapist, the seducer thinks about himself or herself and not about the needs or interests of the person who is the target of the seduction. The intent of the seducer is to beguile the individual and thereby have his or her way with them.

The third arguer is the lover. Lovers differ from rapists and seducers, because they see the other person as human and not as an object, and because they want power parity, rather than a power advantage. Whereas rapists and seducers want immediate personal gratification, lovers want to develop continuing bilateral relationships. Because they have respect for those with whom they argue, lovers acknowledge that those persons have the intellect, ability, and wisdom to decide for themselves what they wish to believe after being exposed to all of the competing arguments. The lover also has self-respect. One who argues from this perspective risks himself or herself in the argumentative exchange. They put themselves on the line for the positions that they believe in, and they argue with a sense of genuineness and conviction that demonstrates argumentative integrity.

Professor Brockriede's metaphor of these different argument styles is persuasive. All of us would prefer to engage in arguments with people who value and respect us, rather than seeing us as objects only to be used. How can you create such a climate for argumentative encounters? We suggest a principle much akin to the "golden rule": "Do unto others as you would have them do unto you," or "if you want a friend, be one." While there will always be manipulative and unethical arguers in our midst, the best way to avoid interacting with them is to avoid becoming one yourself. If enough people embrace this philosophy there will be fewer unethical, deceptive, and coercive arguers in our society.

Ethical arguers are honest arguers. They seek to carefully discover and investigate the relevant facts. They do not misrepresent those facts, they do not conceal information that would cause people to interpret their arguments differently, and they do not attempt to persuade others to embrace positions or viewpoints that they themselves know are not true. Ethical arguers do not try to get people to do things that work against those people's best interests, or, at least, they freely acknowledge the possibility that if certain actions are taken they could prove incompatible with people's best interests.

Ethical arguers enter the argumentative marketplace with the assumption that the other persons already selling their own ideas there are persons of integrity and good will, persons who will be open to other ideas. They acknowledge that force and coercion do not lead to effective decisions, and that people will make the best decisions if given the opportunity to carefully and systematically consider the issues on both sides of a question.

Learning how to argue effectively means learning how to argue in an ethical and positive manner. Set high standards for yourself as an arguer and treat others with respect and dignity, and we believe that the people who interact with you will be more likely to treat you in the same way. In the process, the argumentative marketplace will become a more civilized and valuable place for the free exchange of ideas, and for the pursuit of policies and programs that will improve all our lives.

Summary

The ability to argue is necessary if people are to solve problems, resolve conflicts, and evaluate alternative courses of action. While many people are taught that arguing is a counterproductive activity and that arguments should be avoided, we believe that arguing is an essential and fundamental human activity. Learning how to argue effectively entails learning not just the strategies and principles of analysis and logical reasoning, but also the importance of arguing in a positive and socially constructive fashion.

Key Terms

arguing   ethics   values
arguments   symbols

Activities

1. Keep a log for a day. Record the occasions on which you were exposed to advocacy.
   a. How many times were you exposed to advocacy?
   b. What was the form of the advocacy? Was it written, oral, or nonverbal?
   c. What individual decisions were you called upon to make?
   d. What decisions were you called upon to make as a member of a democratic society?

2. Recall a recent situation in which you engaged in argumentation2 (an interaction characterized by disagreement).
   a. What was the point of disagreement?
   b. What values were reflected in your viewpoint? What values were reflected in the views of the other individual?
   c. How did you resolve the disagreement?
   d. Were you satisfied with the outcome of the interaction?

3. Go into a building on campus you have never entered before. As you walk through the building, try to get a sense of what takes place in the rooms. How is the building similar to others that are familiar to you? How is it different? What labels help you to make sense of this new experience?

4. Make a list of the five values you hold most dear. Now rank order them. Ask a friend, classmate, sibling, parent, or significant other to make a similar list.

Then compare the two lists.
a. How many values appear on both lists?
b. How similar were your rankings?
c. What accounts for the similarities?
d. What accounts for the dissimilarities?

Recommended Readings _____

Brockriede, Wayne. "Characteristics of Arguments and Arguing." *Journal of the American Forensic Association* 13 (1977): 129–132.

Cox, J. Robert and Charles Arthur Willard, eds. *Advances in Argumentation Theory and Research.* Carbondale: Southern Illinois University Press, 1982.

Ehninger, Douglas. "Argument as Method: Its Nature, Its Limitations and Its Uses." *Speech Monographs* 37 (1970): 101–110.

Goodnight, G. Thomas. "Toward a Social Theory of Argument." *Argumentation and Advocacy* 26 (1989): 60–70.

Trapp, Robert and Janice Schuetz, eds. *Perspectives on Argumentation: Essays in Honor of Wayne Brockriede.* Prospect Heights, IL: Waveland, 1990.

Willard, Charles Arthur. *A Theory of Argumentation.* Tuscaloosa: Alabama University Press, 1989.

Notes _____

1. Suzanne Langer declared, "[Language is] . . . that great systematic symbolism . . . that sets men apart from their zoological brethren. The line between animals and men is, I think, precisely the language line." Cited in: Joyce O. Hertzler, *A Sociology of Language* (New York: Random House, 1965), p. 21. See also: Kenneth Burke, *Language as Symbolic Action* (Berkeley: University of California Press, 1966), p. 3.
2. Joyce O. Hertzler, *A Sociology of Language* (New York: Random House, 1965), p. 28.
3. For a more complete discussion of this concept, see: Daniel J. O'Keefe, "Two Concepts of Argument," *Journal of the American Forensic Association* 13 (1976), pp. 121–28.
4. Wayne Brockriede, "Where is Argument?" *Journal of the American Forensic Association* 11 (1975), p. 179.
5. Sally Jackson and Scott Jacobs, "Structure of Conversational Argument: Pragmatic Bases for the Enthymeme," *Quarterly Journal of Speech* 66 (1980), pp. 251–65.
6. Kenneth Burke, *Attitudes Toward History* (Boston: Beacon Press, 1937, rpt. 1961), pp. 3–4.
7. Milton Rokeach, *Beliefs, Attitudes and Values* (San Francisco: Jossey-Bass, 1968), p. 124.
8. Rokeach, p. 124.
9. Rokeach, pp. 123–126.
10. Joseph W. Wenzel, "Toward a Rationale for Value-centered Argument," *Journal of the American Forensic Association* 13 (1977), pp. 150–158.
11. Malcolm O. Sillars and Patricia Ganer, "Values and Beliefs: A Systematic Basis for Argumentation," in J. Robert Cox and Charles Arthur Willard, eds., *Advances in Argumentation Theory and Research* (Carbondale: Southern Illinois University Press, 1982), pp. 184–201.

12. One of the most complete discussions of the role of values in human argumentation was offered by Chaim Perelman and L. Olbrechts-Tyteca. Their book, *The New Rhetoric: A Treatise on Argument* (Notre Dame: The University of Notre Dame Press, 1969), stresses how arguers can learn how to develop their argumentative skills so that they can improve the quality and criticism of argumentative claims in value disputes. See especially: pp. 54–114.
13. Nicholas Rescher, "The Study of Value Change," in E. Lazlo and J. B. Wilbur, eds., *Value Theory in Philosophy and Social Science* (New York: Gordon & Breach, 1973), pp. 14–16.
14. Wayne Brockriede, "Arguers as Lovers," *Philosophy and Rhetoric* 5 (1972), pp. 1–11.

2

The Foundations of Argument

Ill arguments have value implications because all arguments reflect the ways people construct their views of the world and give shape to their experiences. Consequently, an analysis of arguments will give us insights into the people who create them and the people who accept them as convincing.

People are constantly trying to make sense of the world and of the events they experience in their daily lives. Events acquire meaning for us as we think about them, interpret them, and most importantly, as we talk about them to others. It is through discussing our experiences that human culture is created, shared, and thereby recreated.

Human values develop as they do, largely because those who came before us have witnessed and learned the utility of living their lives in accordance with certain principles. Some of these principles are revealed through the teachings of religious prophets, priests, and other clergy. Other values are learned from proverbs, fables, and historical lessons. Still others are taught to us by parents, teachers, and civic leaders. Finally, our values are influenced by our experiences and our interactions with our friends. That people's values differ reflects how their experiences and cultures differ.

Our primary task in this chapter is to consider how values influence people's arguments and the argumentative marketplace. We believe that people come to understand their world and their values in **narrative** (or **storytelling**) form. Throughout our lives, we both hear and tell **stories.** Some stories we believe, enjoy, and find useful, and because we find them appealing we repeat them. Other stories we find unbelievable; these we discredit and discard. Through storytelling we give form to the world around us. These stories not only come to reflect our reality, they actually become our sense of what is real.

Some stories are simple and straightforward, like the proverbs we learn in childhood. All of us can probably recall the story of the three little pigs, one of whom built a house of straw, another of sticks, and a third of bricks. Only the pig

15

who took the time and effort to build the secure brick home had shelter when the strong winds came (in the form of a wolf with immense blowing ability). Obviously, the point of this story goes far beyond the relative merits of alternative porcine dwellings. The intended moral is that hard work will be rewarded, and that people, like pigs, need to exert the energy to prepare for their future. From such stories, children learn important lessons that should help them later in life.

Children learn by listening to and by telling stories not only moral lessons, but also how to reason in narrative form. As their intellects develop, and the problems they face become more complex, so too the stories that they tell become more complex, yet the nature of the narrative reasoning process remains fundamentally the same.

When President George Bush wanted to justify sending American troops to the Middle East to counter Iraq's aggression against Kuwait, he argued that troops were needed to prevent Saddam Hussein of Iraq from capturing Saudi Arabia and the other nations of the region, stealing their oil reserves, and oppressing their people. He claimed that Hussein was utterly ruthless and had no respect for the sanctity of human life. Hussein was said to have seized power by force, to have silenced all his critics, and to have used chemical weapons against the Kurdish citizens of his own nation.

Even these claims of brutality, however, would probably have been insufficient to justify American military intervention. There have been countless other brutal dictators in the world whom we not only tolerated, but befriended—men such as August Pinochet of Chile, or Ferdinand Marcos of the Philippines. How were the apparent inconsistencies between President Bush's intentions toward Hussein and these other stories reconciled?

The decision to send troops was justified in large part on the basis of arguments that likened the Iraqi ruler to Adolf Hitler. Hitler is recalled as perhaps the most notorious figure in history, embodying deliberate evil in its most horrific form. The claim that Hussein is another Hitler gains its power by encouraging the American people to recall the lessons of the World War II experience, lessons continually relived in the stories of that great conflict. These stories almost always begin with accounts of how the British Prime Minister, Neville Chamberlain, sought to appease Hitler and to negotiate with him in order to prevent a broader conflict. Ultimately, of course, Hitler could not be appeased and full scale war was necessary. Surely, the lessons of history relate, it would have been better had Great Britain, France, and the United States responded more aggressively to Hitler much earlier, before he had acquired so much power. Thus if we extend the comparison between Hitler and Hussein, it would seem far better to respond to Hussein's aggression before he manages to further consolidate his power and strengthen his control over captured Kuwait.[1]

The power of the "Hussein as Hitler" narrative is obvious. Hitler, the most heinous of modern villains, was capable of outrageous acts of genocide, and was completely beyond the reach of any rational argument. He was willing to destroy his own people and his own nation in the pursuit of his own delusional, grandiose plans. Hitler was stopped only by extreme force. If Hussein is akin to Hitler, then he is also an evil force who must be dealt with quickly and definitively. As was demonstrated as the crisis unfolded, arguments that asserted that Hussein was in reality not a mad Hitler clone, or that Iraq was no Nazi Germany seemed less persuasive because they lacked the narrative appeal of the Hitler analogy. As this example demonstrates, we continually seek understanding of world events on the basis of events that came before—events that we believe we understand and can account for—events understood and recalled through stories. This is reasoning through narrative structures.

Stories also serve an important formative purpose both for the people who choose to tell them and believe them, and ultimately for the cultures that come to accept them. For example, Americans have developed an understanding of their identity as a nation on the basis of stories about our founding fathers and, though far too infrequently, stories about our founding mothers. We learn of Benjamin Franklin's inventiveness and ingenuity, George Washington's honesty, Thomas Jefferson's concern for equality and Abraham Lincoln's humble origins and homespun style. That Benjamin Franklin and Thomas Jefferson were philanderers, George Washington a padder of expense accounts, and Abraham Lincoln a successful corporate attorney (representing the railroads—the most powerful corporations of the day) are less well remembered stories, because they serve our contemporary needs less well. In short, the stories that are retold time and again are those that fulfill contemporary needs. Because historical accounts that affirm America's moral greatness as a nation help instill patriotic values in our citizens, and because such accounts are sustained by our celebration of the morality of our founding fathers, such stories have wide appeal.

The telling and retelling of these stories of our birth as a nation, and the accounts of the personal lives and achievements of our founding fathers, invites collective identification among American citizens with their government. It also serves to help citizens identify the morally correct course of action. Thus it is to be expected that the freedom loving American people, the nation descended from the patriotic and selfless Washington, Franklin, and Jefferson will unite to help eliminate evil in the world, whether it resides in Saddam Hussein, Manuel Noriega, or any other puppet dictator intent on thwarting the free will of his or her people.

The confidence that we, as American citizens, have in the moral certainty of our actions is thus a result of our own narrative experience—we have created our world to fit our stories, as much as we have created the stories to fit our world. The purpose of this discussion is not to discredit the stories that make up American history, however; nor do we see the process as a negative one. All humans reason through narratives, which helps to explain why the citizens of Iraq, and apparently of many other Middle East nations, believe in the legitimacy of Iraq's takeover of Kuwait, and admire the courage of Saddam Hussein, a man whom we depict as the modern Hitler. Actions that seem so clearly reprehensible in one society are deemed fair and appropriate to another, making the process of international diplomacy and reasoned argument all the more difficult to conduct.

Even patriotic stories which seem so positive to the values of a political culture—such as the stories about Washington, Jefferson, Franklin and Lincoln mentioned earlier—may, however, have negative consequences. These stories may help to instill an unquestioning faith in the legitimacy of the American experience, an unwillingness to see our own faults, and a temptation to assume that our way is the best way.[2]

Before you surrender to the belief that all attempts at reasoned discourse are futile, however, it is important to recognize that it is quite possible for people to critique and evaluate the quality of the stories they hear and tell. Narrative arguments are rational arguments, and we can learn a great deal about how people reason through stories.

The Narrative Paradigm

We are exposed to literally hundreds of different stories in any given week. We hear stories in conversations with friends and family members, we hear them on the news, we watch them in television programs, and read them in books, newspapers, and magazines.

How do we determine which are true and should guide our lives, and which are not true and should be dismissed? One criteria is whether or not the stories were intended as fictions or not. However, the line between real and fictional accounts often becomes blurred. Some fictions come to be accepted as truths, and are especially useful in shaping our lives and helping us make sense of our experiences. Perhaps one of the best known examples of a work of fiction that was taken as truth was Harriet Beecher Stowe's classic novel *Uncle Tom's Cabin,* a story about the experiences of slavery told through the eyes of a slave family. This book had a tremendous impact on public attitudes towards slavery, and came to be accepted as fact, despite its fictional characters. Upon meeting Harriet Beecher Stowe, President Lincoln is purported to have said: "So this is the little lady who made this great war."[3]

People will accept stories as true if these stories speak to them, and account for their experiences. Walter R. Fisher has argued that people reason through narratives. He referred to this mode of reasoning as the narrative paradigm, which he summarized as follows:

> (1) Humans are . . . storytellers. (2) The paradigmatic mode of human decision making and communication is "good reasons," which vary in form among situations, genres, and media of communication. (3) the production and practice of good reasons are ruled by matters of history, biography, culture and character. . . . (4) Rationality is determined by the nature of persons as narrative beings— their inherent awareness of narrative probability, what constitutes a coherent story, and constant habit of testing narrative fidelity, whether or not the stories they experience ring true with the stories they know to be true in their lives. . . . (5) The world as we know it is a set of stories that must be chosen among in order for us to live life in a process of continual re-creation.[4]

Fisher claims that human reasoning need not be bound to argumentative prose, or to clear-cut inferential or implicative structures, because it is typically achieved through the stories that people tell. Viewed from this perspective, virtually all arguments can be understood and evaluated as stories. One of the most noteworthy aspects of this theory of argument is its assumption that ordinary people, people who are untrained in argumentation techniques, are capable of resolving complex problems because they reason through narrative structures. For purposes of clarification, we will look at both the "tests" of arguments, and the criteria for evaluating "good reasons" that Fisher mentions.

First, people assess arguments by evaluating their **narrative probability.** This concept refers to whether a story seems coherent. Is the argumentative structure of the story satisfying and complete? Does the chronology of events seem credible and convincing? Does the story seem to account for the material facts of the situation in a satisfying manner? How do the primary characters in the story acquire their dramatic motivation? Do the heroes behave in ways that are appropriately heroic? Do the villains behave as villains are expected to behave? Are the actions of the characters reliable? Do their actions seem to follow from the plotline that has been developed? Do their behaviors seem consistent with the values that the plotline has attributed to them?

In our earlier discussion about the Iraqi leader Saddam Hussein, for example, we noted that President Bush cast Hussein as a notorious villain. Using the test of narrative probability would encourage arguers to question whether or not Hussein indeed lives up to our expectations for a villain. Is he the "Beast of Baghdad"? Or is he a patriotic and heroic Iraqi strongman who has earned the admiration of his own citizens and of others in the region by standing up to the developed Western powers? Is the United States fighting for the freedom and self-determination of the people of Kuwait? Or are we merely trying to secure our access to cheap oil?

People seek stories that do not leave loose ends untied, stories that offer resolution and satisfy their need to understand issues and events. Surely you can remember, for example, seeing a film that left you dissatisfied because the plotline simply did not hang together very well. While audiences enjoy films with surprise endings, the best of such films are carefully planned so that afterwards the audience can look backwards and discover the clues that had been planted there all along. Our interest in compelling and satisfying stories is no less intense outside of books or films. Most Americans did not wish to fight a war in the Middle East until they were convinced that the conflict was unavoidable, the objectives moral and justified, and the probability of victory was high.

The second test of stories, **narrative fidelity,** concerns whether or not a story represents accurate assertions about social reality.[5] This dimension of narrative reasoning is firmly rooted in people's capacity for making judgments about issues of value. Fisher argued that people seek to make their decisions in accordance with the values that they hold. They also seek to determine if the supposed "facts" revealed to them in the stories they encounter are indeed facts, if they are reliable and relevant, and whether or not they have been taken out of context.

People thus consider the degree to which any new story seems consistent with the stories that they have heard before and have already accepted as true—stories they have used to explain their past experiences. The "Hussein as Hitler" story, for example, fares well in a test of narrative fidelity for many Americans. While Iraq is not Nazi Germany, and the Iraqi leader may not be the driven megalomaniac dictator that Hitler was, many Americans have believed it quite likely that a negotiated settlement between Iraq and Kuwait was as doomed to failure as were attempts to make peace with Hitler. Hussein's willingness to bomb clearly civilian targets in Israel, killing innocent Jewish women and children, also suggested a blind hatred for the Jewish people that strengthens comparisons between Hussein and Hitler.[6]

As we have already mentioned, Fisher argued that the capacity for narrative argument is present in all humans, because all of us are socialized and taught through stories. The power of this form of argument is often illustrated in the courtroom. Lance Bennett and Martha Feldman, in their analysis of legal argumentation observed that jurors were able to make sense of complicated and sophisticated legal arguments because they evaluated them as stories.[7] A prosecution story, for example, must fashion a structurally complete and internally consistent story that takes into account all the evidence in the case.[8] The defense can succeed if they can find a way to reveal flaws in the prosecution's story. They can achieve this by demonstrating inconsistencies, or by revealing that some important evidence is not accounted for in the prosecution's story.

People are also inclined to find stories that fit their own interests to be more truthful. For example, when a political candidate promises to fund increases in social programs while also decreasing taxes, the story may appeal to voters because it promises benefits without pain. A rival story that says that these benefits will require an increase in taxes will be less appealing to most voters. Only when the first political story is refuted by material evidence—in short, when it fails to meet the tests of narrative probability and fidelity—will people move to accept the second story.

Because the appeal of some stories, and the lack of appeal of other stories, is closely connected to the values and life experiences of people, and of the cultures in which they live, the stories that people come to accept help to shape people's conceptions of themselves. Fisher argued that people will seek out stories which confirm their sense of themselves. Thus stories which justify human motives and which make people feel important and worthwhile will have an easier time gaining public acceptance than will stories which negate a person's sense of self. People will be more readily compelled to action on the basis of stories which make such action and their role in it seem appropriate and just. Skilled storytellers understand that people seek stories that affirm their self concepts. For example, when political candidates go before groups like the American Legion or the Veterans of Foreign Wars, they appeal to the ex-soldiers' sense of pride in their patriotism, sacrifice, and love of country.

A politician who wants to refute a story that we can increase spending on social programs and also lower people's taxes might stress the fact that the numbers will not work out and that the result will be an increase in our budget deficit. Then this arguer could claim that the budget deficit will already pose a hardship on our children. This appeal to a sense of obligation to future generations is persuasive because it addresses our desire to nurture and protect our offspring. This human emotion, and others like it, are natural sources for arguments which will appeal to audiences, and consequently, they are the substance of many compelling stories. More than 2500 years ago, Aristotle wrote that happiness, justice, courage, fear, praise, sympathy, and empathy (among others) were all issues that might influence audiences.[9] Listeners might thus be motivated to accept certain stories as probably true rather than others, simply because these stories appealed to their values, emotions, sense of virtue, or instincts.

If all humans possess an almost instinctive ability to engage in narrative argument—to tell stories, and to evaluate and choose between the stories that they are told—what need is there for a course in argumentation? The answer, we believe, lies in the fact that while all people are capable of arguing through stories, some people are better storytellers than others. While everyone can tell a story, not everyone can write a poem, a novel, or even a short story. The assumption we make is that by learning certain argumentative principles people can hone their storytelling skills, and learn how to become better storytellers (advocates) and better critics of the stories that they are exposed to on a daily basis. The next section is devoted to the benefits of learning argumentation theory.

The Class in Argumentation

The study of argumentation we undertake in this book will help you to further develop your argumentation skills. Among the topics that will be considered in detail in the ensuing chapters are the following: how one determines what issues are worth arguing about, and which issues are beyond argument; how arguers can adjust their arguments to suit their audiences; argumentation and critical thinking; forms of argument; evidence; refutation; and some of the differences in argumentation required in the myriad of different contexts in which arguments are created.

The techniques for argument do, of course, vary from situation to situation. We have taken the position that arguers function primarily from a narrative perspective; that most arguments are presented as stories. However, not all argumentative contexts or situations demand the same kind of stories. In fact, certain argument situations, and certain communities of arguers, have created their own standards for arguing. Thus, the arguments that are developed in the courtroom are substantially different from those developed in a legislative hearing, an academic debate, a classroom, a business meeting, a religious conference, or a discussion between friends or family members. Learning the techniques for effective arguing therefore means developing a sensitivity to the demands of a wide variety of different argumentative contexts.

One of the primary objectives of this text is to help you to explore resources that may be useful as you are called upon to develop arguments in a variety of contexts. We will consider how one finds, selects, and develops appropriate evidence; how this evidence is used to support the analysis and reasoning that strengthens claims; and how these arguments are best organized. We will also be focusing on techniques that will enable you to refute others' arguments, and to defend your own arguments after they have been refuted. Finally, we will offer suggestions that will help you to analyze your audience, enabling you to make the strongest possible case in support of your position. By adapting your arguments to your audience you can present a case that is not only well reasoned, well evidenced, and well organized, but also well suited to your listeners' interests, values, and experiences.

The Limits of Argument

One clear measure of a competent arguer is the ability to recognize when one should argue, and when one should remain silent. Another measure is the ability to recognize a superior argument. A competent arguer knows when an adversary has presented arguments that are superior to his or her own. Learning when to argue and when not to argue will not only make you a more convincing advocate for the positions that you espouse, it may also help you to preserve your friendships. While we will discuss the relationship between argumentation style and interpersonal relationships in greater detail in the last chapter, at least brief attention is devoted to this issue now, because it is so important to developing the skills of effective argumentation.

Often we find ourselves in conversations where someone makes a statement that we disagree with, but our disagreement is so trivial that we need to decide whether the relational tension that might result from a public disagreement is warranted. Sometimes arguments are not worth the effort because the issue about which we differ is not very significant. It may not seem worthwhile, for example, to argue that the color of a couch that you had admired at a friend's house was turquoise, if your girlfriend insists that it was teal. Obviously both turquoise and teal come in many different shades, and our ability to distinguish between them may be limited, as may be our ability to recall what we saw. Breaking into a full-fledged dispute over precisely what the color was may simply not be worth it.

The decision to argue (to engage in argument2) over every trivial difference of opinion will obviously impair your relationships with others. None of us choose as friends, lovers, or even close colleagues, people with whom we find ourselves in constant disagreements over trivial issues. The tension level that results from such disputes can begin to undermine even otherwise healthy relationships.

Still other arguments are not worth having because they do not center around questions that can be readily resolved through disputation, regardless of the relative skills of the competing arguers. For example, an argument over which college football team has gone to the Rose Bowl more often, the University of Southern California, or Ohio State University, is not a dispute that can be resolved through arguments (although such arguments have certainly occupied the time of many a sports fan!). This is an empirical question that can be answered simply by consulting a sports almanac. If, however, the argument concerned which school had established the better football tradition, it would be resolvable only through argument. Empirical evidence to support your position would certainly be helpful to resolve such a dispute, but the nature of the question would also require the evaluation of argumentative claims. For example, in answering this question, evidence of Rose Bowl participation would be relevant, but not sufficient to prove one football program superior to another.

Still another type of argument that might not be worth making is an argument directed toward changing the mind of a genuinely and firmly committed ideologue. Some people hold beliefs so strongly that they are not really open to critical reflection. Many arguments over the merits of particular religious philosophies are of this type. Someone who is, for example, a committed Roman Catholic, and who faithfully adheres to the teachings and philosophies of that faith, is not likely to be very open to arguments about its flaws or errors. Such disagreements will be especially difficult to accept if they come from someone outside of the faith, since one might question both their knowledge of the religious teachings of Catholicism, and their motives for seeking to discredit the faith.

Similarly, arguments between intensely committed political conservatives and equally committed political liberals are often not worth spending the time and energy on, because so little of their disagreement can be resolved through dispute and reasoning. For an effective argumentative exchange to occur both parties must be open to arguments. They need not have suspended their beliefs and become "blank slates," but they must be willing to confront the possibility that the beliefs that they hold could indeed be demonstrated to be wrong. For this reason, all arguments entail risk for those who engage in them.[10]

Our goal is not to discourage you from forming strong opinions, or from engaging in arguments with others who also hold such opinions. Instead, our point is that some assessment of the nature of the argumentative climate is important. Arguers need to make conscious decisions concerning whether or not participation in any given argument will serve their interests. They should ask themselves: will having this argument damage my relationship with this person? And, will the arguments that we make really resolve the dispute? It is, of course, often difficult to predict the outcome of a disagreement, or to determine in advance how it will effect our relationships. Nevertheless, sometimes we can predict quite accurately. We believe that arguers should choose their arguments carefully, based on their own sense of where each is likely to lead, and not permit themselves to be ruled only by their tempers. We believe that this selectivity, along with equally careful selection of the situations in which they will argue and the habit of keeping an eye on argumentative strategy, are all traits of effective arguers.

Summary

The perspective that we have developed holds that all people have the capacity to argue and to evaluate arguments, because people are by nature rational beings. The primary mode for the creation and evaluation of arguments is through storytelling, and our stories are tested through an evaluation of their narrative probability and narrative fidelity. Despite the fact that we all have the capacity for arguing, we can improve our argumentation skills by learning conventions and norms for arguing effectively in particular contexts, and by recognizing that some arguments are essentially unwinnable and hence should be avoided.

Key Terms

narrative   narrative probability   storytelling
narrative fidelity   stories

Activities

1. Watch a Saturday morning cartoon. Then analyze the characters and elements of the story.
   a. Who is the hero of the cartoon? Is the hero male or female? What ethnicity is the hero? What are the personality characteristics of the hero?
   b. Who is the villain of the cartoon? Is the villain male or female? What ethnicity is the villain? What are the personality characteristics of the villain?
   c. What do the depictions of the hero and villain say about these types of individuals?
   d. What was the moral of the cartoon?
   e. What values does the moral of the cartoon teach?

2. Make a list of what you think are the traditional values of American culture. Now select a different culture or subculture. Make a list of the values of that culture. If you are not familiar with another culture, ask someone who is to make the list instead.
   a. Are there differences in the values of the two cultures?
   b. How are these differences manifested in behavior?
   c. Are there similarities in the values of the two cultures?
   d. Are these similarities manifested in similar behaviors?

3. Think about the last movie you saw.
   a. Were there points in the plot of the movie that did not seem to fit together?
   b. Were there subplots that where left unresolved?
   c. Did the characters act the way you think real characters would?
   d. How do these aspects of the story reflect Fisher's concepts of narrative probability and fidelity?

4. Pick a public issue from the headlines of the local newspaper. Discuss the issue with a classmate or friend. Then analyze your discussion.

a. Were there points on which you disagreed with your partner?

b. Did you voice all such disagreements or did you keep some of them to yourself?

c. If you voiced all of your disagreements, what effect did this have on the discussion?

d. If you kept some points of disagreement to yourself, why did you do this?

Recommended Readings

Fisher, Walter R. "Clarifying the Narrative Paradigm." *Communication Monographs* 56 (1989): 55–58.

Fisher, Walter R. "Rationality and the Logic of Good Reasons." *Philosophy and Rhetoric* 13 (1980): 121–130.

Fisher, Walter R. "Toward a Logic of Good Reasons." *Quarterly Journal of Speech* 64 (1978): 376–384.

Rokeach, Milton. *Beliefs, Attitudes and Values.* San Francisco: Jossey-Bass, 1970.

Rowland, Robert C. "Narrative: Mode of Discourse or Paradigm?" *Communication Monographs* 54 (1987): 264–275.

Rowland, Robert C. "On Limiting the Narrative Paradigm: Three Case Studies." *Communication Monographs* 56 (1989): 39–54.

Wallace, Karl C. "The Substance of Rhetoric: Good Reasons." *Quarterly Journal of Speech* 49 (1963): 239–249.

Wenzel, Joseph W. "Toward a Rationale for Value-Centered Argument." *Journal of the American Forensic Association* 13 (1977): 150–158.

Notes

1. For an excellent discussion of the power of the comparisons between Adolf Hitler and Saddam Hussein, especially of the effect that this comparison had on President Bush, who was himself a young Navy flier during World War II, see James Gerstenzang, "World War II Lessons Helped Form Bush Strategy," *Los Angeles Times,* 14 January 1991, p. A8.

2. We may become so blinded to our conceptions of ourselves as moral actors that we are unable to see in ourselves the same faults that we are quick to condemn in our enemies. Some have argued that this may, for example, have led to the terrible atrocities committed at My Lai during the Vietnam War, and to the relative ease with which military commanders accepted these events, at least until a full public airing of them prompted further investigations. For a summary of this position, see Seymour M. Hersh, *My Lai-4* (New York: Random House, 1970).

3. There is no evidence that Abraham Lincoln ever read *Uncle Tom's Cabin,* or that he ever saw the play based on the book. Lincoln was, however, very much aware of the impact the book had on the American public. For a discussion of his conversation with the author Harriet Beecher Stowe, see Thomas F. Gossett, *Uncle Tom's Cabin and*

American Culture (Dallas: Southern Methodist University Press, 1985), especially pp. 314–315.

4. Walter R. Fisher, *Human Communication as Narration* (University of South Carolina Press, 1987), p. 5.
5. Fisher, p. 105.
6. For a discussion of these similarities, see Gerald F. Seib and Walter S. Mossberg, "Iraqi Missiles Hit Israel and US Presses Air Attacks," *Wall Street Journal,* 18 January 1991, p. 1A.
7. W. Lance Bennett and Martha S. Feldman, *Reconstructing Reality in the Courtroom* (New Brunswick, NJ: Rutgers University Press, 1981), p. 5.
8. Bennett and Feldman, p. 97.
9. *Rhetoric and Poetics of Aristotle,* trans. W. Rhys Roberts. (New York: The Modern Library, 1954), see *Rhetoric,* Book I.
10. Wayne Brockriede, "Where is Argument?," *Journal of the American Forensic Association* 9 (1975), p. 181.

3

Audiences and Fields
of Argument

Arguments are created to change someone's opinion, influence behavior, or to justify the arguer's beliefs or actions. Thus, all arguments should be developed with an audience in mind. This is not to say, however, that arguers are always aware of their audiences. The exchange of arguments, like many other human activities, sometimes becomes so reflexive that we do not take the time to carefully think through our argument strategies. One of the goals for this book is to help you to become more strategic in the arguments that you choose to develop. To achieve this goal, and to enhance the effectiveness of the arguments that you create, you need to think about the audiences you want to influence with your arguments.

We have already established that humans reason by assessing the quality of the competing claims that they hear in rival stories. Some stories hold together better than others. Their plotlines are more compelling, their characters are given clear and distinctive roles to play and they play them in accordance with our expectations. These stories are judged to have met the test of narrative probability. Likewise, some stories are especially believable and credible to us because they seem to confirm and explain the experiences that we have had in our lives. These stories ring true to us, and because they correspond with our prior experiences they lend a sense of predictability to our lives. When confronted with such a story we know how to respond, because we have seen how such stories can be expected to turn out. These stories are judged to have narrative fidelity.

While we believe that all people reason by testing the quality of the stories they encounter in their daily lives, we also know that alternative stories appeal to different people. An arguer who seeks to prove a story's credibility must find a way to appeal to the values, experiences, and beliefs of his or her audience. Arguers must construct their stories so that they conform to the requirements of a coherent, complete, and satisfying story, and they must do so in such a way that it resembles other stories that the person whom you are trying to convince has already heard and experienced, stories that he/she already believes to be true.

27

Thus, arguers must create stories that affirm the self-concept and self-interest of the person(s) they are trying to convince.

Knowing Your Audience

One of the first challenges that you face as an arguer is to identify the **audience** for your arguments. Sometimes this is easy. If, for example, you are having an argument with a close friend about how the two of you should spend your evening together, the target for your arguments is obvious. In other argument situations, however, identifying your audience is much more difficult. The salesman who is showing the new car to a married couple, for example, may be guilty of directing his comments primarily to the husband, not realizing that the car will be driven primarily by the wife, or that she will make the decision about what kind of car they will purchase. The misdirected arguments, and of course, the sexist attitudes that they reveal, could result in the alienation of the couple and a lost sale.

As the argument situation becomes increasingly complex, even identifying the appropriate audience for your arguments becomes more difficult. In a political campaign, for example, candidates conduct expensive, complicated, and time-consuming public opinion polls in order to identify the values, beliefs, and interests of potential voters. Candidates must address the issues that voters believe are important. This was a challenge in the 1992 presidential election, when President Bush wanted to emphasize his foreign policy experience, but the voters wanted to talk about the economy, an issue that favored his rivals. Candidates also shop for votes among the uncommitted. They seek to identify voters who have not yet made up their minds and then try to see what issues these voters believe are most important. The candidates then try to discuss these issues in a way that appeals to these voters.

Political candidates must, of course, address arguments to those voters who already share their ideology. In primary races candidates are often appealing to voters who are highly partisan, already committed to the values that shape the agenda of their parties. Once the nomination is secured, however, the candidate must attempt to appeal to voters who are far less committed to a particular viewpoint. These independents and crossover voters actually decide most closely contested elections. Identifying precisely who these voters are is a vital part of the campaign process.

If the people most likely to vote for you are primarily suburbanites working in white-collar jobs, you will want to make very different arguments than you would if they were mostly blue-collar residents of big cities. Candidates sometimes develop such sophisticated knowledge about their audiences that they construct appeals that are explicitly targeted toward very specific audience segments. They might, for example, emphasize child care issues because they know that a substantial number of potential voters are single parents who must worry daily about balancing their responsibilities as wage earners with their responsibility to provide care for their children.

The primary consideration in identifying the audience for your arguments is to determine who is in the position of enabling you to achieve your objectives. By focusing on that specific audience, you can better construct your message to appeal to those decision makers.

Assessing Your Audience

While it is often difficult to know precisely what values and opinions people hold, you should probably begin assessing your audience by considering its demographic characteristics. While demographic differences are far from reliable predictors of people's attitudes and values—sometimes these differences even mislead arguers—some of them do help predict attitudes and values. The following demographic characteristics are potentially useful: age, social affiliations, gender, education and knowledge, background and experience, and culture.

Age

In his book, *The Rhetoric,* written in the 4th century B.C., Aristotle discussed the differences between trying to persuade the young, the elderly, and those in the prime of life. He described how the young were more likely to have volatile tempers, how the old were more likely to be stubborn and set in their ways, and how those in their prime were typically free from the extremes of either.[1] While Aristotle's delineation of how people's attitudes and values change as they age might seem a bit simplistic and stereotypical today, his comments continue to have some validity.

Common wisdom suggests that people's age might have significant influence on the values that they hold, and on how open they are to arguments suggesting alternative views. An audience composed of older persons will likely have more conservative views than one of younger persons. Also, because audiences are most likely to be concerned about issues that directly affect them, young persons might be especially concerned with issues such as the draft or the availability of federal funds to help them finance their education. Middle-aged persons might be especially concerned with issues such as child care or property taxes. Older persons will likely be more concerned about issues such as the cost of medical care or retirement benefits. An especially interesting example of an issue that affects persons of different ages very differently is falling interest rates. The young are delighted that interest rates are low. Lower rates make buying a home much easier. Older people often find themselves living off the income from their investments, however, and lower interest rates means that they get a much smaller return on these investments. Thus, economic conditions that greatly benefit one age group can pose serious problems for another.

Social Affiliations

People belong to a variety of groups, and these memberships may give you some insight into their attitudes and values. Obviously, you can learn something about people if you learn what political party they belong to, if they are religious or not, what church they might attend, what groups they belong to, etc. A member of the National Rifle Association probably would have very different values than would a member of the Sierra Club, even though both groups share a concern for the preservation of wetlands. People who belong to Jerry Falwell's Moral Majority, and people who belong to the gay rights group ACT UP, probably have little in common.

Knowledge gained about the specific group affiliations of your audience will help you to construct your arguments to be maximally effective. Such knowledge might also reveal that you are attempting to appeal to an audience who either already agrees with you, or who may be beyond persuasion, regardless of the best arguments that you can muster.

Gender

While it might be difficult to ascertain someone's values on the basis of their gender, gender often influences our values and attitudes, and the degree to which certain arguments appeal to us. For example, one might expect female audiences to be offended by male chauvinist comments, and sexist jokes. One might also expect that women would be more sympathetic to arguments in support of women's issues than might an audience of men.

Women are more likely than men to have experienced gender discrimination, and consequently we can expect that they would be more sensitive to it. While male attitudes on issues such as acquaintance rape, sexual harassment, and domestic spouse abuse are no doubt changing, it is likely that these issues will still be more compelling for an audience of women than for an audience of men. This was certainly revealed by the public responses to the confirmation hearings of Supreme Court Justice Clarence Thomas. When Justice Thomas was accused of sexual harassment by Anita Hill the charges were investigated by the Senate Judiciary Committee, composed entirely of men. Many women were outraged when the committee seemed to turn on the alleged victim rather than the accused perpetrator. After Thomas's nomination to the Court was confirmed many women lambasted the Senate as a "boys club" and declared that women could not expect a fair and impartial hearing by such a group of men.

Education and Knowledge

Arguers must seek to adapt their arguments to the educational and intellectual level of their hearers. Not only might persons of different educational backgrounds harbor different attitudes and values, but they may process arguments differently. The more sophisticated and educated an audience is, the more likely that they will be able to follow and to evaluate complex argument forms.

Those who share knowledge about a subject also share the ability to communicate in the jargon of that discipline. Thus, an audience composed of physicians can have an argument about alternative treatments for patients with AIDS that is far more sophisticated than that which might occur among the general public. Arguers should also recognize the fact that certain educational experiences might predispose some toward certain beliefs. An audience composed of scientists, for example, would be more inclined to place their faith in science as a means to solve social problems than might an audience composed of musicians. Even a shared appreciation of the scientific method might not be sufficient to facilitate shared understanding, however, for an audience of nuclear engineers is more likely to favor the continued development of nuclear power than would be an audience composed of biologists.

Background and Experience

Because people are constantly engaged in assessing the arguments that they hear as stories, they compare them to other stories that they have heard or personally experienced. Consequently, the background and experience of audience members will have tremendous influence on their attitudes and values. An audience member who has had a friend or family member killed by a drunk driver, for example, may have far stronger opinions about the need to tighten controls on those who drink and drive than might someone else. Likewise, a parent who is raising a rebellious teenager might be more sympathetic to the parents of a gang member than might the parents of a docile and well adjusted teenager.

People screen the arguments and the stories that they hear through their own experiences, and the more knowledge you have about the experiences of your audience members the more effective you can be in adjusting your ideas to them.

Culture

One especially important factor that influences people's evaluation of arguments is their culture. The culture in which they are raised and socialized often influences them without their knowledge. For instance, people raised in the American culture have very different values, attitudes, and opinions than those raised in the Middle East, Asia, or even Europe. Given the tremendous differences in the environments, religious beliefs, governmental forms and traditions, and political systems of these regions, it should come as no surprise that people from these different cultures experience and evaluate arguments differently.

Research has suggested, for example, that Chinese arguers use very different strategies and argumentation styles than do Westerners. Chinese arguers are more likely to mask their emotions, they are more likely to use silences to punctuate their differences, and they are far less likely to display their disagreements or negative feelings.[2] Westerners frequently misunderstand what Chinese arguers are actually communicating. Westerners assume that the absence of direct disagreement or the lengthy silences communicate that the Chinese arguers agree with them, when in fact they may not.

Arguers should be aware that in our world people from different cultures are more and more frequently coming into contact with each other. The world's great cities—for instance, London, Paris, Amsterdam, Rome, Hong Kong, New York, Los Angeles—are becoming increasingly diverse. In addition, new global economic forces are changing the way nations must conduct business. People can no longer live in isolation. The management of our social and political life and the public policies that must be designed to maintain social harmony, increasingly demand that arguers be sensitive to differences in culture.

People Evaluate Arguments Differently

We have already asserted our claim that people evaluate arguments in accordance with the principles of storytelling. It is understandable that people evaluate these stories based upon their own unique backgrounds, experiences, age, interests, affiliations, and culture. If arguments must appeal to such a wide range of viewpoints, what is an arguer to do? How can one ever learn enough about his or her audience to be able to tailor one's arguments to suit them? Furthermore, how can an arguer avoid alienating some people in the effort to appeal to others?

The Belgian philosopher and legal theorist, Chaim Perelman and his colleague L. Olbrechts-Tyteca, observe:

> Argumentation aimed exclusively at a particular audience has the drawback that the speaker, by the very fact of adapting to the values of his [sic] listeners, might rely on arguments that are foreign or even directly opposed to what is acceptable to persons other than those he is presently addressing.[3]

Perelman and Olbrechts-Tyteca suggest that arguers direct their appeals to a **universal audience.** This "universal audience" is not an actual, existing one, but is created in the mind of the arguer. They believe that by creating this abstract audience as a reference point for evaluating arguments, one could tailor arguments to a broad range of potential audience members. Perelman and Olbrechts-Tyteca stress that "argumentation addressed to a universal audience must convince the reader that the reasons adduced are of a compelling character, that they are self-evident, and possess an absolute and timeless validity, independent of local or historical contingencies."[4]

To create arguments for this universal audience, one should seek to create claims that will appeal to all reasoning persons. Though not an easy task, this is an appropriate goal for arguers to pursue. So how should an arguer do so?

Perelman stresses that one should seek to develop arguments that make use of **objective facts**—facts that are knowable and uncontested—and by forming these facts into **obvious truths,** or generalizations that are commonly shared and understood. Perelman acknowledges the difficulty in finding such readily agreed upon "facts" and "truths;" as he observes, there are significant differences among people in this regard.

Perelman argues, "everyone constitutes the universal audience from what he [sic] knows of his fellow men, in such a way as to transcend the few oppositions he is aware of. Each individual, each culture, has thus its own conception of the universal audience." The universal audience is thus a construction of the arguer—a self-conscious test that the arguer should submit any argument to in order to make it as strong as possible.

Perelman also recognizes that, on rare occasions, there might be audience members who do not recognize the "objective facts" or "obvious truths" present in the arguments that you create. To some extent he feels that it would be legitimate to dismiss these recalcitrant few as stupid or abnormal. The danger in this is that you may find yourself making arguments designed to persuade fewer and fewer people, because you have castigated as stupid all those who do not agree with you and see the world as you see it.[5]

While Perelman's conception of the universal audience will not resolve all of your challenges in adapting your arguments to different viewpoints, it should help you to create arguments that will appeal to the largest number of people. Arguers should therefore be aware of not only the unique interests, concerns, and beliefs of their particular audiences, but also the need to create arguments that will convince the broader universal audience. Arguers need to continually search for objective facts and obvious truths, because the very process of argumentative investigation can only serve to strengthen arguments and to help create stronger cases.

The Principle of *Presence*

Perelman also proposes that arguers consider the notion of **presence.** This concept of presence involves making arguments seem especially important to your audience. Perelman suggests that the simplest way to achieve presence is through repetition. Arguers can emphasize points by stating them repeatedly. One can also accentuate important arguments or passages, by tone of voice, or by pausing just before uttering them.[6]

Even if you have created your arguments with the notion of a universal audience in mind, it is helpful if you can find a way to make your arguments uniquely appealing to the particular audience that you are addressing. We have already detailed the ways in which different people might be expected to have different responses to the arguments that they encounter. How then do you accomplish this task? How do you create arguments that have universal appeal, but that also uniquely address the concerns of your particular audience?

To a certain extent, the notion of presence suggests concern for the stylistic dimensions of creating and communicating your arguments. It is typically helpful to seek to communicate with your audience, rather than to adopt a preachy or highly judgmental tone.

Arguers should also seek to pique the interests of their audiences, to provoke their sympathy or their feelings of empathy, to construct arguments so that audiences really feel them. Perelman illustrates the concept of presence with a Chinese proverb: "A king sees an ox on its way to sacrifice. He is moved to pity for it and orders that a sheep be used in its place. He confesses he did so because he could see the ox, but not the sheep."[7]

One of the rescue missions that provides assistance to the homeless in Los Angeles sends out mailings to potential donors to raise funds to support their efforts. Even though most of the recipients of the aid, and indeed most homeless people in Los Angeles, are men who abuse and have become dependent on alcohol or drugs, the mission's solicitations often emphasize the plight of homeless children. In this way, the mission creates greater presence as to the problem of homelessness in the city, and probably gains more donations—it is much easier to provoke concern for the plight of the homeless when you emphasize victims who did not make choices that led to their own suffering.[8]

As an arguer, your goal should be to develop arguments and a style of presentation that will make the issues that you raise seem uniquely important to your audience so that they will choose to devote their attention to them. During the 1992 presidential campaign, for example, President George Bush sought to convince the American voters that the achievements in foreign affairs that were made during his presidency were so great that they should earn him a second term. He spoke at length about the end of the cold war, the nuclear arms treaties he negotiated with the Russians, and his successes in the war against Iraq. Unfortunately for the President, he discovered that foreign policy issues had very little presence for most voters at that time. Most Americans were so unhappy and fearful about the state of the economy and the lingering national recession, that this was the issue that they most wanted to hear about, and which most influenced their votes. They cast their ballots for the candidate whom they believed most likely to effect a change in economic policy—Bill Clinton.

Identifying which arguments will have presence for your audience, and finding ways to present your arguments in a style that maximizes their importance, requires knowledge of your audience and of the techniques for presenting arguments. It also requires that you discover the appropriate techniques for a variety of argument situations.

Argument Fields

Another view of how people make argumentative judgments was developed by the philosopher Stephen Toulmin. Trained as a logician, Toulmin became increasingly frustrated with the limitations of formal logic. He felt that the principles of formal logic were useful, but did not reflect the ways in which people actually reasoned in forming everyday decisions. Toulmin's fellow logicians believed that logical models were the most appropriate means for rationally arriving at conclusions and that the requirements for a rational argument did not change from one context to another. Toulmin argued, however, that different contexts—which he came to refer to as **fields**—demanded different standards for arguments:

> The trains of reasoning that it is appropriate to use vary from situation to situation. As we move from the lunch counter to the executive conference table, from the science laboratory to the law courts, the "forum" of discussion changes profoundly. The kind of involvement that the participants have with the outcome of the reasoning is entirely different in the different situations and so also will be the ways in which possible outcomes of the argument are tested and judged.[9]

Arguments can be considered to be in the same field when the data and conclusions are of essentially the same logical type. They will be in different fields when the data and conclusions are markedly different, or in a case where the same data leads to different conclusions.[10]

To understand Toulmin's view of argumentation theory it is important to determine what he meant by the term "fields." Toulmin viewed argument fields and the term "disciplines" as roughly synonymous. His claim was that physicists argued similarly because they shared training in physics. Likewise, attorneys argued in a similar fashion, members of the clergy shared an argument style, as did historians, physicians, engineers, and so on. These disciplinary boundaries are not always formal or predictive. For example, physicists might be expected to argue in a similar fashion to engineers, biologists, chemists, and perhaps even physicians, because the scientific method underlies their shared fields.

Still other complications can occur because people are often members of several different argument fields simultaneously. Someone may be, for example, both a fundamentalist Christian and a scientist. As a Christian, this person might accept the biblical account of the creation of the universe as outlined in the Book of Genesis. As a scientist, on the other hand, this person might be inclined to accept the Charles Darwin's theory of evolution. In such a situation the person who belongs to the incompatible fields is continually forced to reconcile the tensions that may occur between them, and also to decide from situation to situation which field's argument standards to apply.

Other argumentation theorists have suggested that it would be useful to consider argument fields from a broader perspective than that of disciplines. Charles Arthur Willard has suggested that fields should be seen as sociological entities. Willard says that fields encompass terms such as "groups," "organizations," "frameworks," and "relationships," particularly when these entities come to share a "constellation of practices."[11]

Willard claims that the practices of any field are consensually developed as its members come to agreements regarding how their day-to-day work proceeds. Thus, chemists forge appropriate techniques for resolving disputes in the field of chemistry as they conduct their daily work. Likewise, accountants discuss their daily challenges and responsibilities, and then they propose appropriate means for addressing the problems that they share, so that they continually hone the standards and practices of their profession.

Willard acknowledges that while some fields may simply take a body of knowledge for granted, most seek to perfect and improve the knowledge in the field.[12] Thus for example, chefs argue about the best way to prepare a souffle, orthopedic surgeons about the best way to treat a herniated disc, and hairdressers about the best way to color hair so that it looks natural.

Willard also stresses that even the decision to participate in a particular field (which may even be an unconscious decision) may end up constraining your ways of thinking about and approaching problems. To participate in a field entails surrendering a certain amount of one's freedom, because one begins to see the world from the perspective of that field. Consequently, the attorney is always seeing problems from the perspective of questions of law, the scientist from the perspective of scientific inquiry, and the artist from the artistic perspective.[13]

Just as their audiences are composed of persons who represent fields or perspectives, arguers themselves represent particular fields or perspectives. Awareness of the implications of field theory should help you to become more aware of the degree to which your own experiences, beliefs, training, membership in certain groups or organizations, etc., influences your argumentative techniques.

A few arguments may be so compelling that they meet the requirements for argumentative proof in all fields. Toulmin calls these arguments "field-invariant."[14] For example, most of us would accept as true the claim that parents who love their children naturally want to protect them from harm. This claim could be called field-invariant. Even a claim that seems as clear cut as this one, however, may not indeed always be true. As an illustration, let us recall the religious cult called the Branch Davidians.

In 1993, members of the Branch Davidians holed up in a compound outside of Waco, Texas. When agents of the Bureau of Alcohol, Tobacco and Firearms tried to serve a search warrant on them to investigate claims that the group was dealing in illegal guns, the cultists opened fire on the federal agents, killing several of them. The FBI then surrounded the compound and for fifty-one days sought to convince the cultists to surrender. Finally, the government decided to fire tear gas into the compound to try to force the occupants to leave. Instead, the people inside set fire to the compound killing almost one hundred persons, including twenty-four of their own children, seventeen of whom were under age ten.[15] It was extremely difficult for the rest of the world to understand how parents could intentionally cause the deaths of their own children, especially in such a terrible manner. To those of us who did not share their beliefs, who did not participate in the Branch Davidians' field, it seemed that these parents did not love their children enough to try to save them.[16] To members of the cult, however, the decision to perish in the fire may have seemed very rational, and the taking of the children's lives might have been an expression of their love for them. The fiery end to this siege confirmed the biblical prophesy that fire would consume the earth, and that the true believers of Christ would find their way to heaven.[17] Thus, for the Branch Davidians, fiery Armageddon represented not the end of their children's lives, but the promise of a new beginning in heaven. Even this argument which seemed to be field-invariant, is thus found to be "field-dependent."[18]

Arguers should therefore try to be sensitive to the requirements for establishing claims in the argument field in which they are participating, and should seek to create arguments which will satisfy the audience by appealing to their identification with a particular field. When dealing with people from different argument fields, or when it is difficult to determine what field's standards should be applied, it is desirable to create arguments that will appeal to people in as many different fields as possible. In a sense, this is the pursuit of arguments that appeal to the universal audience.

Another interesting task that arguers sometimes face is the need to translate arguments from one field to another. Frequently this process means creating stories that appeal to people from different fields. An illustration of this process would be a scientist attempting to find scientific explanations for biblical stories: an astronomer, for instance, speculating on any events in the heavens on the night that Christ was born that could explain the story about the three wise men following the path of a star to find the newborn baby.

Summary

Arguers should carefully consider the values and attitudes of their audiences in forming their arguments. While it is sometimes difficult to know your audience's values and attitudes in advance, it is useful to study their demographic characteristics, because these demographic factors may provide insight into their interests, needs, and experiences. Arguers should also attempt to emphasize and give greater presence to those aspects of their arguments that are most likely to appeal to their listeners. In addition, arguers should recognize that people respond to arguments differently, and often use different standards for evaluating arguments based upon the fields to which they belong. Your goal should be the creation of arguments that will appeal to the universal audience of reasoning persons. While this does not assure that you will convince all your listeners, it does seem to be as effective a standard as can be created.

Key Terms _____

audience	objective facts	presence
fields	obvious truths	universal audience

Activities _____

1. To practice analyzing an audience, conduct a demographic analysis of your class.

    a. What is the age span of your class? The average age?
    b. What are the social affiliations of the class members?
    c. What is the educational background of the class?
    d. What are the cultural perspectives of your classmates?

2. Select a recent public controversy. Based on the information gleaned above, predict how the class will view the controversy. Then answer the following questions:
    a. Would the audience's views change if the audience were older? younger?
    b. Would the audience's views change if they had different social affiliations?
    c. Would the audience's views change if they were better educated? less well educated?
    d. Would the audience's views change if they were part of a different culture?

3. Take a position on the public controversy identified in the preceding exercise. Now imagine supporting your position with two different audiences. If the only difference you knew about the two audiences were that they differed in age, how might you adapt your argument so as to gain the adherence of each of these two audiences? Repeat this for each of the audience variables identified in this chapter.

4. Listen to an argument interaction by, for instance, listening to a radio talk show, watching a talk show on television, attending a public meeting of local or student government, or observing your friends engaging in argument. Now analyze the interaction.
    a. List the objective facts—those facts that are knowable and uncontested by the disputants.
    b. List the obvious truths—those generalizations that are commonly shared and understood.
    c. What facts and truths were contested? Were these points of disagreement resolved? If so, how? If not, how might they have been resolved?

5. To learn more about the nature of argument fields, attend a meeting of your local government and observe a criminal trial.
    a. What are the differences, if any, in what constitutes acceptable evidence in the two fields of argument?
    b. How do the participants introduce facts?
    c. How do the participants challenge the facts introduced by another participant?
    d. Are there controls on who may speak or on what they can say?

Recommended Readings

Dearen, Ray D. "Perelman's Concept of Quasi-logical Argument: A Critical Elaboration." In J. Robert Cox and Charles Arthur Willard, eds. *Advances in Argumentation Theory and Research.* Carbondale: Southern Illinois University Press, 1982. 78–94.

Farrell, Thomas B. "Validity and Rationality: The Rhetorical Constituents of Argumentative Form." *Journal of the American Forensic Association* 13 (1977): 142–149.

McKerrow, Ray E. "Rhetorical Validity: An Analysis of Three Perspectives on the Justification of Rhetorical Argument." *Journal of the American Forensic Association* 13 (1977): 133–141.

Measell, James S. "Perelman on Analogy." *Journal of the American Forensic Association* 22 (1985): 65–71.

Scult, Allen, "A Note on the Range and Utility of the Universal Audience." *Journal of the American Forensic Association* 22 (1985): 83–87.

Toulmin, Stephen E. *Human Understanding.* Princeton: Princeton University Press, 1972.

Toulmin, Stephen E., Richard Rieke, and Allan Janik. *An Introduction to Reasoning.* New York: MacMillan, 1979.

Notes

1. *Rhetoric and Poetics of Aristotle,* trans. W. Rhys Roberts. (New York: The Modern Library, 1954), pp. 121–126.
2. Michael J. Cody, Wen-Shu Lee, and Edward Yi Chao, "Telling Lies: Correlates of Deception Among Chinese," in J. P. Forgas and J.M. Innes, eds., *Recent Advances in Social Psychology: An International Perspective* (North-Holland: Elsevier Science Publishers, 1989), pp. 359–368.
3. Chaim Perelman and L. Olbrechts-Tyteca, *The New Rhetoric* (Notre Dame: The University of Notre Dame Press, 1969), p. 31.
4. Perelman and Olbrechts-Tyteca, p. 32.
5. Perelman and Olbrechts-Tyteca, p. 33.
6. Perelman and Olbrechts-Tyteca, p. 144.
7. Perelman and Olbrechts-Tyteca, p. 116.
8. We are not suggesting that there are not significant numbers of homeless children and families in Los Angeles, or in any other city. Nor are we suggesting that the missions in Los Angeles do not provide assistance to these families. We do not believe this is a deceptive appeal for support. Instead, we see it as a conscious decision to try to capitalize on the public's understandable concern for the welfare of disadvantaged children.
9. Stephen E. Toulmin, Richard Rieke, and Alan Janik, *An Introduction to Reasoning* (New York: MacMillan, 1979), p. 7.
10. Stephen E. Toulmin, *The Uses of Argument* (Cambridge: Cambridge University Press, 1958), p. 14.
11. Charles Arthur Willard, "Argument Fields," in *Advances in Argumentation Theory and Research,* J. Robert Cox and Charles Arthur Willard eds., (Carbondale: Southern Illinois University Press, 1982), p. 30.
12. Willard, p. 30.
13. Willard, p. 38.
14. Toulmin, p. 36.
15. For a description of the siege and its fiery conclusion, see J. Michael Kennedy, "Waco Cultists Perish in Blaze," *Los Angeles Times,* 20 April 1993, p. 1.
16. For a discussion of public reactions to the tragedy in Waco, see J. Michael Kennedy and Lianne Hart, "In the Eye of the Cult Firestorm," *Los Angeles Times,* 20 April 1993, p. 1.
17. Kennedy and Hart, p. 1.
18. Toulmin, *The Uses of Argument,* p. 38.

4

The Language
of Argument

The spring of 1992 will be remembered for one of the most violent civil disturbances in American history. Thousands of Los Angeles residents viewed the acquittal of four Los Angeles police officers indicted for beating African-American motorist Rodney King as an instance of blatant social and racial injustice. Their anger at joblessness, inadequate housing, poor medical care and discrimination led them to the streets. The looting and violence that followed captured national attention and shut down the second largest city in the country for four days.

Trying to understand why Americans would set their own city afire was difficult. Was there a collective message being sent here? Or were these merely random acts of violence? The labels that the media, city officials, and community leaders placed on the events are instructive.

Some referred to what was transpiring as a "rebellion." To others it was a "civil disturbance." Some called it "anarchy." And still others contended it was "gang-inspired thievery." Perhaps to most of us it has come to be known as the "L. A. Riots."

What's in a name? Everything. Think for a moment of the different images that these labels conjure up. Is there a difference between a rebellion and a riot? Doesn't one convey organization and the other the lack of it? Isn't the former purposeful and the latter meaningless? Would we respond differently to the events of that spring if we considered them a rebellion rather than a riot?

We believe the answer to each of these questions is yes. The objective facts (those which are knowable and uncontested) of what transpired in the spring of 1992 do not change with the different labels. But which facts are given presence (made especially important to an audience), and how those facts are interpreted, changes as a result of the language used to describe them.

In the previous chapter we discussed how strategic arguers analyze their audience and the argument context so that they may adapt their arguments and increase their effectiveness. In this chapter, our goal is to enhance your ability to create arguments that audiences find compelling. We begin by discussing the importance of language in argumentation, move on to considering how language influences the components of a good story, and conclude by examining a special type of argument: metaphor.

Understanding Language

The symbols we use to make sense of our experiences are rich with meaning. They reflect our thoughts and values, and they direct us how to act. A label, or more appropriately, language, is a template that constrains what we think and what we know.

Language Defined

Language is a shared symbol system. This rather simple statement has profound ramifications for the study of argument. First, language is symbolic. In Chapter 1 we defined *symbols* as special types of signs that call attention to significances: they relate to what has been perceived; they point to, indicate, or denote something other than themselves. Because symbols relate to what has been perceived, they are, as Kenneth Burke argues, partially a reflection of reality. But we choose which words will represent the thing perceived, and choice reflects values. Therefore, symbols are also a deflection of reality.[1] By this Burke means that language intervenes between the thing and the arguer. Nor is this intervention benign. Rather, language has an **epistemic function.** That is, the language we learn and employ shapes and constrains our understanding of what constitutes reality. What is real to us is that which we express linguistically, and the language we possess influences how we make sense and what we make sense of.[2]

Nevertheless, language itself has no inherent meaning. We agree that the object speakers stand behind when delivering a speech is referred to as a *podium,* but we could have called it a *smerl.* The word *podium* has only that meaning which we have agreed to give it. The groups agreeing to share a meaning may be as large as a culture, or as small as a clique which creates its own lingo: *surfers, bikers, rockers, heads, punkers,* and the like.

A culture's agreed upon word meanings are usually detailed in a dictionary. Unfortunately, not everyone has read the entire dictionary. And even if they have, there are frequently multiple definitions for a single word. As a result, there can be misunderstandings.

For example, you might think that there would be little confusion over what the term *mother* means. *The American Heritage Dictionary* defines mother as "a female that has borne an offspring." But the dictionary also acknowledges a mother as "a female who has adopted a child or otherwise established a maternal relationship;" as "a woman having some of the responsibilities of a mother;" and even, as "qualities attributed to a mother, such as the capacity to love." Which sense of the term did you think of initially?

How then do we make sense of the words that others use? One answer is that the symbols we share are governed by the *system* of language: grammar. The rules of language use help us to ascertain which of the various meanings of a word is intended. This rule of linguistic context permits a single word to be used in a multitude of ways. In fact, as I. A. Richards wrote, "Most words, as they pass from context to context, change their meanings; and in many different ways. It is their duty and their service to do so."[3] Understanding the rules of grammar enables us to make sense of the context and assign meaning to the words.

But understanding the definition of a word is only part of the game. For dictionaries provide only the **denotative** meaning, that is, the content level of the word. Dictionaries do not always convey the value judgments which are often embedded in words. Nor do they relate how an individual feels about a word. These are considered the **connotative** meanings of the word.

Think about the various definitions of the term *mother*. None of the dictionary definitions relate how an individual may feel about it. Were your experiences with your mother or as a mother positive? Then perhaps for you the term *mother* evokes a warm sense of security. But it is possible that another individual in the class was abused or neglected by their mother. For that individual, the term may awaken negative or ambivalent feelings. So words may have different meanings even for people who have generally agreed to the denotative meaning of a word.

Abstraction

Just because language is shared does not mean that arguers and audiences always understand each other. One reason for the failure to achieve shared understanding arises from the principle of **abstraction.** The word *pen* is more specific or concrete than *writing implement*. The more abstract the term, the more meanings it conveys; and, the more opportunity for confusion or obfuscation.

Confusion can arise when an arguer or advocate uses language which is more abstract than necessary. This lack of precision can lead an audience to believe they understand an advocate when they do not. Unscrupulous advocates sometimes take advantage of imprecise language to purposely mislead audiences. An illustration is the politician. W. Lance Bennett argues that political campaign discourse ritualistically uses abstract language.[4] Candidates often use broadly based appeals, says Bennett, so that different constituencies can take the candidate's message to mean whatever they want to hear. When a candidate calls for eliminating waste in government, audience members are authorized by the broad language to fill in the specifics themselves. Voters are thus encouraged to interpret the targeted wasteful programs as those which benefit others, while presuming those which are beneficial to themselves or those they love will be considered truly essential and preserved.

Understanding the possibility of ambiguity, the skilled advocate chooses words carefully. If the advocate wants the audience to have a more precise understanding, the advocate uses more precise language. If the opposite is desired, then more abstract language is employed. Since our code of ethics calls for us to openly appeal to the intellect of audiences and argue like lovers (see Brockriede's metaphor, in Chapter 1), we advocate the use of precise language.

Advocates who wish to enhance understanding can not only select more concrete language, they can also build in redundancy, repetition and restatement. Being careful to adhere to the grammatical rules of sentence structure also contributes to comprehension.

Since the meanings that we assign to phenomena vary depending on the language used, then the way we depict the characters, scenes, and events can be crucial to how audiences understand them. And how audiences understand argument, influences whether or not they grant adherence to the claims advanced. We consider all of this in the next section of this chapter.

Language and Good Stories

One of the foundational assumptions of the narrative orientation we employ in this text, is that all argument is story. There are three central elements to any story—characters, scenes, and events. We consider how language influences each in turn.

Depicting the Characters in Stories

Central to the narrative perspective is the belief that all humans are social actors. As such, they assume roles, create images and act in accordance with the impressions they wish to sustain. They are **characters** in the stories of social life. Dan Nimmo explains,

> The dramatistic viewpoint regards all social relationships as dramatic action.
> A person in a social drama (be he [sic] in a political setting, religious ceremony,
> business–labor negotiation, marital contract, or even in the bedroom) performs
> in accordance with the image he wishes to leave on his audience.[5]

There are two components to the characters of stories: roles and character types.

A **role** is a set of assumptions about how an individual should act, based on his or her position, occupation, behavior, and status. We don't expect teachers and students, doctors and patients, parents and children to behave the same way. What behavior we do expect of them is influenced, to an extent, by the roles the individuals are playing. Another constraint on how we act in a social drama is the **character type** we assume.

In his analysis of American literature, Orrin Klapp concluded that there are three major American social types: heroes, villains, and fools.[6] Klapp argued that Americans are guided by their desire to emulate positive social types and to avoid negative ones. Thus, these social types serve as models for how Americans should behave.

We believe that American audiences look for similar depictions in the stories they hear. Walter Fisher defines social, or character types as "an organized set of actional tendencies."[7] Because certain character types tend to act in characteristic ways, audiences develop expectations of how these characters are supposed to act. If they don't behave as we expect them to, we may question whether their presentation is accurate.

There are three basic character types in any argumentative drama: heroes, villains, and victims. Of course, within each of these character types there are a variety of subtypes. For example, heroes can be reluctant or willing. They can succeed through physical strength or intellect. They may be glib or taciturn.

Think for a moment of two heroes of recent American generations. In the 1939 movie classic *Mr. Smith Goes to Washington,* Jimmy Stewart plays a bashful individual upon whom the role of hero is thrust. It is a role he is decidedly uncomfortable with. Yet, reluctantly, he assumes the character type and acts out his part. Through honesty and determination he brings Washington corruption to its knees.

Compare this character, with that played by Sylvester Stallone in the Rambo movies. It is physical strength that enables this character to enact the hero role. With violence, instead of words, Rambo rights the wrongs of a world and military bureaucracy out of control.

Villains come in different shapes and sizes, too. Klapp differentiates, for example, between villains who symbolize a threat to social order and those who use that order to accomplish their evil deeds. The desperado, outlaw, or gangster uses violence to cause harm and is antithetical to order. If we all acted like these villains there would be no order, only anarchy.

The authoritarian, the dictator, and the manipulator, on the other hand, adhere to the established order, but achieve elevated status by using the rules to control others. The result is a denial of freedom or worse, but order is preserved.

Finally, victims may be of various sorts. Some are innocent and unsuspecting, while others are willing martyrs. Still others bring ruin upon themselves because they are unwary, ignorant, or uninvolved.

Successful arguers understand the importance of character types and depict the actors in the social dramas they describe accordingly. Ronald Reagan's reference to the Nicaraguan contras as "Freedom Fighters" was an attempt to transform the public's negative conception of these individuals into something more favorable. Americans in the 1980s did not want to be involved in another Central American conflict. The fighting in El Salvador seemed interminable despite American military supplies and advisors. Yet, Reagan sought to solidify support behind the contras by calling them Freedom Fighters.

If the contras were truly Freedom Fighters, we could not abandon them, for to do so would be to abandon freedom itself. Freedom Fighters, much like our Founding Fathers, are heroes. Heroes require our support, especially if they are fighting the common enemy—the communists. Reagan had trouble sustaining this label, however. Evidence that the contras illegally mined harbors, blew up schools and roads, and trafficked in drugs, undercut Reagan's depiction. Yet, for some, the language was powerful.

And, recall how President George Bush described Saddam Hussein in the fall of 1990 (see Chapter 2 for additional information on this depiction). Bush took pains to depict Hussein in ways that painted him as a desperado-villain, even explicitly labeling Hussein as a new Hitler—arguably history's greatest villain. The Kuwaitees were portrayed as innocent victims, and the forces of the Coalition were presented almost as policemen (heroes) enforcing the laws of the new world order. We believe these depictions were critical to rallying support for American intervention in this conflict.

Depicting the Scene in Stories

In addition to presenting the actors in terms of the character types they play in the story, arguers also construct images of the **scene**. *Scene* refers to what is transpiring on the stage. This may include the immediate context, the larger international scene, even the broad sweep of history. The arguer selects what elements of the scene to give presence, and how to present them.

In justifying the transition from Desert Shield to Desert Storm (from economic sanctions to military intervention), Bush vividly described the scene in Kuwait. The continuing barbaric acts of killing and destruction warranted, Bush argued, immediate military action. On the broader, international scene, Bush stressed that Hussein posed a threat to the world's oil supply. This threat not only jeopardized American oil supplies, but that of NATO and Japan as well. The U.S. military, therefore, would not act alone. Rather, the initiation of the Persian Gulf War was the result of consultation with the coalition of nations opposed to Hussein's armed violation of sovereign territory. Arguably, the depiction of a different scene could have resulted in a different audience response.

For example, if Hussein's actions threatened only American interests, then we might have acted alone. That was the apparent case in Panama and Grenada, two situations in which the United States intervened on its own. But the circumstances in the Persian Gulf, according to Bush, warranted a different course of action. Bush argued that Hussein's invasion of Kuwait threatened the free world's petroleum reserves in Saudi Arabia. Thus, it would be the free world's militaries who responded.

Notice how this depiction of the scene dovetails nicely with the kind of action Bush called for. If the situation had not been urgent, a different kind of hero might have been more appropriate. Instead of using military power, the proper course might have been diplomacy and economic strangulation. The hero in a less urgent scene would be one who avoided needless loss of life.

The decision Bush made on how to present the scene in Kuwait fit together well with his characterization of Hussein as villain and justified, in Bush's view, military action. While the validity of the president's characterization of the actors and scene might be debated, there is no doubt that it succeeded in convincing the American public that military engagement was the appropriate course of action.

Depicting the Events in Stories

The third element of a story is the **events,** or the actions engaged in by the characters. As with the first two components of a good story, the language one uses in this aspect of the argument is important. Change the terms and you change the argument. For example, the Korean War was originally labeled a *police action*. Why? Because the connotations of this term are generally more positive than those of the term *war*. To a nation tired of war (remember, World War II was a recent memory), intervening in a dispute between two halves of a nation, like a police officer might in a domestic dispute, is psychologically more comfortable than waging another war.

For another example, the revelation that Oliver North had supervised the illegal sale of arms to Iran so as to raise money to circumvent laws prohibiting the assisting of the contras, was originally called "Irangate" by some media pundits and Democratic politicians. The linking of the Reagan administration problems with the scandal that plagued the Nixon administration, was a powerful argumentative tool. It suggested presidential involvement, a cover-up, a smoking gun, and the possibility of impeachment. Getting the media and the public to label the events the "Iran-Contra Affair" instead was no small achievement.[8] Thus, the labels we give our experiences are powerful in shaping our understanding of these events, and, to the extent that we share these labels with others through our advocacy, we can influence the way they make sense of their world as well.

This is not to say that we can materially change the nature of the world simply by changing the way we label something. We cannot change water into wine merely by changing the label, for the tests of what constitutes truth, or what is rational, are still the same; the labels to the elements of the story (characters, scene, events) must make coherent sense, and the evidence and depictions must ring true with the stories we know to be true. But because the choice of language influences what we believe the story is, we urge you to consider carefully the terms you employ in constructing your arguments.

In analyzing any controversy, audiences naturally ask themselves who are the actors, what are the events, and how are each depicted? These characterizations are then scrutinized to determine whether the grounds warrant the portrayal. Having reached a conclusion, an individual would then use these depictions to present his/her argument to his/her audience. An example will clarify.

Suppose you were confronted by two advocates debating solutions to the American drug crisis. In analyzing their arguments you might discover the following characters: drug addicts, drug suppliers, enforcement personnel, and the public. Having listed the characters, you would then determine how the respective advocates describe them, paying particular attention to the motives given to each.

One side in the controversy, that which supports greater enforcement of existing laws, portrays addicts and pushers as villains, the police as heroes, and the public as victims, citing evidence in support of this depiction. For example, some present details of crimes and violence perpetrated by addicts and drug syndicates. They describe addicts as being lazy and no-good, pushers as seeking success the easy way, the police as heroically fighting overwhelming forces, and a public being preyed upon by the drug culture. Two secondary villains are also introduced: the artists (music and film) and media elites who glamorize drug use, and casual drug users.

On the other side of this illustrative controversy, are advocates who favor the legalization of cocaine. Frequently, arguers on this side present both the public and addicts as victims; the police as misguided; but they may agree that pushers are the villains. These advocates present evidence such as the social conditions that lead to drug use (unemployment and discrimination), the lack of prevention (education) and treatment (detoxification centers), the futility of enforcement efforts, and the fact that pushers are despicably motivated by money.

Note that each story fits together in a coherent way. If addicts are villains, then police efforts to apprehend and incarcerate addicts are logical and narratively coherent (see Chapter 2). On the other hand, if addicts are victims, then police efforts to punish them are inappropriate. We don't punish victims, we try to save them. But, if both characterizations pass the test of narrative coherence, where does truth reside?

The story you grant adherence to is the one whose depictions ring true with the other stories you believe to be true. This is what we call narrative fidelity (see Chapter 2). For example, if you think that many addicts turn to drugs because the world offers them no positive role models, provides them with an inadequate education, discriminates against them, bombards them with the message that the individual is defined through material possessions, but denies them the ability to achieve material success, then you are likely to find greater fidelity with those advocating legalization than those advocating greater enforcement. If, on the other hand, you believe in the truth of stories that present addicts as villains, you will must likely find the case for greater enforcement more convincing.

Having reached a decision as to who is telling the better story, you might feel ethically compelled to become an advocate. If so, you would seek additional evidence which supported the depiction you wished to convey. Thus, the way claims are phrased and organized, and the way grounds employed, are determined, in large part, by how we wish to present the actors in the story.

Once the character types have been determined, the events of the story fall into place, for heroes do heroic acts; villains engage in villainy. They do so because their motives reside within their character. Since the character labels contain social values (heroes are good, villains are bad, victims should be protected), the appropriate audience response is determined once a characterization is accepted.

Actions that are contrary to the character depictions threaten the coherence of the characterizations. Characters must act characteristically, or we begin to doubt the depiction, and may even reject the whole story. For example, portrayals of the police as heroes are undercut when audiences are confronted with videotapes of police brutality, such as the beating of Rodney King in Los Angeles.[9]

In short, as we have previously indicated, audiences make sense out of the world by actively evaluating discourse as story. A skilled advocate recognizes this and takes care to direct audience sense-making along the lines that enhance the effectiveness of his/her advocacy. The advocate therefore carefully presents the particular characters that will convey the story he or she wishes the audience to accept.

Characterizations refer not only to how an advocate characterizes the social actors, events and scenes, but also to how the advocate presents themselves. In his analysis of Ronald Reagan's presidency, Walter Fisher accounts for the success of Reagan's advocacy, in large part, in terms of how the audience saw Reagan.[10] Despite inconsistencies, contradictions, and inaccuracies in Reagan's rhetoric, Fisher notes that he was (and still is) immensely popular. Why? Because, for many Americans he is a heroic figure, one they trust, admire, and identify with. Audiences forgave or ignored the argumentative flaws that would have doomed another advocate. As Fisher notes,

> Obviously, Reagan enjoys a popular perception, and many citizens find comfort in identifying with him. He is perceived as a man of goodwill, and this perception overrides other features of traditional ideas of ethos-credibility, specifically, the "rational" components of intelligence and expertise.[11]

In contrast, some recent vice presidential candidates (for instance, Geraldine A. Ferraro and J. Danforth Quayle) were criticized for their inability to sustain the character type in which they were presented. As is typical for vice presidential candidates, each was introduced as the best individual for the job. Some voters thought that neither candidate had the political experience to legitimize this characterization. Consequently, some members of the audience, which in these cases was the electorate, doubted the validity of their candidacies.[12]

Metaphor

Savvy arguers recognize that there are special forms of argument which can enhance their effectiveness. One such case is the metaphor.

You probably learned all about metaphors, similes and other figures of speech in English classes. They are often referred to as ornaments of language. Saying a classmate "roars like a lion" (simile) and "is bullheaded" (metaphor), communicates information about the classmate in a manner which many might find more interesting than merely saying the classmate is very loud and strong-willed. (Of course, these examples are trite cliches that probably should be avoided.) But the metaphor is far more useful in argumentation than as a mere ornament of language.

If we say, "Peter is as strong as an ox," we are only comparing one aspect of Peter—his strength—with one aspect of the ox—its strength. No one would surmise that Peter walks on four legs, pulls carts behind him, and has a tail suitable for making soup. And the point of comparison is figurative only—Peter certainly does not have the same strength as an ox. But when President Reagan called us to see the Soviet Union as "the evil empire," he meant the comparison to be taken far more literally.

The **ornamental metaphor** thus asks us to see that phenomenon A has some characteristic which resembles phenomenon B. The **argumentative metaphor** contends that phenomenon A should be seen *as* phenomenon B. The argumentative metaphor is a powerful tool, for it influences how we make sense of our world.

Had we accepted that the Soviet Union of the early to mid-1980s was an "evil empire," then we would have interpreted their actions accordingly. If they acted perniciously, then their actions confirmed the metaphor. If, however, they acted charitably, the underlying belief that the Soviets were evil makes even these actions suspect—because evil people cannot be trusted.

Thus, the metaphor acts as a template for interpreting new information. Viewing A as B limits, shapes, and constrains our understanding of A. We "know" A (the Soviet Union) with respect to what we "know" about B (an evil empire). And the values embodied in B are transferred to A through this sense-making process.

An illustration of the sense-making power of a metaphor was provided in a recent study of a child's use of metaphor. Despite her mother's efforts, the child in question could not comprehend the death of her father. Only when the child lost a helium-filled balloon did the child comprehend, metaphorically, the finality of death.[13]

Steven Perry provides an example of rhetoric that successfully incorporated an argumentative metaphor. Perry argues that the writings and speeches of Adolf Hitler are permeated with a view of the Jewish people as an infestation. While we find the rhetoric repugnant we agree with Perry that this metaphor is central to understanding Hitler's argument,

> . . . these figurations are more than stylistic devices: Hitler's critique of the Jew's status as a cultural being, for example, is not illustrated by the metaphor of parasitism, it is constituted by this metaphor and the figurative entitlements it carries. The Jew's cultural inferiority, that is, is never argumentatively demonstrated in propositional fashion by reference to real events or rational principles, but is rather only there to be inferred from Hitler's use and elaboration of parasitism imagery. The figurative language employed by Hitler is not supplementary or subordinate to some argumentative or discursive structure; it is itself Hitler's argument.[14]

The power of the metaphor lies in its completeness. If an audience accepted this abhorrent depiction, the response and the desired course of action are implicit in the metaphor—infestations, as negatively valued entities, call for containment and eradication.

A more recent example of an advocate successfully using metaphor occurred during the confirmation of Clarence Thomas to the United States Supreme Court. As we recalled in Chapter 3, after Thomas had testified before the Senate

Judiciary Committee, allegations that he had sexually harassed Anita Hill were made public. When Thomas returned to the Senate hearing, he defiantly characterized the proceedings as a "high-tech lynching for uppity Blacks who in any way deign to think for themselves."[15]

The effect of Thomas's use of the lynching metaphor was to cast all attacks on him as an attempt to put down African-Americans who do not remember their place. Since his main antagonists were liberals, who tend to be sympathetic to issues of discrimination, recalling images of the struggle for civil rights made arduous questioning less likely.

The attempts by Senate Republicans to convincingly label Hill are also instructive. If Thomas were indeed innocent, then there must be some reason Hill made the allegations. Yet, one by one each label they applied—lunatic, opportunist, scorned woman, and fantasizer—seemed to slip away. The segment of the public that accepted Hill's accusations as real, did so, in part, because these labels just did not fit with the poised professor of law they saw testifying before the committee.

Unlike the figurative or ornamental metaphor, in which only one characteristic of A is seen in terms of B, the argumentative metaphor views all of A as B. This gives the metaphor a **generative capability.** That is, if we know some of the characteristics of A in terms of B, we can infer (or generate) other characteristics. This makes the metaphor a powerful argumentative tool, for it enables us to evoke in an audience a deep, intense response, simply by noting a superficial connection between A and B.

An example will help to clarify. Lakoff and Johnson write that Americans conceive of argument as war.[16] This can be seen in the language we use to describe arguments:

> "Your claims are indefensible."
> "He attacked my argument point by point."
> "I demolished his argument."
> "I've never won an argument with her."
> "He preempted my argument."

It can also be seen in how we prepare and conduct arguments. And in the personal stake we sometimes feel in the arguments we advance. If our position is defeated, we might feel personally lessened. These are some of the consequences of seeing argument in terms of war. If you can come up with other similarities between how we argue and how we wage war, then you've proven the generative capability of the argumentative metaphor.

Argumentative metaphors and analogies, which we discuss more fully in Chapter 6, are not the same. Both entail comparisons and both have generative functions, but the literal analogy compares cases of a phenomena which are materially similar. Metaphor, like the figurative analogy, compares cases which are materially dissimilar.

When citizens expressed concern that the Persian Gulf War might become another Vietnam, they were arguing analogically. Both were cases of American military intervention in a foreign nation. Respondents countered by arguing the analogy was flawed because military objectives were definable in the Gulf. On the other hand, when others argue that homelessness is a plague sweeping the nation, they are not literally arguing that homelessness is a contagious disease, only that it is useful to conceive of one in terms of the other.

Summary

In this chapter we have considered the way advocates can use the language to increase the effectiveness of their arguments. Language shapes understanding, and therefore, strategic advocates must judiciously select the language with which they wish to construct their arguments. We have specifically discussed the qualities of language, how good stories utilize language, and we have considered a specific type of argument, the metaphor.

In this chapter we viewed argument from the perspective of the advocate. In the next chapter we will turn to a specific examination of how consumers of argument can critically examine a discourse. Of course, once we have analyzed an argument, we may be moved to engage in argument ourselves.

Key Terms

abstraction	events	generative
characters	language	capability of
character type	epistemic function of	ornamental
connotative meaning	metaphor	role
denotative meaning	argumentative	scene

Activities

1. In this chapter we discussed language and indicated that each culture or subculture creates its own characteristic way of talking about the things it considers important. For example, think about the kind of music you like to listen to? How do you describe it? What label do you use for music you consider good? How do you label music you consider bad? Now, select a subculture with which you are familiar. List some of the unique language that culture employs and provide a definition of these terms. If you are unfamiliar with the language of a subculture, you may need to interview someone to complete this exercise.

2. Provide your own definition for each of the following terms and indicate whether the term evokes positive feelings for you or negative ones. Now ask a friend or classmate to do the same. Are there differences? Discuss the source of the similarities and differences.

freedom
government
welfare
retirement
marriage
children
charity
religion

3. Select and read an editorial or opinion piece from your local newspaper. Then answer the following questions about its narrative form:
   a. Who does the advocate think are the heroes?
   b. Who does the advocate think are the villains?
   c. Who does the advocate think are the victims?
   d. What qualities does the advocate assign to these characters in their respective roles?
   e. What are the acts that each of these sets of actors engage in?
   f. How does the advocate describe the scene?

4. Throughout the day, you enact many roles. Think about your day and list the roles you fill (for instance, student, parent, child, worker, sibling). Now select two of these roles and consider how they influence your behavior.
   a. Are some behaviors acceptable in one role but not in the other?
   b. Are there differences in the amount of power you have in the two roles?
   c. Are there differences in whether or how you express your feelings in the two roles?
   d. Do others respond differently to you when you enact the different roles? For example, are you more likely to be listened to in one role than in the other?

5. Try to discover the influence of metaphors in your life. For example, if you work, think about your place of employment and how your boss talks about it. Does your boss talk about the workers as part of team? Then perhaps a sports metaphor is being invoked. If your boss uses military terminology, then perhaps your boss wants the work environment to function like the military. List examples of the metaphors your employer uses. Then try to understand what else these metaphors reveal about how your boss wants the workers to act. If you have the good fortune of not having to work, or if you are the boss, then try to analyze the use of metaphors in a different environment. Perhaps you belong to a fraternity or sorority, or some other group with leaders who employ metaphors.

Recommended Readings ⎯⎯⎯⎯⎯⎯⎯⎯⎯⎯⎯⎯⎯⎯⎯

Blankenship, Jane. "The Search for the 1972 Democratic Presidential Nomination: A Metaphorical Perspective." In Jane Blankenship and Howard Stelzner, eds. *Rhetoric and Communication*. Urbana: Illinois University Press, 1979. 236–260.

Burke, Kenneth. *Language as Symbolic Action: Essays on Life, Literature, and Method.* Berkeley: California University Press, 1966.

Farrell, Thomas B. and G. Thomas Goodnight. "Accidental Rhetoric: The Root Metaphors of Three Mile Island." *Communication Monographs* 48 (1981): 271–300.

Fisher, Walter R. and Richard A. Filloy. "Argument in Drama and Literature: An Exploration." In J. Robert Cox and Charles Arthur Willard, eds. *Advances in Argumentation Theory and Research.* Carbondale: Southern Illinois University Press, 1982. 343–362.

Longinus. *On the Sublime.* Trans. A. O. Prickard. London: Oxford University Press, 1907.

Osborne, Michael. "Rhetorical Depiction." In Herbert Simons and A. Aghazarian, eds. *Form, Genre, and the Study of Political Discourse.* Columbia: South Carolina University Press, 1986. 79–107.

Ricoeur, Paul. *The Rule of Metaphor: Multi-disciplinary Studies in the Creation of Language.* Trans. Robert Czerny, K. McLaughlin, and J. Costello. Toronto: Toronto University Press, 1977.

Notes

1. Kenneth Burke, *Language as Symbolic Action: Essays on Life, Literature, and Method* (Berkeley: University of California Press, 1966), 45.
2. See, for example Susanne K. Langer, *Philosophy in a New Key: A Study in the Symbolism of Reason, Rite, and Art* (Cambridge: Harvard University Press, 1942); Kenneth Burke, *Language as Symbolic Action* (Berkeley: University of California Press, 1966); and Richard A. Cherwitz and James W. Hikins, *Communication and Knowledge: An Investigation in Rhetorical Epistemology* (Columbia: University of South Carolina Press, 1986).
3. I. A. Richards, *The Philosophy of Rhetoric* (London: Oxford University Press, 1936/1981), p. 11.
4. W. Lance Bennett, "The Ritualistic and Pragmatic Bases of Political Campaign Discourse," *Quarterly Journal of Speech* 63 (October 1977): 219–238.
5. Daniel Nimmo, "The Drama, Illusion and Reality of Political Images," in *Drama in Life: The Uses of Communication in Society,* James E. Combs and Michael W. Mansfield, eds. (New York: Hastings, 1976), p. 261.
6. Orrin E. Klapp, *Heroes, Villains, and Fools: The Changing American Character* (Englewood Cliffs, NJ: Prentice-Hall, 1962).
7. Walter R. Fisher, *Human Communication as Narration: Toward a Philosophy of Reason, Value and Action* (Columbia: University of South Carolina Press, 1987), p. 47.
8. Kevin Baaske, "Analogic Argument in Public Discourse: A Reconsideration of the Nature and Function of Analogy," in *Proceedings of the Second International Conference on Argument,* Frans H. van Eemeren, Rob Grootendurst, J. Anthony Blair, and Charles A. Willard, eds. (Amsterdam: Sic Sat, 1991), pp. 411–415.
9. Another excellent example of an individual having difficulty maintaining a characterization is presented in Kathryn M. Olson, "The Controversy over President Reagan's Visit to Bitburg: Strategies of Definition and Redefinition," *Quarterly Journal of Speech* 75 (May 1989): 129–151.
10. Fisher, esp. pp. 143–157.
11. Fisher, p. 148.
12. See, for example, Kevin Baaske, "The Rhetoric of Character Legitimation: Geraldine A. Ferraro and the 1984 Vice-Presidential Campaign," an unpublished dissertation, University of Southern California, 1989.

13. B. Moore, "A Young Child's Use of a Physical-Psychological Metaphor," *Metaphor and Symbolic Activity* 3 (1988): 223–232.
14. Steven Perry, "Rhetorical Functions of the Infestation Metaphor in Hitler's Rhetoric," *Central States Speech Journal* 34 (1983): 230.
15. *Los Angeles Times,* 12 October 1991, p. A1.
16. George Lakoff and Mark Johnson, *Metaphors We Live By* (Chicago: University of Chicago Press, 1980).

5

Argumentation and Critical Thinking

In the preceding chapters we have focused on argumentation as a form of storytelling. We have emphasized that people are naturally gifted storytellers, and that they are able to create and test competing stories. Although this is true of all people, some people are more gifted arguers than others. Just as in most other human endeavors, people do have different argumentation talents. Some are more articulate than others, some use more vivid examples than others, some have better vocabularies, some have better memories, and so on.

You can enhance your arguing skills if you understand some of the techniques for creating reasoned arguments. Different argument fields often demand different argumentation styles, strategies, and techniques. In addition, several different analytical techniques are available to you to help you to improve the quality of your claims, and to assure a more systematic analysis of the arguments that you encounter. Our objective in this chapter is to enhance your critical thinking skills—to sharpen your analytical abilities—so that you create better arguments, evaluate others' arguments more carefully and, ultimately, so that you make better decisions. This chapter will explore alternative principles for the evaluation of propositions, suggest how arguers can make strategic decisions regarding how they can best express their own arguments and their disagreement with others' arguments and, finally, discuss some alternative methods for the analysis of arguments.

Argumentation theory, like any other discipline, can be formally taught and learned. Our shift in focus—to the examination of argumentation as a set of principles that can be learned, rather than as a naturally occurring human activity—does not contradict our earlier claims about argumentation. We continue to believe that humans are by nature storytellers, and that arguments are primarily created and understood through stories. In fact, the theories that we will now discuss can be understood as a unique style of storytelling that is especially appropriate for evaluating argumentative propositions.

While people do not require specialized training to engage in arguments in conversational settings, for instance with friends or family members, such training will help them to become more effective arguers in meetings, when writing papers or reports, in formal debates, or at rare but important occasions such as a visit to traffic court or small-claims court.

Propositions

A natural starting point for the consideration of any argumentative interaction is with an investigation of the proposition under dispute. A **proposition** is a statement that expresses the subject of the dispute. The degree of formality in the actual wording of a proposition will vary in accordance with the formality of the setting.

In a casual conversational setting, for example, the proposition might be stated very simply and informally: "I think we should go to the movies," or the rival proposition: "We always end up at the movies, I think we should see a play." As the setting becomes more formal, however, there will be a more careful statement of the proposition. For example, in a curriculum committee meeting, which is likely to follow parliamentary procedure, a participant would probably state the proposition to be argued as a formal motion: "I move that all students be required to complete a course in argumentation." In a court of law the proposition would probably be stated even more formally: "The State contends that the accused Michael Smith did, on April 7, 1991, commit a second-degree sexual assault, which is a felony according to criminal statute." In an academic debate the proposition would also be stated formally: "Resolved: That the federal government should provide a program of comprehensive medical care for all persons in the United States."

There are several benefits to formally stating or expressing a proposition for argument, even in an informal interaction. First, a formally stated proposition clearly establishes the issues that are in dispute. In casual interactions arguments may rage even when the participants lack a clear understanding of precisely what they are disputing. For example, in the informal argument cited above, one person is arguing that they should go to a movie while the other is arguing that they should go see a play. The dispute, however, may have less to do with the specific entertainment than with the underlying tensions in the relationship. Thus the claim, "we always end up at the movies, I think we should go to a play," might really be a disguised version of a different proposition: "you always get to decide what we will do when we go out, I think that I should have the opportunity to decide this time." If the disputants were to fully state their actual propositions, they might discover the precise cause for their disagreement, and thus reach a resolution sooner.

Second, a formally stated proposition serves to divide the ground between the disputants. The advocate of the required course in argumentation (no doubt a faculty member from the Speech or Communication Department), for example, might well be pitted against someone who believes that if students are taught how to argue better they might become more disagreeable. Or, the opponent might believe that students should not be saddled with specific requirements, but instead should have a high degree of freedom to design their own programs of study. Someone who favors increasing the foreign language requirement might oppose the argumentation requirement on the ground that it would overload the curriculum and therefore diminish the likelihood that a foreign language requirement could be enacted. In any case, the explicit statement of the proposition brings to the participants a clear understanding of the specific motion at hand before moving on to the consideration of alternative motions.

Third, explicitly stated propositions help disputants to see what might result from the completion of an argument. For example, if the legal proposition mentioned earlier is proven true, and Mr. Smith is found guilty of the charge of sexual assault, he can expect to face the State's penalty for this crime. If, on the other hand, his defense attorney is able to establish that Smith could not have committed the alleged act, or that the act which Smith did commit was of a very different character than that which the prosecution alleged, namely that it did not fit the requirements of the State's charge of second-degree sexual assault, Smith will be acquitted.

Finally, a formally stated proposition helps to facilitate clear argumentative clash, or sharply focused disagreement between rival positions. The proposition lays out the issues that are disputed, directs the advocates in how to develop their arguments, and reveals the issues likely to be used to support the opposing cases.

Types of Propositions

There are three different types of propositions, each appropriate to the particular types of issues that may be in dispute.

Propositions of Fact

Whenever there are disagreements about factual statements, a **proposition of fact** is in dispute. For example, two friends who are having an argument about the hottest place in the United States, are disputing a proposition of fact. Thus the statement, "Death Valley is the hottest place in the country," is a proposition of fact. The rival proposition, "Corpus Christi is the hottest place in the country," is also a proposition of fact. While propositions of this type readily lend themselves to argument, they are also typically resolvable through the appropriate empirical evidence. In this case, for instance, the National Weather Service keeps records of the average temperatures of reporting stations around the United States. However, even when this data is introduced, there might still be room for interpretation and disagreement. For example, advocates could still dispute the appropriateness of year-long versus decade-long averages, the hottest single days, the use of comfort indexes that include humidity and average wind speed, and so on. As anyone who has ever engaged in such an argument knows, the possibilities for avoiding resolution are as unlimited as are the creative energies of the arguers. However, all such disputes are open to being proved or disproved by the appropriate factual evidence.

Legal disputes are typically stated as propositions of fact, and almost all focus on issues that have already occurred (except for cases in which people seek court injunctions to prevent something from occurring). The jury called upon to decide defendant Smith's guilt or innocence in the sexual assault case would seek to determine whether or not the offense had occurred and, if it had, would then consider whether it met the legal definition for the charge, and whether Smith perpetrated the attack.

Arguers sometimes differ over propositions of future fact, although such arguments are always speculative in nature and therefore do not lend themselves to tidy resolution. We could assert, for example, that at some point during your lifetime you will see the election of the first woman or the first African-American president of the United States. This claim of future fact is certainly arguable. The resolution of such an argument, however, rests on the arguers' prognostications about the changing political landscape in the United States and its future consequences, and not on verifiable material evidence.

Propositions of Value

Closely related to propositions of fact are **propositions of value.** The primary difference between the two types of propositions is that, while factual propositions hinge upon verifiable evidence, value propositions can only be resolved on the basis of the opinions and beliefs of the arguers. For example, the claim "the Los Angeles Lakers were the winningest NBA team of the 1980s" is a proposition of fact. It may be verified by consulting an almanac listing the win-loss record of NBA teams. On the other hand, the proposition "the Los Angeles Lakers were the best NBA team of the 1980s" is a proposition of value. This proposition can only be decided based upon the arguer's conception of what the term "best" really means. A team's win-loss record would certainly be one consideration, but so might be several other factors: the record in the playoffs, the quality of the other teams in the division in which they competed, the quality of key players or of the bench, the quality of the coach, and—perhaps most importantly—whether the person you were arguing with resides in Los Angeles, Boston, or Detroit!

Because propositions of value focus on subjective beliefs and judgments they can be difficult to resolve. Disputes have raged for generations over such value propositions as: "abortion is morally wrong," "capital punishment is morally justified," and "our obligation to protect the first amendment outweighs our concerns about pornography." In any complex, multicultural, and diverse society we can expect that values will be disputed.

People often seem eager to avoid engaging in value disputes for this very reason—because they seem impossible to resolve. We believe, however, that the failure to argue and reason about value differences leaves us with no alternative but to fight over them. We prefer reason!

To analyze value propositions, ask yourself the following questions:

1. What are the foundations for the value under dispute? Is the value expressed in civil, religious, or natural law? If so, is it consistently expressed across these contexts?
2. How closely is the value adhered to, and by how many persons? What sorts of people ascribe to this value? Have they particular expertise in the subject under dispute?
3. How important is this value in the hierarchy of values? People are influenced by many values, how central is this value?
4. Is this value absolute? Are there situations in which this value is set aside? For example, most of us believe that killing is morally wrong, yet the Supreme Court has upheld the State's right to execute convicted murderers, when certain criteria are met. What criteria, if any, must be met for this particular value to be suspended?
5. How might an advocate go about establishing that these criteria have been met? Are these criteria formally established (as in the case of legal burdens that must be met), or are they informally agreed upon?[1]

Even when these questions are systematically asked and answered, however, some value differences are so fundamental that they cannot be easily minimized or overcome. The outcome of many value disputes is that those arguing must simply agree to disagree.

Propositions of Policy

A **proposition of policy** is a statement outlining a course of action that the advocate believes should be taken. Such a statement can range from the informal: "we should go to the movies tonight," to the complex, "Resolved: that the federal government should provide a system of comprehensive medical care for all United States citizens." Propositions of policy imply such value judgments as movies are a worthwhile way to spend one's time, and medical care is a right that the government should guarantee to all its citizenry. These propositions may also imply factual judgments—that not all citizens currently receive medical care, for instance.

Propositions of policy always concern the future, and they typically state that a certain policy change should occur. The best formulated propositions of policy are those that specify the precise change that should occur, and also the agent of that change. The following are examples of well formulated policy propositions:

Resolved: The State of Indiana should legalize casino gambling.

> Resolved: The NCAA should permit student athletes to receive a payment for their services, such payment to be generated from the revenues produced by their respective sports.
>
> Resolved: That the federal government should legalize the sale, cultivation, and possession of marijuana by any person over the age of 21.

If our goal is to produce the fairest and best argumentation on an issue, then we should strive to create explicitly and carefully worded propositions. A precisely worded proposition is easier for arguers to dispute. In order to best assure clash on an issue, a proposition should be worded so that it leaves ground on both sides. A very narrowly worded proposition might not make for very effective clash, and might also not result in effective public policy:

> Resolved: That the federal government should fund a program to provide polio vaccines for all Hopi Indian children residing in Arizona.

There are two problems with this proposition. First, it is difficult to justify limiting the program to only Indian children, let alone the children of only one tribe that reside in only one Western state. An advocate who opposed this proposition could make the case that all children need protection from the polio virus. If that advocate was able to show that other children also failed to receive polio vaccines this might be an effective argument against the adoption of this proposition, or at least an argument for rewriting and expanding the proposition.

Second, this proposition severely limits its advocates' ground. Why create a program to vaccinate children for only one disease, rather than a program to vaccinate children for many diseases? The proposition would make more sense if it were worded:

> Resolved: That the United States government should create a program to provide immunizations against contagious diseases for all children living in poverty.

This wording does a better job of dividing ground to enhance clash on the issue, it focuses on the problem in a way that makes it easier for all the advocates to find materials to support their arguments, and it would probably lead to more effective and responsible health management policies. While there may be times when a narrowly worded proposition is warranted—for example, when advocates already have extensive expertise and knowledge of the subject, or when a preliminary investigation has already warranted a narrowing of policy options— in most cases a broader proposition facilitates better clash on the issues.

The Techniques for Analyzing Propositions

Once the proposition to be disputed has been created or discovered, it is time to begin the process of **analysis.** It is through analysis that arguments in support of or against a proposition are created. This process is the most interesting and creative dimension of the argumentative enterprise. In his theory of rhetoric Aristotle referred to this process as invention, meaning the invention of arguments to support the position that you want your listeners to accept. As you are aware, both weak and strong arguments can be advanced in support of almost any proposition. Your task as an advocate is to create the best arguments that you can, and to create arguments that will appeal to your audience. In short, you must invent arguments that cast your claims into stories that your audience finds appealing and believable given their experiences and values.

Defining Key Terms

The first step in the analysis of a proposition is to define the key terms. For purposes of illustration, we will go back to the proposition that we just created.

> Resolved: That the United States government should fund a program to provide immunizations against contagious diseases for all children living in poverty.

There are several important terms that must be defined for this proposition to be understood. For instance:

"United States government": the federal government—not state or local governments or private industry

"fund": to create the monetary support for, and not necessarily to administer or operate

"a program": an ongoing effort, as opposed to a one-time event

"immunizations against contagious diseases": prophylactic injections to prevent people from becoming infected with a broad range of diseases, including polio, tuberculosis, diphtheria, influenza, measles, and tetanus

"children living in poverty": children under the age of 18 from families whose incomes fall below the existing federal poverty standard

The foregoing are only examples of reasonable interpretations of the key terms in this proposition. Different disputants would almost certainly choose to define some of these terms differently in order to stake out the ground that they wished to argue. For example, an advocate could use term definitions to try to limit the discussion to the medical problems faced only by children in rural America. This advocate's opponent, however, might argue that it is unreasonable to focus only on rural children and exclude urban children.

Another narrow interpretation of the immunization resolution might emphasize only children who do not receive measles vaccines. Again, an opponent could argue that it is unreasonable to limit discussion to only one disease when the explicit wording of the proposition is: "diseases."

In most argument situations, arguers do not formally define their terms. Instead they rely upon their own notions of what the terms mean, usually by recalling the contexts or stories in which they have previously heard them.

Definitions are, in other words, shaped by popular usage. Terms acquire their meanings from their use in conversation; this accepted use gives us our common-sense notion of what terms mean. In some cases, however, arguers may need to define their terms more systematically. Arguers can consult a number of different sources in order to create definitions for key terms. They can consult a dictionary, although dictionaries typically offer several independent definitions in descending order of commonality, and many of these will not be equally acceptable to all audiences. Arguers can also consult specialized sources in the relevant literature of the field. On a topic about medical care, for example, they can consult the journals and periodicals of the medical profession. On issues of law they can consult a legal dictionary or legal periodicals. On an issue pertaining to education policy they can consult journals in that field.

Definitions themselves are often the subject for argument. If during the course of an argument your adversary challenges your definitions of the key terms of a proposition, it is helpful to cite the source for your definitions and to argue their reasonableness and appropriateness by example.

Establishing the Point of Clash

Once you have defined the key terms in the proposition, the next task is to decide where you will choose to draw your point of clash. This is known as establishing your point of **stasis.** In your analysis of any proposition you need to decide what issues you wish to advance. This is the point of stasis, or the place where you choose to differ from the opposing view.

Turning again to our example about immunization policy, an advocate for a federal program to provide immunizations for poor children might stress the severity of the debilitating effects of childhood illnesses, and how frequently poor children go unvaccinated. This would be a logical and appropriate point of stasis. Those who wished to oppose the proposition might contend that almost all children who need vaccinations currently receive them either through existing public assistance programs at the state and local level or through private insurance. They might also argue that a large and unwieldy federal program might only increase the government bureaucracy, and not be the best way to help these children.

One of the greatest challenges for the arguer is to make the best choice about where to attack the opponent's argument. This decision should be based upon your research on and knowledge of the proposition, your understanding of argumentative techniques, and your awareness of the attitudes and beliefs of the audience you are seeking to convince. The key, of course, is to attack arguments at their most vulnerable point.

Hermagoras—a Greek philosopher, rhetorical theorist, and teacher of rhetoric, who lived during the 2nd century, B.C.—developed a sort of checklist for determining where to draw stasis.[2] He suggested that there were four different levels for considering claims:

1. Conjecturing about a fact At this level the arguer seeks to dispute or establish a material claim. The advocate arguing for or against the claim that significant numbers of poor children are not vaccinated, and suffer diseases because their parents cannot pay for required medical care is conjecturing about a fact.

2. Definition At this level the arguer contends that while a material fact may be true, it is not described or defined precisely as it should be. For example, an advocate might admit that significant numbers of poor children are not vaccinated, but argue that this is not because there are no programs available to provide the vaccinations. Instead, the advocate might assert that they fail to receive vaccinations because their parents do not take advantage of the existing programs, perhaps because they lack awareness of their availability, because they do not understand their importance, or because of other barriers such as inadequate transportation, or cultural skepticism about modern medical techniques.

3. Quality At this level the arguer asserts that while the material facts might be true, and while the material evidence is correct, other aspects influencing the material quality of the claims might lead to different interpretations. An advocate arguing from quality might admit that poor children are not vaccinated, and that there are inadequate programs to provide for vaccinations, but contend that the failure to vaccinate is not a significant factor in the children's health. Instead, he or she might argue that poverty itself leads to poor health. This advocate could then detail the effects of poverty: poor diet, substandard housing, low birth weight babies, drug or alcohol addicted parents, and so on.

4. Objection This is a decision to draw stasis at the level of interpretation. An advocate who draws stasis here might concede that poor children are not vaccinated and suffer disease as a result, that the problem results from a lack of government programs to provide health care, and that this failure to vaccinate is responsible for a significant number of deaths of these children. They might contend, however, that the health statistics are not reliable, and that as a result many of these children may have died from other diseases for which no immunizations were available.

As should be clear from the examples provided, these levels of stasis are presented in descending order of their strength. Consequently, it is better to be able to argue at the level of fact than it is to have to argue at the level of definition. Both are stronger arguments than those directed at the issue of quality, and the weakest type of argument is one that relies on objection. Because Hermagoras was fundamentally concerned with inventing arguments he focused almost exclusively on the quality of the logical claims that the arguers made, and he stressed that appropriate logical techniques could be learned and taught to others.

Whether we argue in support of a proposition or oppose it, we must decide where and how to draw our point of stasis. The decision is an important one, for once you have developed the primary argument strategy that defines your case—your central story—it is difficult to change your mind later and move off in some new direction. There is no substitute for careful planning and preparation when developing your arguments.

The Stock Issues

One approach which has been developed to assist arguers in the analysis of policy propositions is the use of **stock issues.** Stock issues are those that readily lend themselves to consideration and focus in policy disputes—they are issues that recur throughout history and that always seem to draw the attention of arguers and audiences.

Many argumentation theorists adhere to the perspective, originally developed by John Dewey in 1910, that thinking, and thus decision making, follows five logically distinct steps: (1) recognition of a felt difficulty, (2) location and definition of the difficulty, (3) suggestion of a possible solution, (4) development by reasoning of the bearings of the suggestion, (5) further observation and experiment leading to its acceptance or rejection.[3] The notion that policy changes occur in response to the location of a felt difficulty, or the identification of a problem in existing policy, led to the formulation of the stock issues perspective.

The stock issues perspective was developed by Lee Hultzen, based upon Dewey's reflective thinking model.[4] The stock issues are the ill, the blame, the cure, and the cost. We will discuss each in turn.

Ill.   The stock issue of an **ill** challenges the advocate to analyze the proposition by considering the inadequacies or problems in the existing system. Turning again to our earlier example, when the advocate demonstrates that poor children are contracting infectious diseases, especially when these diseases might have been prevented by vaccination, he or she is demonstrating the existence of an ill in current health care policy.

The identified ill must also be shown to be significant. An advocate can demonstrate two different types of significance. One type is quantitative significance—that large numbers of children are affected. The other type is qualitative significance—that those affected are harmed in a serious way, perhaps that they are permanently disabled, suffer grievously, or even die. Ideally, an advocate should demonstrate both quantitative and qualitative significance, increasing maximally the impact of his or her arguments. It is the task of the opposing advocate to attempt to undercut this significance, and to demonstrate that few people suffer from the supposed ill, and/or that those who do suffer do not suffer severely.

Blame.   When considering the stock issue of **blame,** the advocate attempts to assign responsibility for the existence of an ill. In a policy dispute an arguer claims that an established policy should be changed to address and eliminate an established harm or ill. To succeed, the advocate must prove that this current policy fails to achieve its stated purpose. In most cases the arguer seeks to identify a problem that is inherent in the present system. The notion of inherency suggests that the problem will certainly repeat itself unless the policy is changed. This is a powerful suggestion, since, normally, policy makers would not concern themselves with ills that would probably repair themselves if left alone.

There are two types of inherent ills. The first is structural inherency. A program may be said to have structural inherency if it results from the very design of the current policy or from the lack of an established policy. The ill of our lacking an immunization program for children living in poverty might be shown to have structural inherency if the advocate points out that there is currently no single governmental agency responsible for providing medical services to poor children. Instead, we have a patchwork of medical programs operating at the federal, state, and local levels, supplemented by inadequate private charities and private health insurance. As a result, many poor children may slip through the cracks and not receive the necessary immunizations against devastating diseases.

A second type of inherency is attitudinal inherency. An ill may be said to result from attitudinal inherency if an advocate can demonstrate that while there may be a policy in place to correct the ill, that policy is being undermined by the attitudes or values of the people who administer it, and as a result the policy is ineffective. In the case of the vaccinations, for example, an advocate might argue that while we have programs that are intended to provide medical care for the poor, those programs are flawed because they have a crisis orientation. Children receive medical care when they are grievously ill, often in an overcrowded emergency room at a public hospital, but they do not always receive the preventive care that might have decreased or even eliminated the risk of disease. This attitudinal bias could be shown to exist in those who administer the programs, in the physicians who actually treat the children, or even in the parents if they do not seek care for their children until they are already ill.

Structural inherency is typically more compelling than attitudinal inherency, because it supports the claim that a policy change is needed to remedy the structural deficiencies which led to the existence of the ills. If attitudinal inherency is claimed, it is better if the advocate can demonstrate that these attitudes result from characteristics of the existing policy that are themselves caused by structures. If the attitudes are caused by the structures, then amending the structures might change the attitudes. If the attitudes are not a result of the structures, however, and merely reside in the people, it is more difficult for an advocate to demonstrate that these attitudes can be changed and the problem solved through policy change.

The primary purpose for analyzing a policy proposition from the perspective of the stock issue of blame is to focus your attention on specific deficiencies in existing policy that might be remedied through the adoption of new policies—policies that are outlined in the wording of the proposition being argued.

Cure. Once the advocate has identified an ill and placed the blame for its existence on the deficiencies of current policies, it is time to propose a **cure.**

The cure is the new policy which you believe will remedy the ill. The cure proposed should be developed to address the specific ill that has been outlined, and to overcome the inherent factors that were shown to cause the ill. If the inherency is structural, your cure should include the creation of a new structure which replaces, remedies, or modifies those now in place. If the inherency identified is attitudinal, the cure must correct the blighted attitudes that led to the problem.

In the case of the inoculation program for children in poverty, the cure might be a program funded by the federal government that required all children to be given their vaccinations. A bureaucracy to staff and administer the program might be established, and a means to locate and treat the children created. This policy would address the structural indictments made—such as that no program currently exists that makes vaccinations against communicable diseases its primary mission—and would reshape the health care bureaucracy. If the advocate has argued an attitudinal barrier—for instance, that parents do not take advantage of existing medical assistance programs and do not seek vaccinations for their children—then the advocate must propose a policy that will either change or circumvent those attitudes. He or she might, for example, argue that in addition to the program outlined above to locate and treat the children, a health education and awareness program is needed to reach parents in maternity hospitals, through welfare and social workers, at schools, and in the workplace and convince them of the importance of preventive health procedures.

The greatest challenge to the advocate who proposes a new policy is to argue in a convincing way that this new policy will remedy the specific ills cited, and overcome the inherency barriers claimed as flaws in the existing policy. There is no merit in changing policies if doing so will not remedy the problems plaguing the current policies.

Cost. The final stock issue is **cost.** While most of the previous stock issues were developed primarily to assist advocates who favored policy changes, the stock issue of cost is of great benefit to the arguer who seeks to refute the need for a policy change. This stock issue asks us to consider what the costs of the proposed policy will be. The issue of cost can concern purely the monetary cost of the new program. How much would it cost to undertake the new health initiatives outlined above? Given the size of our current national budget deficit, and the many other pressing social problems that our society faces (homelessness, declining educational systems, deteriorating highways, rampant crime, and so on) is this the best way to spend public money? An advocate should not simply ask this question, of course, but should argue that this either is or is not the way to spend public money, and that a program to provide vaccinations for children either will or will not produce enough benefits to make the costs worthwhile.

Another way to think about the costs is to consider the disadvantages that might result from the adoption of a new policy. An arguer could assert, for example, that there is actually a certain amount of danger from inoculations, and that some people might actually contract diseases or suffer illness as a result of adverse reactions to the vaccines. These are difficult arguments to make given this proposition, because the research is quite conclusive that vaccinations save lives, but they might serve to weaken some of the advocate's claims by indicating that some lives will be lost even after the vaccinations.

When considering the issue of the costs of new policies you should allow your creative energies to direct you, and you should consider a wide range of potential outcomes from a change in policy. The fact that a program such as the one proposed would be costly, for example, might allow you to develop arguments about the implications of these costs. You might argue that the government is so short of money that money spent for one program will almost certainly mean less to go around to pay for other programs. Then you could argue that spending more money on health might prevent increased spending on education, and that without improvements in education these children will be locked into a cycle of poverty. You might also argue that there are inadequate laboratories to produce the vaccines, and that by encouraging pharmaceutical companies to gear up to produce more vaccines you might divert their attention and resources from the production of other medicines that are even more badly needed.

The Stock Issues Decision Calculus

Arguers who use stock issues as starting points for the analysis of propositions should be mindful of the decision calculus that will be applied to the arguments that they develop. That decision calculus can best be summarized as:

Ill (Significance of Harm)
  Mitigated by Cure (degree to which new policy reduces ill)
    Less Cost (problems or disadvantages of new policy)
      Equal Benefits of Policy Change

The stock issues perspective is a tool that guides arguers in the application of cost benefit analysis to a study of policy issues. Like all other tools of analysis, however, it works only as well as the person who is using it permits it to work. The advocate who is thorough, creative, and thoughtful in the application of the stock issues perspective will create better arguments than will the advocate who is sloppy, indifferent, or uncreative. Another consideration is that this approach strongly values the quantification of argument claims. The very notion of costs and benefits suggests the importance of empirical verifications of arguments. There are certain intangible dimensions of arguments which might have a dramatic effect on listeners beyond their empirical significance, however, and advocates need to keep this in mind. In the example about vaccinations, for example, an advocate would want to keep in mind that these are children we have been arguing about—children who are exposed to serious and preventable diseases; children who may suffer and die from these diseases. Cold calculations about the costs of policy change may not sufficiently account for the moral, ethical, and philosophical values bound up in public policy issues such as this one.

An arguer who chooses to utilize cost benefit analysis should remember that arguments still must be adapted to their audiences, and that listeners respond to arguments by evaluating them as stories. The stories of suffering children can be very compelling indeed, even when the best case for the high costs of a program of treatment has been presented.

Systems Analysis

An alternative approach for the analysis of propositions, especially propositions of policy, is provided by general systems theory, and the method known as **systems analysis.** A system is defined as: "an assembly of objects all of which are related to one another by some form of regular interaction of interdependence so that the assembly can be viewed as an organic or organized whole." When applying the principles of systems theory in propositional analysis, the advocate attempts to identify, study, and evaluate the constituent parts of the system in order to determine their effectiveness.

There are several important underlying assumptions that must be understood before systems theory can be applied. First, systems theory presumes that the constituent parts (often called components) of a system are interdependent on one another. Thus if one component is changed, one might expect that the other components of the system will also be influenced.

Second, systems are characterized by an ordered sequence of events. Because systems (both naturally occurring ones—such as the human body; and created ones—such as a university) are designed to achieve some purpose, their component parts must all function in accordance with their established purpose. When one or more components fails to carry out its assigned functions the entire system may begin to falter.

Third, a system's components are connected to and controlled by each other. Because systems are often extremely complex, they must contain procedures for communication and control that keep the system operating and in a state of balance. Thus, a system might begin to fail either because a component is not performing its assigned function, or because the networks of communication and control intended to link the components to each other are failing.

Fourth, systems entail both a structure and a set of processes.[5] The structure of a system is determined by the processes that the system must carry out, and likewise, the processes of the different components in a system are determined by the structures that are present. Thus, if the structures are inadequate for the processes that need to be performed, those structures must be changed, or if the processes underway do not reflect the maximum utilization of the characteristics of the structures, the processes must be changed.

Because systems theory is a tool of analysis, it is of benefit to an advocate only if it is artfully and creatively applied to the study of a proposition. Systems theory is applied to describe the operations of the existing system, and it can also be utilized to evaluate the effectiveness of that system and compare it with possible alternative systems.

A MODEL FOR SYSTEMS ANALYSIS[6]

Function	Terms	Definitions
	Components	the discrete, unique, or constituent parts that compose a system
Description		
	Relationships	the identity that exists between two or more components; the action of a system, that is, the nature or characteristics of the activity between two or more things taken together
	Goals	the stated or operational objectives, designs, aims, or intentions of the people interacting with their environment; the critical decision-making process is designed to achieve these goals
Evaluation		
	Effects	the assessment, fulfillment, accomplishment, impression, or outcome of a system as a result of certain components interacting in relationships toward certain goals; an evaluation of the elements of the system as measured against the goals of the system

A Systems Analysis of a Policy Proposition

An advocate who chooses to use systems theory to analyze a policy proposition should first describe the components of the existing system and their relationship to each other, and then evaluate them in terms of their effectiveness in meeting their goals. To illustrate the process we will suggest steps for analyzing the proposition,

> Resolved: That the federal government should establish a program to provide sex education, birth control information and access to contraceptives in clinics in all public secondary schools in the United States.

The advocate should first seek to detail the components of the system that currently provides sex education and contraceptives to teenagers. This advocate would likely find that many different organizations, with very different objectives, provide information and services. Following are the components of the present system:

1. Existing clinics in public schools A few schools might have precisely the kinds of clinics that the advocate would like to see throughout the nation. These clinics might provide teenagers with information on avoiding sexually transmitted diseases and preventing pregnancy, and they might also have the facilities and staff to provide medical examinations. These clinics could serve as pilot projects to illustrate the benefits of school-based programs. Currently, however, these programs would be limited in number and able to serve only a fraction of the total number of teenagers.

2. Sex education classes in public schools More schools might have programs that provide information about contraceptives, the prevention of sexually transmitted diseases, and so forth. These schools, however, would probably not provide medical services or contraceptives, and it is not likely that they would be found in all school districts.

3. Planned Parenthood and other volunteer organizations In many communities, schools do not provide information or contraceptives to teenagers, but these groups may fill in the gap. The challenge is to make students aware of these programs, and to make them convenient, so that they will actually take advantage of them.

4. Churches and religious groups Many communities have sex education programs sponsored by churches, religious denominations, or religious support groups. Such programs may focus primarily on trying to prevent teenagers from becoming sexually active and may also seek to counsel them against electing to terminate unwanted pregnancies. Because of their stated purpose these programs may leave many problems unaddressed.

5. Parents, friends, and others For some teenagers there may be no access to information about sex from organized external sources. These students may get their information from their parents or other relatives, their friends and neighbors, or even from comparative strangers. Since many parents feel uncomfortable discussing sex with their children, and may not want to believe that their children are sexually active, they may put off the discussion. Furthermore, these sources may provide teenagers with incomplete or misleading information.

Once the advocate has identified the different components of the system that exists to provide sexual information and services to teenagers, he or she can begin to assess how these different components function in relationship to each other. One will likely find, for instance, that only a small number of teenagers have access to the kind of comprehensive education and services that school-based clinics can provide. Perhaps sex education programs are in existence at some schools, but not in all schools, and voluntary organizations such as Planned Parenthood, while available in most communities, are inadequate to serve all students. Consequently, the advocate might learn that most teenagers get most of their information about sex from their parents or their friends, and that they must use their own initiative to secure contraceptives.

An analysis of the goals of the present system would also help inform the advocate. For example, the goal of many current sex education programs, and the focus of much of the instruction provided to teenagers, is to prevent them from becoming sexually active. Many parents and religious groups, for example, do not tell teenagers much about sex beyond preaching the merits of abstinence. The advocate can critique the system, however, by observing that many teenagers do become sexually active despite this instruction, and that they need information to help them avoid pregnancy and disease. Thus, the advocate might find that the very goals of the present system limit its effectiveness in solving the problems that society faces.

Through an analysis of the effects of the current system, the advocate can identify the problems left unresolved by the existing policies of sex education. Current policy leaves the design, implementation, and administration of sex education programs to individual communities, school districts, and parents. We have soaring rates of teenage pregnancies, sexually transmitted diseases have reached epidemic levels, and the specter of AIDS looms over the entire population. It may well be time to propose a more comprehensive program to address these problems.

The final task for the advocate is to utilize systems theory in designing an alternative to the current system. In this step the advocate seeks to enact the resolution to the stated problems through a new system. The school-based clinics mentioned earlier might be seen as the most effective way to provide information and health services because they are easily accessible to students and meet them on their own turf.

Systems theory can also be utilized by those who seek to defend the current system. Often advocates can argue that the system either functions well as currently designed, or that only minor alterations in the existing system would address the problems, so that a new system is not needed and might even prove to be counterproductive.

The Benefits of Systems Theory

While the traditional theory of stock issues presumes that change occurs only when there is some recognizable need, "felt difficulty," or ill; systems theory suggests that change is always occurring and must be managed in the best way possible. It presumes that minor policy corrections are inevitable and desirable. Consequently, some have argued that systems theory is a more desirable way to evaluate policy arguments in contemporary society.[7]

Another benefit of systems theory is that it more accurately reflects the increasing complexity of modern life. We have so many layers of government involved in decision making today, with state and local governments, regulatory agencies, and the federal government all making decisions that influence our lives, that it is useful to employ a tool of analysis that reflects this complexity and the characteristics of contemporary decision-making structures.

Both systems theory and the stock issues theory are best understood as tools of analysis. They are useful because they guide both advocates and critics in the careful and thoughtful consideration of arguments.

Summary

This chapter considered the different types of propositions that may be argued: propositions of fact, propositions of value, and propositions of policy. It also discussed the importance of defining the key terms of any proposition, and the process of analysis. The chapter offered suggestions for how advocates should select the point of stasis (or the point of clash) in an argument, and it discussed two systems for propositional analysis, the stock issues perspective and the systems theory perspective.

Key Terms

analysis	stock issues
proposition	ill
of fact	blame
of policy	cure
of value	cost
stasis	systems analysis

Activities

1. As practice in writing propositions, select controversies from your local or

student newspaper. Try to locate the main points of stasis for each controversy. Phrase these differences in terms of propositions of fact, value, or policy, depending on the nature of the stasis.

2. Examine the following propositions, identifying whether each is a proposition of fact, value, or policy:
   a. The weather today is nice.
   b. The high temperature today was fifty-three degrees.
   c. If you don't wear a coat today you will be cold.
   d. You should wear a coat today.
   e. Parents should require that children wear coats when the weather is cold.
   f. Failing to wear a coat when it is cold can cause illness.
   g. Protective clothing keeps a person warm.

3. Select a public controversy and analyze how the key terms of the controversy might be defined. Note the differences, if any, in the alternative definitions, and consider how the differences may influence the argument process. Consult each of the following, as appropriate:
   a. your own personal definition
   b. a popular dictionary definition
   c. a specialized dictionary definition from the appropriate field (for example, a legal dictionary)
   d. how advocates engaged in the controversy define the key terms

4. Select an article in which an advocate is calling for a change (for example, an editorial or opinion piece). Then examine the way the advocate identifies the ill, the blame, and the cure. Are all three stock issues presented? Does the advocate rebut potential costs?

Recommended Readings _____

Benoit, William L., Steve R. Wilson, and Vincent F. Follert. "Decision Rules for the Policy Metaphor." *Journal of the American Forensic Association* 22 (1986): 135–146.

Kline, Susan L. "Toward a Contemporary Linguistic Interpretation of the Concepts of Stasis." *Journal of the American Forensic Association* 16 (1979): 95–103.

Klumpp, James F., Bernard L. Brock, James W. Chesebro, and John F. Cragan. "Implications of a Systems Model of Analysis on Argumentation Theory." *Journal of the American Forensic Association* 11 (1974): 1–7.

Lichtman, Allan J. "Competing Models of the Debate Process." *Journal of the American Forensic Association* 22 (1986): 147–151.

Lichtman, Allan J., and Daniel M. Rohrer. "The Logic of Policy Dispute." *Journal of the American Forensic Association* 16 (1980): 236–247.

Mader, Thomas F. "The Inherent Need to Analyze Stasis." *Journal of the American Forensic Association* 4 (1967): 13–20.

Pfau, Michael. "The Present System Revisited Part One: Incremental Change." *Journal of the American Forensic Association* 17 (1980): 80–84.

Notes

1. For a more complete discussion of criteria for the evaluation of value propositions, see Thomas A. Hollihan, "An Analysis of Value Argumentation in Contemporary Debate," *Debate Issues* 14 (1980): 7–10.
2. For a discussion of the principle of stasis, see Ray Nadeau, "Some Aristotelian and Stoic Influences on the Theory of Stasis," *Speech Monographs* 26 (1959): p. 248. See also George Kennedy, *The Art of Persuasion in Greece* (Princeton: Princeton University Press, 1963), pp. 303–309.
3. For a discussion of Dewey's reflective thinking model see Bernard L. Brock, James W. Chesebro, John F. Cragan and James F. Klumpp, *Public Policy Decision Making: Systems Analysis and Comparative Advantages Debate* (New York: Harper and Row, 1973), pp. 3–4.
4. Lee S. Hultzen, "Status in Deliberative Analysis," in Donald C. Bryant, ed., *The Rhetorical Idiom* (New York: Cornell University Press, 1958), pp. 97–123.
5. Brock, et. al, p. 27–29.
6. Brock, et. al, p. 50.
7. Brock, et. al, pp. 1–22.

6

Types of Arguments

Humans are natural arguers—we have an affinity for making, using, and evaluating arguments. Despite this natural proclivity for arguing, however, learning the basic components of arguments can enable decision makers to more systematically dissect and evaluate argumentative claims. Learning argumentation principles will also enable arguers to construct stronger arguments. In this chapter we discuss the reasoning process and consider arguments as complete logical claims.

From a logical perspective, arguments are considered rational when they correspond with accepted standards of reasoning. The reasoning process involves three separate elements. First, you must identify the data or grounds that will be used to develop your claim. Second, you must reason from that data through logical induction or deduction. Third, you must offer a claim or conclusion that builds upon the data and which constitutes a new and original insight. This chapter focuses primarily on the second step, the inductive and deductive reasoning process.

Inductive reasoning might be described as arguing from specific cases to more general conclusions. **Deductive reasoning** is essentially the opposite process, and entails moving from overall theories or generally accepted principles to conclusions about specific cases. Both inductive and deductive arguments occur frequently and naturally, because they are typically embedded in the stories that people tell to make decisions, resolve disputes, or identify solutions to their problems. Both forms of reasoning can be equally compelling and persuasive, and neither form is preferred over the other. Instead, arguers create inductive or deductive arguments in response to the problems that they face and the purposes for the arguments that they are creating.

Inductive Arguments

When you are faced with a situation where you have knowledge or information about a number of specific cases, but you lack an understanding of the factors that might unite those cases into a general theory or principle, you can utilize the inductive reasoning process to seek conclusions. There are three types of arguments that you may utilize to reason inductively.

Arguments by Example

An **argument by example** examines one or more cases within a specific class and reasons that if these cases have certain features then other, as yet unknown, cases in that class will also have those features. All arguments by example are based upon generalizations from these known cases to unknown ones. Here are some examples:

◆ Susan Jones, Ann Harper and Liz Kent are members of the Delta Delta Delta sorority, and they are all on the dean's list. Tri-Delts are good students.
◆ My friends Bill, Dianne, and Lynn were communication majors and they all got into good law schools. Communication must be a good pre-law major.
◆ The last time I tried to get help from the Advising Office I got passed around from one person to another. No one knew the answer to my question. That department is incompetent.
◆ When the standards for disposing of hazardous waste in the United States become more stringent, or when the government increases the regulations to increase worker safety, American companies ship the hazardous waste overseas or build their manufacturing plants in places that are not so well regulated. American corporations don't care about worker safety or the environment.

As can be seen in the foregoing examples, the process of arguing on the basis of examples is familiar and common. Not all arguments from example are strong or convincing, however, and several tests of these arguments can and should be applied.

First, are there a sufficient number of examples offered to support the claim? Obviously there is a great danger in arguing from a very limited number of cases to a more general conclusion. All of the arguments offered above might be challenged on the basis of the sufficiency of the examples cited. The arguer who reasons from only a limited number of cases always risks making judgments about those cases that may not be true for other unknown cases. For example, there are hundreds of communication majors who apply to law schools each year. Knowing that three of them got into good law schools may not tell us very much about how good communication really is as a pre-law major.

Second, are the examples cited typical of the category or class that the arguer is trying to generalize to? Because one individual asked a question of the Advising Office that the staff was unable to answer does not necessarily suggest that this office is typically unable to answer questions. What previous stories have you either experienced personally or heard about the Advising Office? It might simply be that this student's question was so unusual that they had never before encountered it.

Perhaps there was no established policy to provide such an answer, and therefore the fact that this office had no answer was only to be expected.

Third, are negative examples or rival stories sufficiently accounted for in the argument? For example, the Delta Delta Delta sorority might indeed have three members who are on the dean's list. This same sorority might also have three, or perhaps even more, members who are on academic probation during any given semester. It might be just as reasonable to argue that the students on probation reflect the scholarly capabilities of the sorority as it is to argue that the gifted students do.

Fourth, are the cited examples relevant to the claim being advanced? Many factors might, for example, influence a company's decision to shift their operations overseas. Increased environmental safety or worker safety legislation might indeed be a factor in this decision, but companies might also be seeking to benefit from lower wage rates, transportation variables, access to foreign markets to sell their products, among other things.

Arguments by Analogy

An **argument by analogy** seeks to identify similarities between cases that might on the surface seem to be quite dissimilar, in order to permit an inference to be drawn. Analogies are typically literary and creative devices that appeal to the listeners' experiences and beliefs, and they are often used to embellish our stories. There are two types of analogies, literal and figurative.

A literal analogy is a statement drawing a direct comparison between two or more cases. The following are examples of literal analogies:

♦ In business circles there is a new awareness of customer service. It is time for professors to begin thinking of students as the customers of the university.
♦ Students who want an education only to prepare them for careers are like apprentices attaching themselves to a carpenter. That is not what a liberal education should seek to achieve.
♦ Gorbachev, Yeltsin, and the other leaders in Russia who tried to create democratic institutions in their country faced the same kinds of problems that Thomas Jefferson, Benjamin Franklin, and our other forefathers faced two centuries ago.

A figurative analogy is a statement that makes comparisons between classes that are materially dissimilar from each other, but which are nonetheless suggestive of each other in some characteristic or manner. The following are examples of figurative analogies:

♦ The Communist flood washed over the shores of Southeast Asia until the entire region was swamped. The domino principle was considered inapplicable by American liberals, but in Asia it seemed quite accurate.
♦ The builders and developers have attacked the undeveloped hillsides north of the city like hungry locusts.
♦ Many senators responded angrily to the bill limiting their income from outside sources. They are like drug addicts demanding their daily fix.

Both literal and figurative analogies are especially compelling types of arguments because they correspond to people's ability to create stories and to test those stories when they argue. There is an important dramatic element to an effective analogy, for it creates a vivid picture in the minds of the audience. Consequently, analogies readily lend themselves to the tests of narrative probability and narrative fidelity that we have already discussed in great detail.

In addition to these narrative tests, however, analogies can also be tested by asking two questions. First, are the compared cases alike in some meaningful way? Is it really useful, for example, to think of students as customers? Customers are typically passive consumers who expect the businesses they patronize to wait on them. Students, on the other hand, are active participants in the learning process. Education is not something that can be done for you; it is something that students must largely do for themselves. While this analogy might appeal to students, it might not be a very compelling argument for all listeners, especially the professors to whom it is perhaps directed!

Second, are the compared characteristics accurately described? For example, in the argument about the "Communist flood" in Southeast Asia, the reference is drawn to an onrushing tide of Communist takeovers that paid no regard to national borders. In Southeast Asia, however, the Communists took over only in Vietnam, Laos, and Cambodia, and not in the region as a whole. Furthermore, the regimes in two of these nations, Cambodia and Vietnam, were so much at odds that they went to war against each other. This hardly suggests a faceless sea of undifferentiated Communists.

Arguments from Causal Correlation

An even more sophisticated form of inductive reasoning is the **argument from causal correlation.** This type of argument examines specific cases, classes of cases, or both, in order to identify an actual relationship or correlation between them. Most research in the scientific tradition adheres to the principles of the inductive causal correlation argument, or its deductive cousin, the causal generalization, which we shall discuss in the next section.

The following examples might help you to identify arguments from causal correlation:

◆ Children who are exposed to excess levels of lead, either from eating paint chips or from air pollution, often suffer serious brain deficiencies and learning disabilities as a result.

◆ Excessive exposure to violence on television leads to a willingness to accept violence as appropriate behavior and decreases people's sense of revulsion towards violence in real life.

◆ People today are given so many different antibiotics to combat infections that they are increasingly becoming inured to them. All too often the result is the development of resistant strains of diseases which are much more difficult to cure.

There are several tests of causal correlations that enable an arguer to assess this type of argument. First, is the association proposed between cause and effect consistent? For example, do all, or even most people who watch violent television shows become more accepting of violence? Do people who are more inclined toward pacifism watch the least television violence? These questions are all designed as tests of causal correlation such as those that were first proposed by the English philosopher and logician John Stuart Mill. Mill claimed that causal correlations could be tested on the basis of three canons that assess the strength of the association being claimed. The questions posed above all assess what Mill described as concomitant variation.[1] This test says that if increased exposure to violence is claimed to increase one's acceptance of violence, then decreased exposure to violence should also mean a decreased acceptance of violence. Mill believed that there should be a predictable pattern and relationship between a cause and its alleged effect.

Mill also claimed that the consistency between cause and effect could be tested by discovering whether the "method of agreement" between the cases was the same. He thus claimed, "If two or more instances of the phenomenon under investigation have only one circumstance in common, the circumstances in which alone all the instances agree is the cause (or effect) of the given phenomenon."[2] Turning again to the argument about violence on television and violent behavior, an arguer would seek to determine if the subjects in the argument were alike in their television habits and in their proclivity toward violence, but dissimilar in other respects such as social status, income, children in single parent homes, residence, and lifestyle. This inquiry might lead one to conclude viewing violence on television was or was not a more important factor in shaping attitudes toward violence than these other factors studied.

Finally, according to Mill, the consistency between cause and effect can be tested by considering whether the method of difference between the cases compared is consistent:

> If an instance in which the phenomenon under investigation occurs, and an instance in which it does not occur, have every circumstance in common save one, that one occurring only in the former, then the circumstance in which alone the two instances differ is the effect, or the cause, or an indispensable part of the cause of the phenomenon.[3]

Returning again to our test case, one might cite an example of two boys who both grow up in a violent inner city neighborhood, in single-parent homes, and with one abusive and alcoholic parent. One child becomes a violent felon and is sent to prison. The other becomes an ordained priest. The argument about the relationship between television violence and real life violence would be supported if the arguer could establish that the priest's parents had not owned a television set, and he was, consequently, seldom exposed to the television violence that was the other boy's constant companion.

All three of Mill's canons—concomitant variation, method of agreement, and method of difference—are essentially subsumed under the first test of a causal correlation, the test of the consistency of the association between cause and effect.

A second test of a causal correlation argument asks: Is the alleged association a strong one? This is often an empirical test. There are, for example, many children who watch violence on television who do not become violent adults. What percentage of those who see violent programs do become violent? How much violent programming do they watch? Is there some point up to which watching violent programs may not be harmful, but beyond which it is? Is there a certain age at which violent television programs become either more or less dangerous? All of these questions seek to determine the degree to which the statistical association between watching violent television programs and committing violent acts can be predicted.

A third test of a causal correlation asks: Does the movement of cause to effect follow a regular and predictable time sequence? For example, if one argues that children who are exposed to higher levels of lead suffer learning disabilities as a result, one should be able to argue definitively about the length of time it takes for the exposure to cause the harmful effect. Does it take hours, weeks, days, or months for the symptoms to manifest themselves? Furthermore, how long do the symptoms persist? Does the damage that a child faces from lead poisoning correct itself over time? Or can one expect that a child once so injured will suffer throughout his or her life?

Recent research into the AIDS virus has demonstrated the importance of carefully considering time frame as a test of argument. Doctors now understand that AIDS is unlike most other diseases. First, it takes a long time for medical tests to confirm that the patient has been exposed, because doctors can determine that a patient has the disease only after they begin to develop antibodies to fight the infection. Second, even after these antibodies appear, most patients will continue to be healthy for many months or even many years before beginning to develop symptoms of the disease. Finally, even after patients develop AIDS symptoms, it may be another extended period before their condition is identifiable as full-blown AIDS. In the early years of AIDS research, doctors interpreted this time lag as an indication that many, if not most, of the people who became infected with the virus would probably not come down with the disease. Doctors assumed that because these patients had been infected but showed no symptoms, they would probably be able to fight the disease off on their own. Early estimates based on this reasoning predicted that only 10 percent of those infected with the virus would succumb to the disease. Then, as more and more patients became ill, doctors kept increasing their estimates—20 percent, then 30 percent, and so on. Ultimately, the doctors researching AIDS have realized that virtually all patients who are HIV-antibody-positive will eventually come down with the disease. As a result, the notions about the lag time from exposure to the onset of the disease have been extended. Only with this new realization of the ways in which the disease progressed (the cause) was the real severity of the AIDS crisis in the United States understood (the effect).

The final test of causal correlation asks: Is the alleged association between cause and effect coherent? Essentially this tasks the arguer to offer a persuasive explanation for the relationship between cause and effect. For example, several years ago in San Francisco an enraged city supervisor named Dan White murdered Mayor George Moscone and a fellow supervisor named Harvey Britt. The defense attorney claimed during the trial that White committed the murder because he was addicted to, and had been on a binge, eating junk food. This junk food, the attorney claimed, produced such a "sugar high" that the murderer could not be held responsible for his actions. This so-called, Twinkie defense, won wide attention from the media but was criticized by nutritional experts as largely spurious. These experts argued that while there might be some association between physical behavior and diet, there was no coherent explanation to support an association between willingness to commit violent acts and one's diet.

Now that we have introduced the three primary forms in which inductive arguments might be developed, it is time to consider the different forms in which deductive arguments occur.

Deductive Arguments

In deductive arguments one generalizes from theories or principles believed to be true to claims about individual cases. There are two types of deductive arguments.

Arguments from Sign

An **argument from sign** relies on the presence of certain attributes observable in a specific case to prove that it can be related to a generalization that is assumed to be true. When using this form of argument one identifies certain characteristics or signs and then seeks to account for them by tying them to a conclusion or claim. Consider the following examples:

- ◆ The lack of respect for other people's property—the graffiti and vandalism, as well as the increased incidents of violence—suggests that many American youths lack values.
- ◆ Bob is suffering from excessive fatigue, diarrhea, swollen lymph glands, night sweats, and he has a yeast infection in his mouth. He must have contracted AIDS.
- ◆ The students were hunched over their desks in apt concentration, and the quiet in the room was almost deafening. It was obvious that they were taking their required competency examinations very seriously.

There are three separate tests that can be used in the evaluation of a sign argument. First, are the cited signs always indicators of the general theory being cited? The symptoms cited in the example about AIDS, for example, might also be symptoms of many other medical conditions, none of them as alarming or as serious as AIDS. A doctor would not want to mention the possibility that the patient had contracted AIDS until these other possibilities had been eliminated. It would be cruel to cause a patient to worry unnecessarily.

Second, are there enough signs present to support the conclusion offered? The students who are hunched over their desks taking the examinations, for example, might simply be exhausted from a night of intense partying, and might not be concentrating on their tests after all. One might want to determine whether or not there are other signs that the students took the examinations seriously. For instance, did they study for them? And how well did they score?

Third, are contradictory signs present and, if so, have they been carefully considered? With regard to the argument about AIDS, for example, it might be that Bob is gaining weight despite all of his other symptoms. As it is highly unusual for an AIDS patient to gain weight, the arguer would need to account for the weight gain in order to support any conclusion ventured about the underlying cause for Bob's medical symptoms.

Arguments from Causal Generalization

The second type of deductive argument is the **argument from causal generalization.** The causal generalization is the direct counterpart of the causal correlation. While the causal correlation argues inductively from specific cases to seek to identify a connection between these cases, the causal generalization argues deductively from some general principles that are assumed to be true, to judgments about specific cases under consideration. The following are examples of causal generalizations:

◆ It is well known that the AIDS virus is transmitted by the exchange of bodily fluids. This frequently occurs when drug addicts share hypodermic needles. Bob was an IV drug user which probably accounts for his infection with AIDS.
◆ Steven is bound to abuse his children because he was himself abused as a child.
◆ It is unwise to raise interest rates. Every time interest rates have been substantially raised a recession has followed.

There are three tests of arguments from causal generalization. First, is the cause that is identified sufficient to produce the effect? The fact that Steven was abused as a child might influence his parenting style, for example, but there are many persons who were abused as children who are very good parents and who do not abuse their children. As a result, one can question whether his own abuse experience is sufficient to explain his behavior.

Second, might the cause result in other quite different effects? Perhaps Steven has such negative recollections of his own childhood experiences that he will be especially motivated to avoid them with his children. He might become a parent who is unusually sensitive and kind to his children precisely because his own parents were far less sensitive and kind.

Third, might intervening factors preclude the expected relationship between the cause and the effect? In some cases an adjustment upwards of interest rates will stabilize and ultimately strengthen the economy. The increase in interest rates might slow demand, reduce inflation, and help to strengthen the banks. All of these factors might actually serve to keep the nation out of a recession.

The Deductive Syllogism

We can test all deductive arguments, whether arguments from sign or arguments from causal generalization, by phrasing them in syllogistic form and then examining their structural properties. A **syllogism** is a formal, logical type of reasoning. A syllogism consists of three statements. The **major premise** states a generalization: *All men are mortal.* The **minor premise** relates a specific case or class to the generalization: *Socrates is a man.* And the **conclusion** is deduced from the two premises: *Socrates is mortal.*

The example about Socrates is what is known as a *categorical syllogism*—one that makes a statement about all cases within a given category. The major premise asserts a generalization that prescribes the category, the minor premise locates a specific case being argued within that category, and the conclusion is the deductive judgment that presents itself when these two premises are rationally or logically evaluated. The categorical syllogism is thus a very straightforward and simple deductive judgment. Another example of a categorical syllogism is:

Major Premise	All Christians believe in God.
Minor Premise	Fred is a Christian.
Conclusion	Fred believes in God.

Analyzing deductive arguments as syllogisms enables an arguer to quickly assess their validity. (A valid syllogism is one that meets the required characteristics of argumentative form.) As we will discuss in detail later, logical validity is not the same as material truth. A syllogism that is not true may be valid, and an invalid syllogism may be materially true. Nonetheless, tests of logical validity are very useful to arguers, and are easy to learn because they are often intuitive. These tests can be summarized as follows:

First, to be valid, a categorical syllogism must in its major premise so define the category in question that it can be determined for certain that the specific case cited in the minor premise will fall within it. In the most recent example, the category defined "All Christians" is so clear that once the minor premise labels Fred as a Christian we can immediately conclude that he believes in God. If, for example, the major premise had asserted only that some Christians believe in God, it would have been impossible for us to know whether or not Fred fell within that group.

Second, no term can be found in the conclusion that is not found in one of the premises. For example:

Major Premise	All tennis players are athletic.
Minor Premise	Jim is a tennis player.
Conclusion	Susan is athletic.

This syllogism cannot be presumed valid because the specific case Susan is not specified in either the major or the minor premise. We do not know from this syllogism whether Susan is a tennis player or not. Thus, her specific case cannot be deduced from a generalization about tennis players.

Third, the major and the minor premises cannot both be negative statements. If both statements offer negative judgments it is impossible to derive a positive conclusion about a specific case from them. See if you can think of one for this example:

> *Major Premise*   No Republicans favor tax increases.
> *Minor Premise*   Matt is no Republican.
> *Conclusion*   (Who knows?)

Fourth, whenever the major or the minor premise is a negative statement the conclusion must also be a negative statement. For example:

> *Major Premise*   No Democrats favor cuts in social programs.
> *Minor Premise*   Mary is a Democrat.
> *Conclusion*   Mary does not favor cuts in social programs.

You have no doubt discovered by now that most of these categorical syllogisms are fairly easy to evaluate. In order to further guide your assessments of the validity of a syllogism, however, you can construct what is known as a Venn diagram, named for its creator, the nineteenth-century mathematician John Venn. In a Venn diagram one takes the broadest category, established in the major premise, and draws it in a large circle. One then takes the more specific term of the major premise and draws it in a smaller circle. Finally, one takes the particular case that you are seeking to categorize and draws it in the smallest circle. For example:

> *Major Premise*   All Christians believe in God.
> *Minor Premise*   Fred is a Christian.
> *Conclusion*   Fred believes in God.

The Venn diagram would be constructed as follows:

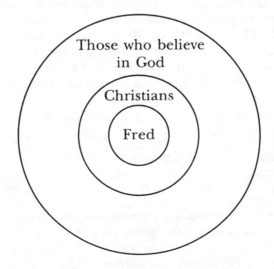

The Venn diagram reveals that this is a valid syllogism because the three circles, are located within each other. We can thus visually determine that Fred, as a Christian, falls within the category of those who believe in God.

A Venn diagram can also reveal the invalidity of a syllogism:

Major Premise	No Republicans favor tax increases.
Minor Premise	Matt is no Republican.
Conclusion	Who knows?

The Venn diagram for this syllogism would look like this:

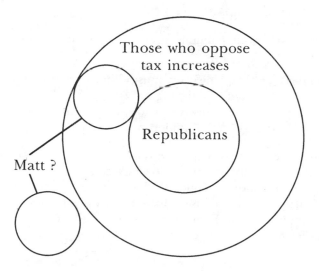

Because, in this case, we cannot place the term we are seeking to define (Matt) within the circles representing the two proposed defining characteristics, this Venn diagram reveals that the syllogism docs not meet the requirements of formal validity.

The Conditional Syllogism

A conditional syllogism might best be described as an "if/then" syllogism. This type of syllogism asserts that if a particular thing occurs then some other particular thing will follow:

Major Premise	If students study they get better grades.
Minor Premise	Students will study.
Conclusion	Students will get better grades.

The antecedent, or "if" premise, sets up the reasoning process that makes the syllogism function. If the consequent, or minor premise, affirms the antecedent the syllogism is presumed valid. However, if the consequent denies the antecedent, the syllogism cannot be presumed valid:

Major Premise	If students study they get better grades.
Minor Premise	Students will not study.
Conclusion	Students will get better grades.

Since, in this example, the consequent does not meet the conditions specified in the antecedent, the syllogism is invalid.

The Disjunctive Syllogism

A disjunctive syllogism contains premises that are essentially either/or statements:

Major Premise	The University must either raise tuition or cut faculty and programs.
Minor Premise	The University is unwilling to make cuts.
Conclusion	Therefore tuition must be increased.

The disjunctive syllogism may be judged valid when the major premise includes all of the possible alternatives thereby allowing a conclusion to be drawn through the process of elimination. Frequently there are more alternatives than are provided for in the major premise. This flaw is less a failure of the syllogistic reasoning than it is a test of the material truth or falsity of the syllogistic claim, however. This leads us to the next issue for discussion.

Structural Validity versus Material Truth

The evaluation of syllogistic form is useful as a demonstration of explicit logical deduction. By applying the tests of syllogistic reasoning, an arguer can readily determine whether or not a conclusion argued in a syllogism is valid. The same tests are not effective in determining the material truth underlying the argumentative claim, however, because material truths are assumed in the formation of premises. Consider the following example:

Major Premise	All cats have three legs.
Minor Premise	Felix is a cat.
Conclusion	Felix has three legs.

The syllogism is valid. It meets all of the tests of a categorical syllogism. Obviously, however, the syllogism is not materially true since we know that cats have four, not three, legs. The arguer who wishes to test syllogisms needs to remember that a syllogism's being valid does not make it true. The truth or falsity of a syllogism must also be evaluated by an examination of the material truth of the premises, and the degree to which these observations are supported.

The Toulmin Model

Another approach to viewing arguments has been suggested by Stephen Toulmin, and has come to be known as the **Toulmin model,** or diagram, of argument.[4] (We have already discussed Toulmin's field theory of argument in Chapter 3.) While few artifacts of argument exhibit all the elements of the Toulmin model, and while abstracting an argument from its social context in order to diagram it risks distorting and oversimplifying it, the Toulmin model is a useful tool for understanding the components of argument, and it provides real insight into the reasoning process that arguers use. Once you understand the elements of an argument you can critically evaluate each one in turn. The six components are:

Claim: The conclusion of the argument; that statement which the advocate wishes the audience to believe

Grounds: The foundation or basis for the claim, the support

Warrant: The reasoning that authorizes the inferential leap from the grounds to the claim

Backing: The support for the warrant

Modality: The degree of certainty with which the advocate makes the claim

Rebuttal: Exceptions that might be offered to the claim

Before discussing each of these elements in greater detail we will examine an entire argument and diagram it.

Sue: The Braves will probably win the National League Pennant this year. (claim)

Tim: What are you basing this claim on? (request for grounds)

Sue: They have the best pitching. (grounds)

Tim: Maybe, but how does the fact that they have the best pitching lead you to believe they will win the pennant? (request for the warrant)

Sue: The team with the best pitching usually wins. (warrant)

Tim: How can you make that claim? (request for backing of the warrant)

Sue: Well, that is what has happened the last few years. (backing)

Tim: How sure are you that they will win? Do you want to bet on it? (request for modality)

Sue: Well, I did say probably, so I don't want to bet too much. (modality)

Tim: Well, you seem pretty confident. Why won't you make a nice big wager?

Sue: There is always the possibility that the Braves will have a lot of injuries. (rebuttal)

Following the Toulmin model, this argument would be diagrammed in this way:

```
Grounds————Warrant————Modality————Claim
               |                       |
            Backing                 Rebuttal
```

Claims

The first component of an argument is the *claim*. The claim is the statement the arguer seeks to convince the audience to accept. Claims may be made in past, present, or future tense. The following are examples of claims:

It is time for you to start working on your term paper.
The recession should be over by next spring.
We should probably give more foreign aid to the Russians.

Each of these claims is a declarative statement that expresses the advocate's belief. Claims are not always expressed in declarative statements, however. "Won't deficit spending ultimately come back to haunt us?" is another way of asserting that it *will* come back to haunt us. There are several different types of claims that can be argued:

Fact: Claims of fact are potentially verifiable assertions as to the nature of things.
◆ There are currently six million unemployed Americans.
◆ The number of high school dropouts is increasing.
◆ Millions of Americans have no health insurance.

Value: Claims of value indicate preference or judgment. Often values are predicated on facts, but they also contain valuative judgments.
◆ We should not tolerate a situation in which so many are unemployed.
◆ The large number of dropouts demonstrates that our schools are failing.
◆ It is unacceptable that some persons are denied access to health care because they cannot afford it.

Policy: Claims of policy are assertions that something should be done. They are easily identified because they usually contain words like *should* or *ought*.
◆ We should create a jobs program to find people work.
◆ We should revise our school curriculums so that students will want to stay in school and get their diplomas.
◆ The federal government ought to create a program of national health insurance.

The first objective in analyzing a claim is to determine whether it is a claim of fact, value, or policy. Once you have identified the claim and categorized it you can determine whether you wish to challenge it.

Sometimes an advocate's claim is not readily apparent in their argument. This may occur simply because an argument is poorly developed and expressed. Often advocates themselves are not sure what they are arguing. On other occasions arguers are reluctant to explicitly state their claims for strategic reasons. They may have a hidden agenda. In such situations you must infer from the information available to you what the arguer is claiming. This inference process is, of course, subject to great error, so the arguer who wishes to be clearly understood should explicitly state his or her claim.

Grounds

When asked, "What are you basing your claim on?" you are being asked for the *grounds,* or foundational assumptions, underlying your argument—the evidence you offer in support of your claim. The grounds may include examples or signs that you cite and then generalize from. Evidence should consist of such things as factual statements, statistical proof, the statement of accepted principles, and testimony.

Each type of evidence can be subjected to tests evaluating its quality. The grounds for arguments, and the appropriate tests of evidence will be discussed in far greater detail in Chapter 7.

Warrants and Backing

The next two elements of the Toulmin model are called the *warrant* and the *backing.* Just as a judge may issue a warrant authorizing the police to conduct a search of a suspect's dwelling, a warrant authorizes an advocate to make a claim based on the grounds provided. A warrant is the reasoning that permits an inferential leap; it works like a bridge connecting the grounds to the claim.

Backing refers to the support for the warrant. If a warrant has backing there is reason to believe that the warrant is legitimate. In essence, a warrant is a secondary claim. The backing for the warrant is thus the grounds for this secondary claim. There are several different types of warrants, which correspond to the different forms of reasoning we discussed in the beginning of this chapter. One can reason warrants from examples, analogies, signs, and causal correlations or generalizations. In addition, however, an arguer can use warrants that are drawn from authority (this claim is true because a significant, respected, and qualified source says it is true) or from principle (this argument is true because it depends upon a principle that virtually everyone would accept as true).

Earlier in this chapter we discussed the tests to which arguments from example, analogy, causality, and signs could be subjected. There are also tests to evaluate arguments from authority and principle. Arguments from authority depend upon the quality of the authority cited, and arguments from principle depend upon the principles' being readily accepted and shared. These tests for arguments from authority and principle will be considered more fully in Chapters 7 and 9.

Modality

The fifth element of the Toulmin model is called the *modality* and refers to the degree of certainty the advocate has that the claim is true. Words like *probably* and *possibly* are illustrations of modal qualifiers. The absence of a modal qualifier in an argument makes a claim unequivocal, that is, certain.

Consider the following adverbs and adverbial phrases. Which communicates the greatest certainty? the least?

very possibly
apparently
it would seem
certainly
presumably
quite likely

When attempting to discern the modality of an argument artifact you must be careful not to confuse those adverbs which modify other elements of the argument with those that modify the certainty of the claim. Modality refers only to those that modify the claim. For example, an advocate could argue "I definitely smell smoke, so it is likely that there is a fire." The modality of this argument is expressed by the word *likely,* and not *definitely.*

Modal qualifiers are a very important element of the argument model. Claims that are absolute, about which the arguer is certain, leave no room for doubt. The grounds must be equally certain. By diagramming an argument and identifying whether or not a modal qualifier is present, and what its relationship to the grounds is, one can begin to assess both the merits and the weaknesses of the argument.

Rebuttal

The final component of the Toulmin model is called the *rebuttal.* The rebuttal refers to exceptions, cases in which the claim would not be true. Understanding the nature of rebuttals, and being able to identify them, is important to the evaluation of arguments for two reasons. First, some advocates admit to rebuttals when presenting their arguments. For example, an advocate could argue that current deficit spending by the federal government has significantly drained capital resources (grounds), and that unless new sources of capital are discovered (rebuttal) continued deficit spending will bankrupt the economy (claim). In this case, the advocate has admitted that there could be an intervening factor which would deny the validity of the claim. If an advocate admits to a rebuttal, a critical audience can consider the possibility that this rebuttal will negate the claim. If the outcome suggested in the rebuttal actually appears probable, the arguer will probably not win adherence to his or her argumentative claim.

Rebuttals are also important to opponents of an argument because they highlight a potential point for refutation. Since to all arguments there may be exceptions that make their claims invalid, critical thinkers should draw upon their own knowledge and experience to identify and create rebuttals. Giving presence to the role of rebuttals in arguments facilitates such critical thinking.

Summary

This chapter has considered arguments as complete logical claims, and has focused on the ways in which such claims can be constructed and analyzed. Two primary modes of argument, inductive and deductive claims were discussed. Inductive arguments might be developed from example, analogy, or causal correlation. Deductive arguments can be developed from signs or from causal generalization. Each type of argument can be tested, critically assessed, and responded to.

In addition, the chapter focused on the deductive syllogism as a formal test of argumentative reasoning. Principles for constructing and evaluating syllogisms were specified. Finally, the chapter discussed the utility of Toulmin diagrams as a means for arguers to both develop and analyze the component parts of argument claims.

Key Terms

deductive reasoning	argument by analogy	Toulmin model
argument from sign	argument from causal	claim
argument from causal	correlation	grounds
generalization	syllogism	warrant
inductive reasoning	major premise	backing
argument by	minor premise	modality
example	conclusion	rebuttal

Activities

1. Find an editorial or argument artifact in your local or student newspaper. Select a major argument advanced in the artifact. Identify what type of argument it is, and apply the appropriate tests of reasoning provided in this chapter.

2. Select a major argument from one of the debates provided in the appendices of this text. Identify the type of argument you selected, and apply the appropriate tests of reasoning provided in this text.

3. Locate a causal claim in an argumentative artifact such as one of the debates in the appendices. Utilize the tests of causal correlation or causal generalization to assess the validity of the claim.

4. Construct a categorical syllogism which is both structurally valid and sound.

5. Find a song with which you are familiar and try to diagram it using the Toulmin model. What is the claim advanced by the songwriter? What grounds does this advocate provide as the basis for the claim? Is there a warrant provided? What type of reasoning does the warrant employ? If the warrant is not explicit, can you provide it? Are any other elements of the Toulmin model included in the advocacy?

Recommended Readings

Lee, Ronald and Karen King Lee. *Arguing Persuasively*. New York: Longman, 1989.

Reinard, John C. *Foundations of Argument.* Dubuque, IA: W.C. Brown, 1991.

Rieke, Richard D. and Malcolm O. Sillars. *Argumentation and Critical Decision Making.* 3d ed. New York: Harper Collins, 1993.

Rybacki, Karyn C. and Donald J. Rybacki. *Advocacy and Opposition.* 2d ed. Englewood Cliffs, NJ: Prentice-Hall, 1991.

Warnick, Barbara and Edward S. Inch. *Critical Thinking and Communication.* New York: Macmillan, 1989.

Ziegelmueller, George W., and Jack Kay, and Charles A. Dause. *Argumentation: Inquiry and Advocacy.* 2d ed. Englewood Cliffs, NJ: Prentice-Hall, 1990.

Notes _____

1. John Stuart Mill, cited in George W. Ziegelmueller and Charles A. Dause, *Argumentation: Inquiry and Advocacy* (Englewood Cliffs, NJ: Prentice-Hall, 1975), p. 100.
2. Mill, p. 101.
3. Mill, p. 102.
4. This model of argument was originally discussed in the book, Stephen E. Toulmin, *The Uses of Argument* (Cambridge: Cambridge University Press, 1958). It was later modified, and it is this modification that is discussed here. See Stephen E. Toulmin, Richard D. Rieke, and Allan Janik, *Introduction to Reasoning* (New York: MacMillan, 1978).

7

The Grounds
for Argument

In the latter half of the twentieth century, humans across the globe have begun to ponder the consequences of their actions on the biosphere. One result of this environmental focus is an ongoing debate about global warming.

One side paints a bleak picture. Humanity's heavy reliance on burning fossil fuels, they say, is releasing large amounts of carbon dioxide into the atmosphere. The result is the greenhouse effect: carbon dioxide traps the earth's heat, causing the planet to warm. This, they contend, will melt the polar ice caps, and lead to starvation, wars over resources, and significant economic dislocations. These advocates claim that we should therefore immediately discourage the use of fossil fuels.[1]

The other side tells a different story. Current evidence, these individuals argue, does not support significant actions to discourage fossil fuel use. The data available to us now is insufficient to justify actions which could have significant adverse economic repercussions.[2]

The stasis of the dispute between these two views is in what should be done now. Each side might agree that global warming is undesirable, and that if it were certain to happen, policy initiatives would be, thereby, necessitated. However, they disagree about the nature of the evidence used as the foundation for their claims. This dispute illustrates how disagreement over the facts can be at the center of a long-standing, intense debate.

In the previous chapter we described how individuals reason from grounds to a claim. We also indicated some ways in which the critical listener might evaluate the reasoning of an advocate. Finally, we suggested that those wishing to enhance their decision-making and argumentative effectiveness should take these aspects into consideration both in evaluating the arguments of others and in constructing their own.

In this chapter we will continue this process by focusing on the support or grounds advocates use for their claims. We will identify the types of grounds used by advocates, present the tests many critical consumers of argument typically employ to assess the validity of grounds, and suggest ways advocates choose supporting data that will increase the likelihood they will gain adherence to their claims.

The Nature of Grounds

When an advocate is asked, "What are you basing this claim on?" The advocate is being asked for the grounds or evidence supporting the argument. Whether the argument is inductive or deductive, **grounds** serves as the evidence, support, or foundation for the claim. According to Aristotle, the basis for a claim may be one of two types depending upon where it originates.[3] If the advocate is the creator of the support for the claim, it is considered **artistic proof.** If the starting point for the argument comes from someone else, it is considered **inartistic proof.** Both types of evidence include premises, examples, statistics, and testimony. We will consider each in turn.

Premises

All evidence acts as the premise or starting point of a claim. But as a premise grounds function as an established point of agreement between advocates and audiences. A **premise** is therefore a point accepted without additional support.

The premises an advocate can use to support a claim are based on two types of knowledge: personal knowledge and cultural knowledge.[4] **Personal knowledge** is that which we know to be true because we have firsthand experience with it. Personal knowledge is an artistic proof.

We know fire is hot, ice is cold, rain is wet, and so on, because our senses provide this information. We had to learn the labels, but the senses give us the basic information. Personal knowledge extends beyond such sensory data however. We know when times are tough, because we are unemployed, or we know someone who is unemployed, or we worry that we, like others around us, might become unemployed. We believe these things because we have experienced them. When an advocate uses a premise that taps into our personal knowledge, we are likely to find fidelity in the argument, for the premise rings true with what we know to be true.

There are other things we believe to be true that we have not experienced ourselves. Yet, we hold these views because we are part of a culture. This **cultural knowledge** may be shared values, or shared truths. It may be explicit—codified into rules, principles, or laws—or it may be derived from our conduct. It is contained in the stories we tell about ourselves, who we are, where we have been, and where we are going. A defining aspect of any culture is the stories it tells about itself.[5]

In our culture we teach a multitude of stories to our children: from the Pilgrims at Plymouth Rock, to the patriots at Valley Forge, from Abraham Lincoln at Gettysburg, to Teddy Roosevelt at San Juan Hill, from the marines at Iwo Jima, to John F. Kennedy in Berlin. Through each story we reveal a little more about what it is to be American. In this fashion we inculcate American values in our youth. And these values and "truths" about our public experiences are the premises advocates use in their arguments.

Another way a culture reinforces its shared knowledge is through rituals. **Rituals** are behavior patterns so often repeated that the participants come to know them by heart and expect them to be performed at precise times. From who sits where at a family meal, to the inauguration of a president, many of our practices are scripted by ritual.[6]

When you successfully complete your college degree, you may participate in a commencement ritual. Participants will be suitably garbed in the vestments of the tradition, speakers will laud the accomplishments of the students, and friends and family will cheer as you receive your diploma and ceremoniously move your tassel to signify completion of the process of graduation. Through such a ritual the university communicates the value of learning and admits you to the ranks of educated elite.

Symbols are yet another way a society teaches its values. Visit any capital and you will undoubtedly see great monuments and halls devoted to governance. Must executives of state reside in stately homes like the White House? Is it necessary to construct huge buildings with stately rotundas and lofty ceilings? Of course not. But these vestiges of monarchial tradition are perpetuated to convey the seriousness of the business conducted in these settings and the importance of the individuals engaged in the country's governance.

Shared premises enjoy **presumption** with audiences. That is, audiences tend to believe these premises until convinced otherwise. This is the concept of presumption. It is the idea that most people, most of the time, are comfortable with the way things are. We generally are apprehensive about the unknown. We stick to familiar beliefs, values, and policies until sufficient reasons are presented for change.

Advocates can successfully build arguments upon shared premises by invoking them through their own argument (artistic) or by citing evidence which calls upon shared premises (inartistic). For example, most of us have little personal experience with censorship. But just because we have not actually been arrested for something we have said does not diminish the fervor with which we support freedom of speech. In this culture, unlike some cultures with backgrounds of authoritarian leadership, we cherish the right to express our views. Consequently, an advocate arguing against censoring recordings of popular music can draw upon this shared premise.

Where can an advocate discover premises? A good source are adages or proverbs we all know. Here's a short list. You can undoubtedly think of additional examples.

Good triumphs over evil.
Experience is the best teacher.
Love conquers all.
Hope for the best, but prepare for the worst.
Good things come to those who wait.
Haste makes waste.

The manifestos we profess faith in are another source of premises. Look, for example, to the articulation of our beliefs in the Declaration of Independence and the Constitution. We believe in equality, in freedom of speech and religion, in due process, in the liberty to pursue happiness, in the rule of law, among other things.

Although audiences generally grant adherence to premises, arguments predicated upon accepted premises will not necessarily win automatic agreement. Critical consumers of argument and advocates constructing discourse will evaluate the use of premises. We identify three tests of the use of premises.

Testing Premises: Shared Premises

First, the premise employed by an advocate must be truly shared by the audience. While the definition of a premise presumes agreement, beliefs are not static. Some things that we believe now, we may have once rejected. We once scoffed at the idea that the earth is round, and that the earth revolves around the sun, rather than the reverse. But we do not have to go so far back in history to see beliefs change.

In 1976, 1980, and 1984, Ronald Reagan campaigned for president by arguing against big government. He contended that government was the problem, not the solution to problems. By his third campaign, this premise was widely shared. But twenty years earlier government was looked upon by most Americans as the best way to address the ills of society. This latter "liberal" view became so widely denigrated that the 1988 Republican campaign did considerable damage by labeling Michael Dukakis a *liberal*. So, audiences and advocates must determine whether the premise being invoked is currently regarded as true.

Another difficulty with assuming that all audiences share the same premises arises from the influx of competing cultures. Alan Bloom and E. D. Hirsch, among others, have lambasted the American educational system for no longer teaching the values of Western culture.[7] These individuals argue that Americans do not share the same Western values because we do not read the same Western classics in literature courses, and because higher education now teaches that the values of other cultures are equal to Euro-American values. The result, these advocates contend, is a society without strong values.

Others have called for even greater inclusion of Eastern and Southern culturally shared beliefs in American education.[8] Teaching from a multicultural perspective, they argue, validates the experiences of minority students and makes all individuals more sensitive to the differences between people.

The continuing debate in higher education over the teaching of cultural perspectives, reveals the difficulties in assuming that all audiences share the same premises. There may be differences between and within audiences because the audiences collectively or separately represent divergent cultures.

Testing Premises: Contradictory Premises

A second concern with the use of premises as evidence for a claim is that there are contradictions among them. Bromides reflect American values; they also reveal the tension between competing wisdoms. Consider the belief that you should "Look before you leap," versus "He who hesitates is lost." Similarly, is it "Absence makes the heart grow fonder" or "Out of sight, out of mind"?

On a more serious level, Walter Fisher argues that the dominant belief of this culture is in the American dream.[9] But Fisher maintains that the American dream is actually derived from two frequently contradictory beliefs. The first is the belief in America as the land of opportunity. The opportunity to achieve unlimited material success is the cornerstone of capitalism. The haves of American society have achieved more than the have-nots. The second belief is that there must be equality of opportunity. This is the moralistic dimension of the dream. There are times when the materialistic and the moralistic components of the dream are in opposition. For example, some argue that affirmative action programs are moralistic attempts to redress inequities at the price of impinging on the materialistic endeavors of non-minorities.

In fact, the most hotly contested contemporary disputes have contradictory premises at their core. The dispute over whether or not to punish the rock group 2 Live Crew for the lyrics they used, centers on the conflict between our belief in freedom of expression and the importance of parental control; and, stasis for the abortion controversy resides, in part, in the conflict between the view that a woman should have control over her own body, and the view that the unborn also have rights. Clearly, advocates who predicate their arguments on premises that are contradicted by other widely accepted beliefs risk the rejection of their advocacy.

Testing Premises: Public vs. Private Beliefs

Finally, there are often discrepancies between our public and private beliefs. The values that a culture shares are not always exemplified in the actions of the individuals who comprise the culture. As a society, we abhor racism and bigotry. Yet, it would be naive to think that America has no racists or bigots. The politically correct movement may have partially purged public language and behavior of antisocial or insensitive conduct, but the attitudes remain. Social actors may have merely learned acceptable code words with which to express their prejudice. An audience that privately rejects the publicly shared belief is not likely to find appeals to that belief compelling.

Advocates confronting uncertain situations must take pains to support the premises they employ. Simply stating what one believes to be a widely shared premise may not be enough. Proving the premise, and then using the premise as the foundation for the next claim would be preferable.

Examples

Examples are specific instances or occurrences of a given phenomenon. They may be detailed or cursory. The advocate may provide an example from personal experience (artistic proof), or derive the example from another source (inartistic proof). In Chapter 6 we identified the inductive process of using examples to reason to a generalization. In that chapter we discussed four tests for reasoning from examples:

1. Are there a sufficient number of examples offered to support the claim?
2. Are the examples that are selected typical of the category or class that the arguer is trying to generalize to?
3. Are negative examples sufficiently accounted for in the argument?
4. Are the examples that are cited relevant to the claim being advanced?

In addition to these tests, we would admonish advocates to provide whatever details are necessary to gain the audience's adherence. Listing several specific examples may enhance the validity of the claim for a given audience. On the other hand, detailed examples (also called *extended illustrations*) can give power to a claim by making it more memorable and by arousing the audience's emotions.

Consider the effect of briefly listing the names of five students who have died in alcohol-related automobile accidents. The use of these examples may provide sufficient basis for a claim that students should not drink and drive. But providing an extended illustration of how one student lost his or her life may have the same persuasive effect. In addition, hearing the details of the accident, may enable the audience to visualize the events, and that may stir their empathy for the individual. Thus, more fully explaining an example may humanize—and strengthen—the argument.

Advocates can also seek to bolster the audience's faith in the examples by drawing them from sources the audience considers credible (inartistic proof). In this way they combine examples and testimony. Some advocates even attempt to emulate statistical methodologies and select examples randomly from the set of possible examples.

Statistics

Since the use of multiple examples may enhance the likelihood of their acceptance, and since time constraints may limit the number of specific cases that may be presented, advocates may choose to present statistics instead.

Statistics are numeric expressions of examples. There are two basic types of statistics: descriptive and inferential. **Descriptive statistics** are numeric representations that represent the entire set of instances of a phenomenon. When advocates present the number of AIDS victims, they are attempting to describe the entire population of victims. Similarly, the number of workers laid off, the number of handgun accidents, the number of starvation victims in Somalia, the number of traffic fatalities, all attempt to describe all of the cases.

Inferential statistics are numeric representations that attempt to infer the properties of a population from inspection of a sample of it. The advocate who cites public opinion polls is providing inferential data. These numbers do not literally present the views of the entire public. Rather, a presumably representative sample or subset of the public is selected and described. Then the pollster infers that the descriptions of the samples accurately represent the views of the entire public.

Testing Statistics: Methods of Gathering

Both kinds of statistics are useful as proof, and both have potential weaknesses. Whether advocates are presenting their own statistics or those from other sources, meeting certain tests enhances the likelihood that critical audiences will accept the data.

First, it may be important to know how the statistics were gathered. Understanding the methodology employed in counting the cases may reveal weaknesses in the evidence. One way statistics are often gathered relies on individuals reporting instances of the phenomenon. This method can lead to misleading statistics, due, for instance, to the problem of **underreporting** wherein disincentives for reporting instances of the phenomenon result in artificially low numbers. For example, how much child abuse was there in the United States last year? Law enforcement and social service agencies compile the number of cases reported to them, but are all instances reported? Unfortunately, many abused children do not come forward, and most abusers, their spouses, and their relatives are reluctant to report the abuse. So, are the official counts an accurate reflection of the actual cases of such abuse? Obviously not. Underreporting of child abuse means that the true numbers are certainly far larger than official statistics indicate.

There also may be incentives for **overreporting** cases of a phenomenon. During the Vietnam War, American soldiers were told to report the number of enemy soldiers they witnessed killed in action. Critics argued that the military's desire to show that the U.S. was winning the war resulted in an exaggerated body count. Thus, when the statistical method is to collect individuals' reports, the motive of those doing the reporting must be considered.

Inferential statistics rely on describing a subset of the population and inferring that what is true of the sample, is true of the general population. The method by which this subset is selected is consequently very important. The sample must be representative of its parent group, or else any general conclusions drawn will not be valid. Thus, most researchers use random samples. A **random sample** may be defined as a sample in which each element of the larger group has an equal and independent probability of being selected.[10] Let's assume we wanted to discover who students thought was the best teacher at a particular university. We could question all of the students on the campus (descriptive statistic) or select a representative sample of all of the students, question them, and infer that their answers closely mirrored the entire student population. Since it would be difficult to survey all of the students, it makes sense to use inferential statistics.

There are several ways to select a random sample. One way to assure that all students have an equal chance of being included in the study is to use a technique called **simple random sampling.** Researchers using this method employ a random numbers table. This is a list of numbers randomly generated by computer. For example, by assigning all of the students on campus a number, we could select a predetermined number of students as their numbers are chosen. If the number of students in our sample is large enough we are relatively certain that we will have a sample that roughly mirrors the student body.

A second way researchers generate random samples is by using an **interval sampling** system. With interval sampling we might construct our sample of students by including every twentieth student on the roster. As long as we randomly determine where to start choosing the students, each student would have an equal chance of participating.

Equality of participation, however, does not guarantee that we will have a representative distribution of graduate students, undergraduate students, part-time students, and so on. To make sure that such groups are included in numbers proportionate to their size, we could use a modification of the random and interval procedures called **stratified sampling.** Instead of sampling from the entire student population, in stratified sampling we would divide the population into groups which we might want in the sample. Once the population has been stratified, we could select students from each stratum using either the simple random number technique, or the interval technique.

Another technique is called **multistage sampling.** In this method, usually used when complete lists of the population are unavailable, the researcher randomly selects clusters or groups and then randomly selects a sample from each group. In trying to select the best teacher, we might list all of the majors at the university, randomly select a predetermined number of majors, and then randomly select students from within each of the chosen majors. However, since there is a chance that any random sampling will produce an unrepresentative group, methods which require multiple levels of sampling also run the risk of providing an unrepresentative sample at each layer.

Professional pollsters and researchers employ sophisticated sampling techniques to assure the reliability of their results. When they report their findings they usually identify the **margin of error** as well. Harris, Roper, and Gallup polls of voter preference during presidential campaigns, for example, will acknowledge that their statistics may be off by 2, 3, or 4 percent. If a poll has a margin of error of 4 percent, a candidate that it shows having the support of 52 percent of the potential voters may actually have as much as 56 percent of the potential electorate behind them—or as little as 48 percent. Polls which do not reveal their margins of error should be viewed with suspicion.

Presidential preference polls are further complicated by respondents who change their mind or do not vote. This can account for some of the inaccuracies of the predicted vote totals.

Some periodicals also report the results of surveys of their readers. The use of these polls as evidence of what the population believes is dubious, however, because the survey participants are self-selected. Only the readers of the periodicals are asked to fill out the questionnaires, and only those sufficiently motivated do so. Thus, the conclusions drawn in the survey are biased by the self-selection process and may bear little resemblance to opinions of the overall population.

Similarly, phone-in polls have become increasingly popular on television and radio shows. CNN has a nightly phone-in poll, and some television networks have asked viewers to phone in their thoughts on who won presidential debates. Yet only those with phones, who watched the show, who could afford to spend fifty to seventy-five cents per call, and who bothered to phone in, are included in these polls. Callers can also make as many calls as they care to, skewing the results at will. Special interest groups, like political campaigns and the National Rifle Association coordinate how their members will participate in such phone-ins. Campaigns have been known to set up phone banks and have their members make call, after call, after call. Naturally, excessive participation by any segment of the population distorts poll results.

The results of such phone-ins are not scientific because they do not approximate the overall population. Broadcasters often mention this, yet, surprisingly, they continue to cite the results—often treating the totals as legitimate news items. If the results are essentially meaningless we wonder why they bother. The effect can only be to mislead.

Testing Statistics: Defining Categories

In addition to problems with how the statistics are gathered, there is the second and equally troublesome problem of how the categories are defined. If the categories are not exact, the count of cases will be inexact.

When researchers assign particular occurrences to categories, they often must make judgments about those occurrences. Sometimes the categories are forthright—"alive" or "dead", for instance. Yet there are often gray areas. For example, "employed" or "unemployed" appear to be pretty discrete categories requiring little interpretation by the researcher. Appearances are misleading.

If you are on a payroll and your salary is reported to the government, you are clearly employed. If you have been laid off and you are collecting unemployment, which requires that you be actively looking for a job, you are unemployed. If, however, your unemployment has run out, or you have quit looking for a job because there are none, or you are not really looking for a job but would take one if you could find one that would accommodate your school schedule, or if you are a housewife, or a student, you are neither "employed" nor "unemployed." Even though you are not employed, you are not unemployed because none of these situations matches how the government defines "unemployed."

We all know there are far too many cases of sexual harassment in the workplace. But how many cases are there? Since experts disagree as to what constitutes harassment, it is difficult to know what to include and what to exclude from the count. Thus, statistical reports as to the amount of sexual harassment in the workplace vary widely.

Testing Statistics: The Time Frame

The third test of statistics relates to **time frame.** When one begins and ends the counting of the statistics can directly influence what the statistics reveal. At the beginning of this chapter we discussed the issue of global warming. Some argue that the climate is warming, while others point to data that says it is not. There is clear evidence that the Northern Hemisphere experienced cooling in the 1940s and 1970s. Advocates who begin and end their statistical evidence with these two decades might convince an uncritical audience that the earth's climate is cooling. But when researchers look at longer periods of time, the entire twentieth century, for example, they see overall warming.[11]

In Chapter 6 we also raised the time frame question with regard to the AIDS crisis. We noted that early in the crisis medical experts mistakenly believed that only some AIDS patients would develop full-blown AIDS. This occurred because it can take many years before the disease ultimately claims its victims.

Americans generally have faith in science and scientific methods, though this may be waning. Consequently, American audiences often find statistics compelling. But Americans are also aware that statistics are susceptible to distortion— remember the adage, "There are lies, damned lies, and statistics."

Skilled advocates recognize that, though susceptible to distortion, statistics are compelling argumentative tools. They do not hesitate to use them, or to provide as much detail as possible about the method used to gather and categorize the data, as well as the time frame of the analysis.

Testimony

A fourth type of grounds utilized by advocates is the provision of testimony. **Testimony** consists of observations and/or judgments by the advocate or sources cited by the advocate. Testimony may be descriptive or interpretative. **Descriptive testimony** relates the observation of supposedly factual (verifiable) information. **Interpretive testimony** involves making judgments or drawing inferences from the facts in discussion. In each case, a similar set of tests can be applied.

Before accepting an advocate's arguments, critical audiences evaluate the credibility of the advocate and any authorities she or he cites. **Credibility** refers to the audience's assessment of the competence and trustworthiness of the source. It is important to emphasize that sources do not possess credibility, rather, audiences attribute varying levels of credibility to them. Thus, a source may be quite credible to one audience, and wholly lacking in credibility to another.

The first dimension of credibility is **competence.** Audiences assess whether or not the source, be it the advocate or a supposed expert, is competent to make the proferred observation or interpretation. This assessment entails judgment of capability and ability.

Capability refers to whether or not the source is capable of making the observation. Have you heard someone claim to have seen something, when they could not have done so? Did you doubt the veracity of their claim? Then you have applied the test of capability.

Whether the source has any particular ability or expertise is a second measure of competence. Ability may be the result of education, training, or life experiences. Most Americans believe physicians have more ability to diagnose illness than do witch doctors. Why? Because anyone can claim to be a witch doctor, but physicians are required to complete years of specialized education and training. Does that guarantee the physician will be correct and the witch doctor wrong? Not necessarily. But most American audiences would probably find the physician more credible.

Of course, physicians may know less than witch doctors about herbal medicines. This illustrates the concept of field dependence in competence. Experts are only authoritative in their own fields. Dr. Benjamin Shockley, who received widespread notoriety for his theories on the genetic differences between African- and Caucasian-Americans was a Nobel Prize winner. But his Nobel Prize was for the transistor, not genetics. Thus, many rightly questioned his ability in genetics.

Celebrities testifying outside of their fields lose the enhanced ability of their expertise. Nevertheless, we frequently see sports figures or movie stars asked about political and social issues. Do you think they necessarily know more about these issues than you do? Perhaps, but their prowess in sports or on the screen does not make it so.

Competence does not, however, require extensive training. People whose life experiences make them experts are often favorably viewed by audiences. If we wanted to know what it was like to be homeless, for instance, we might consult scholars who have written on the subject. But the testimony of a homeless person on the subject might seem even more authoritative.

The second dimension of credibility is **trustworthiness,** which is an audience's assessment of the integrity of the source. Source integrity concerns the source's motives. Is the source willing to report his or her observations and judgments fairly? Sometimes sources have something to gain from what they report. This potential may influence what they say, causing *source bias.*

When Congress holds hearings before enacting legislation, they invite experts to present their views on the issue at hand. If the issue is mileage requirements for new automobiles, experts from the big three auto makers would probably testify. Their statements, however, might reflect mostly their own biased interests. In such cases, Congress might also hear testimony from environmental and consumer groups. While their testimony might also reflect their own agenda, the net effect, we all hope, is that our representatives hear all of the conflicting views. They can then (again, hopefully) make up their minds impartially, after carefully considering all the evidence.

When audiences hear advocates make self-serving statements, or hear them quote biased sources, they generally consider such statements less reliable than testimony that is not motivated by the needs of the source. In fact, many audiences consider **reluctant testimony,** that testimony given grudgingly because it does not serve the motives of the source, as the most reliable kind. Individuals who step forward and admit misdoings are generally considered more credible, for example, than those who admit culpability only after they have been confronted with incontrovertible evidence.

Evidence that is **internally consistent,** that is, free from self-contradiction, is usually considered better than testimony from a source that contradicts itself. The police rely on this test of the integrity of suspects. If a suspect changes his or her story when retelling it, the police will often consider this internal inconsistency evidence of duplicity. Parents have learned the same lessons. Consequently, they often ask their children to repeat their stories in the hopes of discovering an error.

The ability of advocates to provide several sources which concur with their positions is likely to encourage an audience towards a positive evaluation of the argument. This demonstration of **external consistency**—showing that the testimony is consistent with the testimony of others—strengthens the credibility of each cited source, since none is alone in its observations. Corroboration by other experts reduces the likelihood that the evidence is not trustworthy.

Verifiability is another component of trustworthiness. A source that cannot be verified, because it is either not available or not properly identified, is not likely to be received well. For example, in the legal field hearsay evidence (testimony given by witnesses concerning what they heard others say) is, with few exceptions, considered inadmissible because, in part, the statements are not verifiable.

A final test of the trustworthiness of testimony is **recency.** Some advocates and audiences assume that the date of testimony is critical to its value. But recency is only partly concerned with when the testimony was given. Some evidence is outdated almost as soon as it is presented; other testimony seems perpetually valuable. The test of recency asks whether anything has happened between the date of the evidence and when it is used in advocacy that would make the testimony invalid. If nothing has changed significantly, then the observation or judgment is still relevant.

This morning's stock prices may already be useless. Yet, we still use the judgments of Aristotle. Why? Because nothing has happened in the intervening years to invalidate some of Aristotle's views. Utilizing evidence which passes the test of recency indicates a concern that the audience receive only relevant information and reveals the good intentions of the advocate.

Of course, there are additional steps advocates can take to enhance their credibility. Research reveals that audiences are likely to view speakers who present well organized arguments more favorably than those who are disorganized. This seems compatible with Brockreide's arguers-as-lovers metaphor (see Chapter 1). Advocates who care (trustworthiness) about their audiences do not try to seduce or rape in their arguments. Rather, since they have nothing to hide, they are explicit and clear.

Research further indicates that audiences are more inclined to grant adherence to claims advanced by an advocate who is likable and dynamic. If advocates seem personable and friendly, we may make allowances for them and grant them greater credibility than ones for whom we have no feelings. Think about how you respond to your friends as opposed to people you hardly know or, worse yet, dislike. We tend to find the claims of those we like more compelling.

Advocates who are excited and animated about their claims indicate that they believe their own arguments. This aspect of sincerity speaks to their integrity. Of course, we are generally suspicious of those who attempt to conceal the weakness of their arguments by resorting to a dynamic delivery, like the smooth-talking salesman, so, even dynamism must be measured, lest it boomerang.

Summary

In this chapter we have considered the grounds used by advocates when they make claims. We identified four specific types of grounds: premises, examples, statistics, and testimony. And we pointed out that each type of evidence is subject to tests to determine the likelihood that critical audiences will accept or reject it. Critical decision makers will consider the grounds presented before they render a judgment on the advocacy of others. And advocates seeking to maximize their effectiveness will consider what kinds of grounds are most likely to sway their audience.

Now that we have laid out the types and tests of grounds, how can advocates locate and record inartistic evidence to use in support of their advocacy? In Chapter 8 we discuss the steps to formulating a successful research strategy.

Key Terms

artistic proof	multistage sampling	descriptive
competence	overreporting	inferential
credibility	personal knowledge	stratified sampling
cultural knowledge	premise	symbols
examples	presumption	testimony
external consistency	random sample	descriptive
grounds	recency	interpretive
inartistic proof	reluctant testimony	time frame
internal consistency	ritual	trustworthiness
interval sampling	simple random sampling	underreporting
margin of error	statistics	verifiability

Activities

1. Examine an argumentative artifact. Once you have ascertained the claim, determine whether the grounds provided are artistic, inartistic, or both. Next,

identify the kind of grounds that are presented: premises, examples, statistics, or testimony. Then apply the appropriate tests to determine whether or not you find the grounds compelling.

2. Find a public opinion poll in a newspaper or magazine. Examine the polling sample, the questions asked, and the definitions of the statistical categories. Does the statistical evidence pass the appropriate tests?

3. Examine a speech by a public figure. (You can find speeches in the periodical *Vital Speeches of the Day*). Identify the types of data the speaker employed and apply the appropriate tests to determine whether or not you find the grounds compelling.

4. Look through a popular magazine and locate three advertisements. What kinds of grounds do the advertisers utilize? Apply the appropriate tests to determine whether or not you find the grounds compelling.

5. Select a public controversy of interest to you. Take a position in this controversy and then find grounds of each of the four kinds to support your position.

Recommended Readings _____

Aristotle. *Rhetoric and Poetics of*. Trans. W. Rhys Roberts. New York: The Modern Library, 1954.

Bettinghaus, Erwin P. and Michael J. Cody. *Persuasive Communication*. 5th ed. New York: Holt, Rinehart and Winston, 1994.

Bettinghaus, Erwin P. *The Nature of Proof*. 2d ed. Indianapolis: Bobbs-Merrill, 1972.

Burke, Kenneth. *Attitudes Toward History*. 2d ed., rev. Boston: Beacon, 1959.

McKerrow, Ray. "Richard Whately and the Revival of Logic in Nineteenth-Century England." *Rhetorica* 5 (1987): 163–185.

Whately, Richard. *Elements of Rhetoric*. Rpt. Carbondale: Southern Illinois University Press, 1963.

Williams, Frederick. *Reasoning with Statistics*. 4th ed. Fort Worth: Harcourt, Brace, Jovanovich, 1992.

Notes _____

1. See, for example, Jeremy Leggett, *Global Warming: The Greenpeace Report* (New York: Oxford University Press, 1990).

2. See, for example, National Research Council, *Global Environmental Change: Understanding the Human Dimensions* (Washington, D.C.: National Academy Press, 1992).

3. *The Rhetoric of Aristotle*, trans. Lane Cooper. (Englewood Cliffs, NJ: Prentice-Hall, 1932), p. 8.

4. For additional information on this subject, see Michael Polanyi, *Personal Knowledge* (New York: Harper & Row, 1964); John M. Ziman, *Public Knowledge* (Cambridge: University Press, 1968); and Lloyd Bitzer, "Rhetoric and Public Knowledge," in *Rhetoric, Philosophy, and Literature*, Don M. Burks, ed. (West Lafayette, IN: Purdue University Press, 1978), pp. 67–93.

5. See, for example, Clifford Geertz, *The Interpretation of Cultures* (New York: Basic Books, 1973).

6. For interesting discussions of the importance of rituals see, for example, Mircea Eliade, *Cosmos and History: The Myth of the Eternal Return* (New York: Harper Torchbooks, 1954) and Joseph Campbell, *Myths We Live By* (New York: Bantam Books, 1972).

7. Alan Bloom, *The Closing of the American Mind* (New York: Simon and Schuster, 1987); and E. D. Hirsch, *Cultural Literacy: What Every American Needs to Know* (Boston: Houghton Mifflin, 1987).

8. See, for example, M. Gibson, "Approaches to Multicultural Education in the United States: Some Concepts and Assumptions," *Anthropology and Education Quarterly* 7, no. 4 (November 1976): 7–18; and N. Appleton, *Cultural Pluralism in Education: Theoretical Foundations* (New York: Longman, 1983).

9. Walter R. Fisher, "Reaffirmation and Subversion of the American Dream," *Quarterly Journal of Speech* 59 (April 1973): 160–167.

10. Gene V. Glass and Julian C. Stanley, *Statistical Methods in Education and Psychology* (Prentice-Hall, 1970).

11. For a discussion of the issue of global warming/cooling see, for example, Robert Silverberg, "The Greenhouse Effect: Apocalypse Now or Chicken Little," *Omni* July 1991, pp. 53–88.

8

Building Arguments

Perhaps something about life or the social conditions of living has struck a responsive chord within you, and you wish to share your views with others. You know what you want to say, but you need supporting materials to make your claims more compelling. Or perhaps you are not sure what to believe and are searching for the best conception of truth. In either case, the opportunity and obligation to investigate the issue necessitates that you be familiar with the process of research.

In this chapter we will describe the research process, give some suggestions as to what to look for, and discuss how you can organize your research results to increase the likelihood that your arguments will gain the adherence of your audience.

Defining Research

We have previously explained that rational arguments contain three basic elements: the grounds used as the basis or premise to develop a claim; the reasoning which justifies the inferential leap from grounds to claim; and the claim itself, which is the conclusion built upon the grounds and reasoning. Thus, grounds refers to the foundation or support for the claim the advocate wishes an audience to grant adherence to (see Chapter 6). Like a house, an argument is only as solid as its foundation. Thus, it is imperative that you provide grounds that will move your audience. But where do these grounds data come from?

The best answer is: from our life experiences. We argue based on what we know; what we have read, studied, and lived. That is why American universities generally emphasize a liberal arts education—so that students can draw from a variety of perspectives. Use what you know as the basis for your claims. And take the time to expand that storehouse of information; read! Be an informed citizen. It will make you both a better advocate and a better consumer of argument.

Nevertheless, no matter how well read you are, or even how well you have lived, there will come a time when your personal knowledge will be insufficient to convince an audience. In some circumstances your life experiences may even be contradicted by the life experiences of another. Then, to be convincing, you will need to look elsewhere for support. Or perhaps you have been asked to give a more formal presentation of your views. And, if you wish to be an ethical advocate and present what you consider to be the best conception of truth, you are obligated to take the time to discover what that truth is, and to make your advocacy of it as compelling as possible. In each situation you will need to supplement your own knowledge with the facts and opinions of others. Doing this is what we call **research.**

Planning the Research Process

Once you have decided to explore the ideas of others, you will need to decide where to begin. The information available in American libraries can be overwhelming. This is not just a happy circumstance. It is the result of a conscious decision to preserve individual liberties. Without ready access to the latest information, we would be forced to make decisions in a vacuum. The chance that we would err or be misled would be significant. That is why societies led by dictators restrict access to information. Nevertheless, if the millions of holdings in a library are to be useful to you, you must have a **research plan** or strategy for determining what you need and the best way to obtain it.

Our advice is to start with general sources and move to more specific ones as your research progresses. By **general sources** we mean those that give a broad understanding of all aspects or sides to the controversy.

There are five benefits from starting with more general sources. First, getting a broad overview of the controversy will enable you to understand sources you consult later. Authors write because something in the ongoing conversation prompts them to contribute. Sometimes they will tell you what that thing was. Sometimes their agenda is less clear.

For example, authors may be directly responding to the arguments their opponents have previously presented. Or they may be anticipating and preempting arguments their opponents might raise. You can understand why such information would be very valuable to your research. You can also probably see how easily you might miss this information if you don't understand the whole controversy. The result can be poor argumentation, or the necessity that you reread some material. Neither outcome is desirable.

A second benefit of starting with more general sources is that doing so will enable you to generate a list of topic headings and synonyms. This can be invaluable because when you consult indexes you may need to look under several headings. A lack of familiarity with the overall picture can frustrate good faith efforts to research a topic. We once had a student group assigned to research "ethos." They returned to class confused by the lack of material in the library on what they had been told was a major element of public speaking. As is turned out, the students had only looked under "ethos" in the indexes they consulted. A second attempt, this time looking under "public speaking," "source credibility," and "Aristotle," yielded better results.

The broad understanding of the controversy yielded by general sources offers the third benefit of enabling you to select those lines of inquiry which seem most promising. There may be many reasons, for example, to support gun control in the United States. If you have less than ten minutes to convince an audience, however, it probably makes sense to limit the scope of your advocacy to a couple of positions. That means selecting the most compelling reason or reasons. Knowing your options early in your research can save you a lot of time and the time you do spend more productive.

A fourth benefit is the discovery of potential critical responses to your advocacy. In order to gain the adherence of a critical audience, you will need to know what the likely objections are to your arguments. Researching only one side of the controversy may not prepare you adequately. Whereas understanding the arguments from both sides to the dispute should enable you to anticipate refutation and prepare for it.

The fifth and final benefit: you will most likely find that general sources are easier to read than more specific writings. General sources tend to be written for lay audiences. If the authors use jargon, they explain it. More specific writings may assume a level of knowledge which is beyond you. The language, references, and style may also limit your comprehension.

So start with sources which give you a broad understanding of the controversy and move to more and more specific information as you continue your research.

What to Research

Interviews

Having decided that you wish to start with broader sources of information, the next question is where to find this information. Some might recommend interviewing experts. On any given campus it is likely that there are faculty members knowledgeable about the controversy you wish to investigate. They will make excellent subjects to interview. So will public interest groups. If your topic is really a controversy in society, then there could easily be groups of citizens who have literature advocating one side of the controversy or the other. However, while interviewing such experts will be valuable, it may not necessarily be a good starting point.

If you make an appointment with a university professor or some other expert, and then ask her or him to tell you everything they know about some controversy, he or she may not know where to begin. Instead, this person will ask you what you already know. If you know so little that you cannot ask specific and knowledgeable questions, you are undoubtedly wasting this expert's time. Even if the expert is willing to spend the time with you the results may not be particularly useful. Save such interviews until you have enough background to make them productive.

In addition, statements made in personal interviews are frequently not accepted as valid by educated audiences. Since the advent of the printing press, Western culture has been dominated by the written word. It is as if appearing in black and white on the printed page makes an idea intrinsically superior to the same thought delivered in speech.[1] Neil Postman notes that in the academic world the published word is given greater credence than the spoken word. This emphasis, he argues, stems from the transitory nature of oral communication.

> What people say is assumed to be more casually uttered than what they write. The written word is assumed to have been reflected upon and revised by its author, reviewed by authorities and editors. It is easier to verify or refute, and it is invested with an impersonal and objective character . . .; that is to say, the written word is, by its nature, addressed to the world, not an individual. The written word endures, the spoken word disappears; and that is why writing is closer to the truth than speaking.[2]

This emphasis on the written word accounts, perhaps, for why so many of us are not particularly good at monitoring what we say. When the spoken word constituted the preferred form of communication, we were probably better at communicating orally. Now that the emphasis has shifted to the written word, we are better writers, perhaps, but possibly less effective at communicating orally.

Just as we may suffer discomfort when we hear our recorded voice or see ourselves on videotape, it can be disquieting to see one's spoken words written out in black and white. A frequent, and understandable reaction to transcribed conversation is to wish to rephrase an utterance. In some cases we deny that such words could have come out of our mouths, or insist that the words are misleading without the other words which surrounded and contextualized our thoughts. We are convinced that this accounts, in part, for the claim that reporters misquote celebrities.

A final reason why educated audiences look dubiously on statements made in personal interviews derives from their lack of verifiability. Published statements are potentially available to all and can be checked for veracity. Personal interviews are not. So save the interviews until you have specific questions, and then ask the expert to identify sources in which the information they mention is published.

General Sources

Having postponed interviews until later in the research plan, we still need to find general sources which give a broad view of the topic. Where do you turn in the library? Let the journalistic ethic be your guide.

Reporters are generally taught to report both sides of a controversy. Presenting the competing views is considered balanced coverage. For our purposes, that means you should begin your research with sources that report the controversy, rather than those advocating a single, particular viewpoint. Newsmagazines, such as *Time, Newsweek, U.S. News and World Report,* tend to offer both sides in their stories. The stories are also accessible to the general reader. The same goes for background pieces in newspapers. You can find articles in news sources such as these by consulting the *Readers' Guide to Periodical Literature* or the *Public Affairs Information Service* (PAIS). Newspapers are also indexed individually, so consider consulting indexes for the *Chicago Tribune,* the *Christian Science Monitor,* the *Los Angeles Times,* the *New York Times,* the *Wall Street Journal,* the *Washington Post,* or your local newspaper.

When newspapers take positions on controversies, they do so in editorials. Editorials are indexed by newspaper. Or, you can find a national sample of these in *Editorials on File.*

Specialized Sources

Once you have read what some general sources have to say about your topic you will be ready to conduct a more focused search of **specialized sources.** These publications are usually targeted for specific segments of the population. Their readers typically have some, and often a lot of, background knowledge in the field. Having covered a number of general sources, you should now fit that description too. So why not stop there? There are four reasons why it will be beneficial for you to continue your research by consulting specialized sources.

First, articles written for the general public often report the conclusions of experts in the field. But they do not go into the controversy in depth. While breadth means more individuals know a little about the topic, to discover where truth resides, or to find the material to help you gain the adherence of others, you need more than that. You need to learn the rationale behind the conclusions experts reach.

Second, as you gain more knowledge of your topic, you may begin to discover the unstated assumptions of the experts. We remember when it was widely reported that U.S. oil reserves would be exhausted in less than seventy-five years. We may well run out of oil in less than seventy-five years—or else the assumptions could be flawed. Upon delving deeper, however, it becomes apparent that these estimates were based on projections of continually increasing consumption, and, most importantly, predicated on current prices.

Perhaps the prognosticators are correct. But only through focused research can the assumptions be unearthed and the veracity of the story fully examined.

Third, this additional research will help you find the specific information necessary to solidify the arguments you wish to convey. General sources may give you most of the information you need to justify your position, but there may be gaps in your knowledge. For example, newsmagazines may provide basic information about the importance of childhood immunization programs, but they may not provide the details to make the argument compelling. Consulting journals devoted to public health could yield statistics on the efficacy of immunizations, examples of the consequences of failing to immunize children, or the procedures necessary to fully protect youngsters.

The most important benefit of consulting specialized sources of information may be the opportunity it affords you to discover more about your topic than you might think you need. Have you heard the saying, "A little knowledge is a dangerous thing"? This adage stems from cases in which individuals, with some general knowledge of a topic, enter into discussions assured that they "know" the truth, when they may only know a part of it. A wiser idea is to approach arguing as the negotiation of shared realities. Perhaps the other participants in the discussion are right and you are wrong. Or maybe the best conception of truth is somewhere else. Getting a more thorough grasp of the subject by conducting more focused research should help you to avoid sounding like you know it all when you don't.

Having made the decision to pursue the lines of research your general reading has indicated will prove profitable, you need to decide what types of sources to consult and how to go about finding them. We will present three types of specialized sources, but this is not meant to convey that there are no others. However, these three should get you going on most topics.

Scholarly Journals. In any academic discipline, scholars are expected to contribute to the understanding of the field by publishing the results of their research in professional journals. These articles are not usually written up for the general public. But readers familiar with the controversies which prompt research can gain valuable insight by reading them. Check the list shown in the box that follows, or consult your reference librarian for the index to the journals in the topic that interests you.

Of course, there are a wide variety of popular magazines which publish in-depth articles and editorials on almost any subject. You can access these articles through the *Readers' Guide* or the *PAIS*. Such pieces tend to be relatively one-sided, but at this point in your research, that is what you are ready for.

SELECTED INDEXES TO SCHOLARLY JOURNALS

ABC: Political Science Index
Abstracts in Anthropology
Applied Science and Technology Index
Education Index
Humanities Index
Index Medicus
Index to Legal Periodicals
Philosopher's Index
Social Science Citation Index

Government Sources. Other, more specialized sources that can be immensely useful are government publications. The United States Congress holds hearings on almost anything of national concern. At these hearings experts from both sides of the controversy present sworn statements and answer questions from members of Congress. The experts usually testify as advocates in favor of, or opposed to, federal legislation. Consequently, these sources contain practically everything an advocate could need to construct compelling arguments.

To locate government hearings you need to consult the *Congressional Index Service (CIS)*. This publication is divided into indexes and abstracts for a given year. More recent publications are indexed monthly and quarterly. First, look up your topic in the index. (Remember, you may need to consider several synonyms or related aspects of the particular topic that interests you.) When you find your subject, you will also find a number. If the number begins with *S*, it refers to a publication of a Senate committee. If the number is preceded by an *H*, the document comes from the House of Representatives. Or the listing may start with a *J*. This refers to a joint committee composed of members from both the Senate and the House.

Having located a number, turn to the abstracts for the same year and look it up. You will find the citation for the document and, in most cases, a summary of what is contained in the document. If it is a hearing, then the abstract may direct you to certain pages for testimony relevant to your topic (See box).

Congress also prints a record of the debates that take place on the floor of Congress. The *Congressional Record* is indexed to help you find information you may find useful. The *Congressional Record Index* combines subject and author, so you can look up either the congressperson who made the speech or proposed the legislation, or you can look up the subject. Looking in the index yields the page number where the speech can be found. As in the *CIS*, the page number is preceded by a letter. *S* would indicate a speech in the Senate, *H* a speech to the House, *E* an extension or revision of remarks by a congressperson, and *D* a notation on the Daily Digest of events. Since senators and representatives can revise and extend their remarks, and even insert documents for the record, you can find a lot of information in the *Congressional Record*.

Documents issued by all government agencies, including the executive branch, also can be found in the *United States Government Publications Monthly Catalog*. This is a cumbersome index, but it works much like the other government indexes. You first look in an index, obtain a number, and look that number up in the abstract. This provides a call number which you can use in either finding the document in the library, or purchasing it from the Government Printing Office.

Of course, some controversies that interest you may be more prominent in local discourse than in national discourse. Your state may publish information about their proceedings. Consult your reference librarian for more information.

A SAMPLE *CIS* SEARCH

CIS INDEX 1992

Looking under "Railroad Accidents and Safety" yielded the reference number H401-44. The *H* reveals that this is a publication of the House of Representatives. The first number indicates that this is a hearing related to government operations; the second number that this is the forty-fourth hearing of the year in this category.

CIS ABSTRACT 1992

Looking under H401-44 provided the title of the hearing, "Adequacy of Laws and Regulations Governing Rail Transportation of Hazardous Materials." The hearing was held July 31, 1991 before the Subcommittee on Government Activities and Transportation. The summary revealed that the hearing concerned two rail accidents in California. The detailed summary of testimony reported who testified before the committee and what the essence of their testimony was.

The citation indicated that this hearing was available to library depositories and if the library had purchased this hearing it would be listed under the call number *Y4.G74/7:L44*. If the library did not purchase this hearing, it could be purchased from the Government Printing Office for $5.00.

Books. In addition to periodicals and government documents, most libraries have—not too surprisingly—books. Books published on the controversy can also be very helpful. But we have listed them last because there are limitations to what you can obtain in books. First, reading books can be very time-consuming. While thorough research necessitates reading almost everything published on the subject, for most of us that is a luxury we cannot afford. We need to obtain the greatest possible return for the time we invest. Because of their length and depth, books may not be as profitable as other sources.

Second, a book will generally offer you the perspective of only one author. The same time invested in reading journal articles is likely to offer a number of perspectives.

Finally, it can take a long time to get a book into print. For some controversies, especially those focused on events in history, this is not necessarily a problem. But in current events the question of recency can be critical. On some topics, where government is acting, or the problem fluctuates, by the time a book reaches the public, it may already be out of date.

So, yes, read books. But don't turn to them too early in the research process. And weigh the pros and cons of such research. Books can provide a wealth of information, but they have their limitations too.

Computer Searches

The Technological Age is clearly upon us. One benefit of this is that many libraries are now equipped to conduct computer searches for source materials. The indexes these searches access are extensive. And a computer search can literally tell you everything that has been published on your topic. Of course these searches require a lot of computer time, so they can be very expensive. To offset these charges, libraries sometimes limit computer searches, or assess fees for them. But an increasing number of libraries now make computer searches available to students without charge. Other students conduct searches from their home computers by connecting to research indexes over a modem. If you have not conducted a computer search yet, you probably will soon.

Each computer system has its own procedures, so it is best to consult your librarian. However, most searches have some factors in common. First, they have databases. Some databases are limited to selected recent periodicals, much like the *Readers' Guide*. Others are far more extensive. The bigger the database, the longer, and therefore more expensive, the search. Second, each on-line search system has to have a way to search the data. Usually this requires that the searcher provide key words that narrow the data fields.

For example, one of the most popular systems is called LEXIS®/NEXIS®. This is an extremely extensive and sophisticated data system. The researcher must first select from seventeen different categories of data, called libraries. There are libraries devoted to topics such as, industry, people, business, medicine, politics, patents, and six different categories of law. Each library has subsets of holdings too.

Once researchers have selected the data set they wish to investigate, they provide the key terms for the search. These can be as simple as a single word, or as complex as asking only for those articles in which two specified words appear within a specific number of words. LEXIS®/NEXIS® then searches for these terms in the headlines, bylines, dates, and texts of the articles in this data set. The researcher is then notified as to the number of articles that meet the search specifications.

If the number and nature of the articles found is too broad, the researcher can modify the search to refocus it. Additional words can be added to the search, or certain types of stories can be excluded. Each time the search is modified the number of matches is narrowed until only the articles of greatest interest are isolated.

At any point in the process, the searcher can take a quick look at the articles, or go through the articles fully. The option of paying for copies of the actual articles is also available.

Obviously, selecting the key terms is a critical component of this process. This again illustrates the importance of beginning your research with some general sources. Finding the right key terms for your computer search can result in a major time savings. As you become proficient at such searches, you will find these databases invaluable.

A SAMPLE LEXIS®/NEXIS® SEARCH

Research Topic

The need for immunizations to prevent the transmission of the hepatitis B virus by pregnant women to their unborn (prenatal) and newborn (perinatal) offspring.

Key Research Terms

hepatitis B virus, immunizations, prenatal, and *perinatal.*
(1) Select Library: Medical: General Medical
(2) Select from the Full Text Update Journals
    JNLS: All updated journals
    AJDC: American Journal of Diseases of Children
    JAMA: Journal of the American Medical Association
    PHRP: Public Health Reports
(3) Conduct Search
Level One: hepatitis w/seg immunizations
    Result: 445 articles contain these two terms within the same segment of the article.
Level Two: w/seg B Virus
    Result: 196 articles contain the terms from level one and the term B virus within the same segment.
Level Three: w/20 perinatal
    Result: 31 articles contain the terms of levels one and two, plus the word perinatal within 20 words of the previous terms.
Level Four: w/20 prenatal
    Result: 15 articles contain all the terms identified by the four searches.
Kwic View: enables researcher to get a quick look at the article. If it is relevant, the searcher can examine the text of the document in its entirety

---

How to Record the Evidence

Having located an article that interests you, it is time to record whatever information you will need later on. In addition to recording the verbatim quotation (more about this later), there are five components to a complete citation.

1. Author's Name The first thing to record is the author's complete name. Some style manuals require that you provide only the author's last name and the initials of their first and middle names.[3] Others require the full name. Regardless of the style you will eventually use, it is useful to record the full name. That way you have it if you need it.

What do you do when there is no author identified? This frequently happens in newspapers, newsmagazines, and pamphlets. It means that the source, the newspaper, magazine, or group that produced the pamphlet, should be considered the author. The same goes for articles written by staff writers. The words in such articles are, in a real sense, the words of the source.

2. The Author's Qualifications None of the official style manuals require or permit the inclusion of an author's qualifications in the reference section. These citation systems make no judgment about the quality of the sources an advocate consults. But audiences do evaluate the quality of the sources an advocate uses. Advocates who cite sources the audience views favorably (that is, sources which the audiences finds credible), benefit from a "halo effect." If a source the audience considers trustworthy and competent agrees with your argument, it makes both your argument and you look better. Of course, the reverse is also true. Consequently, it is important that we record the author's qualifications. As we do this, we can decide for ourselves whether our credibility will be enhanced or reduced by using this source.

Occasionally, you will not know the qualifications of an author. All you may know is that he or she wrote a book or article. Well, start with that information. It may be one of the times it is desirable to tell your audience the title of a book or article. But chances are you can find out more about the author by consulting some additional indexes. *Who's Who* and *Who's Who in America* provide biographical information on a variety of authors. There are other such biographical indexes as well. Once you record the qualifications of the sources you intend to use, be sure to use them in the text of your advocacy. Your audiences may not know your sources are expert unless you tell them. Therefore, it is to your advantage to include enough about the author, when you actually use the author's words, ideas, or statistics, to convince your audience of his or her credentials.

3. The Source Style manuals require that you provide enough information about the source so that members of your audience could locate it themselves. For a book, this usually necessitates the full title and the name and location of the publisher. For an article the title of the article, and name and volume of the periodical are usually required.

To be safe, you should consult the style manual you will be using for the required information before you conduct your research. This is especially the case for unusual sources like pamphlets, recordings, translations, edited volumes, videotapes, and the like.

4. The Date In Chapter 7 we discussed the test of evidence called *recency*. We argued that the date of the material is not as important as what has transpired since the material was written. Thus, some recent data is already outdated, while some will always be current. Nevertheless, it is important to record the specific date of the reference. Not only is this required by style manuals, to make it easy to locate the original source, it is frequently useful to include the date of the evidence in the text of your advocacy. Audiences may be impressed if your evidence is very recent. And if the date of the evidence is somehow germane to the argument being advanced (if, for instance, you are quoting the reactions to a speech) the date of the evidence may be critical.

5. The Page Number If you intend to quote or paraphrase an author, style manuals require that you provide the specific page where the passage appears in the original source. In addition, the reference page may require you to provide the beginning and ending page numbers for articles and chapters in books. So be sure to record this information.

What to Look for When Researching

You have found great articles and recorded the important citational information. Now you are reading the text. What do you record and what do you ignore? These are essentially questions of relevance. They are difficult questions and experience is the best teacher, but there are some suggestions we can make.

Considering What Is Necessary to Gain Adherence

We have previously discussed the role of stasis and stock issues in argumentation. Think about the issues that must be addressed and where there is likely to be disagreement. To illustrate this, we will consider the case of policy analysis.

The first stock issue of traditional policy analysis concerns the existence of a problem or an ill. This issue generates several questions:

How many people are affected by the problem?
How are they affected?
To what extent are they affected?
How are these affects manifested?
What are the likely consequences of the affects?

Such questions get at the heart of the stock issue. If you are trying to convince an audience that the status quo needs to be changed, you will want to show them the nature and extent of the problem. After all, there is no sense in changing the status quo if the problem is not particularly significant. Evidence that directly answers these questions should be recorded.

The second stock issue is blame. This issue concerns the cause of the problem and why our current policies are inadequate. Some questions to consider here include:

What is the main cause of the problem?
Why are other potential causes unimportant?
What is the status quo policy toward the problem?
Why is this policy inadequate?
Can the status quo policy be saved with minor changes?

The third stock issue is cure. This deals with whether or not the proposal would solve or ameliorate the problem. Questions like the following appear relevant:

What specifically should the agent of change do?
What proof is there that it would work?
Has the policy been tried elsewhere? With what effect?

Finally, consider the stock issue of cost. Remember, this issue asks the question "Are there any disadvantages to the proposal that outweigh the advantages?" Consider evidence that addresses the following:

Will the proposal cause any new problems?
Will the proposal exacerbate any existing problems?
Will the proposal delay some desired outcome?
Is the proposal ethical?
What is the likelihood that there will be some disadvantageous, unintended consequences?
Are there adequate answers to possible disadvantages?

Recalling the requirements of the various stock issues will help guide your research and help you discover where probable truth resides.

If you are motivated to share what you have learned with others you will need to consider the kind of materials that will prove compelling. This is what we address next.

Considering What Is Likely to Gain Adherence

Your focus here should be on the audience you anticipate addressing and the field of argument where the advocacy will be made. Merely having the relevant facts may not be enough. Remember, facts are subject to interpretation. You must not only secure that which is necessary to gain adherence, you must make sure that what you find is sufficient to move the audience. That means, first of all, finding evidence that helps you to present the actors, events and scene in the light you find most effective.

If you are depicting the government as heroic, find data that supports this characterization. If government is the villain, then evidence which presents this view is desirable. Similarly, the data you use as the foundation for your portrayal of the events and the scene should reflect and support your view. Quotations can be particularly effective, for the language of the authority may embody the label you wish to depict.

In addition, remember the importance of examples and analogies, which we have previously discussed (See Chapter 6). Not only do they serve as proof, they also make the argument comprehensible to an audience. Consequently, it is useful to record examples and analogies you find compelling. You will probably convey these in your own words, so it won't be necessary to record them verbatim. But you will wish to acknowledge the source of this information. To do so can enhance your credibility and guard against allegations of plagiarism.

When we discussed examples, however, we noted that a single example may not be typical of the set of possible examples. Even a few examples might lead to a hasty generalization. Statistics, the numeric expression of examples, reduce the likelihood of such errors. So record statistics that show the extent of the point you are trying to make. But, since statistics alone are rather cold and might not move an audience, it is useful to combine them with examples. Examine your readings to see if there are statistics and examples you can combine. Then you can not only illustrate your claim, you can quantify it. (Keep in mind that with statistics it is often desirable to relate to an audience a little something about how the statistics were gathered, and by whom. So record this information, too.)

Authoritative opinions can also be compelling. Examine what your experts say. A concise quotation that directly supports a point you are trying to make can be very effective, if the audience accepts the source as an authority. Thus, again, it is important to record the qualifications of the source.

Be careful when recording these quotations that you include more than the author's conclusions. The reasoning engaged in by the author is as important as the conclusion he or she reached. Audiences may find the reasoning compelling itself while they would reject a concluding statement from the same author. After all, the reasoning is the author's argumentation. Merely quoting the author's claim assumes that the audience will be convinced by the author's credibility alone. Perhaps they will. But a knowledgeable advocate would probably hedge that bet by including the author's reasons.

Lastly, when selecting data to record, be sure to consider the tests of data we presented in Chapter 7. Audiences are more likely to grant adherence to data that passes these tests.

In sum, we think the best advice is this: think of the kinds of claims you will need to advance to make your arguments compelling to your audience. Then, find data that directly demonstrates these claims to be well founded.

Recording the Text of the Evidence

After deciding what evidence you need, and finding it, you will need to record the text of the information. You can do this on sheets of paper, on note cards, or by making photocopies of the desired pages. There are pros and cons to each of these.

Sheets of paper and note cards are inexpensive. But both require time and effort on the researcher's part. Photocopies are faster, and more accurate since there is little risk of transcription error, but can be expensive.

Note cards can ease the process of organization. Each note card has a specific quotation on it. As you accumulate more and more information, you can easily reorganize the note cards to follow your developing thoughts on your subject. Working with stacks of paper and photocopies is much more cumbersome. And, since each sheet of paper or photocopy may have several quotations on it, finding the right quotation when you want it can be difficult and inefficient.

Debaters, who must work with vast amounts of evidence, often resort to a combination of note cards and photocopying. By cutting the photocopy apart and gluing it to note cards, the debaters obtain the accuracy and speed of photocopies, and the flexibility of note cards. There is the time lost, however, in cutting and pasting the evidence to the note cards. So, there is no perfect system. What works best for you is what you should use.

Organizing Your Advocacy

Even the best argument will fail if an audience does not understand it. That is why it is important that you construct your advocacy carefully. Part of this certainly entails making lucid and succinct claims. It also includes discovering relevant and convincing evidence. But even good argumentation must be organized well if it is to move an audience.

Exactly how you choose to organize your advocacy will depend on several factors: the occasion, the audience, your subject, and you. Each of these factors constrain the advocate, so each will be considered in turn.

The Occasion

Some occasions, circumstances, or situations lend themselves to structured arguments. Others do not. Clearly in the middle of an interpersonal discussion it would be inappropriate to launch into an extended speech advocating a specific point of view. Even in public speaking situations, which lend themselves to prepared addresses, there may be times when pointed advocacy is inappropriate.

We recently heard a commencement speaker receive a mixed reaction because he argued for a change in the way the city was administered, rather than celebrating the achievements of the graduating class. Perhaps a more appropriate approach would have been a combination of the two. The speaker might have argued, for example, that the graduating class could be the ones to accomplish real change since they had succeeded thus far. The speaker was less successful because he failed to consider the expectations of the audience adequately.

The Audience

The fact of the matter is that audiences do not approach the argumentive situation as blank slates. They bring with them a host of experiences, values, attitudes and beliefs. Even those willing to suspend judgment and give a full and impartial hearing do so within the value framework and experiences that have shaped their lives. Advocates need to assess this in order to organize their arguments effectively.

The audience will also reveal something about the field of argumentation. We explained in Chapter 3 that the assumptions about the nature and tests of argument vary from field to field. The type of argument expected or even demanded in one field, may not be accepted in another. So the advocate must take into consideration the field of argument embraced by the audience.

The Subject

We have identified three kinds of claims: fact, value and policy. Each type of claim would lend itself to different organizational patterns. Questions of fact generally are organized into main points, each of which constitutes reasons why an advocate believes some statement of fact to be correct or not.

Value questions usually involve setting criteria for evaluation and arguments in support of or against the value judgment. For example, an advocate who claimed that Jack Nicholson was America's best male actor would be required to offer two lines of argument: the first would involve establishing the criteria for selecting the best American male actor; and the second would demonstrate how Jack Nicholson met this criteria. These two lines of argument would most likely lead to two major points in a speech.

Finally, there are questions of policy. There are five ways policy advocates typically organize their advocacy. Each reflects a pattern of reasoning. The first method is called the **need case.** With this organizational pattern advocates tailor their arguments around the three stock issues they need to address.

A second organizational format, which stems from systems analysis, is called the **comparative advantage case.** In this approach, advocates present their policy proposal and compare the status quo to the status quo as modified by the proposal. The advocate's goal is to demonstrate that this second state (the status quo plus the proposal) is potentially more advantageous than the status quo.

A third approach is a variant of the comparative advantage case called the **goals case.** With this approach, the advocate attempts to convince the audience that they are all committed to a particular goal (ending discrimination perhaps). If the advocate can convince the audience that his or her proposal has a better chance of achieving the goal than the status quo alone, then the audience will likely find the case compelling.

A fourth organizational pattern used by policy advocates is called the **criteria case.** When audiences agree that a problem exists (or can be convinced of this by the advocate), but disagree as to what to do about the problem, the advocate may select to present and defend criteria for making this determination. The criteria may be fairly self-evident: the new policy should be reasonably inexpensive, easily administered, and likely to be successful. Or, the criteria may be complex. For example, policies to support expansion of manufacturing might entail criteria that includes sensitivity to environmental needs, regional development plans, employment needs of minority workers, relations with competitive foreign manufacturers, and so on.

Once the advocate establishes the criteria, he or she then presents the policy supported and argues that it meets the criteria the best. This organizational pattern thus entails three main points: review of the problem, presentation of the criteria, and application of the criteria to the policy proposal.

Summary

In this chapter we have argued that research is an important component of the argumentation process and we have attempted to equip you with the basics of library research. We began by defining research and urged you to construct a research plan. We specifically recommended that you begin with general sources and move to more specialized materials. Next we considered what to research and how to go about it. We also identified the elements of full citation and advised you to consider, as you research, what is necessary to prove an argument and what is likely to be effective in gaining adherence. We evaluated various methods for actually recording the text of the evidence. The final section of this chapter was devoted to how advocates can organize their discourse.

In the next chapter we switch roles from that of advocate to that of respondent. For it is not enough to just construct what you believe to be a compelling argument. You may need to point out why someone else's argument is deficient.

Key Terms

comparative
  advantage case
criteria case

general sources
goals case
needs case

research
research plan
specialized sources

Activities

1. Select a controversy you wish to research. Construct a research plan. Be sure to indicate what sources you will consult for each step of the plan: general and specific research.

2. Make a list of key terms and synonyms you will use to conduct a search of the controversy you have selected.

3. Find an article relevant to your research in each of the following reference aids:
   a. the *Readers' Guide to Periodical Literature*
   b. the card catalog
   c. a newspaper index
   d. an index to scholarly journals
   e. a legal or government index

4. Record the full source citation and text of five quotations relevant to your research. Be sure to include the qualifications of the author whenever possible.

5. Find a policy argument presented in an argument artifact and attempt to reorganize the advocacy using the four policy organizational formats provided in this chapter: need case, comparative advantage case, goals case, and criteria case.

Recommended Readings

Chesebro, James W. "Beyond the Orthodox: The Criteria Case." *Journal of the American Forensic Association* 7 (1971): 208–215.

Chesebro, James W. "The Comparative Advantages Case." *Journal of the American Forensic Association* 5 (1968): 57–63.

Dresser, William R. "The Impact of Evidence on Decision Making." *Journal of the American Forensic Association* 3 (1966): 43–47.

Lewinski, John D., Bruce R. Metzler, and Peter L. Settle. "The Goal Case Affirmative: An Alternative Approach to Academic Debate." *Journal of the American Forensic Association* 9 (1973): 458–463.

Kruger, Arthur N. "The Comparative Advantage Case: A Disadvantage." *Journal of the American Forensic Association* 3 (1966): 104–111.

Newman, Robert P. and Dale R. Newman. *Evidence.* Boston: Houghton-Mifflin, 1969.

Smith, Craig R. and David M. Hunsaker. *The Bases of Argument: Ideas in Conflict.* Indianapolis: Bobbs Merrill, 1972.

Zarefsky, David. "The 'Traditional Case'-'Comparative Advantage Case' Dichotomy: Another Look." *Journal of the American Forensic Association* 6 (1969): 12–20.

Notes

1. A number of scholars have commented on the influence of the printing press on the communication process. See, for example, Marshall McLuhan, *The Gutenberg Galaxy* (Toronto: University of Toronto Press, 1962).
2. Neil Postman, *Amusing Ourselves to Death* (New York: Penguin, 1985), p. 21.
3. There are a number of different style manuals. See, for example, the style manuals of The Modern Language Association (MLA), the American Psychological Association (APA), and the *Chicago Manual of Style.*

9

Refuting Arguments

Occasionally, you may find yourself privately disagreeing with the public statements of another individual. You may be in a committee or a kitchen, a boardroom or the bedroom, a lounge or a living room, or even a classroom. When this occurs, you must first decide whether voicing your disagreement is worthwhile. If you conclude it is, you will probably formulate your own argument and present it. Unfortunately, that may not be enough to persuade the other individual. Our experiences indicate that disputants are rarely wowed into silence because a well crafted counterargument is presented. Thus, in addition to constructing and presenting your ideas, you will also need to be able to point out the weaknesses in the arguments of others. This is called *refutation*.

Even when you do not have the opportunity to directly interact with an advocate, we believe that you automatically subject the advocacy of others to the same refutational processes. Why? Because it is natural that you evaluate what others say to you. Humans are not sheep who can be led wherever and whenever another wants to lead them. Humans are actors; they have choice over their actions. And as actors, we naturally evaluate the claims advanced by others because acting on an uncritical acceptance of advocacy can lead to undesirable consequences. So we scrutinize the messages we receive. Some we accept, others we reject. Understanding the refutation process will enable you to more carefully evaluate the arguments that you encounter, and it will give you the tools to identify why you reject a claim, should you choose to verbalize your concerns.

In this chapter we will, first, define the refutation process. Then we will systematically guide you through the steps necessary to critically evaluate an argument, formulate a response, and verbally present your refutation.

The Refutation Process Defined

To refute an argument is to deny its validity and refuse to agree with it. The **refutation process,** therefore, is a series of actions culminating in the denial of the argument advanced by another. It is not simply attacking another's argument, for how do you know what to say or how to say it? We believe refutation involves four steps:

1. listening in a focused way
2. critically evaluating arguments
3. formulating a response
4. presenting the response

Focused Listening (Step One)

Listening vs. Hearing

Have you had a conversation in which you remember hearing the other person talking but could not recall what it was they said? Of course you have. How about in the classroom? Have you ever heard a lecture but not really tuned in to it? You were hearing, but not really listening. Hearing is passive. We have no control over it. We cannot choose to not hear. But listening is active. It requires concentration or focus. This applies to reading too. If you ever find yourself rereading something because you do not remember what you just read, it could be because you lost your concentration. There are several reasons why people may be poor listeners.

Factors Affecting Listening

Selective Exposure.   Psychologists tell us that we seek out discourse with which we agree, and avoid that with which we do not. It is simply more cognitively comforting to believe that we are correct in our thinking, than the opposite. Consequently, we may not even expose ourselves to messages which we sense are contrary to our beliefs.

Distortion.   If we are exposed to messages we disagree with, it can be unsettling. Since we prefer not to be unsettled, our minds may help us by distorting the message into something more palatable. We may also distort messages because we anticipate the rest of a message prior to to actually hearing it. Did you notice that the word *to* was repeated in the previous sentence? Some readers will skip right past that because they anticipate the end of the sentence. We can distort another's argument the same way—by thinking that we know what they are going to say, prior to actually hearing it all.

Intrapersonal Argument. Another reaction we may have to controversy is to turn our attention from the discourse, to a discussion within our own heads. When we argue with ourselves, or focus on what we are going to say, instead of attending to the advocate, we are not likely to do as good a job listening.

Externalities. Distractions can also prevent us from being good listeners. Noise draws our attention away. It can prevent us from hearing another's argument correctly. If we wish to maximize our listening skills, we need to minimize those things which may distract us from our task.

Internalities. Just as external factors can interfere with your reception of messages, internal factors can distract you too. If you are upset about something, it is unlikely you'll be a very good listener. You might also be distracted if you allow the person you're arguing with to trigger a response by hitting your "hot buttons." "Hot buttons" are those sensitive, psychological points that invariably upset you. Our relatives are usually very adept at hitting those buttons and seem to know just what to say to rile us up. But when we react emotionally to these triggers, we are not being good listeners.

So the first step is to attend to the discourse so that we can comprehend it and understand exactly what it is the advocate wants us to agree to. But active listening is only half of being a critical listener. Once you decide to listen to advocacy, you should do so with a critical ear. The critical ear is one that is listening, even searching for flaws.

Critically Evaluating Arguments (Step Two)

In this text, we have been trying to teach you to be skeptical of the advocacy of others. Many of the things we have been working on in this book come together in the refutation process. Listening actively is a good start, but it is only a start. The product of active listening is accurate reception of the other person's argumentation: you will correctly hear what the other individual has said. But you still need to evaluate the message you've just received.

Determining What the Advocate Is Arguing

To evaluate another's arguments you should begin by trying to determine what it is that the other individual is actually arguing. Sometimes this is not as easy as it sounds.

Some advocates just do not argue well. As a result, they can be difficult to follow. Others deliberately try to conceal their objectives. We call an intentional attempt to disguise or conceal one's real argument **obfuscation.** There are two reasons for obfuscating, to be kind and to be tricky.

Advocates may deliberately use language which is not explicit because they wish to shield the listener from unnecessary pain or discomfort. One way this is accomplished is through the use of euphemisms. A **euphemism** is a mild or inoffensive term in the place of language which might offend or suggest something unpleasant.

There are many examples of language that is used euphemistically for relatively benign purposes. Think of the language used to refer to someone dying: people pass away, go to a better place, move on, go to sleep. Such terms soften the impact of saying someone has died.

This culture also has a plethora of names for what individuals do in bathrooms. The printable examples include: powdering one's nose, going to the john, going wee-wee, freshening up, and answering the call of nature. In fact, the entire process of excusing oneself from a group so that one can perform natural bodily functions is an interesting cultural ritual.

At other times language is used perniciously to confuse or conceal. This is sometimes called **doublespeak.**[1] Both sides in the Persian Gulf War used language in this way to hide what was occurring. Saddam Hussein called the hostages taken during the war "restrictees." The term, while perhaps more civil, did not obscure the fact that these individuals could not leave Iraq, nor did it remove the threat to their safety.

Likewise, when reporting the success of air strikes against strategic targets in Iraq, the American military spoke of "collateral damage." What did this term mean? It meant that some U.S. bombs hit civilian targets, like homes, schools, and businesses. Why did the military use a term that did not clearly convey what some of the bombs were actually hitting? Because the military feared the American public might not support bombing civilians. Remember, President Bush had argued that our conflict was not with the people of Iraq, but with its leaders and military.

The following are two specific ways in which language can conceal.

Ambiguity. When advocates deliberately employ language that is overly broad or unclear, they are utilizing **ambiguity.** This results in our having only a vague understanding of what it is they are actually advocating. Politicians, who wish to avoid alienating voters, often speak so vaguely as to be essentially meaningless.

Supporting family values was a popular rallying cry for conservatives early in the 1992 presidential campaign.[2] But what did that mean? Different politicians gave the term different meanings. What family values did single parents lack? How were Republicans more committed to family values than Democrats? In fact, the term was so vague, that each audience could give it whatever meaning it wanted.

The Democrats were equally guilty of employing ambiguous language. Candidate Bill Clinton spoke of increasing government "investments in education and jobs."[3] What did he mean by "investments"? In an earlier era they would have been called "public spending," and were by Clinton's opposition. But voters were reluctant to elect a "tax-and-spend liberal," hence the decision to rename the proposal in more ambiguous language.

Equivocation.   Making the same word mean two different things at two different times is **equivocation.** Sometimes people, like political candidates, equivocate so that different audiences assign different meanings to the same words. In this fashion, they try to ensure that potential voters are not alienated. Other times, individuals equivocate in an attempt to avoid having words they have spoken earlier used against them.

During the 1992 presidential campaign George Bush frequently accused Bill Clinton of equivocating. Bush attempted to give presence to Clinton's equivocation by charging Clinton with waffling on the issues. Bush even went so far as to give a speech outside of a Southern restaurant called The Waffle House.

Thus, advocates may use language which is purposely confusing to hide their real agenda. In such cases, it may be necessary to ask questions of the advocate, or read between the lines. Look for clues as to the real claim in the information you have available to you. Can you glean anything from your knowledge of the context or of the advocate? Do any other messages shed light on what the advocate is seeking?

Once you have determined what the advocate is actually arguing, you can subject the reasoning to critical scrutiny.

Evaluating the Reasoning

We have previously discussed the reasoning process (Chapter 6) and the data used to support claims (Chapter 7). These are the starting points for the critical assessment of ideas which is central to the refutation process. Breaking an argument down into its component elements enables us to scrutinize each element for weaknesses. We will consider each in turn.

Introduction to Fallacies of Reasoning.   In Chapter 6 we presented different forms of inductive and deductive reasoning. The first step to evaluating the reasoning employed by the advocate is to determine what kind of reasoning is being used, and apply the appropriate tests: example, analogy, causal correlation, sign, or causal generalization. If the reasoning appears to pass the tests we provide for each of these patterns of reasoning, consider the additional tests presented below. An argument that uses flawed reasoning is *fallacious,* and the tests below are known as *fallacies of reasoning.*

Argument scholars have identified many examples of what are generally considered fallacies. While each audience, in each field, determines for themselves whether they will grant adherence to a story or not, it is useful to understand the recognized fallacies of reasoning. We present three categories of fallacies and several illustrations of each.

Fallacies of Irrelevant Reasoning.   Some advocates base their claims on what most argument scholars consider irrelevant reasons. We identify seven.

1. **Ad populum** If an advocate attempts to prove a claim is correct by arguing that most people agree with the claim, the advocate is committing the ad

populum (appealing to the people) fallacy. For example, poll data indicates the majority of Americans believe public schools do not do a good job of educating students. To use this data as proof that public schools are failing, may be fallacious. The majority could be wrong. More important is why the people believe the claim to be correct. What are their reasons? When the reasons for the public perception are presented, they can be examined like any other reasons. Simply because a majority believes something does not make it correct.

2. Ad hominem We remember hearing Jose Canseco talking about baseball, and an acquaintance labeled Canseco's ideas as "so much nonsense." When we asked the acquaintance why, he said "Because Canseco is such a jerk." Canseco may, or may not be a jerk. But the indictment of an individual does not necessarily invalidate his or her ideas.

If an advocate argues that an idea should be rejected and offers as justification, not something wrong with the idea, but something wrong with the person presenting the idea, they are engaging in ad hominem (attacking the person). Even the worst person can have a good idea. If, however, the attack on the person is presented to show a motive for bias, or indicts the ethos of the source, the attack may be relevant.

3. Appeal to pity Occasionally the only basis for a claim is pity. When the claim calls for compassion, pity is a relevant reason. When the claim calls for something else, like a higher grade on an exam, pity is probably not relevant.

4. Appeal to fear The threat "your money or your life," relies on fear to convince us to agree to the claim. Such appeals do not provide real choice, thus, they are not really reasons for agreement—even if they are sometimes successful in gaining compliance.

5. Tu quoque Defending one's actions by pointing out others acted in a similar fashion is not really a defense (tu quoque means, you're another). We know an individual who frequently leaves newspapers scattered all over the house. When criticized for this behavior by his wife, he responded that she too left things scattered around the house. We could not help but notice his use of an irrelevant reason. Maybe both individuals are messy, but accusing the accuser of similar behavior does not invalidate the initial claim.

6. Appeal to tradition Because something has always been done a particular way may or may not be good reason to continue to do it that way. We can only know if we examine the reasons why it is always done that way. We recently suggested having a post-commencement reception for students and their families. One faculty member objected, pointing out, "We usually just greet people outside the building." Perhaps that was a better idea than a reception. But merely invoking tradition is probably an insufficient reason for the rest of us to grant adherence to the claim.

7. Slippery slope If you have ever started down an ice-covered hill and been unable to stop, then you have experienced how difficult it is to stop an action once it starts. When an advocate objects to something not because it is undesirable but because it may eventually lead to something else that is undesirable, the advocate is recalling this experience. But, if you have ever stopped before reaching the bottom of the ice-covered hill, you know why this is fallacy: we *can* stop before reaching the undesirable end. Therefore, an undesirable but not inevitable outcome is an irrelevant reason to reject an otherwise desirable idea.

Fallacies of Miscasting the Issue. Sometimes advocates commit errors in reasoning by casting the dispute in fallacious terms. We present three such fallacies.

   1. Fallacy of composition This fallacy is committed when an advocate argues that what is true of the parts is true of the whole. The fact that faculty at a university are creative in dealing with problems does not necessarily mean that the university is creative in dealing with problems.

   2. Fallacy of division This fallacy is the reverse of the fallacy of composition. The advocate who claims that what is true of the whole must be true of the individual parts is committing the fallacy of division. The military may be committed to discipline, but to conclude that all soldiers are committed to discipline is probably fallacious.

   3. Fallacy of false dichotomy Life is rarely all black or all white. There often are gray areas. An advocate who casts an argument in either-or terms may be falsely dichotomizing the issue. In the 1992 presidential debates George Bush argued that Bill Clinton must either accept or reject the North American Free Trade Agreement. Clinton responded that there was a third alternative, modify the agreement and then accept it.

Fallacies of Misdirecting the Issue. The final category of fallacies concerns those occasions when advocates avoid proving their own claims by distracting the audience.

   1. Shifting the burden of proof Instead of proving their own claim, some advocates challenge audiences to disprove the claim. "There is no end to the universe. And I challenge you to prove there is!" Perhaps the claim is true. But the advocate advancing the claim bears the burden of proving it. There is no burden to rebut an unproven claim.

   2. Begging the question An advocate who essentially restates the claim as the reason for the claim is guilty of begging the question. "I think I should have received an A on this paper," said a student. When we asked "Why?" The student said, "because it was an A paper." The student's reason was the same as the claim. The argument had not been advanced. Had the student given some data, such as: the paper was thorough, well researched, organized and well written, these would have constituted reasons for the claim. As it was, the student essentially gave the claim in support of the claim. And that is not how argument works.

3. Straw man fallacy How difficult is it to knock over a man made of straw? Not very. Nor is it particularly difficult to refute an opponent's argument if you get to present it in an undesirable fashion. Some advocates have attacked arguments for reform of medical care in this country by calling them attempts to socialize medicine. They then attack socialized medicine. Unless the original proposal really is for socialized medicine, this is a fallacious attempt to redirect the dispute.

In each of the foregoing fallacies the reasoning is flawed, therefore the argument is a **non sequitur,** which means that the conclusion does not follow.

Having subjected the reasoning to critical scrutiny, critical consumers of argument turn their attention to the grounds or evidence offered in support of the evidence.

Evaluating the Narrative

In Chapter 4 we examined how advocates usc language to construct their arguments. We specifically discussed the elements of a narrative: actors, scene, events. With each, we discussed what constituted effective argument. As the audience of another's argument you should also carefully examine these depictions. Analyze how the advocate depicts these narrative elements. Are the characterizations fitting? Are they consistent? Are there alternative and more appropriate constructions? Similarly, if the advocate employs a metaphor, the critical consumer will evaluate whether this particular metaphor is appropriate. Are there weaknesses in the comparison it makes?

Evaluating the Grounds

In Chapter 8 we presented four types of data which advocates use in support of their arguments: premises, examples, statistics, and testimony. We also identified ways in which you can test the data to see whether audiences will consider it compelling. You should now scrutinize the data to see whether it is valid.

Formulating a Response (Step Three)

Once you have discovered what it is that an advocate has said, and evaluated the discourse to determine whether the argument is faulty or not, you must determine how you wish to respond. If the argument is not faulty, the appropriate response seems to be agreement. If, however, you disagree, you still must make a decision.

Sometimes the best response is no response. Sometimes the opponent's argument is so weak it falls on its face, and at other times the price you pay by engaging in argument is too great. Individuals who continually find fault with the advocacy of others are considered argumentative. Most people prefer not to associate with argumentative people. So choose the arguments you wish to initiate wisely.

If you decide you wish to refute an argument, you must decide upon a strategy and the tactics to present your ideas.

Strategy

Your first decision now is which of your opponent's arguments you wish to attack. They are probably not all faulty, but even if they were, you might not want to spend the time and energy required to attack them all. Your choice will likely vary with the argumentative situation, the nature of the argumentation, and the audience.

If you are engaging in interpersonal argument then you may have little time to present your views before you are interrupted. In such circumstances, you would probably be wise to decide what the most critical point is, and start there. If you are engaging in an audience debate you may have more time, and you may be able to advance a number of objections. So, consider the situation when deciding upon a strategy.

You must also consider the nature of the dispute. Is the disagreement over a claim of fact, value or policy? The stock issues for each kind of dispute are fairly well established (see Chapter 5), and you may choose which of them you wish to dispute. Policy advocates, for example, must convince neutral audiences that there is a problem with the status quo, that the current policies cannot solve the problem, that the proposed policy will solve the problem, and that there are no significant disadvantages to the proposal. If you are attempting to refute policy argument of this nature, you can choose which of these stock issues to address. You need not refute them all. There is no reason to adopt a new policy if the policy will not solve the ill (cure), or if the current mechanisms can solve the problem (blame), or if there really is not a significant problem with the current policy (ill). Selecting the point of stasis is an important component of strategic planning.

Finally, take into consideration the values and beliefs of the audience. The field of argument determines the standards for what constitutes good evidence. Arguments that might work in a legal context, accusations of hearsay evidence, for example, might be irrelevant in interpersonal argument situations. Further, the values of the audience will certainly influence the efficacy of your argumentation. You may believe that capital punishment is immoral, but if you know your audience does not, this should influence the way in which you construct your argument.

Tactics

Having decided what you wish to refute, you must now go about the business of refutation. You still have choice of tactics however.

1. Refutation by denial Sometimes an advocate is completely wrong. In such cases, you would be justified in selecting a strategy of denial, attempting to prove that the conclusions offered by the advocate are erroneous. This will, in all

likelihood, necessitate that you have material which supports an opposite conclusion. But such support alone is probably not enough. Your opponent or your
audience would be left with contradictory arguments but no basis for determining which conclusion is the better one.

To be successful in refutation by denial, you must account for the two
conclusions. Perhaps the advocate's position makes erroneous assumptions. Or
perhaps the evidence you use is superior. It behooves you to provide the rationale
for deciding which contradictory view is correct.

2. Refutation by mitigation The effect of refutation by mitigation is to
minimize the impact of the advocacy in question. Perhaps the problems identified by the advocate are exaggerated. Maybe the reasoning is dubious, the
characterizations are spurious, or the evidence is questionable. In any case, it is
doubtful that these arguments alone will convince the advocate or a neutral
audience that the advocate is completely wrong. At best such refutation will
diminish the strength of the advocate's claims, but some probative argumentative
force will probably remain. Thus, the strategy of mitigation must be used in
conjunction with other arguments.

3. Refutation by additional consideration The advocate may be quite correct, in which case it may not be possible to deny or mitigate their position. This
does not leave you without recourse. The advocate's reasoning may be incomplete. We will consider two possibilities.

a. Reducing the argument to absurdity The Latin term for this is reductio ad
absurdum. With this tactic you take the advocate's reasoning to its logical
conclusion, which hopefully reveals how it is flawed.

Consider the arguments advanced for legalization of cocaine. One of the
reasons offered by supporters of this position is that anti-drug laws are unen-
forceable. You might argue that the assumption of this argument is that the
inability to enforce the law justifies giving up. It would be possible for you to
argue that if your opponent is correct, then this reasoning should be logically
extended to other comparable situations such as: laws against speeding, drunk
driving, and violent crimes. Examining the advocate's reasoning this closely may
illustrate the faulty assumption of the argument—in this case, that inability to
adequately enforce the law means the behavior it prohibits should be legalized.

b. Turning the tables It is possible that the advocate is correct, as far as the
reasoning goes, but the consequences he or she opposes are actually desirable.
In academic debate this is called a turnaround. It simply means taking a negative
position and making it a positive.

Suppose an advocate argues that some policy has adverse consequences for
the American economy. The negative effect of this could be a lowering of the
American standard of living. But is this necessarily bad? Americans might think
so, at least initially. But people living in the less developed countries competing
with Americans for scarce resources might disagree. And when we consider the
adverse environmental impacts of the wasteful American standard of living, even
American audiences might agree that forcing ourselves to make do with less
through conservation and recycling might not be all bad. In this way a negative,

a lower American standard of living, might be turned into a positive, a better world standard of living and a cleaner environment.

Preparation for Refutation

Deciding upon the strategy and tactics will be much easier if you have had the opportunity to prepare for the refutation process. While this is unlikely in the interpersonal argument context, it is possible in fields like debate and the law. In such situations you should anticipate what your opponent might argue and prepare contingencies: consider the stock issues that need to be addressed. Gather supporting materials ahead of time. These may be prepared in briefs or blocks, or organized on note cards.

Briefs are a series of arguments, claims and the requisite support, organized to support a specific point of clash. You will probably have many more briefs or blocks than you actually use because you will need to prepare for a variety of contingencies. Lawyers anticipate the witnesses the opposition might call, and outline the line of cross-examination they intend to follow. Debaters anticipate the arguments their opponents will raise, prepare responses, and in some cases, anticipate what the opposition will say to the brief and prepare extension briefs that answer those points.

SAMPLE BRIEF

If you were to argue that the ozone layer is being depleted and that this is bad, an opponent could argue that the layer is not being depleted very rapidly. You might then construct a brief which contains the claims and data you would present in refutation of your opponent's claim.

Responses to "the ozone layer is not being depleted quickly."
1. Old estimates are outdated.
Sharon Begley, Staff Writer, "On the Wings of Icarus," *Newsweek*, May 20, 1992, p. 60.

The vanishing ozone layer is fast approaching just such a worst-case scenario. Stratospheric ozone, which screens out the sun's ultraviolet rays, is disappearing twice as fast as was predicted only two years ago.

2. The evidence is overwhelming
Michael Lemonick, Staff Writer, "The Ozone Vanishes," *Time* February 17, 1992, p. 60.

The evidence is overwhelming that the earth's stratospheric ozone layer—our shield against the sun's hazardous ultraviolet rays—is being eaten away by man-made chemicals far faster than any scientist had predicted.

Presenting the Response (Step Four)

Only when you have completed the first three steps are you really ready to actually present your arguments. We will now discuss two processes for refuting an advocate's arguments: declarative refutation and refutation by questioning.

Declarative Refutation

The first refutation process involves the systematic assertion of one's objections to an argument. In a well organized, thorough, carefully reasoned manner, one "declares" a series of criticisms, or beliefs that counter the opponents'. There are four steps to presenting refutation declaratively.

1. Identify point to be refuted The first thing you must do is tell the advocate and audience what argument you are responding to. Is it a specific point or subpoint of his or her advocacy? Are you grouping a number of points together? Are you responding to the essence of the entire advocacy?

2. Label and signpost your refutation What is the essence of the point you want to make? Try to state it succinctly. This is the claim you are making about the advocate's argument. If there are several points to your refutation you need to enumerate them to preserve clarity.

3. Support the refutation You have already labeled the argument, now you must develop it. What is your reasoning? What supporting evidence (premise, example, statistic, or testimony) can you present? Repeat steps 2 and 3 until your case is complete.

4. Show the impact of the refutation(s) What effect do your arguments have on the entire dispute? Did you win this particular argument? Did you mitigate it? What must the advocate do to answer your refutation? If you win this point, what effect does this have on the other issues of the dispute? Do not trust the advocate or the audience to determine this. They may see the controversy differently. You need to direct them.

These four steps should be repeated for each point you wish to refute. When you have presented your refutation you should have convinced a neutral audience of the veracity of your position.

Refutation by Questioning

Asking questions is an important part of almost all argumentative interactions. In academic debate and the law, questioning is known as **cross-examination.** Each of these fields has specialized guidelines for the process. We will present some general orientations that apply to all contexts in which arguers use questioning.

Philosophy. The chance to question an opponent can be very inviting. Some individuals get swept up in the process and engage in tactics which undermine their credibility and likability. We admonish you to remember the golden rule and treat the opposing advocate the way you wish to be treated: Do not badger. Ask questions that can be answered. And allow him or her time to answer.

Purpose. We believe that questioning can be used for three purposes: to clarify what an opponent has argued, to probe an argument for weak points, and to highlight weaknesses you already know of. This latter purpose can be very useful for setting up arguments that you will make later. It is unlikely that opponents will concede the argument during questioning, so that is not listed as a purpose.

Procedure. Just as verbal refutation has several steps, so does questioning.

   1. Identify the point about which you wish to question your opponent Don't just ask questions out of the blue. Something your opponent said is prompting the question. Tell your opponent and the audience what it is.

   2. Ask your question succinctly Try to be brief. The most effective questions are direct and specific. Avoid asking compound questions or questions that require elaborate preparation. They will take too long to set up and you may be interrupted. You should also avoid asking loaded questions. **Loaded questions** are those which direct your opponent how to respond, such as "Do you support wasting millions of dollars on space research?" No one would answer this affirmatively. But if your opponent favors space research, he or she won't take this question lying down. He or she will object to the phrasing and you'll have lost ground.

   3. Ask followup questions Only occasionally will one question accomplish all that is needed. Listen to the answer and probe it. Try to uncover its unspoken assumptions. Probe the characterizations and reasoning.

   4. Move on When you have accomplished what you can you should not continue to ask questions. Just as moving on too quickly can prevent you from exposing weaknesses, dwelling too long on a point can undercut your effectiveness and waste time.

   5. Use the information you acquire The information you glean from questioning can help you to construct subsequent arguments. In some argument contexts, like academic debate, cross-examination is only effective to the extent that answers are used in subsequent speeches.

   Whether you present your refutation declaratively or through questioning, if you have chosen your strategy and tactics well, and conveyed the refutation clearly, you will be in a position to reap the rewards of your thoroughness.

Summary

In this chapter we have considered the process of refutation. It is our philosophy that both those who will engage in refutation and critical consumers of argument profit from considering the refutation process.

We defined the refutation process as a series of actions culminating in the denial of the argument advanced by another. This process includes four steps: focused listening, the critical evaluation of argument, the formulating of a response, and lastly, the presenting of the refutation.

In following chapters we will examine specific contexts of argumentation. Each chapter is designed as a self-contained unit capable of being mastered by anyone who has a thorough understanding of the first nine chapters of this text.

Key Terms

ad populum	euphemism	refutation by denial
ad hominem	fallacy of composition	refutation by
ambiguity	fallacy of division	mitigation
appeal to fear	false dichotomy	refutation process
appeal to pity	loaded question	shifting the burden of
appeal to tradition	non sequitur	proof
begging the question	obfuscation	slippery slope
cross-examination	reducing to absurdity	straw man fallacy
doublespeak	refutation by additional	tu quoque
equivocation	consideration	turning the tables

Activities

1. Observe two or more individuals engaged in argument on a radio or television talk show. Try to find indications of flawed listening, then identify which of the factors affecting listening provides the best explanation for it.

2. Assess your own listening behavior. Listen to an individual engaged in public advocacy on a talk show. As you listen to the advocacy, apply the five factors which affect listening to your own listening behavior.

3. Construct one example for each of the fallacies of reasoning presented in the text.

4. Select a public controversy which interests you and take a position on one side of the controversy. Identify a claim made by the opposition. Now construct a brief attacking the opponent's claim.

5. Have a friend or classmate help you to practice your questioning technique. First, reread the section of the text on questioning, then have your colleague

take a position on a public controversy and ask them questions. Be sure to follow the golden rule. To practice answering questions, reverse the process.

Recommended Readings ────────────────────────

Bridges, Dick A. and John C. Reinard, Jr. "The Effects of Refutational Techniques on Attitude Change." *Journal of the American Forensic Association* 10 (1974): 203–212.

Cragan, John F. and Donald C. Shields. "The Comparative Advantage Negative." *Journal of the American Forensic Association* 7 (1970): 85–91.

Dudczak, Craig A. "Direct Refutation in Propositions of Policy: A Viable Alternative." *Journal of the American Forensic Association* 16 (1980): 232–235.

Hollihan, Thomas A. "The 'Turnaround' as Argument Strategy: A Rationale for Use and Standards for Evaluation." *Speaker and Gavel* 22 (1985): 45–51.

Johnstone, Henry W. *Philosophy and Argument.* University Park: Pennsylvania State University Press, 1959.

Wellman, Francis L. *The Art of Cross-Examination.* 4th ed. New York: Collier, 1936, republished 1962.

Notes ────────────────────────────────

1. The National Council of Teachers of English give an annual award to the most egregious example of doublespeak. See also William Sparke and Beatrice Taines, *Doublespeak: Language for Sale* (New York: Harper's College Press, 1975).

2. The reference, of course, is to Dan Quayle's criticism of the television comedy "Murphy Brown" in which the title character decides to have a baby out of wedlock. This theme, however, was also dominant at the Republican Convention. See, for example, the text of Quayle's acceptance speech, *Los Angeles Times* 21 August, 1992 p. A10.

3. While Clinton used this phrase repeatedly throughout the campaign, his acceptance speech at the Democratic Convention is an excellent summary of why he wanted to be president, *Los Angeles Times* 17 July 1992 p. A10 (See Appendix A).

PART II

Argumentation
in Specialized Fields

Theremaining chapters will focus on argumentation in selected specialized fields. As we have already discussed, the norms and practices that characterize argumentation differ according to context. You would not argue the same way in an ordinary conversation between friends as you might in an academic debate, as a candidate engaged in a political campaign, in a court of law, or in a business organization. The requirements for establishing acceptable proof, the style of presentation, and the criteria for evaluating knowledge claims are substantially different in each case.

The fields selected for discussion in the following chapters are intended to reflect some of the differences found when one argues in alternative settings. Thus the selection is representative, rather than exhaustive. We do not claim that it represents all the important differences found in argument fields, and in fact, we could have selected other fields for discussion. We chose these fields because they are substantially different from each other, and because it is likely that you will come into contact with them at some point during your lives.

Chapters 10 and 11 consider the field of academic debate. Chapter 10 provides the rudiments of debate as a field, and Chapter 11 gives you a glimpse of some of the more complex theoretical issues that emerge in debate competitions. Many teachers of argumentation assign debates as class requirements, because these contests provide an outstanding way to teach students the practical skills of argumentation. Academic debate was first developed as a kind of model of what well reasoned argumentation should look like. It is a contest activity designed to teach the skills of research and oral argumentation. We encourage you to read these chapters and to try your hand in debating. It truly is enjoyable as well as educational.

Chapter 12 focuses on the arguments that surface in political campaigns. These arguments fix our attention on the vital political issues of the day, and involve all of us as citizens and also, hopefully, as voters. They shape our public life and our collective social energies. These arguments represent the very essence of our system of pluralistic democracy. Warts and all, the political campaign practices of today represent the culmination of more than 200 years of experimentation in representative democracy. This chapter should interest all of you, and should help you to fulfill your civic responsibilities.

Chapter 13 considers the argumentation that takes place in our courts. These arguments also involve all of us. Some of you may become litigants, others may become attorneys or judges, and many more will serve as jurors. But all of us will be affected by the argumentation that takes place in the courts because it reflects our social values, and because our courts create what passes for justice in our frenzied contemporary society.

Chapter 14 examines argumentation in business and organizations. This chapter is included because almost all of you will someday find yourselves working in an organization. Your effectiveness in achieving your career goals may be very much influenced by how well you can represent your ideas through both spoken and written arguments. While we would caution all readers that organizations differ, and that the specific requirements for arguing in any particular organization may be unique to that organization, we believe that there are general characteristics to arguments created in business organizational settings. You can learn these and, once mastered, they will make you a more effective organizational member.

Finally, Chapter 15 discusses arguing in interpersonal relationships. This chapter also affects all of us, because we are all engaged in creating, managing, nurturing, and sometimes disengaging or terminating interpersonal relationships. The method for managing the disagreements or conflicts in these relationships is argument. Our goal is to make you a more effective, sensitive, and strategic arguer in these interactions—in short, to help you win friends and influence people!

10

Basic
Academic Debate

Many classes in argumentation culminate with participation in academic debates. Others require observation of debates. Since academic debate is a special field of argumentation, distinguished by the problems it addresses and the methods used to evaluate disputes, it is best to study the nature of this activity prior to attempting it. This chapter is devoted to that study. We will discuss the role of the debate proposition, identify the respective burdens of the participants, and present aspects of the format of this specialized form of argumentation. In the next chapter we will focus on some aspects of debate which may be of interest to more advanced students.

In this text, we have approached argumentation as part of the natural process of life. It is one way we make sense of our world, and negotiate our understanding with others. Our intent has not been to teach you how to win arguments, rather, we have given you the tools to reach your own decisions and to construct your own advocacy. We have also contended that through argument you can discover the best conception of probable truth.

Academic debate is a somewhat different proposition. It is a laboratory for practicing the skills of argumentation. Students are frequently assigned to debate both sides of a controversy; clearly, their arguments do not necessarily reflect their own conception of truth. Rather, debaters offer the best arguments they can find for the view they must defend. While the result will hopefully lead to a better understanding of truth, the focus is competitive. The intent of debate is to have fun, refine your argument skills in a structured environment and, if your skills are up to the challenge, to win.

Although there is widespread agreement among the argumentation community as to the value of academic debate, there are few explicit rules governing the activity of debating. Consequently, if you will be involved in academic debating, your instructor will likely give specific instructions regarding how you should engage in debate.

The Resolution

The focus of any debate is the proposition. The proposition is a statement that expresses the subject of the dispute. In academic debate the proposition is called the **resolution.** Because debate is a formal setting for argument, the resolution is explicitly worded prior to the debate. It may be a proposition of fact, value or policy. Most debates utilize either value or policy resolutions, so we will focus on these.

The purpose of the resolution is twofold. First, it announces to all participants the topic of the debate. This gives both teams an equal opportunity to prepare for the debate. Second, it divides the ground for the two teams, delineating their argumentative tasks.

Affirmative Burdens

The team which supports or affirms the resolution is called the **affirmative.** Since the resolution typically proposes a change from current value or policy, the affirmatives are also known as the advocates of change. Their burden is to persuade the audience that the resolution is correct.

Negative Burdens

The resolution also conveys certain argumentative obligations to the opposing, or **negative,** team. Their burden is to negate the affirmative team's arguments. As representatives of current belief, negatives are not required to persuade the audience that the resolution is false. They are merely obliged to rebut the story advanced by the affirmative. Negative debaters may show the affirmative narrative lacks probability or fidelity. This may be best accomplished by presenting a competing narrative. If a competing story better accounts for the facts, then it will seem likely that the affirmative narrative is not true.

Presumption and the Burden of Proof

While all arguers have a burden to support their arguments, affirmative debaters have **the burden of proof.** They must prove the resolution true. This necessitates that they present and defend a **prima facie case:** a narrative which, on its first presentation, would meet the burdens necessary to persuade a reasonable audience that the resolution is true.

Affirmatives have the burden of proof because they must overcome **presumption.** In the field of law, this principle assumes an individual is innocent until proven guilty. In debate, we presume that current beliefs are justified until there is good and sufficient reason for a change. In most debates, presumption resides with the negative and against the resolution.

Assume the resolution for an academic debate is: *Resolved: that the United States should significantly strengthen its trade restrictions with Japan.* Both teams would know that the affirmative team would be calling for the imposition of stronger trade restrictions by the U.S., and that the negative team would be obliged to rebut their imposition. The burden of proof would be placed upon the affirmative, for the affirmative is advocating a change in policy. Presumption would be against such change. Both teams would also know that the debate would focus on U.S.-Japanese trade policies. This would enable them to investigate the relevant literature to discover and prepare for the issues likely to figure in this debate.

Two Types of Academic Debating

Policy Debate

In **policy debate** the affirmative team is generally asked to present a specific proposal or plan to implement the change called for in the resolution. Imagine the resolution is: *Resolved: that the United States should substantially change its development assistance policies toward one or more of the following nations: Afghanistan, Bangladesh, Burma, Bhutan, India, Nepal, Pakistan, or Sri Lanka.*[1] The affirmative would present a plan that detailed how they think the United States ought to substantially change its development assistance policies for one or more of the identified countries. They would also need to identify the current policies and argue that they are somehow inadequate compared to the proposal.

Value Debate

In **value debate** the affirmative asks the audience to agree to a judgment made in the resolution. There are two components to this judgment: a value object and a value judgment. For example, the topic may be: *Resolved: that the welfare system exacerbates the problems of the urban poor in the United States.*[2] In this case the value object is the relationship between the welfare system and the problems of the urban poor. The value judgment is that this relationship is adverse. Whether you think the welfare system exacerbates, or worsens, the plight of the urban poor depends upon what is important to you; on what you value. Debates on this topic would focus on two major questions: By what criteria should we determine whether or not the welfare system exacerbates the problems of the urban poor?; and then, using this criteria, Did the welfare system make the problems of the urban poor better, worse, or leave them unchanged?

Format

Most academic debate is conducted by two-person teams, although other formats of debate also exist. One-on-one debate, known as Lincoln-Douglas debate is very common, and will be discussed in Chapter 11. The nature of speeches, the speaker order and the time limits of each speech are referred to as the **debate format.** There are three components of a debate: constructive speeches, rebuttal speeches, and cross-examination. While there is some variety in the length of speeches, there is consensus as to the basic type and order of speaking (see sample format).

A SAMPLE DEBATE FORMAT

First Affirmative Constructive Speech	8 minutes
Cross-Examination by a Negative Speaker	3 minutes
First Negative Constructive Speech	8 minutes
Cross-Examination by an Affirmative Speaker	3 minutes
Second Affirmative Constructive Speech	8 minutes
Cross-Examination by a Negative Speaker	3 minutes
Second Negative Constructive Speech	8 minutes
Cross-Examination by an Affirmative Speaker	3 minutes
First Negative Rebuttal Speech	5 minutes
First Affirmative Rebuttal Speech	5 minutes
Second Negative Rebuttal Speech	5 minutes
Second Affirmative Rebuttal Speech	5 minutes

Because they are generally the advocates of change and therefore have the burden of proof, affirmatives both initiate and conclude the debate. This advantage is offset by the negative team retaining presumption.

Constructive Speeches

Each student presents a **constructive** speech. In this speech you can present any argument you consider relevant. This is the opportunity to construct the positions you believe should be the focus of the debate. It is also the occasion for presenting your initial responses to the positions developed by the opposition.

Rebuttal Speeches

Each student also presents a **rebuttal.** In this speech you will rebuild your initial constructive positions and extend your attacks on the opposition. Because rebuttal speeches take place in the latter part of the debate, debaters are prohibited from initiating new arguments. You can extend your own arguments and refute your opponents'; you can even read new evidence in your rebuttal, but you cannot start a brand new argument.

For example, consider the trade topic illustration we used earlier. If the negative had not discussed in their constructive speeches the possibility that

Japan would respond to new American trade restrictions by implementing their own, it would be too late to bring this up in rebuttals. If this is an important argument, it should have been introduced earlier, while there were still several speeches to be made. Then the likelihood of Japan's acting in this way could have been fully explored. The prohibition against new arguments in rebuttals also prevents the affirmative from coming up with new reasons for their policy in the last rebuttal.

Rebuttal speeches are shorter than constructive speeches. This means that you must adapt to the rebuttal situation. Sometimes this means offering a little less explanation. Sometimes it means choosing which arguments you believe you need to discuss—but remember, if you don't discuss an argument in your last rebuttal, it is likely that the audience will not consider this argument when deciding who won the debate.

Final rebuttals are also the last opportunity for you to convince the audience why you have won. This means that you should explain why you have won certain issues, and what it means to have won them. Putting the arguments together into a coherent story at this point is an effective strategy.

Cross-Examination

Most debate formats incorporate question periods. In debate this is called **cross-examination.** Each debater asks questions of, and is questioned by, the opposition. The individual asking the questions is called the questioner. The debater who has just concluded a constructive speech and is now being questioned is called the witness.

You may decide to use this time to clarify what the opposition has argued, asking for copies of the evidence read, and the like. While this may be necessary—after all, one cannot refute what one has not heard—it is not the most effective use of cross-examination time. Asking questions that probe an opponent's argument can be a more profitable use of this time. Arguments and evidence often are predicated on unproven assumptions. Discovering these may permit you to dispense with arguments expeditiously. Also, if you know what the weaknesses of an opponent's arguments are, it can be useful to highlight these during questioning, before you make the argument in your next speech. Then you can reference the admission gleaned in your crossexamination.

We discussed questioning in depth in Chapter 9, but debate cross-examination is a little different. In most contexts argument is regulated by the norms of polite conversation. If you are abusive or uncooperative, people will probably stop interacting with you. Two rules govern the cross-examination required of debaters, and they are quite strict.

First, the cross-examination period is controlled by the questioner. If you are the questioner, you get to ask the questions, the witness does not. You can also politely interrupt the witness if you feel the need. This may happen because you think you have the answer you need, or because the witness is not answering the question you thought you had asked. But you may not badger the witness or demand yes-or-no answers. Some questions cannot be adequately answered with a "yes" or "no," so it is unfair to make such a request. You are not permitted to read new evidence during cross-examination, even if you intend to give the witness a chance to respond to it. Evidence must be read during a speech.

Second, witnesses must cooperate as fully as possible. This means that if you are the witness you should answer the questions as clearly and as succinctly as possible. You should not attempt to stall or obfuscate. Nor are you permitted to read new evidence. Of course, you are permitted to refer to the evidence you presented in your speech.

Time Limits

Each team receives an equal amount of speaking and cross-examination time. These time limits are strictly enforced, and when your speaking time has expired, you must end your speech.

Now that you have an idea of how a debate operates, we can discuss in greater detail the types of debate arguments typically advanced.

The Nature of Debate Arguments

As one might expect, most of the arguments advanced in debate focus on the reasons why the audience should accept or reject the resolution. These are called substantive arguments. There are some arguments, however, that may precede the substantive one.

Procedural Arguments

Procedural arguments are those that must be resolved prior to consideration of substantive issues. These arguments must be initiated in the first two speeches (first affirmative constructive or first negative constructive). The most important procedural argument is topicality. We will also discuss criteria arguments which are used in value debating. Other less common procedural arguments are discussed in Chapter 11.

Topicality Arguments. We have already noted that the affirmative burden is to prove the resolution. If the arguments presented by the affirmative deal with something other than the resolution, the affirmative will not have proved the resolution true. A negative argument alleging that the affirmative has strayed from proving the resolution true is called a **topicality** argument.

Typically, the affirmative first defines the key terms of the resolution and then develops the arguments supporting the resolution. In policy debate the plan proposed by the affirmative, or the policy change under consideration, is the focus of the topicality question. If the plan is topical, that is, if the proposed plan does what the topic calls for, the advantages which flow from the plan would prove the resolution true. If the plan is not topical, the advantages would not be relevant, and they would not serve as reasons why the resolution ought to be implemented.

For example, if the affirmative defined trade restrictions as tariffs and quotas, the plan must specify how U.S. tariffs and quotas would be modified. The advantages of such a policy must then be shown to stem from these changes.

In value debate there is no plan. Thus, a different determinant of topicality is used. With value resolutions the issue of topicality focuses on the relationship between the definitions and the arguments advanced by the affirmative in support of the resolution. Let's take, for example, the resolution *Resolved: that the welfare system exacerbates the problems of the urban poor.* The affirmatives would define the key terms: *welfare system, exacerbates, problems,* and *the urban poor.* The affirmatives would then present reasons why they think the resolution is true. If they argued that public schools do not adequately prepare the urban poor for careers, and the negative team did not think schools are part of the welfare system, the latter could issue a topicality argument.

Although topicality is an affirmative burden, it is generally presumed that an affirmative will present a topical case. Thus, it is the first negative speaker who initiates a topicality argument if one is called for.

Criteria Arguments.   In value debates there is a special kind of definition presented, a definition of the value term. Since a term like *exacerbates* is subjective, a means must be proposed for determining whether it applies or not. Affirmatives debating value resolutions are therefore required to present **criteria** for determining the value term in the resolution. For the topic *resolved: that implementing the United Nations' universal declaration of human rights is more important than preserving state sovereignty,*[3] the affirmative would need to provide a way to evaluate the value judgment "more important." An affirmative might present a paramount value, such as preservation of life, and argue that this is the most important value. The affirmative could then contend that whichever concept (the U.N.'s universal declaration of human rights or state sovereignty) preserved life better should be considered more important.

Alternatively, instead of a paramount value, an affirmative could choose to present several values in a hierarchy or value system. For example, if you were debating the U.N. resolution, you might choose to present the utilitarian value system as your criteria for determining whether the U.N.'s universal declaration of human rights or state sovereignty is more important. (The utilitarian value system stipulates that the concept which provides the greatest good for the greatest number of people is the more important concept.)

First negative speakers can respond to affirmative criteria arguments by accepting or rejecting them. If they accept the affirmative criterion then the audience will use it as a filter to evaluate the arguments presented in the debate. If preservation of life is paramount, then the audience will look first to determine whether the affirmative or the negative arguments uphold this value best.

Arguments which address other values, such as human rights, would not flow through the criteria filter, and should therefore not enter the debate. Since the affirmative can select their criteria, and since this selection often provides a strategic benefit, many negatives choose to clash with the criteria.

Negatives who elect to reject an affirmative criterion can choose how they will do so. First, they can present a **value objection:** an argument that says the affirmative value is a bad value to use. For example, some affirmative values focus on the rights of individuals. Negatives could argue that basing decisions on individual rights is a bad idea because individual rights reinforce the notion that individuals are more important than the group. This, some authorities contend, has adverse consequences on society. They contend that our wasteful, throwaway, pollution-filled society is the result of elevating the individual above the group. Therefore, they maintain, a criterion which focuses on individual rights should be rejected. Without a criterion, there is no way to make the value judgment presented in the topic, and therefore, the negative can argue that the affirmative fails to prove the resolution true.

Negatives can couple their attacks on affirmative criteria with the presentation of counter-criteria. In this situation you would argue that an alternative criterion is superior to the affirmatives', and therefore, the counter criterion should be used as the filter for the debate. Of course, this counter-criterion is selected by the negative and gives them an advantage in the debate.

Whether a criterion is presented by the affirmative or the negative, it should be defined and the rationale behind its selection should be presented and defended. The team which does the better job of debating about criteria will convince the audience to use their criteria for evaluating the debate.

Substantive Arguments

While topicality and criteria arguments are both potentially decisive, most debates focus on the **substantive arguments** which remain. In substantive debate on policy the affirmative is called upon to envision and depict two worlds: the world of the status quo, and that of the status quo plus the plan. In substantive debate on matters of value the vision may be only of the status quo. We will consider each in turn.

Substantive Issues in Policy Debates.

In examining the status quo, the policy affirmative presents a story about the world as they see it. This entails describing the actors, the scene and the events in narrative terms. The affirmative may show the status quo to be inadequate either because it has problems that cannot or will not be solved by the present system, or because it compares poorly to the world that would exist following the adoption of the affirmative proposal.

Traditionally, affirmatives presented a world with problems that needed to be solved. An affirmative story of this type is called a **needs case.** These problems (the stock issue known as the ill) must be significant and inherent to the status quo (the stock issue known as blame). If the ills of the status quo are insignificant then there would be no sense enacting a new policy. If the problems are not inherent to the present system, that is, if we do not know the cause of the problem and why current policies are inadequate, then a new policy might not solve the problem. Finally, we must have good reason to predict that the proposal will actually solve the identified problems (the stock issue known as the cure). If the plan accrues no advantage, then it ought not to be enacted.

It is much more common now to tell a narrative which merges these three stock issues (ill, blame, and cure) and presents **comparative advantages.** In such an approach, the affirmative presents a plan and argues that the advantages of the plan compare favorably to the status quo. Thus, there does not have to be a significant problem (ill) with the present system, just a significant advantage (cure) which results from enacting the plan. The question of blame becomes part of the solvency issue. If the plan compares favorably with the status quo, then the inherency burden has been met—unless the negative can show that the same inadequacies that thwarted status quo efforts will also thwart the affirmatives'.

Substantive Issues in Value Debates

Once the criterion has been presented, affirmatives in value debate must show that the status quo should be negatively evaluated. This is usually accomplished through the presentation of a story which demonstrates the validity of the value judgment. For example, in arguing that the welfare system exacerbates the problems of the urban poor, an affirmative could present independence as the value to look to when determining the truth of the resolution. Then in their arguments they would need to show that the welfare system frustrates the achievement of this value by the urban poor. This would probably entail the presentation of several ways in which the welfare system fostered dependence.

The relationship between the procedural and the substantive issues in value debate should now be clear. The substantive elements of the case demonstrate the failings of the present system with regard to the value criteria presented earlier.

The first substantive decision the negative must make is how to respond to the affirmative's depiction of the status quo (the issues of ill and blame). Suppose the affirmative is claiming that health care assistance programs in Pakistan are failing and that, as a result, thousands will die. There are three potential responses to this claim. First, the negative can accept this depiction but clash with another aspect of the affirmative case. This is risky because it grants the affirmative the point that the problem they address is significant. If their case shows even the potential to protect thousands of lives, they have gained an important advantage.

Second, the negative can attempt to deny the depiction. Perhaps there is evidence that, contrary to the affirmative's claim, health assistance programs in Pakistan are working. Usually when teams are contending polar opposite positions there is some explanation for the differing views of experts. Sometimes it is a question of conflicting definitions, sometimes there is a time frame difference between the two competing views, sometimes the qualifications of the experts explain the divergence of opinion, and sometimes it is a matter of unstated assumptions behind the conclusions. Negatives should try to figure out why their position is contradictory to the affirmatives' and strive to explain why the former is superior.

Third, negatives can attempt to minimize the significance of the affirmatives' depiction. It could be that the numbers presented are a worst case scenario, and that the loss of life will probably be significantly less.

Minimization is a strategy that must be accompanied by some other tactic. Negatives are not likely to win by saying only that the problem in the status quo is not as significant as the affirmative depicts. An audience is likely to conclude that, even if the negative wins their arguments, there are still sufficient problems in the status quo to warrant the plan.

The negative may pursue, either in combination with attacking the depiction of the status quo, or alone, the substantive route of assaulting the prediction of the status quo plus the plan, i.e., addressing the issue of cure. There are two ways of doing this.

First, the negative may try to deny that significant advantages will result from implementing the plan. Such arguments challenge the affirmative prediction that the proposed policy will solve the problems of the status quo, hence they are called **solvency** attacks.

There are several reasons why a plan may not accrue the advantages predicted by the affirmative. Negatives must research the proposals to find out why they have not already been adopted. If the proposal really is likely to accrue significant benefits, there is a good chance that we would have adopted it already. Usually there is a reason it has not been.

Sometimes the plans are not practical. If one scholar or policy analyst has argued for a specific proposal, it is possible, even likely, that another has critiqued the proposal. If the plan is modeled after a policy in a foreign country, examine that model to see if it is actually working.

Sometimes proposals are not adopted because special interests oppose them. Debaters may be able to argue that the plan will not work because it is open to **circumvention**—people will only get around it. To construct a circumvention argument you need to show that there is both a motive and the means for someone to get around the proposal. For example, during Prohibition people had the motive and means to circumvent the law. As a result, the policy was largely ineffective. If an affirmative suggests a similar prohibition—or, for instance smoking or excessive campaign contributions—the motive and means may exist for circumvention of that policy as well.

Policy debaters are not particularly interested in determining the likelihood that their proposal would be enacted. Rather, they prefer to concentrate on the merits of the policy. Policy topics do not say that the policy *will* be enacted, just that it should or "ought to" be. So don't spend your time trying to determine whether or not Congress might actually pass the policy, focus on whether or not they should.

Failing to clash with solvency concedes the entire solvency claimed by the affirmative. Then the negative must attempt to outweigh the solvency through the third, and final, substantive argument: cost.

This is an issue raised by the negative. It asks, "Are the disadvantages of the proposal insignificant?" A **disadvantage** is a story that argues that there will be undesirable consequences should the policy be adopted. Disadvantages usually assume affirmative solvency. But predicating a disadvantage on the conditional acceptance of solvency does not preclude attacking solvency. Rather, our understanding of the negative contention is that even if the plan is solvent we would not want to do it because of its disadvantages.

There are several types of disadvantages. Each disadvantage is a story involving actors, events, and scenes. Debaters must be cognizant of how they depict the actors in their arguments. Inconsistency can destroy the validity of the story.

Sometimes proposed policy actions might create problems where none currently exist. For example, you could argue that banning guns might leave the citizenry defenseless against an invasion by a foreign power. Perhaps this is currently not a concern, but the policy could make it important.

At other times, new policies exacerbate existing problems. Pollution in already a serious concern. But you could argue that an affirmative plan which increases economic growth in the United States may significantly worsen environmental conditions.

New policies also may be a step in an undesirable direction. America may be moving toward a more egalitarian state. Plans which reinforce patriarchal attitudes thwart this desirable movement. You could argue on this basis that the plan should be rejected.

Finally, plans can be attacked on moral or philosophical grounds. This necessitates developing a value justification. If you are arguing against a policy which calls for the death penalty for drug pushers, you could oppose the plan on moral grounds. If so, you would have to argue that capital punishment is immoral, and that the morality of a plan is an important consideration.

Regardless of the type of disadvantage, the negative must meet several burdens. First, the negative must demonstrate a clear **link** to the affirmative policy. This means that you must show that there is a clear causal connection between the affirmative plan and the disadvantage. Second, the disadvantage must be **unique.** To be unique, the affirmative plan must be the sole cause of the disadvantage. If many things can cause the disadvantage, you would have to show the unique increment in the disadvantage that the affirmative plan causes. Third, the negative must show the affirmative plan is sufficient to cause the disadvantage. There are two ways this may be accomplished.

Some disadvantages presuppose that the present system is on the **brink,** or precipice, of a disadvantage. With this kind of argument, you would need to contend that the affirmative action is enough to push us over the cliff. For example, you might be able to present evidence that any new expensive federal program will destroy the budget deficit accord and send the U.S. into an economic depression. The affirmative can deny the validity of the brink if they can show an expensive new program that should have caused the disadvantage, but did not.

Other disadvantages are **linear.** This means that each increment is undesirable. We know additional pollution would be a bad thing, so if an affirmative policy causes additional pollution it would seem to be a bad idea. With such disadvantages you may be required to show how much more pollution the affirmative would cause and the impact of this additional increment of pollution.

Finally, **time frame** may be critical. If the affirmative plan may cause a significant disadvantage before it accrues its advantage, that could be a reason to reject the proposal. If the affirmative advantage has a shorter time frame than the disadvantage, the audience may decide to accept the eventual risk of the disadvantage for the nearer term benefit of the affirmative proposal.

Negatives must be wary when presenting disadvantages, for an affirmative has two options for response. One option is called a **take out.** This is an argument which simply denies the chain of events in the story. Its name stems from the idea that if you take out one link in a chain, the chain falls apart. Similarly, if you break the sequence of events in the story a disadvantage tells, you deny the validity of the story. If the negative story is that assisting Pakistan may anger the leaders of India and lead to war, the affirmative could agree that India would be angered, but deny the next step in the story: that India would go to war.

The second kind of affirmative response to a disadvantage is particularly dangerous to the negative. Affirmatives may present arguments called **turnarounds.** A turnaround is an argument that takes a disadvantage and turns it into an advantage for the affirmative. There are two ways a disadvantage can be turned.

First, an affirmative may turn the link. If a negative argues that implementing the U.N.'s declaration on human rights is undesirable because it reinforces the domination of male leadership in the world, an affirmative may respond by claiming that, rather than reinforcing the patriarchy, the U.N.'s declaration is a tool for enhancing the role of women in the world because it extends the protection of women to corners of the world where women are still viewed as male possessions. Thus, if patriarchy is a bad thing, it is more advantageous to implement the declaration than not to. In this line of argument the impact of the disadvantage is untouched, and is claimed as an advantage by the affirmative.

The second kind of turn is an impact turn. If the negative argues that changing health aid to Pakistan is disadvantageous because the new health aid will foster internecine conflict there, an affirmative could grant this scenario but claim that rather than a disadvantage, such civil unrest would be desirable because it would prevent Pakistan from obtaining nuclear weapons. Thus the impact, internal strife, is turned from an undesirable outcome, to a desirable one.

Flow Sheeting as Systematic Note-Taking

When good students listen to lectures they take notes so that they may return to this information later and study for examinations. Debaters must also take notes, but their notes do not have to be as complete because they will be using their notes in a few minutes. The system of note taking in debate is referred to as **flowing.** It is a very important part of the debate process. In order for a debater to be sure that they have answered all of the arguments raised by their opponents, and to be sure that they have extended all of their own, they must write down what people have said. And they must record this in a fashion that makes it easy to read while they speak. In addition, they must write it down quickly enough that they succeed in recording everything important that their opponent argues. This is not an easy task. But it should be clear that it is an essential task.

Here are some tips that may make the process a little easier.

1. Use at least two legal pads. Draw lines which divide the paper horizontally into eight equal sections. You now have room to record the arguments advanced in each of the eight speeches of the debate. Do not worry about flowing cross-examination, but be sure to listen to it. One pad will be the **case flow.** The other pad will be the **off-case** flow. On the case flow you will record the first affirmative and all of the arguments, negative and affirmative, which directly deal with the affirmative case. On the off-case flow you will record all of the procedural arguments and any disadvantages or value objections.

2. When you record a speaker's arguments, do not cross the lines you drew on the flow pads. To avoid crossing the lines you will need to write very small and you will need to abbreviate.

3. Record the enumeration employed by a speaker. If a speaker says this is the "first argument," write down: #1. If a speaker says "subpoint A" write it down too. We suggest you also circle the enumerated structure of the affirmative case as presented in the first affirmative constructive and all subsequent references to the affirmative case structure. That will make these numbers stand out. Then in later speeches when a debater says, "On their B subpoint I will have three responses," you can easily find the B subpoint on your flow.

4. Leave space between groups of arguments. Sometimes arguments expand as the debate develops and you may want more room to record them. Leaving space also helps you to find the group of arguments quickly.

5. Use arrows and lines to show which argument applies to which. If the first negative speaker has three arguments against the IB2 subpoint of the first affirmative case, it helps to draw a line to that subpoint.

6. Record the number and claim of the argument. As you get better you will be able to record the source citation and the essence of the evidence as well. If you miss something, ask your partner or ask about it during cross-examination.

7. Alternate the colors of the fine point pens you are using, one color for the affirmative arguments and another for the negative arguments. That way you can tell at a glance who said what.

8. Before it is your turn to speak, try to write down the arguments you intend to make. If you have your arguments on the flow pad, all you have to do is read your flow from left to right. You will have, right in front of you, what your opponent said and what you plan to say.

TRUNCATED SAMPLE FLOW

Topic: Resolved that implementation of the United Nation's universal declaration of human rights is more important than preserving state sovereignty.

First Aff Const	First Neg Const	Second Aff Const
① Definitions UN- intern'l org implmt- fulfill UDHR- doc of HRts presrv- sustain st sov- legal concpt of governance	① OK	① granted
② Crit- HRts Ⓐ HRts prereq 4 civilization - humanity & progress tied to recog of HRts	② Ⓐ 1. must arise w/in -only when fought 4 are rts valued	② Ⓐ implmnt=assist & ed so = arise w/in
Ⓑ HRts O/w st sov - states trample HRts & that's bad	Ⓑ 1. only sov guar safety -purpose of sov to presrve st & Rts of people	Ⓑ 1. demo=guar too eg, USA 2. Rts more imprtnt fight to presrv Rts
① UDHR protects Democracy Ⓐ UDHR respcts other views - when writ=respct 4 divrgnce	① Ⓐ OK	① Ⓐ granted
Ⓑ UDHR plants seeds of Demo - adopted by all to accpt demo goals	Ⓑ & Ⓒ Demo Bad 1. aid=dependency - aid fosters reliance 2. — ! repression - aid—alignmnt of classes, presrvd w/repression	Ⓑ 1. nations do move away -eg, Korea 2. others ask for aid -many nations reqst aid 1. aid=rep past exmpls prove 2. UDHR solves rep - purpose=protct Rts
Ⓒ Demo=freedom - demo protcts a variety of Rts		

note: this truncated sample flow only shows parts of the first three speeches of the debate.

Explanation of Truncated Sample Flow

The First Affirmative Constructive

Observation ① Definitions

UN—United Nations

implmt—implement

UDHR—Universal Declaration of Human Rights

presrv—preserve

st sove—state sovereignty

Observation ② Crit—Criteria; HRts—Human Rights

  The affirmative is arguing that "more important" will be determined by
    examining which preserves human rights better, implementing the
    UDHR or state sovereignty

Subpoint Ⓐ HRts prereq 4 civilization—Human Rights are a prerequisite
    for civilization

  evidence: humanity and the progress of humanity throughout history
    have been tied to a recognition of human rights

Subpoint Ⓑ HRts o/w st sov—Human Rights outweighs state sovereignty

  evidence: nation states have trampled human rights and such abuse is
    not warranted

Contention ①. UDHR protects Democracy

Subpoint Ⓐ UDHR respects other views

  evidence: when then UDHR was written it was written with a recognition
    of and respect for divergent viewpoints

Subpoint Ⓑ UDHR plants seeds for Democracy

  evidence: the UDHR has been adopted by all of the members of the UN
    and that means they all accept the goals of a democracy

Subpoint Ⓒ Democracy preserves freedom

  evidence: democracies are established to protect a variety of rights of
    their citizens

First Negative Constructive

Observation ① OK—we have no arguments with the definitions

Observation ②

Subpoint Ⓐ

  claim: human rights must arise from within a nation

  evidence: only when people have fought to obtain them are rights valued
    by the people

Subpoint Ⓑ

  claim: only state sovereignty guarantees the safety of the people

  evidence: the purpose of sovereignty is to preserve the state and the
    safety of the people and in doing so, it preserves the rights of the
    people

Contention ①

Subpoint Ⓐ OK—we have no arguments with this subpoint

Explanation of Truncated Sample Flow *Continued*

Subpoint Ⓑ and Ⓒ are grouped together
  claim #1: foreign aid promotes dependency in the recipient nation
  evidence: a nation which receives aid from other nations becomes
    dependent on that aid
  claim #2: dependency leads to increased repression
  evidence: aid leads to class differentiation, the haves and the have nots.
    Those who administer the aid attempt to perpetuate their status
    through repression

The Second Affirmative Speech

Observation ① the negative granted our definitions
  explanation: the definitions cannot be challenged in subsequent
    speeches

Observation ②

Subpoint Ⓐ
  claim: by implementation we mean assistance and education
  explanation: our definition of implement was to fulfill the UDHR
    through assistance and education, so the rights will arise from within
    the nation

Subpoint Ⓑ
  claim #1: democracy guarantees safety too
  explanation: the United States is a democracy and it guarantees the
    rights of its citizens
  claim #2: Rights are more important
  explanation: democratic nations have gone to war to fight to preserve
    the rights of the people. This shows that rights are more important
    than safety

Contention ①

Subpoint Ⓐ The subpoint was granted by the negative

Subpoints Ⓑ and Ⓒ

First Negative Argument #1
  claim #1: many nations do move away from aid
  evidence: at one time South Korea received significant American aid.
    It has now become self-sufficient
  claim #2: Other nations ask for aid
  evidence: requests for foreign aid from the U.S. are significant
  explanation: other nations wouldn't request aid if it were so bad

First Negative Argument #2
  claim #1: aid does not lead to repression
  explanation: many nations have received aid without it leading to
    repression
  claim #2: UDHR solves repression
  evidence: the purpose of the UDHR is to protect those rights of
    individual recognized by the UN

If you have been flowing correctly, you will be able to see how an argument unfolds during the course of a debate. You should be able to follow the argument across your paper, hence the term *flow* paper.

In most situations you will need to respond to each argument or group of arguments raised by your opponent, even if only to say "We grant that point to the other team." You will also want to extend your own arguments, especially if your opponent had nothing to say about them. A good flow will enable you to do this.

Summary

In this chapter we have examined the argument field of academic debate. We have presented the theory and practice of fact, value and policy debate. The debate format was identified and both affirmative and negative burdens were generally considered. We discussed the different kinds of procedural and sub-stantive issues that can be raised. In the next chapter we will continue our discussion of academic debate and consider some advanced concepts found in debate. These will be of interest if you intend to continue debating beyond the activities of this class.

Key Terms

affirmative	disadvantage	rebuttal
brink	flowing	resolution
burden of proof	linear	solvency
case flow	link	substantive arguments
circumvention	need case	take out
comparative advantage	negative	time frame
case	off-case flow	topicality
constructive speech	policy debate	turnaround
criteria	presumption	uniqueness
cross-examination	prima facie case	value debate
debate format	procedural arguments	value objection

Activities

1. Select a value or policy proposition and construct an affirmative case for it. Be sure that your case addresses the issues required by the type of resolution you choose. For a guide to the specifics of an affirmative case, see also the debate appendices.

2. Select a point of stasis in the resolution you have chosen and construct a negative brief which addresses this point. Be sure to include the enumerated

claims, the full source citations, and the text of the data you intend to present in your brief.

3. Construct a disadvantage to implementing the change advocated by the affirmative. This should include the structure and data, including the full source citation, which supports the subdevelopment of your argument. For samples of disadvantages, see the debate appendices.

4. Prepare an affirmative brief responding to one or both of the arguments you constructed in the two preceding exercises.

5. Practice taking a flow of a debate by having someone read you the transcript of the sample debates included in the appendices.

Recommended Readings

Bauer, Otto F. *Fundamentals of Debate: Theory and Practice.* Glenview, IL: Scott, Foresman, 1966.

Freeley, Austin J. *Argumentation and Debate: Critical Thinking for Reasoned Decision Making.* 8th ed. Belmont, CA: Wadsworth, 1993.

Kruger, Arthur. *Modern Debate: Its Logic and Strategy.* New York: McGraw-Hill, 1960.

Patterson, J.W. and David Zarefsky. *Contemporary Debate.* Boston: Houghton Mifflin, 1983.

Pfau, Michael, David A. Thomas, and Walter Ulrich. *Debate and Argument.* Glenview, IL: Scott, Foresman, 1987.

Thompson, Wayne N. *Modern Argumentation and Debate: Principles and Practices.* New York: Harper and Row, 1971.

Notes

1. This was the topic debated by participants of the National Debate Tournament during the 1992–1993 academic year.
2. This was the topic debated by participants of the Cross-Examination Debate Association during the fall of 1992.
3. This was the topic debated by participants of the Cross-Examination Debate Association during the winter and spring of 1993.

11

Advanced
Academic Debate

Academic debate is practiced in a variety of contexts: class debates, audience debates, and intercollegiate debate, among others. In Chapter 10 we presented the general information needed to participate in any of these contexts. But to keep the ideas manageable, we also skipped past some of the thornier aspects of debate theory.

This chapter will delve more deeply into seven areas of debate covered in the preceding chapter. The issues we discuss should prove useful to anyone wishing to gain additional insight into academic debate, but are especially geared toward those who are interested in competing in intercollegiate debate.

The Debate Judge as Audience

Throughout Chapter 10 we couched our discussion of debate theory and practice in terms of adapting to one's audience. Since our intent was to introduce students to the general world of academic debate, the nature of this audience was not delineated. Here we discuss more fully the type of audience those participating in intercollegiate debate will encounter.

Intercollegiate debates are evaluated by debate judges. These individuals are usually trained in the theory and practice of argumentation and debate. It is their task to listen to a debate and decide who won. Most judges also consider it part of their responsibility to teach students to be more effective debaters. To their role as debate judges they bring expectations as to how a debate should proceed. For many judges, an important component of these expectations is a judging paradigm.[1]

A **judging paradigm** is a lens through which the judge views the debate.[2] It shapes and guides what the judge perceives, considers important or inconsequential, and how the judge evaluates the debate. We discuss five paradigms common to intercollegiate debate.

The Stock Issues Paradigm

The **stock issues paradigm** traces its roots to classical Roman stasis theory. More recently, John Dewey and Lee Hultzen have contributed to our understanding of the typical points of dispute in policy deliberations.[3] We discussed the nature of the stock issues in Chapter 5. You will recall that we identified ill, blame, cure and cost as the issues arising from stasis.

A debate judge employing this paradigm would focus attention on how these issues were debated, and who won them. If the affirmative wins them all, then the stock issues judge would vote for the affirmative, for the affirmative would have shown that there is a problem in the status quo that cannot be solved by the mechanisms of the stasis quo, but *can* be solved by the affirmative proposal, and for which there are insignificant costs. If the negative can convince the judge that even one of these issues has not been won by the affirmative, the stock issues judge would vote for the negative. Stock issues thus become the distinguishing point of view for judges employing this perspective.

Students debating before a stock issues judge should focus on the resolution of these issues. Arguments which do not impact upon one the stock issues are of less, if any, relevance to this judge. In addition the stock issues paradigm limits the issue of blame or inherency to the location of structures of the status quo that preclude the resolution of the problems by the existing institutions. Thus, affirmatives must present structural inherency to carry the issue of blame.

The Policy Making Paradigm

The **policy making paradigm** presents an alternative viewpoint of the debate. Premised on general systems theory, this perspective views the debate as a comparison of two competing policy systems: the one presented by the affirmative, and the present system (or possibly a counterplan).[4] The critic employing the policy making paradigm evaluates on the basis of the arguments presented in the debate, which policy system is superior.

The policy making paradigm has two major ramifications for debaters. First, with this paradigm affirmatives are charged with contrasting two worlds: the present system, and the present system as modified by the proposed policy. Negative debaters may attack either depiction.

Second, with this paradigm policy impacts are enormously important. Policy making judges not only consider the way the two competing policy systems are presented, they consider the probability, significance, and value of predicted policy impacts.

The Hypothesis-Testing Paradigm

If you view the debate resolution as a hypothesis which the affirmative tries to prove and the negative tries to disprove, then you would be employing the **hypothesis-testing paradigm.**[5] The hypothesis tester approaches the role of the judge as a scientist, evaluating arguments to determine whether or not the data leads one to conclude in favor of, or against the truth of the resolution.

In this perspective any negative argument that denies the validity of the hypothesis wins the debate. The arguments presented by the negative team need not be logically consistent, for the negative is not attempting to defend a policy system. Instead, each argument is considered separately in the search for truth.

This paradigm allows the debater the freedom to argue mutually inconsistent positions. A debater can argue that there is no problem with the way things are, but, if this argument is lost, the next argument can be that there are one or more alternatives (counterplans) which address the problem more effectively. If another paradigm were in use this would be an argumentative flaw, but it is quite permissible in this case.

The Tabula Rasa Paradigm

The fourth way of viewing intercollegiate debate is called the **tabula rasa paradigm.**[6] Judges using this paradigm approach the debate as if they were "blank slates," that is, they permit the debaters to decide the paradigm that the judge should employ. If both teams agree on a paradigm, the tabula rasa judge agrees to use this paradigm, and the debate proceeds. When there is disagreement, the debaters must argue the use of alternate paradigms just as they would any other issue. Since in this case the debaters may not know which paradigm will be used until the conclusion of the debate, they must proceed as if either of the paradigms may be used to evaluate the arguments.

The Narrative Perspective

This text has considered argument as narration, so it should not be surprising that we also believe that argumentation in the field of intercollegiate debate can be profitably viewed from a **narrative perspective.**[7]

Judges employing the narrative perspective view the arguments presented in the debate as competing stories. The affirmative case, for instance, is replete with actors engaging in actions for reasons the affirmative must identify. Negatives have the option of impugning this description by attacking the narrative probability and/or the narrative fidelity of the story. Negative arguments are also understood as stories. Disadvantages, for example, entail both the attribution of motives to actors and predictions about the likelihood of events. Judges operating from the viewpoint of the narrative perspective are concerned with which story is most effectively presented and defended.

The use of the narrative perspective has several implications for how a debate will unfold. First, it means that debaters need to tell a consistent story. Since one important aspect of narrative rationality is how well the story comes together (probability), stories that are inconsistent are not likely to be persuasive. This interest in a complete story should lead debaters to tie up the loose ends of their narratives. This can be especially important in final rebuttals.

A second implication of the narrative demand for coherence is the need for consistency in the characterization of social actors. Actors are not evil in one set of arguments, and benign in the next. If the first affirmative presents industry as concerned with profit only, the affirmative cannot decide, in light of negative attacks, that industry is really compassionate. Changing the characterization of actors undercuts their believability.

Third, the test of narrative fidelity states that audiences compare the stories advocates present with the stories they know to be true. Debate judges try to suppress their own attitudes, values, and beliefs, in order to evaluate the arguments of any given debate as objectively as possible. However, those judges using a narrative perspective give presumption to the stories the culture considers true. These stories arise from the public's understanding of history, biography, culture and character. Since presumption resides in stories, it is not necessarily against the resolution. For example, the public in this culture believes in freedom of speech. If an affirmative advocates the abolition of censorship, audiences would be predisposed to accept this action. However, the presumption can always be overcome through argument.

We have considered the use of paradigms by intercollegiate debate judges. We have suggested that each has implications for how a debate unfolds. Debaters should be cognizant of the use of judging paradigms and how argument strategies and tactics can be adapted to the paradigm employed by specific judges.

The Resolution

In Chapter 10 we identified the resolution as the focus of debate and indicated that the affirmative is obligated to present a topical case. We also suggested that affirmatives present definitions of the key terms of the resolution. We think this is a good idea for beginning debaters. It is more common, however, for experienced debaters to define their terms operationally.

Operational Definitions

When an affirmative uses **operational definitions,** the audience and the negative is expected to ascertain what the affirmative thinks a term means by looking at their plan or their arguments. The definitions are not explicit, they are implicit. If you want to know how an affirmative defines "substantially change its development assistance policies" you look at what the plan modifies. Only if such operational definitions are challenged by the negative will the affirmative present formal definitions.

Constructing Topicality Arguments

In Chapter 10 we also indicated that a negative who believes the affirmative is not debating the resolution fairly can present a topicality argument. This is the argument which communicates to the audience that the affirmative interpretation of the topic is illegitimate. But how is such an argument constructed?

Usually a topicality argument has three components: standards, violation, and impact.

Negatives typically present **standards** that they wish the audience to use when evaluating whether or not the affirmative is topical. Years ago in academic debate all an affirmative team needed to do was argue that their interpretation of the resolution was reasonable. But that is a difficult thing to assess. What constitutes reasonability? How does one determine that an affirmative has crossed the line from reasonable to unreasonable? There is no way to predict what an audience will consider reasonable. Consequently, most scholars now agree that when there is a disagreement concerning what definition to use, the affirmative's or the negative's, the **better definition** should be used. But how does one determine the better definition? This is where standards come into play.

There are a variety of means employed to determine the better definition. We will consider several common standards presented by negatives. These are also used by affirmatives as counter-standards.

Unique Meaning. This argument is premised on the assumption that each word has a **unique meaning.** This seems self-evident. Even Alice in Wonderland knew that we cannot make words mean whatever we want. Yet debaters sometimes interpret the resolution in such a way as to render some words meaningless. For example, if the resolution calls for a change in *development assistance policies,* and the affirmative's interpretation of the topic is that all assistance policies are developmental, then the affirmative has rendered the term *development* meaningless. A better definition is one that preserves the unique meaning of each word in the resolution.

Precision. The **precision standard** argues that the more specific or concrete definitions are, the more clearly they mark the boundaries of what is topical and what is not topical. Arguing that *urban* refers to those who live in cities, rather than those who live near communities, is more precise because it is easier to determine who lives in a city than it is who lives near a community. Therefore, the better definition is that which more precisely defines a resolutional term.

Limiting. The broader the resolution the more latitude affirmatives have in presenting a topical case. The more topical the case, the more difficult it is for negatives to prepare. Consequently, affirmatives gain a tactical advantage if they can broaden the range of topical cases. To offset this advantage, negatives sometimes argue that the better definition is a **limiting** one, which establishes manageable boundaries to the scope of the topic.

If any public assistance program is a part of the welfare system, then negatives will have to be prepared for a wider range of cases than if the welfare system is defined more narrowly as income transfer policies.

Affirmatives usually present the opposite view as their counter-standard, **breadth.** The view here is that broader topics are more challenging, less tedious, and require more research. Broader topics, say affirmatives, mean debaters learn more. The better definition, then, either limits or broadens the topic.

Field Definitions. The **field definition** standard maintains that the better definition is one used by members of the field that is the focus of the resolution. The rationale behind this standard stems from the understanding that each field tends to bring its own meanings to the terms it employs. The term "fantasy" has a different meaning, for example, in psychology than it has rhetorical criticism. Since jargon varies from field to field, it would be better to use definitions from the appropriate field.

Context. I. A. Richards, among many others, has argued that a word gains its meaning from the **context** in which it is used.[8] Defining a word without considering the other words in the sentence will likely lead to error. Define *red* and *herring* separately, and you are not likely to come up with the same meaning as you would for *red herring*. As Richards writes, "A word or phrase when isolated momentarily from its controlling neighbors is free to develop irrelevant sense which may beguile half the words to follow it."[9] Consequently, it makes sense to define words as terms whenever possible.

These common definitional standards are used selectively by affirmatives and negatives. Speakers choose a standard that supports the definition they wish to use in a given debate. If the definition they wish to read does not meet a particular standard, the standard is not presented. Of course, as reasonable as each of these standards sounds, there are indictments of each, so debaters must be prepared to defend them.

Further, just as there is an incentive for the affirmative to define the resolution broadly, there is an incentive for the negative to define it narrowly. If the negative definition is so narrow that the affirmative may not have a reasonable chance to win, the affirmative will argue that this is an unfair standard.

Regardless of the standard or counter-standard presented, debaters must convince the audience that their standard should be used, or they must use the standard of their opponent.

The second component of a topicality argument is the **violation.** Once negatives have presented the standard they wish the audience to use, they must present their definition, state why they think this is a better definition (because it more closely adheres to the standards they have previously presented), and explain why they believe the affirmative violates this specific definition.

If the affirmatives believes they *do* meet the negative definition, they may accept the negative standard and just dispute the violation.

Finally, negatives must indicate, as with all of their arguments, what **impact** this argument has on the debate. In policy debate topicality is a voting issue. This means that if the negatives convince the audience that the affirmatives are not topical, the negatives win. All other arguments then become irrelevant. Why? Because if the plan is not topical, no matter how advantageous it is, the advantages do not prove the resolution true.

In value debate the impact of a topicality argument depends on what part of the affirmative case is not topical. If, for example, an affirmative presents three ways in which the welfare system worsens the plight of the urban poor, and only one of these is not topical, many audiences will simply disregard the non-topical part of the case. What remains may still be sufficient to carry the debate for the affirmative.

Some affirmatives argue that since the negatives can win the debate with a topicality argument, negatives will argue topicality even against cases that most debaters and audiences consider topical. To discourage frivolous topicality arguments some theorists contend that topicality should be a **reverse voting issue.** This means that if a negative loses the topicality argument, the negative should lose the debate. We have found that very few scholars consider this a good idea. Implementing it would make it too risky to argue topicality. This would give the affirmatives even greater lattitude to run cases of questionable topicality. But negatives must be prepared for this possibility.

Justification

There is a second procedural argument we have yet to consider. It is called **justification.** In policy debate the thrust of this argument is that the affirmatives may be topical, but they have not provided sufficient rationale for implementing this resolution. For example, if the topic calls for action by the United States, a negative could argue that the affirmative has not provided sufficient rationale for using this particular agent of action. The individual states, or perhaps a world organization, like the United Nations, could act instead.

In this line of argument the negative contends that another agent *could* be used, not that another agent *should* be used. Arguing that another agent should be used is called a counter-proposal or, more commonly, a counterplan. We will consider counterplans later in this chapter. Rather than deal hypothetically with what agent might be used, most audiences prefer the negative to engage in advocacy. Consequently, justification arguments are not usually effective in policy debate because they are hypothetical.[10]

In value debate a justification argument is made by the first negative speaker when the negative believes that the affirmative has not provided sufficient rationale to believe that the resolution is true.

We have indicated that the affirmative burden is to prove the resolution true. But this claim glosses over a controversy in value debate. In policy debate it is commonly accepted that the resolution serves as a parameter for determining the range of cases that may be presented. As long as the case is topical, the case proves the resolution to be true. This approach has come to be known as **parametrics.** The resolution acts as a parameter, laying the boundaries for what is topical. All the affirmative must do is fall within the parameters to be topical and to prove the resolution true. There may be many cases which prove the resolution true, but the affirmative is only required to present and defend one. In value debate this is not necessarily true.

Value resolutions tend to be generalizations. "Advertising degrades the quality of life," is an unqualified claim; a generalization. If the parametric approach to topicality is used with such a resolution, the affirmative need only select one example of the topic and then prove the truth of this one example.

Permitting affirmatives to argue only one example of the resolution results in at least two potentially significant advantages for them. First, they do not have to defend examples of the resolution that are untrue. For instance, if some advertising degrades and some does not, the affirmative could choose to present only an example of advertising that does degrade. And second, affirmatives can dismiss arguments that are not specific to the case they present. Just as a policy debater can dismiss a disadvantage that does not link to the mandates identified in the affirmative plan, a value debater can dismiss arguments that are not specific to the affirmative case.

We believe the net result of such a focus is to reward teams that have the resources to prepare, both as affirmatives and as negatives, to debate every conceivable example of the resolution. This could potentially limit the ability of some programs to compete effectively. We also believe the theoretical foundation for such an approach is flawed.

In policy debate the focus of the debate is the plan. The plan is the operational definition of the resolution. The resolution calls for a change from the present system, and the plan identifies that change. If the plan is proved to be advantageous, the resolution is proved to be true. Value debate, generally, has no plan. In addition, in argumentation one proves a generalization to be true either by arguing at the level of the generalization, or by arguing inductively from examples to a generalization. An affirmative may therefore present examples of the resolution and argue that what is true of the examples is true of the generalization, or the affirmative may argue the **whole resolution.**

Affirmatives who argue by example cannot dismiss counter-examples, for as we mentioned in Chapter 5, generalizations established by examples must account for counter-examples. And an affirmative who reasons by example may be charged with committing a hasty generalization. Permitting affirmatives to reason by example gives the negative at least two potentially significant advantages.

First, negatives do not have to prepare for the affirmative examples, all they have to do is present the same counter-examples and the same hasty generalization argument in every debate. We do not believe this would promote much learning. And second, it is nearly impossible to find a generalization that divides ground fairly yet does not have some counter-examples. If a single counter-example invalidates an unqualified generalization, then affirmatives would be unable to win some resolutions.

If both the parametrics and the inductive approach are flawed, what is the affirmative to do? The answer seems to reside in resolutional **intrinsicness.** According to this view there are certain qualities that are inherent to the value object.[11] The affirmative should identify these and argue that the value judgment is causally related to these intrinsic attributes. For example, are there certain qualities which are present in all advertising? Does the degradation identified by the affirmative stem from one such inherent quality? All advertising sells. Is selling degrading? All advertising creates a need or desire on the part of the consumer. Does that degrade?

Some scholars contend that there is no suitable way to ascertain the intrinsic qualities of a value object. Consequently, they argue, intrinsicness is not an appropriate definitional standard.[12] There is no consensus at this point in value debate. Consequently, many debates still exhibit theory argumentation as to the burdens of the affirmative.

If you decide to present a justification argument you will need to develop the same three lines of argument as a topicality argument: standards (often the same), violation, and impact.

Proposals and Counterplans

In Chapter 10 we indicated that affirmatives in policy debate are called upon to articulate the details of the proposal enacting the resolutional change. Here we examine the role of plans in detail, as well as the negative's option of presenting their own proposal or counterplans.

Plans in Value Debate

Value debate is arguably pre-policy, and the vast majority of debates remain at that level. Yet it is becoming increasingly common to present quasi-policy proposals in value debate. Consequently, many of the comments we will make about plans and counterplans are relevant to value debate as well as policy debate.

There are two reasons plans are receiving increasing use in value debate. First, they can give affirmatives tactical advantages. (Of course, any theory that gives a team a tactical advantage will eventually be tried.) Plans permit affirmatives to focus the debate on those aspects they consider relevant. For instance, the topic calling for a comparison between implementing the U.N.'s universal declaration of human rights and preserving state sovereignty, resulted in a fair number of affirmatives giving the details of the term *implementation* in something that strongly resembled and sometimes was actually called a plan. This permitted the affirmatives to focus the debate on the process of implementation they selected, and to dismiss methods of implementing the universal declaration of human rights that were less desirable.

Second, plans appear to be warranted by some topics. One way, for example, to reveal the inadequacies of the welfare system (the fall 1992 intercollegiate value topic) is to compare the current system with a modified system, presumably one modified by an affirmative plan.

As a result, the following comments about plans and counterplans are as relevant to value debaters as they are to policy debaters.

Plans

In order to clarify the change being advocated, affirmatives usually specify the elements of the plan of action they support. Plans typically have five components.

1. The agent In this plank of the plan the affirmative identifies who will implement the plan. This may be the federal government or a specific agency of government, such as the Environmental Protection Agency.

2. The mandates These are the specific actions called for in the plan. If the affirmative wishes to change development assistance policies by halting agricultural assistance programs, the details of this action are presented in the plan mandates.

3. Funding If the proposal necessitates the expenditure of monies, some affirmatives specify where that funding will come from. Others rely on the normal funding processes, such as the general revenues of the federal government.

4. Enforcement Policies requiring enforcement may have those provisions identified in this plank of the plan. Enforcement planks may specify the agent responsible for enforcement and the penalties for violating the mandates of the plan.

5. Intent In order to clarify the purpose of the proposal, in case there is ambiguity in its wording, affirmatives may elect to present a summary statement of the plan. This plank derives from the judicial process of examining legislative history in order to clarify the intent of legislation.

Affirmatives occasionally incorporate other components in their plans which preclude disadvantages and/or counterplans. These are called **plan spikes.** They are controversial in that many planks which neutralize disadvantages are not topical actions. Thus, the negative might argue that the plank yields a non-topical advantage.

Fiat

In debate, **fiat** refers to the assumption that if the affirmative can demonstrate a proposal *should* be adopted, we can assume that sensible policy makers would adopt it through normal means. If the agent of action is the United States federal government, then "normal means" refers to the democratic processes typically followed when legislation is enacted. To dispute whether the plan *would* be enacted, rather than *should* the plan be enacted is called a **should/would argument** and is dismissed.

The enactment of legislation is no guarantee, however, that the legislation will be solvent. If adverse attitudes preclude the status quo from accruing the advantages now, the enforcement of the new legislation may be thwarted by the same pernicious attitudes. Fiat is no magic wand. It does not automatically overcome attitudes. It only, theoretically, implements the legislation.

An understanding of fiat is necessary to avoid or point out situations of fiat abuse. We have heard both plans and counterplans that abuse fiat. One plan called for the nations of the world to eliminate their militaries. The United Nations would then be the only entity with a military. Needless to say, the plan was advantageous when compared to the status quo where practically everyone has their own military. Could this plan be implemented through normal means? What are the "normal means" by which the nations of the world abolish their militaries? We believe the plan was an abuse of fiat.

Counterplans

Traditionally, presenting a **counterplan** was predicated on an explicit admission by the negative team that there was a problem in the status quo that could not be solved, but that the affirmative plan should be rejected because there was a different and superior way to solve the problem. In order for the counterplan to be a reason to reject the resolution, it must meet two standards: it must be non-topical and competitive. Usually negatives read the counterplan (it is written, just like a plan) and argue that it meets those standards. Most contemporary scholars believe that these requirements, like procedural arguments, must be presented in the first negative speech.

Negatives can construct non-topical counterplans either by employing a non-topical agent of action, or by advocating a non-topical action. Advocating a topical counterplan provides another rationale for accepting the truth of the resolution. Consequently, topical counterplans are not a reason to reject the resolution.

Competitiveness is a more difficult issue. To be competitive is to support rejecting the resolution. To support rejecting the resolution, counterplans must be mutually exclusive or net beneficial.[13]

For a plan and counterplan to have **mutual exclusivity** they must be unable to coexist.[14] In the 1980s politicians presented two mutually exclusive ways to balance the federal deficit. One group wanted to cut personal income taxes to spur the economy. Another wanted to raise personal income taxes to reduce the deficit. These two plans were competitive because they could not coexist. No one can cut and raise the same taxes at the same time. Raising income taxes while cutting capital gains taxes would not be mutually exclusive because they could coexist.

Some negatives abuse this standard by artificially creating mutual exclusivity. For example, some negatives include a counterplan plank that prohibits adopting both. Others steal the same funding planks. These are arbitrary and artificial because they do not pertain to the substantive mandate planks of the counterplan. Similarly, arguments that the two plans are redundant and/or philosophically incompatible are not tests of whether the plans could coexist. They are arguments that the plans should not coexist, which more correctly fall into the net benefits test.

The **net benefits standard** says that it is more advantageous to implement the counterplan than it is to implement either the affirmative plan or both the affirmative plan and the counterplan. A counterplan that is net beneficial when compared to the affirmative plan does not in and of itself warrant rejecting the resolution. Suppose, for example, the affirmative plan is to establish national health insurance, and the affirmative says that this will save thousands of lives a year. If the negative were to counterplan with a foreign aid plan that saves millions of lives a year, the counterplan would not be a reason to reject the resolution, for we could do both. In this example, the counterplan is not net beneficial when compared to the affirmative plan and the counterplan together. If, however, the negative can demonstrate that the federal government should not do both plans because doing both would destroy the economy, then the counterplan alone would be better than doing both.

If the counterplan cannot coexist or should not coexist, then the counterplan is a reason to reject the resolution and it is therefore competitive. If the counterplan is also not topical, the negative should win.

Permutations

In response to negative counterplans which artificially established mutual exclusivity, affirmatives initiated something called **permutation.** This is a tactic whereby the affirmative illustrates the artificiality of the mutual exclusivity by rewriting the affirmative plan or the counterplan to reveal the lack of clash in the plan mandates.[15]

Thinking Strategically

Since debate is an intellectual contest, it is important that you approach it that way. Some debaters have better tactical skills than others—perhaps they can speak more succinctly or more rapidly, or they have more or better evidence. They may simply have more experience than you. Some of these advantages can be minimized through strategic planning: anticipating how the debate may unfold and preparing accordingly.

Controlling the Ground

Affirmatives have an advantage in that they get to start and end the debate. Starting the debate means selecting how they want to go about proving the truth of the resolution. This is their ground. Anyone familiar with sports will confirm that there is usually a home court advantage. The same is true of academic debate. As much as possible, affirmatives will want the debate to unfold according to their terms. In policy debate, they will construct the plan and case so that the focus is on the issues that they think they are most likely to win. Similarly, in value debate experienced debaters are very adept at presenting criteria that make it difficult for them to lose.

Some negatives are skilled at capturing the ground. If the negative presents several off-case arguments, the focus of the debate can shift from the affirmative case, to the off-case. The off-case is the negative's turf. They get to select from all of the possible off-case arguments, those they feel best able to win. Arguing one's own issues should be an advantage.

Planning for the End of the Debate

What do you think will be the telling issue or evidence at the end of the debate? Thinking in terms of how the audience will eventually make sense of the round may help you decide how or when to present an argument.

When you first begin to debate it is difficult enough to come up with what you can say in your constructive speech. But as you gain experience, you will start to think in terms of what your opponent will say, and what you will say about your opponent's argument. Good chess players think several moves ahead. So do good debaters.

In fact, just as chess players lay traps for their opponents or divert their attention from their real objectives, so do debaters. Knowing what an opponent will say in response to your initial argument enables you to decide, in advance of the debate, what to say to defeat that response. If you cannot beat the response, perhaps you should not make the argument in the first place.

Winning in Rebuttals

Advanced debaters often attempt to narrow the debate to a limited number of issues in the final rebuttals. This means selecting those issues or arguments a team is most likely win.

Negatives often have several arguments that they could choose to extend in the final rebuttal: case arguments, procedural arguments, a counterplan, and/or several disadvantages. Because of time constraints, however, it may be difficult to cover all of them. As a result, many debaters grant answers which destroy the reasoning of a disadvantage or ignore an argument in their final rebuttal. This essentially removes these arguments from the final decision-making calculus. It also permits the debaters to more fully explain and extend the remaining arguments.

The art of deciding what to go for in the last rebuttals is central to understanding what argumentation is all about.

Maximizing Your Strengths

Some basketball teams walk the ball up the court. Others run it. Some football teams like to run the ball every down, while others prefer to throw it. Why? Because they know their strengths and try to play to them. Think about your strengths in debate. Are you good at explaining arguments? Are you a quick talker? Do you have a lot of evidence or a little? Discover your strengths and weaknesses and construct your strategy accordingly.

We have known debaters who were prepared for almost any argument an opponent might raise. Such debaters maximized their strengths by constructing a broad affirmative case. But we have also coached teams whose strength was dealing with a limited number of arguments. Such debaters were better off with a case that invited fewer arguments.

Alternative Debate Formats

Throughout this and the previous chapters we have focused on the most common formats for engaging in academic debate: team policy and value debate. There are two additional formats which merit attention.

Lincoln-Douglas Debate

Most debating in post-secondary education is done by two-person teams. Nevertheless, there is increasing opportunity for one-on-one debate, which is known as **Lincoln-Douglas** or L-D **Debate.** It is named after the historic debates between Abraham Lincoln and Stephen Douglas.

Lincoln-Douglas debate may employ the value or policy topics used nationally, or the sponsoring organization may select its own resolution. Such resolutions may be fact, value or policy. The responsibilities and obligations of the debaters remain the same however. Affirmatives typically have the burden of proof, negatives enjoy presumption. Questions of fact, value and policy are debated much as they would be in team debate.

As with team debate the affirmative speaks first and last, both speakers question and are questioned, and both sides have an equal amount of speaking time.

TYPICAL LINCOLN-DOUGLAS DEBATE FORMAT

Affirmative Constructive	8 minutes
Cross-Examination	3 minutes
Negative Constructive	12 minutes
Cross-Examination	3 minutes
Affirmative Rebuttal	6 minutes
Negative Rebuttal	6 minutes
Affirmative Rebuttal	4 minutes

Parliamentary Debate

Most intercollegiate debate emphasizes argument to such an extent that public speaking skills are too frequently neglected. Not so in **parliamentary debate.** Such debate rewards wit and rhetorical skill. It is modelled after the kind of debating that occurs in the British House of Parliament.[16]

TYPICAL PARLIAMENTARY DEBATE FORMAT

Prime Minister	8 minutes
Leader of the Opposition	8 minutes
Member of the Government	8 minutes
Member of the Opposition	8 minutes
Leader of the Opposition	4 minutes
Prime Minister	4 minutes

The principle distinction, and the reason that speaking skill is rewarded, stems from the audience perspective. Parliamentary debate either utilizes or envisions lay judges, instead of trained judges skilled in the rules and jargon of academic debate.

Another difference lies in the resolutions debated. In traditional intercollegiate team and Lincoln-Douglas debate, a resolution is announced and the same resolution is used for a year, semester, or, at minimum, a tournament. In Parliamentary debate the resolution changes each round. This results in debates that call upon the general knowledge of the participants, rather than on pre-competition research. In fact, inartistic proofs are generally prohibited.

A third distinction is the role of heckling. According to Theodore Scheckels and Annette Warfield, "A heckle is a brief, witty, and somewhat substantive remark hurled at the speaker so that everyone can hear it."[17] The purpose of such heckling is refutation, and a good speaker will respond to the heckling and proceed.

The resolution to be debated may be a sentence or a phrase. It may be fact, value or policy. It may be philosophical, political, or just a silly statement. The topic is announced and the teams are given ten minutes to prepare.

Summary

This concludes our look at some of the more advanced aspects of intercollegiate debate. Some of the issues we have addressed are controversial. Needless to say, we have presented our views of these issues. Readers are encouraged to pursue those issues that interest them by reading the articles footnoted in this chapter, or by consulting the suggested readings.

We have examined more fully the focus on the resolution, discussing such aspects as topicality, justification, hasty generalizations, and parametrics. We have also considered the nature and functions of plans and counterplans. We have moved beyond specific tactics employed in debates to offer advice as to how debaters can think strategically. Finally, we have considered two increasingly popular alternatives to traditional value and policy team debate.

In the next chapter we examine a second argument field, political campaigns.

Key Terms

competitiveness	narrative perspective	breadth
counterplan	operational definitions	context
fiat	parametrics	field definition
hypothesis-testing	parliamentary debate	limiting
paradigm	permutation	net benefits
impact	plan spikes	precision
intrinsicness	policy-making paradigm	unique meaning
judging paradigm	reverse voting issue	stock issues paradigm
justification	should/would argument	tabula rasa paradigm
Lincoln-Douglas debate	standards	violation
mutual exclusivity	better definition	whole resolution

Activities

1. Examine the sample debate presented in Appendix B. Then construct a negative topicality argument against the affirmative case presented. Be sure to include the three elements of a topicality argument: standards, violation, and impact. If you think the affirmative case is topical, then envision a similar, but non-topical case on the same topic.

2. Now approach the question of topicality from the affirmative perspective. Construct an affirmative topicality brief answering the topicality argument constructed in exercise 1. You may clash on one or more of the three elements of the negative topicality position.

3. Examine the sample value debate in Appendix B. Construct a negative counter-criteria argument. This should be supported with data and should include a criticism of the affirmative criteria as well as a counter-criterion for the debate.

4. Construct an affirmative brief supporting the original criteria presented in the sample value debate. This brief should respond to the arguments constructed in exercise 3.

Recommended Readings

Herbeck, Dale and John P. Katsulas. "The Affirmative Topicality Burden: Any Reasonable Example of the Resolution." *Journal of the American Forensic Association* 21 (1985): 133–145.

Herbeck, Dale, John P. Katsulas, and Karla K. Leeper. "The Locus of Debate Controversy Reexamined: Implications for Counterplan Theory." *Argumentation and Advocacy* 25 (1989): 150–164.

Madsen, Arnie. "General Systems Theory and Counterplan Competition." *Argumentation and Advocacy* 26 (1989): 71–82.

Madsen, Arnie and Allan D. Louden. "The Jurisdiction/Topicality Analogy." *Argumentation and Advocacy* 26 (1990): 151–154.

Murphy, Thomas L. "Assessing the Jurisdictional Model of Topicality." *Argumentation and Advocacy* 26 (1990): 145–150.

Perkins, Dallas. "Counterplans and Paradigms." *Argumentation and Advocacy* 25 (1989): 140–149.

"Special Forum, Debate Paradigms." *Journal of the American Forensic Association* 18 (1982): 133–160.

Thomas, David A. and John P. Hart, eds. *Advanced Debate: Readings in Theory, Practice and Teaching.* Skokie, IL: National Textbook, 1992.

Notes

1. We use the word *paradigm* because it is the term commonly used to describe this concept. But we direct the interested reader to a paper critiquing the use of this term. See Patricia Riley and Thomas A. Hollihan, "Paradigms as Eristic," a paper presented at the annual meeting of the Speech Communication Association, 1982.

2. This discussion of the nature of judging paradigms stems from Thomas Kuhn's work on the role of paradigms in science in *The Structure of Scientific Revolutions,* 2d ed. (Chicago: University of Chicago Press, 1970).

3. Thomas Dewey, *How We Think* (Boston: D.C. Health, 1910); and Lee Hultzen, "Stasis in Deliberative Analysis," in *The Rhetorical Idiom*, Donald C. Bryant, ed. (Ithaca, New York: Cornell University Press, 1958).

4. For a discussion of the policy making paradigm, see Bernard L. Brock, James W. Chesebro, and James F. Klumpp, *Public Policy Decision Making: Systems Analysis and Comparative Advantages Debate* (New York: Free Press, 1973); James Klumpp, James W. Chesebro, and John F. Cragan, "Implications of a Systems Model on Argumentation Theory," *Journal of the American Forensic Association* 11 (Summer 1974): 1–7; and Allan J. Lichtman and Daniel Rhorer, "The Logic of Policy Dispute," *Journal of the American Forensic Association* 16 (Spring 1980): 236–247.

5. See David Zarefsky, "A Reformulation of the Theory of Presumption," a paper presented at the annual meeting of the Central States Speech Association, 1972; David Zarefsky and Bill Henderson, "Hypothesis-Testing in Theory and Practice," *Journal of the American Forensic Association* 19 (Winter 1983), pp. 179–185; and David Zarefsky, "Argument as Hypothesis-Testing," in *Advanced Debate: Readings in Theory, Practice and Teaching,* David A. Thomas and John P. Hart, eds., (Chicago: National Textbook Company, 1992), pp. 252–262.

6. See Walter Ulrich, "In Search of Tabula Rasa," a paper presented at the annual meeting of the Speech Communication Association, 1981.

7. For a more complete discussion of the application of the narrative to the debate context, see Thomas A. Hollihan, Kevin T. Baaske, and Patricia Riley, "Debaters as Storytellers: The Narrative Perspective in Academic Debate," *Journal of the American Forensic Association* 23 (Spring 1987): 184–193.

8. I. A. Richards, *The Philosophy of Rhetoric* (London: Oxford University Press, 1936).

9. Richards, p. 55.

10. The use of any hypothetical or conditional arguments is a point of controversy. For a summary of some of the views on this issue, see Thomas A. Hollihan, "Conditional Arguments and the Hypothesis-Testing Paradigm: A Negative View," *Journal of the American Forensic Association* 19 (Winter 1983): 171–178; David Zarefsky and Bill Henderson, "Hypothesis-Testing in Theory and Practice," *Journal of the American Forensic Association* 19 (Winter 1983): 179–185; and Thomas A. Hollihan, "Conditional Arguments and the Hypothesis-Testing Paradigm: A Negative Rebuttal," *Journal of the American Forensic Association* 19 (Winter 1983): 186–190.

11. Kenneth Bahm, "Intrinsic Justification: Meaning and Method," *CEDA Yearbook* 9 (1988): 23–29; and David M. Berube, "Hasty Generalization Revisited, Part One: On Being Representative Examples," *CEDA Yearbook* 10 (1989): 43–53.

12. Bill Hill and Richard W. Leeman, "On Not Using Intrinsic Justification in Debate," *Argumentation and Advocacy* 26 (Spring 1990): 133–144.

13. These are the classic determinants of the counterplan presented by Allan J. Lichtman and Daniel M. Rhorer, "A General Theory of the Counterplan," *Journal of the American Forensic Association* 12 (Fall 1975): 70–79.

14. Kevin Baaske, "The Counterplan: A Reevaluation of the Competitiveness Standard," Western Speech Communication Association, 1985.

15. For a thorough discussion of the issue of permutations, see Dale A. Herbeck, "A Permutation Standard of Competitiveness," *Journal of the American Forensic Association* 22 (1985): 12–19.

16. For a complete explanation of the parliamentary debate, see Theodore F. Scheckels, Jr. and Annette C. Warfield, "Parliamentary Debate: A Description and Justification," *Argumentation and Advocacy* 27 (Fall 1990): 86–96.

17. Scheckels and Warfield, p. 88.

12

Argumentation in Political Campaigns

Uring every election year we hear complaints about the deplorable state of American political campaigns. In the United States, "politics as usual" typically means superficial image-oriented campaigning, negative attacks against one's opponent, and thirty-second spot commercials that distract us as we watch reruns of "Mork and Mindy." Experts note that the rates of political participation in the United States, as measured by the percentage of eligible voters who register and actually cast their ballots, have been dropping for years, in part because citizens are so disgusted with the conduct of political campaigns.[1]

People complain about political campaigns for many reasons. Some are unhappy because they believe politicians do not really listen to them or represent their interests. Others lament the fact that regardless of who they vote for, their problems never seem to end, and things never really change. Still others protest the fact that candidates seem to be so dependent on and responsive to special interest groups that they ignore their constituents. Regardless of the cause or causes for the declining rates of political participation and the dissatisfaction with the political process, however, all of us have an interest in addressing the problem. The stability of our nation and the vitality of our political system, depend upon a fairly high level of political participation and involvement by our citizens. When people do not vote, and do not believe that their votes make a difference, a pervasive feeling that the system does not work develops. If people do not participate in the political process, and in fact feel alienated from that process, then they are less likely to be committed to its preservation. As W. Lance Bennett argued: "Restoring public interest in government, trust in leadership, and commitment to a liveable society for all are essential steps toward real solutions for problems like crime, homelessness, drug abuse, education, economic revitalization, and other obstacles to the 'good life.'"[2]

While it is unlikely that American electoral politics were ever as clean, straightforward, or focused on substantive issues as many critics of present electoral practices would have us believe—there is much nostalgia for a golden age in American politics that never was—there is no doubt that the political landscape in America has changed in recent years. The most dramatic and noteworthy change is that paid political consultants have replaced the political parties as the controlling force in American politics. In the past, the political party bosses and a small group of party activists handpicked the candidates who ran for public office, either behind closed doors or in party conventions. The candidates were selected because they had toiled in the party vineyards by working on past campaigns, or because they possessed wealth or connections that would help them gain election. Candidates were expected to follow the party platforms on issues, and voters were more likely to vote straight party tickets. The power of the political parties diminished for many reasons, including: the demise of urban political machines, the move to primary elections for the selection of party candidates, and the fact that voters now are more independent in their voting choices.

Because voters are less likely to vote for the candidates of only one political party, and because they can now directly participate in choosing the nominees of their own party, they must actively seek information about political candidates in order to make informed choices. Since few voters are sufficiently interested in politics to actually attend a political speech in person, they must depend upon the political information offered them in newspapers, newsmagazines, on news broadcasts, or in the pervasive advertisements that candidates now purchase to become known to the voters.[3]

Those voters who are most politically active and involved—the active electorate, composed of those persons who follow the issues, are informed about the competing candidates, and have strong opinions—tend to decide who they will vote for early in the campaign. These are also the voters who are most likely to get the bulk of their information about the competing candidates from newspaper articles. Those voters who are less interested in politics and who do not have strong positions on the issues are far less likely to read the newspaper coverage of the political campaigns. These citizens tend to decide who they will vote for later in the campaign and they will get most of their political information from the broadcast media, from paid political advertisements, and from their friends and family members.[4] These less informed and less ideologically committed voters—the undecided and loosely committed voters—are the primary targets of the campaigns.[5] Because political advertising, whether in the form of direct mailings, newspaper ads, or radio or television spot ads, is expensive, most candidates must seek to simplify their messages and present them in the briefest possible form. Furthermore, because the undecided voters are the targets of these ads the candidates typically assume that these voters are not well informed and can best be reached via the simplest of messages.[6] The result is a system in which candidates are increasingly packaged into attractive media personalities and then sold to the voters in much the same way that products are sold to consumers.[7]

We have thus entered the era of **image** politics, where elected officials at most levels are evaluated on the basis of their public personalities. George Bush was selected over Michael Dukakis in 1988 because he *seemed* tougher and more experienced; Ross Perot attracted public support in 1992 running against George Bush because he seemed more pragmatic and because his lack of conventional political experience suggested that a Perot administration would not constitute "politics as usual." Bill Clinton was ultimately elected in 1992 because he was a new kind of Democrat who would not, presumably, take us back to the tax-and-spend policies of the past.

Given this public penchant for selecting candidates on the basis of their images rather than their expressed positions on the issues—Perot, for example, admitted during the campaign that he had not yet thought through his positions on many issues, but that he could solve problems that had baffled other politicians "without breaking a sweat"[8]—one might question what role argumentation can play in American political campaigning? The answer, as you should expect given the bias of this book, is a very important one.

We believe that American political campaigns, despite their emphasis on candidate image and on the hoopla of the campaign, are fundamentally rational and argumentative in character. In fact, campaigns are elaborate and carefully orchestrated argumentative exercises aimed at engaging the electorate and convincing voters that their interests and those of the candidate are the same.

Questions of Character

An examination of a candidate's image is in essence an examination of the candidate's **character.** Voters naturally seek to select candidates whom they believe are honest, trustworthy, and competent. We seek elected officials who will keep their promises and be true to their word. Perhaps even more importantly, however, we seek candidates who see the world as we do, candidates who share our stories and who have the same values that we have. In our earlier discussions of the storytelling perspective of argumentation, we emphasized that the world was made up of competing stories, each vying for public acceptance. Electoral campaigns provide excellent settings for watching these competing stories develop and emerge. Larry K. Smith, a former manager of a presidential and several senatorial campaigns, has observed that: "A campaign is a morality play . . . a contest over values and norms, not issues. . . . Every campaign is a story about the candidate and the nation."[9]

Voters seek candidates who share their values, beliefs, and worldview.[10] They want candidates to be like them, but not *just* like them. In short, voters seek candidates who can understand their needs, but who are perhaps just a little better than they themselves are— a bit more intelligent, a bit more experienced, and perhaps even a bit more morally perfect.

For example, during the 1992 campaign, Governor Bill Clinton sought to appeal to the public's need to identify with its presidential hopefuls by emphasizing his humble roots in Hope, Arkansas. In a very moving video presentation at the Democratic National Convention in 1992, he shared his life story: growing up in a poor, lower middle-class home with an outhouse in the backyard; living with his stepfather's drinking, violent mood swings, physical and emotional abuse; and of his own efforts to succeed. Through his own hard work and the unyielding support of his loving mother he graduated from college, became a Rhodes Scholar at Oxford University, and was admitted to Yale Law School. Then, when he could have had a highly paid job in the East, he have up this opportunity to return to his home state and build a career of public service.[11] Here is a compelling narrative which conveys to the public that Bill Clinton is a simple person much like them, but also intelligent, gifted, and ambitious enough to lead them.

The issue of a candidate's character takes on strong moral dimensions. Earlier in the campaign Governor Clinton had been charged with having an extramarital affair. While affairs are certainly common in contemporary America, and no doubt many of the voters had also been unfaithful at some point in their lives, there is a desire in America to hold our political candidates up to moral standards that we may be unable to meet ourselves. So who was this candidate? Was he the unfaithful husband, selfishly pursuing his own gratification outside of the bonds of marriage; a slick politician who would do anything to be elected? Or, was he simply a humble, honest, devoted man of the people? Should an extramarital affair disqualify him from public office? Or should he and his wife gain additional respect from the voters for staying married and attempting to work through their problems?

The voters were also, of course, asking: Who is George Bush? Is he the privileged son of the Eastern establishment and the handpicked choice of corporate America, as the Democrats would have us believe? Or, is he a self-made family man and former war hero who has devoted almost his entire life to public service?

We believe that there is no single answer to these questions because a candidate's image and public character are created rather than merely discovered. Candidate images are created by the candidates themselves in speeches and public statements; they are created by campaign consultants and media experts in advertising messages; they are created by the public statements of their supporters and opponents; they are created in press accounts; and finally, they are created in the conversations that voters have with their friends and family members.[12]

While many critics of the American political system lament its emphasis on candidate character and image, we see it as an inevitable dimension of the storytelling that occurs in political campaigns. An important measure of a story's narrative probability is its **characterological coherence**.[13] In testing a political narrative, voters seek to answer three questions relating to the candidate's character: Is this candidate the person that he or she claims to be? Does this candidate's character suit the demands of the political office he or she seeks? And, can I trust that my interests and the public interests that I hold as most important will be served by this candidate's election to office? These seem to us to be very relevant and important questions for voters to consider before casting their ballots.

Stories of History, the Present, and the Future

All political campaigns provide **historical narratives** that seek to explain our past and how we have happened to find ourselves where we are now. Thus, virtually any candidate's political rhetoric will emphasize those aspects of history that enrich and provide foundational support for the story he or she wants voters to accept. Both Republicans and Democrats draw freely upon the Founding Fathers for their inspirational messages about our political system. In addition, Republicans celebrate the achievements of the great Republican leaders from the past, and the Democrats celebrate the legacy of their great leaders. In fact, after an ex president has been dead for a certain number of years it even becomes possible for him to be claimed by the opposition! Thus, President George Bush invoked the name of Harry Truman, praising his personal character and independence.

These nostalgic recollections for the great political leaders of the past are more than idle memories or naïve memorializing. These leaders have come to represent the ideological history of the different political narratives that live on in American politics. To invoke the name of Franklin Roosevelt is thus to invoke the New Deal dream of proactive governmental involvement designed to enrich the condition of the masses. To invoke the name of John F. Kennedy is to remember the optimism, vitality, and youthfulness of his administration, and of the "New Frontier" thinking that initiated the space race. To invoke the name of Ronald Reagan is to express nostalgia for the time of relative prosperity and pride that marked his administration. Obviously all of these presidents faced opposition during their administrations. Nonetheless we seek to remember a past that was perfect and we try to cite the lessons from that past as part of our moral and political compass to guide our present actions.

When we argue about the events of Watergate, or the Vietnam War, or the invasions of Panama, Grenada, and the Middle East, we are seeking to use these historical events to shape our understanding of the world that we live in today. We are creating historical accounts to serve contemporary needs and interests. Did we fail in Vietnam because it was an immoral war which we never should have entered in the first place? Or did we fail because we lacked the will to see the fight through to the finish? The answer we give to a question such as this one helps to determine what course of action we will consider in future wars. If the lesson of Vietnam is that we should avoid involving ourselves in civil wars supporting puppet dictators, we will conduct our foreign policy very differently than if we tell an historical story that celebrates the moral justice of our involvement and only condemns the fact that we did not fight to win.

Historical stories thus provide material that is drawn upon in interpreting present problems and choices, and also in articulating **future narratives.** All political candidates seek to emphasize that if they are elected, and their proposed policies are enacted into law, the world will be a brighter place and the quality of all our lives will be improved. On important public issues the competing candidates will construct very different but competing depictions of history, accounts of the present, and views of the future. The historical stories must, of course, account for the facts of history, and thus cannot be fabricated to achieve a candidate's purposes.

Likewise, stories of the present must account for life as we know it. For example, former President Bush protested that the doomsayers in the press were responsible for the public's lack of faith in the economic recovery, but voters would not accept his story that a recovery was underway unless they experienced it.

Stories about the future are far more flexible, however, and political candidates always try to persuade voters that the world will be a much more prosperous, harmonious, and pleasant place if they are elected to office. Often arguments of this type refer to our enjoying a world so perfect that we will almost certainly never experience. In his nomination speech for Bill Clinton at the 1992 Democratic National Convention, for example, New York's Governor Mario Cuomo recalled his joy in participating in the parade welcoming our victorious troops back after the Persian Gulf War. But what he'd felt then would be nothing, he indicated, compared to the thrill he would feel when he had the opportunity to march behind President Bill Clinton through the neighborhoods of American cities that were free from the scourge of illicit drugs, where all the streets were safe, where all children had equal access to college educations, where every American had equal access to health care, and where all citizens had well paying jobs.[14] This certainly was an optimistic story about the future, and an obviously appealing one. If Bill Clinton indeed achieves all this, they will have to find room to chisel his face on Mount Rushmore!

Argumentative Themes and Issues

Voters are especially attuned to issues that directly affect their own lives and situations. Thus, farmers are predictably drawn to candidates who support policies that are helpful to agricultural producers, union members seek candidates who are willing to support the rights and power of unions, small business owners back candidates whose positions on issues would likely enhance the profitability of their businesses, and the parents of young children favor candidates who focus on issues such as improved education or day care.

In addition to constituencies such as these, however, political candidates also seek to appeal to voters who hold strong positions on other key political issues. Some voters, for example, are so concerned about abortion that they decide to vote for or against a particular candidate on the basis of that candidate's position on this single issue. For other voters gun control, environmental regulations, or gay rights might be the issue that decides their votes. Candidates must seek to develop positions on these important single issues that will win more votes than they lose. Obviously a pro-life voter is unlikely to vote for a strongly pro-choice candidate. But candidates must be careful not to become so beholden to special-interest or single-issue voters that they ignore the broader constituencies.

Candidates must also attempt to create images, public personas, and stories that are consistent. A candidate who emphasizes certain issues to build support with a particular constituency also attempts to appeal to other voters with similar interests. Candidates develop ideological constituencies in part to preserve a sense of harmony and predictability in the stories that they tell.

Walter Fisher has written that two political **myths** or stories have long dominated American electoral politics.[15] The first he calls the *materialistic myth.* This myth emphasizes economic issues, material well-being, and the drive to succeed and improve one's life in a material sense. We are all concerned about the state of the economy, our job security, the promise of the future, and our ability to support our families today and ourselves in our retirement years. As the old saying goes: "When your next-door neighbor loses his job we are in a recession. When you lose your job we are in a depression." The materialistic myth drives such shared cultural values as our beliefs in the work ethic, self-reliance, initiative, and ingenuity.

The second myth Fisher calls the *moralistic myth.* This myth celebrates the qualities of equality, justice, brother[sister]hood, collective responsibility, and concern for our fellow citizens. While the materialistic myth stresses that government should stay out of our way so that we can take care of ourselves and "do our own thing," the moralistic myth says that government has a responsibility to protect the weak and less fortunate, and to elevate the spirit of humankind.

Fisher says that virtually all Americans have at least some allegiance to both of these myths, and that both of them shape our values, our political identities, the American political culture, and the argumentative appeals that candidates make to voters.[16] Fisher notes that in the 1972 presidential election Senator McGovern's campaign emphasized the moralistic myth while President Richard Nixon's campaign emphasized the materialistic myth. If the 1972 election is seen as a referendum on the two myths, the results are clear: The materialistic myth triumphed. The real message of that campaign, however, was probably that the voters are reluctant to vote for the moralistic myth alone, and that they also need to be convinced that candidates satisfactorily address their material concerns.

The Structure and Form of Campaign Arguments

Because political campaigns are essentially narrative in form, the arguments offered to the voters seldom resemble the more formal arguments that might be discovered in an academic debate, in a courtroom, or even in a business meeting. Political campaign arguments may, consequently, have very loose rules of evidence, lax standards for evaluation, and sometimes seem designed to confuse rather than clarify issues. There is a tendency in much political arguing, for example, to tell only partial truths, or at the very least to embellish and exaggerate in support of one's positions. Maverick political candidate Ross Perot, for example, emphasized how he was born the son of a simple Texas horse trader and grew up to turn a one-thousand-dollar investment into a billion-dollar fortune by forming a company called Electronic Data Systems. Perot has since admitted, however, that the one-thousand-dollar check was only the registration fee that Texas required to charter a new corporation, and that he used a great deal more capital than that to get his company started.[17]

While Perot's autobiographical story might seem like a harmless exaggeration, the great risk is that the exaggerations will be more extreme and consequently more dangerous. Sometimes candidates even convince themselves that they are true. In 1980, for example, Ronald Reagan ran an ad celebrating his qualifications to be elected President of the United States. The ad claimed that during his eight years as governor of California Reagan had "all but saved the state from bankruptcy," decreased the size of state government, lowered taxes, and left behind a huge surplus. The *New York Times* conducted a detailed examination of the ad, however, and asserted that the state had never been near bankruptcy, that the commercial neglected to mention two substantial tax increases that helped create the surplus, and ignored the fact that state spending rose substantially during Reagan's tenure in Sacramento.[18] The Carter campaign eventually prepared its own commercial showing the Great Seal of California and declaring that Reagan had increased state spending by 120 percent, while adding 34,000 employees to the state payroll. The voiceover then declared: "The Reagan campaign is reluctant to acknowledge these facts today, but can we trust the nation's future to a man who refuses to remember his own past?"[19]

Obviously the media has a responsibility to record, listen carefully to, research, and evaluate our political leaders' arguments in order to help us judge the quality and veracity of their rhetorical claims. The media must therefore do more than merely report the campaign as if it were a horse race: they must focus on the issues and arguments advanced by the candidates. The voters, in turn, must act upon the information provided them. Americans have to be encouraged to read the newspaper accounts, listen to news broadcasts, and expend the energy to evaluate the arguments offered by political candidates.

If voters become more attentive to the quality of arguments advanced by candidates there is some hope that candidates will be less inclined to deliver simplistic, sophomoric arguments. As Roderick Hart declared, candidates need to focus less on how "audience predispositions can be exploited" and more on "how citizens' needs can be met."[20] Our political leaders speak for us, and they speak for America. They should be creating arguments that challenge us, stimulate us, and educate us, and not ones that merely massage our egos and self-interests and tell us what we want to hear.[21]

Political Debating

The one format for political argumentation celebrated for its promotion of rational, deliberative discussions of issues is the political debate. Political debates are praised because they provide an opportunity to observe the candidates, in face-to-face interactions, talking about the issues. Certainly these contests have value, but it is misleading to refer to them as debates because they do not resemble formal academic debates, or even parliamentary or legislative debates. Instead, these contests are more like joint press conferences.

In most political debates the candidates respond to questions from a panel of reporters, and the quality of the debates are in large part determined by the resourcefulness of these questioners. If they ask tough, penetrating questions, the candidates will be challenged far more than if they merely lob big, easy softballs at them.

In addition, many political candidates have learned that they can beg the question, skirting the issue by resorting to lines from their standard campaign stump speeches. When this happens the reporter (if given the opportunity for a follow-up question) and the opposing candidate need to be vigilant in pointing out that the original question has not been answered. Likewise, voters need to listen to debates very carefully so that they can assess and critically evaluate candidates' responses in the debates.

Research in political campaign debates has confirmed,[22] and candidates have discovered,[23] that debates are typically "won" by the candidate who can keep the opponent on the defensive. While there are obvious exceptions to this rule, most candidates in debates attempt to attack their opponents. Often candidates are quite haphazard in defending themselves from these attacks because they do not want to seem defensive. The result is that too many debates consist of mudslinging and little in the way of helpful, probing, constructive argumentation.

The other problem with political debates is that they have become mediated campaign events where the press and the voters seem to focus less on the substance of the discussion than they do on the candidates' momentum. The press and the public expend so much energy trying to determine who won the debate, and whose campaign was helped by their performance in the debate, that there is far less emphasis on the actual issues discussed and on the differences between the candidates than there should be. The emphasis on momentum has also led to some interesting consequences. For example, the research has suggested that voters questioned immediately after a debate may have different impressions of it than they will if questioned a few days later. It thus seems clear that voters' opinions are heavily influenced not just by the event itself, but by press reporting of the outcome of the debate.[24]

Yet another problem with current approaches to campaign debates is that the press and public have been conditioned to evaluate the performances on the basis of which candidate may have slipped up and made a critical mistake. For example, in 1976, President Gerald R. Ford declared that Poland could not be considered to be under domination by the Soviet Union. The remark seemed so clearly to be a mistake that the moderator gave the President an opportunity to clarify what he meant. Instead, of admitting his error, President Ford reaffirmed his conviction that Polish citizens would not consider themselves to be under Soviet domination. The postdebate commentary in the press primarily focused on this one remark, all but ignoring the rest of the debate.[25] This focus on identifying, preventing, and punishing candidate gaffes often seems to distract public attention from the more substantive issues in the debate, and sometimes seems to turn the debates into media events, offering voters little true insight into the candidates' abilities to govern.

There has been much discussion in recent years of ways in which political debate formats might be improved. Political debates should be structured to increase and emphasize the substantive ideological differences between the candidates, and their intellectual and communication abilities. This might be achieved by moving away from formats that emphasize the role of the reporters and moderators, and towards formats that encourage direct clash between the candidates. The formats should also encourage a combination of longer and shorter speeches, and more extensive opportunities for the candidates to give rebuttals to the arguments offered by their opponents. Finally, there should be direct questions or cross-examinations between the candidates.[26]

Summary

The quality of the issues and arguments advanced during political campaigns has a profound effect on the vitality of the American political process. Recent data suggests that approximately 80 percent of the American public place little trust in their political leadership. They feel that they have little meaningful choice in, or subsequent control over, their elected leaders.[27] In order to restore public confidence and trust in our political leaders we should strive to improve the substance and the quality of political argumentation. Candidates need to demonstrate greater respect for the intellect and wisdom of the voters, and they need to be honest. Voters need to invest more energy in learning about the issues and the candidates' stands on them. Only an involved and informed electorate can expect to have influence over its elected officials. Voters will not respect elected officials until the elected officials demonstrate their respect for the voters.

Key Terms

character	future narratives	image
characterological coherence	historical narratives	myths

Activities

1. Consider why almost half of the potential voters do not participate in general elections. Write a short essay presenting the reasons for this lack of participation, and suggest changes that might encourage greater participation by the electorate.

2. Read the text of either Bill Clinton's or George Bush's nomination acceptance speech, presented at their respective national conventions (Appendix A). Indentify who each candidate presents in his speech as the heroes, villains, and victims. Describe also how they depict the scene and the events which account for the state of affairs as they stood in the summer of 1992.

3. Examine both Bill Clinton's and George Bush's acceptance speeches at their national conventions. Identify the historical figures they cite and consider what strategic purposes these citations played in their speeches.

4. If the 1992 presidential election campaign took place again today it might have a very different outcome. Construct a new ad campaign for George Bush, Ross Perot, or Bill Clinton. What issues of image or substance would you give presence? How would you respond to negative advertising?

5. Presidential debates are often criticized for being superficial. What changes in the debate format would you propose to force candidates to be more specific?

Recommended Readings _____

Bennett, William L. "The Ritualistic and Pragmatic Bases of Political Campaign Discourse." *Quarterly Journal of Speech* 63 (1977): 219–238.

Edelman, Murray. *Constructing the Political Spectacle.* Chicago: Chicago University Press: 1988.

Graber, Doris A. *Processing the News: How People Tame the Information Tide.* New York: Longman, 1984.

Gronbeck, Bruce E. "Functional and Dramaturgical Themes of Presidential Campaigning." *Presidential Studies Quarterly* 14 (1984): 486–511.

Kraus, Sidney, ed. *The Great Debates.* Bloomington: Indiana University Press, 1962.

Kraus, Sidney, ed. *The Great Debates: Carter vs. Ford, 1976.* Bloomington: Indiana University Press, 1979.

McBath, James H. and Walter R. Fisher. "Persuasion in Presidential Campaign Communication." *Quarterly Journal of Speech* 55 (1969): 17–25.

Nimmo, Daniel. "Elections as Ritual Drama." *Society* 22 (1985): 31–38.

Nimmo, Daniel and James E. Combs. *Mediated Political Realities.* New York: Longman, 1983.

Notes _____

1. Citizens may choose not to cast their ballots for any number of reasons, of course, but some have suggested that the most likely reason for political apathy is that voters see no connection between themselves and political candidates. See Jeff Greenfield, *The Real Campaign* (New York: Summit Books, 1982), p. 30.

2. W. Lance Bennett, *The Governing Crisis: Media, Money and Marketing in American Elections* (New York: St. Martin's Press, 1992), p. 2.

3. R. Joslyn, *Mass Media and Elections* (Reading, MA: Addison-Wesley, 1984).

4. V.O. Key, *The Responsible Electorate: Rationality in Voting, 1936–1960* (New York: Vintage Books, 1966).

5. For an excellent discussion of the issues of political participation, media usage, and campaign strategies see Kathleen Hall Jamieson, "The Evolution of Political Advertising in America," in Linda Lee Kaid, Daniel Nimmo and Keith R. Sanders, eds., *New Perspectives on Political Advertising* (Carbondale: Southern Illinois University Press, 1986): 1–20. See also Sidney Kraus and Dennis Davis, *The Effects of Mass Communication on Political Behavior* (University Park: Pennsylvania State University Press, 1976). See also Kathleen Hall Jamieson, *Eloquence in an Electronic Age: The Transformation of Political Speechmaking* (New York: Oxford University Press, 1988).

6. C. Atkin and G. Heald, "Effects of Political Advertising," *Public Opinion Quarterly* 40 (1976): 216–228.

7. Most experts argue, however, that political advertising is constrained by the voters' preexisting beliefs about the candidates' attributes and the existing political situation. Thus, Kathleen Hall Jamieson argued that, "advertising, whether brilliant or banal, is powerless to dislodge deeply held convictions anchored in an ample amount of credible information." See *Packaging the Presidency: A History and Criticism of Presidential Campaign Advertising* (New York: Oxford University Press, 1984), p. 412.

8. Cited in George J. Church, "The Other Side of Perot," *Time*, 29 June 1992, p. 39.

9. Cited by Wendy Kaminer, "Crashing the Locker Room," *The Atlantic Monthly*, July 1992, p. 63.

10. Bruce E. Gronbeck, "The Presidential Campaign Dramas of 1984," *Presidential Studies Quarterly* 15 (1985): 386–393.

11. The very moving 12-minute-long Clinton video featured footage found in the John F. Kennedy Presidential Library archives showing Clinton, as a 17-year-old high school boy shaking hands with President Kennedy during a visit to the White House in 1963. Clinton also talked about the father he never knew (who died before his birth), and his feelings for his wife and daughter. The video was produced by Harry Thomason and Linda Bloodworth Thomason, and emphasized his small town roots. See David Lauter, "Clinton: Nominee Tries to Show Bush as Failed Leader," *Los Angeles Times*, 17 July 1992, p. A29.

12. Allan D. Louden, "Image Construction in Political Spot Advertising: The Hunt/ Helms Senate Campaign, 1984," Unpublished diss., University of Southern California, 1990, pp. 1–8.

13. Walter R. Fisher, *Human Communication as Narration: Toward a Philosophy of Reason, Value, and Action* (Columbia: University of South Carolina Press, 1987), p. 47.

14. "Text of Nomination Speech by Governor Mario Cuomo," *Los Angeles Times*, 16 July 1992, p. 12A.

15. Walter R. Fisher, "Reaffirmation and Subversion of the American Dream," *Quarterly Journal of Speech* 59 (1973), pp. 161–63.

16. Ibid.

17. George J. Church, "The Other Side of Perot," *Time*, 29 June 1992, p. 40.

18. Cited in Jeff Greenfield, *The Real Campaign* (New York: Summit Books, 1982), p. 254.

19. Cited in Greenfield, p. 254.

20. Roderick P. Hart, *The Sound of Leadership: Presidential Communication in the Modern Age* (Chicago: University of Chicago Press, 1987), p. 200.

21. Hart, p. 201.

22. See Patricia Riley and Thomas A. Hollihan, "The 1980 Presidential Debates: A Content Analysis of the Issues and Arguments," *Speaker and Gavel* 18 (1981), pp. 47–59. Also, Thomas A. Hollihan and Patricia Riley, "The 1980 Presidential Debates:

An Analysis of Argument Types, Issues, and Perceptions of the Candidates," paper presented at the International Communication Association Convention, Minneapolis, May 1981.

23. Greenfield, p. 226.
24. G. Lang and K. Lang, "The Formation of Public Opinion: Direct and Mediated Effects of the First Debate," in G. Bishop, R. Meadow, and M. Jackson-Beeck, eds., *The Presidential Debates* (New York: Praeger, 1978).
25. "The Blooper Heard Round the World," *Time,* 18 October 1976, p. 16.
26. Robert C. Rowland and Cary R.W. Voss, "A Structural-Functional Analysis of the Assumptions Behind the Presidential Debates," in Joseph W. Wenzel, ed., *Argument and Critical Practices* (Annandale, VA: Speech Communication Association, 1987): 239–247.
27. Bennett, p. 203.

13

Argumentation and the Law

The most formalized and ritualized setting for the creation and evaluation of arguments is the courtroom. It is in the resolution of legal disputes that our expectations for arguers are most carefully delineated. Disputants are to carefully research both the facts in their cases and the relevant statutes and laws; they are to present their arguments in accordance with carefully constructed rules; the evidence they introduce is to be probative without being unduly prejudicial; the arguments are to be weighed by independent jurors who typify the values of the community; and the entire process is to be controlled by a trained and impartial judge. The American legal system also allows for appeals. A litigant who loses a case may appeal the decision to a higher court if he or she can establish that the first trial finding was in error.

The United States is a very litigious society. As Ronald J. Matlon observed:

> In 1950, there were approximately 220,000 lawyers in America. That number grew to over 300,000 by the mid-1960s, and stood at nearly 650,000 in 1985. That meant that there were 2.7 lawyers for every 1,000 persons in the United States. By 1995, the number of lawyers in the United States is expected to double, making law one of the fastest-growing professions.[1]

As one old saying describes it, if there is only one lawyer in a city she or he will starve to death, but if there are two they can make enough work for a dozen! Another joke goes: rumor has it that scientists are replacing laboratory rats with lawyers in all scientific experiments, there are so many more of them, they are so much harder to become attached to, and there are some things that even a laboratory rat won't do!

The increasing complexity of modern society, the tremendous number of new regulations created since the 1960s, the fact that the courts have now recognized that defendants in criminal trials have a right to legal counsel, and the fact that there are simply more lawyers today trying to make a living, has led to far more demand for attorneys, and to increasingly crowded courtrooms. The court docket is so crowded in some American cities that it takes more than five years for a case to make it to trial.

There are essentially two types of cases that come before the courts, **civil** cases and **criminal** cases. In civil cases litigants typically sue someone for financial damages that they believe they have sustained as a result of the other party's actions or negligence. You might sue for civil damages if you paid to have a house built and the contractor did not complete all of the work, if a surgeon made a mistake and amputated your right leg when it was your left that had been injured, or if someone ran a red light and hit your car when you were legally driving through an intersection. Criminal cases are, of course, those wherein a defendant is charged with violating the established laws of the community. In these cases litigants are charged by the district attorney on behalf of all of the citizens of the jurisdiction whose laws were violated. Thus a charge of murder filed against the Milwaukee mass murderer Jeffrey Dahmer might be listed on the court docket as: *The People v. Jeffrey Dahmer.*

Before discussing the importance of argumentation theory and argumentation principles in legal settings, we will briefly consider the organizational characteristics of the American judicial system.

The American Judicial System

In the United States we have both courts that are controlled by the states and courts that are controlled by the federal government. Each state has primary responsibility for its own courts, and the decisions in one state court do not impact court decisions in another state. The structure of court systems varies somewhat from state to state, but typically states will have municipal (sometimes called circuit) courts, district courts, and/or superior courts. The municipal or circuit courts are generally reserved for minor criminal cases or civil cases in which the amount of damages sought is fairly small. These courts may be subdivided further into traffic courts (where traffic offenses are adjudicated), probate courts (where wills are ruled upon), domestic courts (where divorces and marital issues are handled), small-claims courts (which rule on small civil suits not requiring attorneys), and petty crimes courts. More substantial and important cases are decided in district or superior courts. The latter typically cover greater territory and jurisdiction, and also are noteworthy because the judges are appointed or elected and may have more stature in the community and in the legal profession. Each state also has state appeals courts and a state supreme court to rule upon the cases that have been decided by these lower courts. There are more than 3,500 courts of general jurisdiction in the United States.[2]

The federal courts resolve violations of federal laws and especially focus on interstate crimes. These include: violations of laws on federal lands or in national parks, as well as such offenses as environmental pollution that crosses state boundaries, immigration violations, income tax evasion, trafficking in drugs, treason, kidnapping that crosses state boundaries, and unlawful flight from one state to another to avoid capture. The federal court system is composed of 94 district courts and eleven federal appellate courts. Decisions from any of these federal courts, or even decisions from any of the state courts, could ultimately be appealed all the way to the United States Supreme Court.

The crush of activity in both the state and federal court systems has given attorneys, judges, and litigants increased incentive to divert cases from the docket and free the courts' time for hearing other cases. Thus in civil cases litigants are encouraged to reach a settlement before the trial begins, and in criminal cases the prosecutors and defense attorneys often agree to a plea bargain (in which a defendant agrees to plead guilty to a lesser offense than the one originally charged) in order to save the time and cost of a full trial. Because of the pressure to settle cases, only a small percentage of the cases that are initially filed, either civil or criminal, actually end up going to trial.

These bargaining and negotiation sessions, in which settlements are agreed upon, are also argumentative, of course, since the attorney has to build as strong a case as possible in order to achieve a settlement that most favors the interests of the client.

The Assumptions of the System

The American judicial system, which was modeled after the British system, is **adversarial** in nature. This model assumes that litigants, each taking incompatible positions, can by presenting the best arguments in support of their cases, present the essential facts in such a manner that the truthfulness of their arguments can be assessed and evaluated. Furthermore, this system assumes that even highly complex and technical legal questions at the trial level can be best resolved by untrained citizen jurors. Different states have created different standards for when litigants are entitled to a trial by jury, but typically, all civil cases beyond a certain level of damages (which varies from state to state), all felony criminal trials, and many misdemeanor trials can be decided by a citizen jury if the litigant demands it. Alternatively, a defendant can waive the right to a jury trial and have the case decided by a judge; such trials are known as "bench trials."

One might ask why we have placed such faith in untrained citizen jurors? Certainly the jury system is costly and troublesome. Citizens do not eagerly come forth and volunteer their time for jury duty. In many jurisdictions it is a constant challenge to the courts to find suitable jurors to fill all of the jury panels needed. Furthermore, the law has become so complex that it might arguably lead to better decisions, especially in such technically sophisticated areas as medical malpractice or antitrust prosecutions, to have cases decided by experts. Instead of turning to experts, however, our system emphasizes the ability of ordinary citizens to make these complex decisions. The reasons for this commitment to citizen jurors are numerous and varied.

First, there is a general belief that citizen jurors are capable of making good decisions. They are careful and conscientious in the verdicts that they render, and they take their responsibility seriously. Research has suggested that judges agree with the verdicts rendered by juries most of the time.[3]

Second, even though the entire court system is organized and structured to assure litigants impartial and fair verdicts that will resolve complex questions of facts, one benefit of the jury system is that jurors are not dispassionate arbiters of fact. Jurors are an important part of our legal system precisely because they temper their judgments with emotion and with pathos. The jurors bring with them into the courtroom the emotions and values of their community. Their judgments are shaped by their sympathy and or anger both for the victims or plaintiffs and for the defendants. In this sense the jurors reflect the public will. The presence of citizen jurors in the process protects the litigants from the potential capriciousness of the state, and ensures that the courts are not merely the instruments of existing state power and control, but reflect the wisdom and the will of the people themselves.

Third, the opportunity to serve on a jury provides a kind of civic involvement that is unrivalled by any other experience in our society. Jurors learn about the legal system, feel themselves much more a part of their government, and are likely to be more committed to the protection and preservation of our important civic institutions.

Because the American legal system involves untrained jurors in the decision-making process at the most critical junctures of cases, the courtroom becomes an interesting field for argumentative study and inquiry. As we have already discussed, different fields develop specific standards for argument evaluation based upon the need to resolve unique problems and to make effective decisions within the objectives of that field. In the law, for example, the key challenge is to decide how to categorize events. This categorization is sought through several kinds of questions. Some of these questions are factual: Did the alleged assault occur? Did the defendant commit the assault? Other questions may focus on the character of the act. Even if it can be clearly established that an assault occurred, and that the defendant committed the assault, one could still question the nature of the assault: Was this action taken in self-defense? What was the character of the situation, and did this situation have implications for the defendant's actions? Did the defendant simply lose control and strike out without thinking? Or was the act planned in advance and coldly calculated? Finally, there are questions of **precedent.** In classifying and categorizing events legal arguers attempt to assure that like actions will be dealt with in like fashion by the courts. If all people are truly viewed as equal under law, an assault by a white defendant on an African-American victim should be dealt with in the same way as an assault by an African-American assailant on a white victim. The courts consider legal precedent as well as statutory guidelines to assure that the law protects the interests of its different constituencies equally well and is applied to events in a predictable and patterned way.

Because the work of the courts is primarily designed to resolve factual disputes and to classify and categorize actions and behaviors, the propositions being disputed are propositions of fact. The specific wordings of the propositions in dispute will be very carefully framed to reflect the demands for legalistic precision. In criminal indictments the proposition considered will be a formal complaint, a charge in which the district attorney alleges that the named defendant broke a specific statute, on a specific date. The **burden of proof** in such a complaint clearly rests with the prosecution, and the prosecutor's arguments must be sufficient to overcome a **reasonable doubt.** What constitutes reasonable doubt is of course a matter of argument. Most judges will advise jurors that it does not mean the resolution of all doubts, but that a reasonable person would be inclined to find the evidence and the arguments presented by the prosecution sufficient proof that the complaint is true.

The complaints filed in civil cases are somewhat less precise than in criminal cases, but still demand that the specific allegation be explicitly understood and spelled out. If, for example, the plaintiff is claiming that the defendant caused her injury when he struck her with his car, the plaintiff's attorney will have to prove that the accident was the defendant's fault, that the resulting injury was sufficiently severe that the plaintiff should be compensated for actual losses and perhaps also for pain and suffering. One important difference between a criminal case and a civil case, however, is that in a criminal case the verdict is typically guilty or innocent, with little opportunity to create a middle ground (although in some jurisdictions, and with some kinds of crimes, a defendant could be convicted but on a lesser offense). In a civil case, on the other hand, verdicts quite often involve compromises in which, for example, the defendant is able to reduce the amount of damages claimed by arguing that while he should shoulder some responsibility for the accident, there was also negligence by one or more other parties in the case. In civil cases a verdict in favor of the plaintiff still leaves the question of the amount of damages to be awarded up to further deliberation. In determining the amount of the financial award, the jurors are asked to temper their findings with feeling for both the plaintiff and the defendant in the case.

The Role of the Attorney

The role of an attorney is, by its very definition, argumentative. Your attorney is your advocate in any legal case; in criminal cases the prosecutor is the "people's advocate," who reflects the community's will in having its laws enforced. From the time an attorney is first introduced to a client, she or he is beginning to construct the case.

During this first meeting the litigant and the attorney discuss the possibility of a case. In a civil case the client seeks out an attorney either in hopes of filing a cause of action against another person, or because someone has filed a complaint against him or her. In a criminal case the prosecuting attorney likely begins by interviewing the police officers who investigated the criminal complaint and identified a probable suspect. Likewise, in a criminal case the defendant is often interviewed by counsel only after a criminal complaint has been lodged.

During the interview the attorney seeks information that will facilitate an assessment as to whether this is a winnable, or deserving, case. Attorneys rarely want to spend their own time or the court's time on a case that they probably cannot win. This is why a defense attorney will urge a settlement or a plea bargain if the facts seem to suggest that it is unlikely that an outright acquittal can be achieved for their client.

The initial attorney-client interview also provides the attorney and client an opportunity to begin to get to know each other. Trust is an important dimension of the attorney-client relationship. Because most citizens lack understanding of the law, and because we typically call upon attorneys only when we really need their expertise, trust is highly important. It also works both ways. Just as it is important that clients trust their attorneys, so it is also important that attorneys trust their clients. It is helpful to attorneys if clients are honest and forthright with them, for there is nothing worse than clients who lie to their attorneys, and then get caught in those lies when their cases go to trial.

The Discovery Phase

Once an attorney decides to represent a client, she or he begins the process of research into the facts of the case to determine if the client's claims are indeed supported by the material evidence that is present. This is called **discovery.** Discovery typically includes additional interviews with witnesses or interested parties, an examination of important documents that might prove or deny the case, and the consultation of law books to both illustrate the specific statutes in dispute and to examine relevant case precedents.

The evidence that the attorneys assemble may take many forms: letters, contracts, legal documents, photographs, statements or affidavits from witnesses, and so on. Sometimes witnesses will be identified so that they can be subpoenaed to testify in court at a later date, and at other times their statements are introduced in the form of sworn depositions, given under oath and in the presence of a trained legal stenographer.

From this vast amount of information, the attorney begins to organize the facts together into a case that supports the client's position. The case should be organized so that the key issues that the case is to turn on are highlighted and accessible for discussion and scrutiny.

Developing the Theory of the Case

What an attorney must be thinking about when interviewing a client is a **theory of the case.** Attorneys use their knowledge of the law in an attempt to adapt general legal principles, statutes, and precedents to fit the specific situation of the client's case. The theory of the case is the underlying idea that unites the legal principles to the factual background, and ties the evidence into a coherent story that puts the client's position in the best possible light. That human decision makers rely on stories in the creation and evaluation of arguments, has already been established. Consequently, it should come as no surprise that courtroom arguments also emerge in the form of stories.

The stories that the attorneys tell, like all other stories that listeners evaluate, will be judged on the basis of their narrative probability and fidelity. With regard to narrative probability, or whether or not the story is coherent: Is the structure of the story satisfying and complete? Does it account for the chronology of events? Does it account for the material evidence that has been revealed? And what of the actors and characters these legal stories present? The attorneys seek to convince the jurors to sympathize with their clients. The plaintiff's counsel or the prosecuting attorney wants the jurors to empathize and feel pity for the victim. They seek to portray the defendant in the worst possible way. The defense attorney, of course, seeks to portray the defendant as sympathetically as possible, and even seeks to demonstrate ways in which the victim does not really suit that role very well.

The second test of stories is that of narrative fidelity. Does the story seem likely to be true; do they coincide with the stories that jurors have known or experienced in their own lives, in the lives of friends or family members, with stories they have read about in the press, and even the fictional accounts of characters that they have come to accept as reasonable and lifelike?

Two researchers, W. Lance Bennett and Martha S. Feldman, observed criminal trials in the Superior Courts in King County (Seattle), Washington, for a year. During their studies, they noted that:

> in order to understand, take part in, and communicate about criminal trials, people transform the evidence introduced in trials into stories about the alleged criminal activities. The structural features of stories make it possible to perform various tests and comparisons that correspond to the official legal criteria for evaluating evidence (objectivity, reasonable doubt, and so on). The resulting interpretation of the action in a story can be judged according to the law that applies to the case.[4]

Bennett and Feldman discovered that attorneys presented their legal arguments in the form of stories, and that stories provided the means by which jurors organized information, recollected that information, and systematically tested and evaluated information.[5]

The greatest benefit to the use of stories as a means of legal reasoning is that:

> Stories have implicit structures that enable people to make systematic comparisons between stories. Moreover, the structural form of a completely specified story alerts interpreters to descriptive information in a story that might be missing, and which, if filled in, could alter the significance of the action. The inadequate development of setting, character, means, or motive can, as any literature student knows, render a story's action ambiguous. In a novel or film, such ambiguity may be an aesthetic flaw. In a trial, it is grounds for reasonable doubt.[6]

The best stories are those which not only account for all of the evidence presented in the case, but those that are also simple, relatively straightforward, and easy for jurors to follow. The more complex a story is, the greater the likelihood that the opposing counsel can find ways to poke holes in it and reveal its flaws.

It is also helpful if attorneys create stories that they themselves find believable. An attorney should try not to argue a case that they do not themselves find plausible, for in doing so they might reveal their lack of faith in the case to the jurors, and as a result, poorly represent the interests of their client.

Because the burden of proof is always placed on the prosecution or the plaintiff, it is especially important that they present a unified, compelling, and forthright story. Complexities, plot twists, inconsistencies of almost any kind, prove especially troublesome to the construction of a compelling case by the prosecutor or plaintiff, because they all enhance the likelihood that a defense attorney can introduce an element of doubt in the jurors' minds.

It is best if the defense counsel can also present a unified defense story which clearly contrasts and is incompatible with the opponent's story, but which also accounts for all of the material evidence that is present. Unfortunately, it is often difficult for the defense to construct such a unified story. In these cases, the defense counsel might choose to present multiple stories all of which compete with and therefore cast doubt on the prosecutor or plaintiff's story. In some cases, the defense attorney might even decline to present any story at all, and might choose instead to present only a refutational case. Such a strategy tries to capitalize on the fact that the prosecutor or plaintiff has the burden of proof, and seeks to demonstrate reasonable doubt only by probing the potential weaknesses in the opponent's case. Because the jurors have such a strong preference for narrative reasoning, however, this is a dangerous strategy for the defense to use. The jurors will likely be seeking to construct rival stories to challenge the prosecution or plaintiff's story on their own. If they are unable to identify such a story, and if the defense counsel has also failed to present such a story, a verdict against the defendant is likely.

The preparation of the case and the pre-trial work that goes into the development of the case, is every bit as important, if not more so, than the trial presentations. Given that very few cases even get to trial, it is clear that most cases are won or lost during the pre-trial investigations and the construction of the case arguments. The decision as to whether or not to take a case to trial is often the most important one an attorney makes, and it can be made only after a careful consideration of the evidence, the appropriate legal statutes, and the theory of the case that is to be advanced.

Selecting the Jury

The selection of the jurors occurs before the trial begins. The attorneys seek jurors whom they believe will be most sympathetic to their case. The assumption of the jury system is that jurors are to represent a cross section of the community, making up, for any defendant, a "jury of one's peers." Consequently, jury panels should include persons of racial, ethnic, religious, economic, and gender approximately in proportion to these groups' share of the general population. Jury pools are drawn from voting registration lists, drivers' license lists, tax rolls, etc., in order to represent all segments of the community. Jury service is a legal responsibility; once called, jurors must serve unless they can get an excuse. One might be excused because of a physical limitation (poor health, disabilities of hearing or sight, and the like), because they have to care for others (children or elderly relatives, for instance), or in some instances because of their professional responsibilities, but most jurors must serve when called.

The lists of jurors are then gathered together into pools in such a way as to reflect the desire to achieve balance. These pools are then slated for specific cases. Trial judges actually seat the jurors on cases following a process known as *voir dire*. During voir dire the attorneys (or, in some jurisdictions, the judge) direct questions to the jurors in order to probe for potential bias. The questions can probe many dimensions of the potential juror's life including: occupation, political beliefs, religious beliefs, personal opinions, hobbies, relatives, reading habits, and so on. During voir dire the attorney seeks to determine if the potential juror is likely to be sympathetic to the client and capable of rendering a verdict in the case. Attorneys also use the voir dire in order to attempt to establish a relationship with the potential jurors. They seek to make a good impression on the jury, and to begin to win their favor.

There are three types of challenges that can be made to prevent someone from being seated on a jury. First, there is a challenge to the *array*. This is a claim that the entire jury panel was selected in an inappropriate way. Such challenges are very infrequent in contemporary society, because most court jurisdictions have become very careful in the selection of jury panels. Years ago, however, jury panels were sometimes selected by means that did not assure that the balance of the community was represented. Minorities were often excluded from jury service, and in some instances people could even volunteer to serve on a particular jury. In both cases the fairness of the jury might be undermined, either because the resultant jury might not be appropriately sympathetic to the litigant's case, or because the jury might then include a juror who already had strong opinions about the case. Challenges to the array are unlimited. An attorney may make as many as he or she wishes, but they are rarely sustained by the judge because the procedure for selecting jury panels is, by now, so routine.

A second type of challenge is known as a "for cause" challenge. In this kind of challenge an attorney can argue to the judge that a particular juror should be excused because he or she might be unable to be impartial. Someone who has been raped might, for example, be excused from jury service in a rape trial. Someone who had a son or daughter murdered might be excused from a jury in a murder trial. Close relatives of police officers might be excused from cases in which there are charges of police misconduct. Any juror who already has an opinion on the outcome of the case, or who has learned a great deal about the case through pre-trial publicity might also be excused for cause. Finally, any juror who admits to racial or ethnic prejudice might be dismissed from a jury for cause. The attorneys in a case have an unlimited number of challenges for cause, but each challenge must be ruled upon by the judge.

The final type of challenge that can be raised is what is known as a *peremptory challenge*. These challenges can be raised by either attorney for any reason, and the reason does not have to be stated. Attorneys may decide to eliminate potential jurors because they did not like their political bias, were concerned about their religious beliefs and how these might influence the jurors' judgment, because they wanted a better or less well educated juror, and so forth. The number of peremptory challenges available to each attorney is strictly limited (although it varies by jurisdiction) so they must be exercised very carefully.

The selection of the jury challenges the attorneys in several ways. Attorneys evaluate potential jurors by considering their appearance, expressions, and answers to direct questions. But they also call upon certain stereotypical assumptions they are likely to have about jurors. Thus, for instance, defense attorneys often seek to find jurors who are like their client in the case, while prosecutors or plaintiffs seek to find jurors who are like the victim. Conventional wisdom also suggests that political liberals tend to favor the defense, while conservatives favor the prosecution. Minorities are more likely to favor the defense, while Caucasians might be more inclined to be sensitive to the prosecution. While there are most certainly exceptions to these stereotypical assumptions, they nonetheless guide the attorneys as they make their selections.[7]

The Trial

Once the jury panel is seated, the trial can begin. The prosecutor or the plaintiff begins the trial by presenting an opening statement. The opening statement provides the attorneys an opportunity to briefly introduce their story of the case, and to offer an explanation as to how the evidence will be drawn together to support the case. The opening statement is probably the most important moment in the case, especially for the prosecution or the plaintiff (for the purpose of clarity, future references will be to the prosecutor, and we will assume a criminal rather than civil action is being described). If the case does not seem clear and comprehensible to jurors on first hearing, before the defense has had its chance to speak, it is unlikely that the case can be won. Most of the trial evidence will be presented through the testimony of different witnesses, and may come out in a somewhat disorganized and chaotic manner. The opening statement provides a framework for jurors to use in pulling this evidence together. An effective opening statement should stay in their minds throughout the case, and should go with them into the jury room. In short, this statement provides the attorney with the opportunity to create the context for the presentation of all of the ensuing evidence in the trial.

The defense counsel may waive the right to make an opening statement, but generally they will seek to make some sort of an opening statement, even if it is just to alert the jury to the fact that the other side has the burden to prove their case. However, the defense counsel will choose not to make an opening statement if, for instance, they do not yet have a clear story of their own case that they wish to advance; they may plan a purely refutational case strategy; or they may wish to wait to hear their opponent's case before they commit themselves to a particular argumentative strategy.

Following the opening statements, the prosecution presents its case. The legal case is presented through the introduction of the testimony of relevant witnesses and the introduction of the physical evidence. The evidence becomes the substance of the legal case, and can consist of physical evidence (such as contracts, the murder weapon, burglar's tools, or the drugs seized), as well as testimony. The evidence is introduced to the court through the question and answer process. The prosecutor introduces the witnesses and builds a case through what is known as **direct examination.** Then, after the prosecution's questions elicit the relevant evidence for the court, the defense attorney will ask questions of the witness. This is known as **cross-examination.** The direct examination and cross-examination portions of the trial are especially important to the trial's outcome, for they are the means by which jurors actually hear the assembled evidence, and also hear the challenges to that evidence.

Unlike on television, however, witnesses rarely melt under the withering questions of the attorneys, and there are usually no profound surprises produced during these examinations. If the attorneys have done their pre-trial homework they have a very good idea as to what the witnesses will say in response to their questions. Neither counsel wishes to risk asking a witness a question that they do not already know the likely answer to, for doing so could jeopardize their case.

In the questioning process, attorneys seek to develop questions that put their cases in the best possible light, and which minimize the credibility of the opponent's stories. Questions are best asked in a fairly simple and straightforward manner, and in such a way as to prevent the witnesses from providing lengthy elaborations which might only confuse the jurors or which might suggest questions that would not otherwise occur in the jurors' minds. The attorneys also seek not to antagonize witnesses, even the opponent's witnesses, because such antagonisms often enhance their appeal for the jurors while undermining the attorney's appeal. The attorney should always interview her or his own witnesses before the trial begins so that she or he knows what answers will be given. The attorney must be careful to avoid coaching the witness, since the witness will be testifying under oath and must tell the truth. However, the attorney should seek both to learn what the witness will testify, and to advise the witness on techniques for presenting that testimony in the most desirable way.

Some people, of course, are better witnesses than others. Ideally a witness should be a person of integrity and good moral character who will be believed and viewed sympathetically by the jury. In addition, a good witness is one who demonstrates a good memory, seems thoughtful and conscientious, is able to provide clear and focused answers, and does not seem to carefully qualify every answer given. Some witnesses pose very special problems to attorneys. These may include problems of character (the convicted felon, the philandering husband, the youth who demonstrates a willingness to fib); they may reflect communication habits (a long-windedness, an antagonistic style, an unpleasant personality), or they may be caused by the witnesses limitations (for instance, age, or infirmities). An attorney who calls such a witness takes a calculated risk as to how such a witness will hold up under cross-examination, and how he or she will be perceived by the jury.

There are many other issues that attorneys must consider in presenting the witnesses in support of their case. Who should be called? In what order should they be called? If more than one witness can corroborate the testimony then how many witnesses should be called? If there are weaknesses in the testimony of the witness, should they be introduced by your side rather than left to be possibly discovered by the opposing counsel? The wise attorney is careful and conscientious in the construction of the case, and weighs the different strategic elements of the case in deciding these issues.

The cross-examination of the witnesses is also a great challenge for the attorneys. When examining witnesses that one has called to testify one has a good idea as to what they will say, having already interviewed them. When examining witnesses who have been called by the other side, however, the situation is far more difficult. You may have learned through pre-trial disclosure what the witness is to testify, but the courtroom sometimes provides the first opportunity to speak directly to this witness. It is dangerous to risk asking questions that may actually strengthen the opponent's case by helping the witness to enhance her or his credibility with the jury. In conducting cross-examinations, the counsel must carefully study the depositions that were introduced and the material evidence that the witness may be presenting. In addition, the counsel should carefully structure and phrase all questions. This is no time for a hunting expedition. A good attorney also knows when to stop questioning a witness, so as not to undercut the progress already made with a line of questioning. Matlon provides the following example of a defense lawyer cross-examining an eyewitness:

Q: Where were the defendant and the victim when the fight broke out?

A: In the middle of the field.

Q: Where were you?

A: On the edge of the field.

Q: What were you doing?

A: Bird-watching.

Q: Where were the birds?

A: In the trees.

Q: Where were the trees?

A: On the edge of the field.

Q: Were you looking at the birds?

A: Yes.

Q: So your back was to the people fighting?

A: Yes.

Q: Well, if your back was to them, how can you say that the defendant bit off the victim's nose?

A: Well, I saw him spit it out.[8]

Attorneys should ask clear and direct questions, they should vary their inflection and pacing so that the examinations do not become monotonous for jurors, and they should always remember that they are working to win jurors over to their side of the case. Consequently, they should not appear to badger or treat the witness rudely, even if the witness is an undesirable character, for they do not wish the jury to begin to sympathize with the witness rather than with them.

The most important thing that attorneys must remember in cross-examination, however, is that they must have a strategy in mind. They must know what they hope to accomplish, they must prepare their questions in advance, and they must be able to use the questioning process to tell their story of the evidence and events.

Once the prosecution has completed its case it is time for the defense to present its case. Often the defense will approach the judge at this point with a motion to dismiss the complaint on the grounds that the prosecution's case is insufficient to overcome a reasonable doubt—in other words, that the prosecution has failed to present a prima facie case. These motions are usually dismissed out of hand by the judge, because as we have already mentioned, the court dockets are so crowded that very few frivolous cases actually make their way to trial. In rare circumstances the defense counsel's cross-examination of the prosecution's witnesses has been so effective that the judge may in fact grant this motion. If it is granted, the trial is ended and the complaint against the defendant is dismissed. More likely, however, the judge will rule that the prosecution has met the burden of overcoming reasonable doubt, and the defense will be instructed to present its case. The defense now has the opportunity to present its witnesses under direct examination, and the prosecutor has the opportunity to cross-examine those witnesses.

After the defense has presented its case, the trial proceeds with the closing statements. These allow the attorneys to pull all of the evidence and testimony together and to tell their stories. The prosecution obviously tries to tell as coherent and complete a story of the events as possible. Loose ends prove especially dangerous to the prosecutor's case, so there is an attempt to demonstrate that the defendant had the motive, means, and opportunity to commit the crime. The defense obviously wants to discredit this story, to find flaws in it that will convince the jury the defendant should not be found guilty.

Attorneys must be careful in closing statements to faithfully recount the facts that were presented in the case. If the evidence is inaccurately described at this point the opposing counsel will almost certainly object. The attorneys also have to decide what the key facts in their case are, and to emphasize those facts, rather than to merely recount the entire case. Finally, it is important that the attorneys attempt to predict the flaws in their own case and seek to preempt arguments that either the opposing counsel or the jurors themselves might advance as they consider the evidence. The attorney who can predict the key turning points in the consideration of the case, and resolve jurors' uncertainties regarding those turning points, will have a much better chance of securing a favorable verdict.

Closing statements also offer attorneys a final opportunity to win over the jurors with their communication skills. Attorneys seek to communicate directly with the jurors, and to impress them with their competence, fairness, and thoroughness in presenting their cases. Often they will resort to emotional appeals in their closing statements in order to win sympathy and/or empathy for their clients or for the victims they represent. If the attorneys made the right choices in jury selection they should have created a panel that will be open to these arguments. They will now seek to take full advantage of these sympathies and to win the jurors over. It is especially important that the closing arguments be simple, straightforward, and easy to follow. Often the attorneys will resort to such well tested argumentation strategies as the use of analogies and metaphors in their closing statements, because as we have already discussed, these argument techniques, in particular, take advantage of the fact that most decision makers rely on a storytelling mode of reasoning.

Once the attorneys have presented their closing arguments, the judge will brief the jurors. This state of the trial is extremely important to the outcome, for the judge essentially creates the context in which all of the other information in the trial is to be considered. Judges direct the jurors about the law, about the admissibility of certain evidence, about their obligations in reviewing the relevant evidence, and about their burdens in delivering a fair and impartial verdict. Because instructions to jurors are frequently cited as places in which the trial judge errs, and they consequently provide the grounds for many appeals, some jurisdictions provide the judge with what are called *pattern instructions*. These instructions are standardized to fit the nature of the charge and to reflect the statutory rules of the particular jurisdiction. Because they are standardized, however, they frequently do not address the needs of the specific case under review, so judges often have to add to these standardized instructions.

Once the judge has charged them, giving them instructions for the consideration of the verdict, the jurors are sent to their chambers to deliberate and to reach a verdict. In the jury room the competing stories told by the opposing counsels are subjected to close scrutiny. The jurors may ask to reread portions of trial testimony, examine the physical evidence again, and ask questions of the judge which are relayed through the court's bailiff. They should not have discussed with each other, or anyone else, their opinions of the case or the evidence, prior to being sequestered in the jury room. Once the case is in their hands, however, the attorneys can have no further effect on the trial outcome and they can only wait along with the victims and the defendants, for the verdict to be reached.

When the jurors have reached their verdict, the principles in the case are reassembled in the courtroom, and the verdict is handed over to the bailiff and announced. The attorneys will often seek to interview the jurors in order to discover why they ruled as they did, and in order to learn why their case strategy succeeded or failed to persuade the jurors.

Summary

The law is an especially important focus for argumentation. Attorneys use their argumentation skills in virtually every dimension of their professional lives, from their initial conversations with their clients, to the negotiations and settlement conferences they conduct, to the depositions and fact-finding phase, and finally in the courtroom itself. Many of the principles of effective argumentation discussed in this text are especially important in the courtroom. The advocates rely on a storytelling argumentative approach, and the jurors make their decisions based upon their judgments of who told the superior story. In this argument field, as in many others, the emphasis should be placed on careful research and preparation, for a well researched and reasoned case theory is likely to win over the jury.

Key Terms

adversarial	cross-examination	precedent
burden of proof	direct examination	reasonable doubt
civil	discovery	theory of the case
criminal		

Activities

1. Diagram the court system in your locale, from municipal to state supreme court.

2. Attend a criminal trial and observe the presentation of the opening arguments. Try to ascertain the theory of the case held by each side. Evaluate these opening presentations in terms of narrative probability and fidelity.

3. Attend a civil court proceeding and compare what transpires with what took place in the criminal court. What differences can you identify? What are the similarities?

4. We have elsewhere described the importance of symbols and rituals. Observe a court proceeding and identify the symbols and rituals of the judicial system. What role do these symbols and rituals play in the American justice system?

5. Visit a small-claims court and compare what transpires there with what went on in the civil courtroom you visited. How does the participation of citizen advocates change the nature of the proceedings? What similarities are there?

Recommended Readings

Beach, Wayne A. "Temporal Density in Courtroom Interaction: Constraints on the Recovery of Past Events in Legal Discourse." *Communication Monographs* 52 (1985): 1–18.

Benoit, William L. "Attorney Argumentation and Supreme Court Opinions." *Argumentation and Advocacy* 26 (1989): 22–38.

Hollihan, Thomas A., Patricia Riley, and Keith Freadhoff. "Arguing for Justice: An Analysis of Arguing in Small Claims Court." *Journal of the American Forensic Association* 22 (1986): 187–195.

Makau, Josina. "The Supreme Court and Reasonableness." *Quarterly Journal of Speech* 70 (1984). 379–396.

Nobles, Scott. "Communication in the Education of Legal Advocates." *Journal of the American Forensic Association* 22 (1985): 20–25.

Saks, Michael J. and Reid Hastie. *Social Psychology in Court*. New York: Van Nostrand Reinhold, 1978.

Taylor, K. Phillip, Raymond W. Buchanan, and David U. Strawn. *Communication Strategies for Trial Attorneys*. Glenview, IL: Scott, Foresman, 1984.

Wellman, Francis L. *The Art of Cross-Examination*. 4th ed. New York: Collier, 1936, reprinted 1962.

Notes

1. Ronald J. Matlon, *Communication in the Legal Process* (New York: Holt, Rinehart and Winston, 1988), p. 2.
2. Matlon, p. 4.
3. Matlon, p. 101.
4. W. Lance Bennett and Martha S. Feldman, *Reconstructing Reality in the Courtroom: Justice and Judgment in American Culture* (New Brunswick, NJ: Rutgers University Press, 1981), p. 4.
5. Bennett and Feldman, pp. 4–7.
6. Bennett and Feldman, p. 10.
7. For a discussion of the jury selection process see Michael Fried, Kalman J. Kaplan and Katherine W. Klein, "Juror Selection: An Analysis of Voir Dire," in Rita James Simon, ed., *The Jury System in America: A Critical Overview* (Beverly Hills: Sage, 1975), p. 47–66.
8. Matlon, p. 236.

14

Argumentation in Business and Organizations

The principles of argumentation that we have been discussing in this text are not merely theoretical abstractions that you can commit to memory, regurgitate on a final examination, and then forget. Instead, these are concepts that you will use—whether you are conscious of them or not—throughout your lives. While most of you will not participate in formal academic debates once you have finished this class, and some of you may never be asked to create or evaluate arguments in a courtroom, all of you will find yourself creating arguments in your workplace. As members of business, governmental, academic, or professional organizations you will often be called upon to develop arguments in support of your positions. As a result, we have designed this chapter to be pragmatic. We want to help you to develop the skills necessary to effective advocacy in the workplace.

This chapter will help you to learn to argue in a business organization. We will suggest how you should prepare your arguments, assess your audience, create and present your messages, defend your ideas, and follow up on your presentations. The goal is to help you to learn how to promote your ideas—and yourself—in an organization.

Storytelling in Organizations

As is the case in other argumentative contexts, organizational arguers typically make use of narratives, and evaluate arguments on the basis of their appeal as stories. In fact, many organizations have "company stories" or **organizational cultures** that are essential to defining the organization vis-à-vis its competitors.[1]

To say that there is a shared company story, however, is not to say that organizations do not have disagreements. Organizations are composed of individuals bound together to perform certain tasks and to produce products or services.[2]

They transform inputs into finished products or outputs. Communication is necessary for organizations to accomplish their tasks and to permit the individuals who make up these organizations to function. Because these individuals have different opinions, tasks, interests, and objectives they frequently find themselves in conflict. Arguments can resolve these conflicts and help make decisions. People differ about how to do their jobs, and about how their organizations are most likely to prosper. Organizations are composed of people with different levels and types of expertise, who may also have different worldviews and objectives.

In a large and complex business organization, for example, you may find a finance division, a research and development division, a manufacturing division and a marketing division. Even though the executives from these different divisions all work for the same company, and should be pursuing the same objectives, their different tasks, personalities, and expertises often lead them to very different views of how their company should be run and what decisions are in the company's best interests. Executives from the finance division, for instance, are especially concerned with the bottom line, and are sometimes referred to disparagingly as the "bean counters." They want to improve the company's income and reduce expenses. They are especially protective of the company's assets and reluctant to commit funds for such things as product development, new plants or equipment, or new employees. Conversely, executives from the research and development division of a company are especially interested in developing new products and improving current products. They are the company dreamers, always speculating about how things could be improved. In an effective organization the research and development executives are highly creative. They also may have little regard for what things will ultimately cost, how hard they may be to manufacture, or who may actually buy them. The manufacturing division's executives, for their part, are keenly aware of how difficult it is to actually produce the new products. They are often reluctant to undertake new product lines, and eager to continue operating as they always have in order to get the product out on schedule, keep a ready flow of spare parts available, and maintain a stable workforce. New products require development money and lead to quality problems. The manufacturing division believes new products will necessitate additional employees, more floor space, and new equipment, which they feel they cannot persuade the "bean counters" to give them. Finally, the executives from the marketing division are concerned with selling the product. Consequently, they want a secure market share, reliable products that meet customers' needs, timely deliveries, and most importantly, products they can sell at a competitive price—which places pressure on all the other divisions.

A well managed company needs strong and articulate executives from all of these different divisions. If any division is poorly led or does not make its interests known, the company will not make the best decisions and will suffer financially as a result. Company chief executive officers often have to make tough decisions and resolve conflicts. Obviously some CEOs make better decisions than others, but a CEO is most likely to make better decisions in an organization that has created a healthy climate for the construction and evaluation of competing arguments.

Organizational conflicts are often productive and necessary.[3] Arguers in organizational settings should not assume that their colleagues already know the facts and understand their thinking. Instead they should view their arguments as an opportunity to enlighten and inform their colleagues. In addition, organizational advocates should not see conflicts as zero-sum games, with winners and losers, but should approach arguing as an investigative process that enables the decision makers to choose the best courses of action. This means that advocates should avoid personality attacks or personalizing the arguments directed against them. Arguments should be seen as a natural and important part of the organization's daily activity.

Preparing Your Arguments

The first consideration for developing arguments in an organizational or workplace setting, as in any other setting, is to clarify your objectives. What do you hope to accomplish? People may argue for many reasons: to advance an issue that they believe is especially important, to effect change in the way the organization conducts its business or operates, to secure resources for a new project or procedure, to promote themselves or their work unit, or to defend themselves or their unit from attack or criticism. It is important for you to have a clear idea of precisely what your purpose is before you go about developing arguments. If your ideas are unclear you risk undercutting your purpose. For instance, say that you want to argue for a new innovation that reduces layers of bureaucracy in order to streamline your company and help it to operate more efficiently and thus more profitably. This argument could, of course, backfire if the executives who have to approve your proposal believe their jobs reside in the layer of bureaucracy that is eliminated! Carefully consider what you hope to accomplish and how you intend to go about accomplishing it before going public with your arguments.

Second, carefully assess the accepted communication or argumentation style of your organization. Organizations may reflect very different communication cultures. Some are very friendly, supportive, and informal. In such an organization the chain of command might be more loosely followed, and the executives quite open to interactions from below. The style of interaction in such organizations tends to be relaxed. Other organizations may be very formal, requiring communication to flow along specific paths that conform to the organization's hierarchy. In such an organization interactions might be fairly tense, people may be somewhat closed toward each other, and there might be great emphasis on the chain of command. Such an organization might repress conflict and discourage disagreements. Still other organizations might be highly contentious. In such organizations not only might conflict be common, it might be accepted as the norm. You need to determine the nature of the organization that you are a member of, and attempt to respond accordingly. Violating the expectations of the organization will diminish your effectiveness as an advocate and might cause both you and your coworkers to feel uncomfortable.

Third, assess the audience for your arguments. Consider who ultimately makes the decisions about the issue that you wish to address. Once you have a clear idea of this, you can attempt to determine what this person is looking for and considering when he or she ponders the alternatives presented. Is this person especially interested in certain kinds of issues? Is there a particular perspective likely to result from the requirements of his or her job? time with the company? academic training? What values or goals seem to influence this individual and your organization, and how might these values and goals shape your arguments?

Often the audience for your arguments in an organizational setting is your immediate boss. Consequently, you should always consider how to make arguments that your boss will find persuasive. Keep in mind, one way for you to prosper in an organization is to make your boss look good![4] Perhaps if you make her or him look really good, he or she will be promoted and you can step into the open position! Remember, in presenting arguments to your boss, that your boss is an ordinary person with biases, fears, preoccupations, goals, strengths, weaknesses, etc. Too often bosses make poor decisions because they have been poorly trained or ill prepared for their jobs, or because they fail to get good information from their superiors and their subordinates. Subordinates may distort the information to protect their own interests, and superiors may keep them in the dark just as you may feel your boss keeps you in the dark.[5] Your role as an arguer is to identify your boss's interests, objectives, and idiosyncracies and to adapt your claims to them.[6] Then make every attempt to supply your boss with the information and analysis necessary to make the best possible decision.

Shaping the Message

Once you have decided what your objective is, and considered the audience to whom your arguments will be addressed, it is appropriate for you to consider what resources you have at your disposal to help sell your arguments. What is your position in the company? How much authority, credibility, and perhaps most importantly, **power** do you really have? If you have just been hired as a clerk in the mailroom you may find that your ideas about how the company ought to be restructured will not receive much consideration. If, on the other hand, you have come to the company in a position of authority, the company's leadership may be expecting great things from you and might be eager to listen to your ideas. A careful consideration of your resources will help prevent you from overplaying your hand and getting yourself in trouble. It will also help you to understand that if you are in an uphill fight against someone who holds a lot more power and influence than you do that you will have to adjust your argument strategies accordingly.

There are some strategies that you can consider using if you find yourself at odds with a more powerful organizational advocate. First, you could seek out a mentor who will sponsor your position and protect you from the flak that your ideas might create in the organization. Ideally your mentor would be someone at least as powerful as your principle adversary. Second, you could present your suggestions to your boss and encourage the boss to take "ownership" and become an advocate for your ideas. One important way to do this is to find a way to convince the boss that your idea was really his or hers all along.

In addition to assessing your power in the organization you should begin to form **coalitions** for support.[7] Before brashly going to the boss you should cultivate support for your arguments with peers and with other people in your organization who can help you and enhance your position. If these persons are supportive of your position they lend credibility to it—they provide "prestige referrals" for you. And, if they are not supportive, this gives you feedback that will help you strengthen your arguments and prepare for the reactions you may get from others.

You should think very carefully about who is likely to resist your arguments. Whose ox is being gored? Whose interests will be undercut? How might these potential adversaries be neutralized? How much power do they have in the organization versus how much power do you have? Who will be your opponent's allies if there is a confrontation? What compromises or accommodations might you offer that will win them over? Certainly it would be preferable not to have determined adversaries, especially powerful ones.

You should also seek strategies for presenting your arguments in a manner that discourages opposition without undercutting your objectives. For example, perhaps you wish to propose a solution to a problem that you have identified in your organization, but you realize that there will be a resistance to your ideas. You might consider presenting two alternative scenarios as potential solutions to the problem. The first scenario might be a conservative, inexpensive, and perhaps easily enacted approach to the problem, but nonetheless inadequate to solve it. The second scenario, in contrast, might be a complex and expensive scenario, replete with "bells and whistles." While this scenario would solve the problem, its cost and complexity will likely make it an unacceptable solution. Then, after your supervisor has shot down these two scenarios, you can introduce a third— the one you actually favored all along—as a compromise alternative to the first two. Scenario 3, which might not have received careful consideration if proposed initially, might now seem like a very reasonable approach compared to scenarios 1 and 2.

In creating your arguments don't forget the importance of careful preparation. To succeed as an organizational advocate you must do your homework. You should begin by reviewing previous arguments that have been made in your organization regarding the issue that you are addressing. When the issue has come up for discussion before how did the advocates phrase their claims? What were the outcomes of these prior discussions? What happened as a result of the decisions made before? Were those results positive or negative? What historical lessons should you and your supervisors learn from those prior discussions?

You must also be careful to tailor your arguments to the decision maker you are addressing. Be mindful of our earlier discussion of field theory. People in different fields often evaluate arguments differently. If you are talking to engineers you need to adapt your arguments to that field. If you are talking to human resources people you need to adapt to that field. You should also take care to assess the extent to which the audience that you are addressing has prior knowledge, expertise, or understanding of the issues that you are raising. Often you will have far greater expertise on the issue being discussed than will the person you are making your appeals to. Do not presume that they fully know what you know: adapt your arguments to their expertise and experience. Pay special attention to your use of technical language or **jargon** in your presentations. If someone docs not share your technical vocabulary they are not likely to follow your arguments, and often they will be reluctant to tell you how little they understand because they do not wish to appear ignorant or uninformed.[8] Be careful, on the other hand, not to demean the intelligence, background, or experience of your audience. Nothing puts people off more quickly than being talked down to. Assess the background of your audience before you begin your presentation, adapt your language to that background, define terms that may be unknown to your audience, and carefully assess the feedback that you receive.[9]

You should also carefully consider the alternative formats available to you for sharing your arguments. Sometimes it is preferable to write a memorandum advocating your position. Sometimes a phone call is sufficient. At other times, however, you might need to prepare a formal briefing. You can decide which form of communication is appropriate based upon several factors. First, how many people will have to be involved to implement your ideas? The more people who need to be involved, the more interaction is probably needed to plan and discuss the proposal. If people are present in the planning of innovations, it is easier to convince them to accept them, and less likely that they will criticize them later.[10] Second, how complex are the issues you are trying to communicate? The more complex an idea is, the more people will need to discuss it in order to feel that they understand it. Third, how many feathers will be ruffled by your arguments? This is a political consideration. How much resistance can be expected? If you expect to encounter resistance to your ideas it is probably best to present them in a briefing meeting. A memorandum can be too conveniently ignored or lost—if they don't wish to act on it people can simply claim that they did not receive it; a phone call can be too easily distorted when discussed with others. A briefing, on the other hand, permits you to explain your position in your own words so that others hear for themselves what you are advocating.

If you decide that you need to make a formal presentation you should very systematically prepare for it. Outline your objectives and prepare supporting **visual aids**—graphs, charts, tables, and so on. In most companies, executives expect business presentations to be made with such supports as handouts, transparencies, and charts.

Do not expect that your audience will be very effective at taking notes. If you wish them to remember key facts or arguments from your talk you should be prepared to provide them with written copies of these. Be careful not to bury them with so much material to read that they focus on reading it while you are speaking, because then they will most likely not follow what you are saying. Few people can read and listen at the same time. Most people will read ahead of the speaker, occupy themselves by flipping through the pages, and then once they have finished reading the document, start doodling all over its edges. If you want them to hear what you are saying and follow along with notes you should either keep the notes skimpy and give them ample space in the margins to jot in additional concepts, or you should pass out the written material section by section so that you have some control over when they receive it.[11]

Too many organizational advocates are sloppy and careless in the preparation of their visual aids. Take care to make your charts clear and easy to follow. Make certain that the photocopier does not cut off the bottom line that explains what the graph measures. Be sure that you catch your spelling errors. If your listeners become so preoccupied counting all of the misspelled words in your handouts they are not likely to hear what you have to say. Remember how important appearances are. If you seem polished, prepared, well dressed, and professional, your arguments are far more likely to be favorably received.

The Oral Presentation

Most oral presentations succeed or fail on the basis of the quality of preparation that has gone into them. The more time and attention that you devote to analyzing your proposition, developing your arguments, marshalling your evidence, structuring and writing the actual presentation, the better your talk will be. There are, however, some other tips that may be helpful.

First, familiarize yourself with the setting for the talk. If it is a conference room or auditorium, visit it and make sure that you can arrange where you will stand and how your visual aids will be placed so that they can be seen by all in attendance. Make certain that the room contains all of the equipment that you need (like overhead projectors) and that it all actually works. Nothing can be more unnerving than to devote hours to making transparencies that you cannot show because the bulb is burned out on the projector or someone has stolen the extension cord.

Second, construct your talk so that you tell them a story that has a beginning, a middle, and an end. This allows you to create a new scenario to explain how things will be different, to paint a future that contrasts with the status quo and with alternative stories and scenarios. Also, preface your story with an overview that lays out your objectives, so that your audience can see where you are going.

Third, consider preparing both long and short versions of your talk. Often presentations are scheduled in meetings at which several other persons are speaking. If their talks run long then you might find that you have only five minutes in which to make your fifteen-minute presentation. Be prepared with a shortened version, and also be prepared to request an opportunity to make the balance of the presentation at a later time.

Fourth, try to keep your presentation as brief as possible. The most frequently heard criticism of business presentations is that they run too long. Seek to determine how much background information your audience really needs and give them just that much. Try to confine your comments to those that are germane to your topic. Never talk for twenty-five minutes when a ten-minute talk will do the job.

Fifth, use humor. Do not try to be Jay Leno—no one expects you to keep them in stitches. But, on the other hand, people do like a little humor. If you do decide to attempt a joke, however, be sure that it is clean and inoffensive. Never tell an off color joke, especially not a joke which ridicules any persons, genders, or ethnic groups; such jokes only serve to embarrass their tellers.

Sixth, make sure that you encourage questions, and always try to leave time for them. Answering questions gives you an opportunity to further clarify your arguments, respond to potential misunderstandings, and to get feedback on how your audience sees your arguments. Often arguers communicate verbally that they are willing to answer questions, while nonverbally sending a message that they are reluctant to answer them. Be careful not to communicate that a question from your audience is stupid or ill informed, for nothing can discourage questions more effectively than a hostile reception. Avoid becoming defensive when asked a question that seems hostile to your position. Answer questions carefully and honestly. If you do not know the answer admit your ignorance. It is far better to admit that you do not know the answer than to make something up that might be wrong and might discredit your entire position. The best response may be: "I don't know the answer to that question right now, but allow me to do some research into it and get back to you." Having made such a commitment, however, be sure that you do in fact get back to the questioner with an answer.

Encountering Resistance

Organizational advocates often face **resistance** to their arguments. As we have already observed, organizations are composed of people with different opinions, interests, and objectives. There will probably be opposition to at least some of your arguments. However, if you carefully researched and prepared your presentation you may have anticipated this resistance and should also be prepared to respond to it.

First, stay calm. Opposition to your arguments is not the same as opposition to you as a person. It does not necessarily mean that the person who opposes you dislikes you, is out to get you, or wishes you to look bad. The more calm and cordial you are, the more likely it is that the disagreement can remain at a professional and respectful level. If you become antagonistic and personalize the opposition, you can expect that your counterpart will respond in kind. If you remain calm, friendly, and professional, your adversary probably will too. If someone is going to lose their temper and their calm, however, it is generally best if it is your adversary and not you.

Second, clarify your position. Sometimes people oppose arguments because of what they think they are hearing rather than what was in fact said. As a result, you may find that a mere clarification of your arguments mitigates the opposition. However, if the opposition is genuine, it still serves your interests and the interests of the decision maker, to fully understand the nature of the disagreement and what prompts it.

Be especially wary of cases in which your adversary gives a false reason for his or her opposition to your argument in a public setting. Often people are reluctant to state the true reasons for their objections to arguments (often referred to as a hidden agenda) because they fear that they will appear selfish, resistant to new ideas, or inflexible. In such situations you need to decide how direct you wish to be. Do you confront someone with your feelings that they are holding something back? Or do you play along, responding in kind by trying to defeat their public objections, and just hope for the best? There is no single right answer to such a problem; it depends on the situation and the persons involved.

Third, be prepared to add new evidence or analysis to support your arguments. Just as in an academic debate, in business or organizational arguments you should anticipate the refutation that your arguments might face and prepare answers to your opponent's arguments and extensions to your own positions. Don't merely retreat to your initial position or repeat your arguments when you are faced with opposition. Instead you should add to your arguments and strengthen them. Remember also the power of storytelling as a means of communication. Be prepared to expand your storyline to include new characters or actions. Think about the power of a shared story. We have been in meetings in which we were surrounded by statistical data that clearly suggested what the appropriate course of action should be, only to have someone in the meeting say: "let me tell you about the last time we attempted to do something similar. . . ." Suddenly this narrative account of shared historical experience becomes far more compelling evidence for which course of action should be followed than all of the statistical data that had been presented.

Fourth, when faced with what appears to be severe or intractable opposition you should seek to minimize the differences between your positions and rival positions. Avoid dichotomies and either-or language. Look for ways to make accommodations and adapt to other views. If **compromise** is possible and will not undercut your argument then offer compromise. Most decision makers are uncomfortable with conflict and resist making decisions that force them to support one strong-willed advocate while thwarting the will of another. Instead they prefer compromise and consensus. Remember also, if you can find a way to compromise your adversary just might come around to agree with the newly modified position. The more "buy in" you get for a decision the more likely people are to stand behind it and not to turn on you when something goes wrong.

Fifth, challenge your opponents to prepare and defend alternative positions. It is much easier to oppose and speak against change than it is to develop and advocate alternatives. Try to force your opponent to present alternatives, and then be prepared to refute them. Make the comparison between the two alternatives the focus of the discussion so that the decision maker can carefully weigh the benefits and disadvantages of the competing alternatives in making a decision.

Sixth, always be a graceful winner or loser. Organizations typically reward people who can get along with their peers and not cause problems. Do not flaunt your successes over those you may have vanquished and do not stew over your losses. Instead take them all in stride. Assume that during the course of a career you will have both wins and losses along the way.

Follow-up Activities

One of the most common problems in organizations is that people do not carefully follow through after a decision has been reached. If you win support for your arguments or concessions to your positions, for example, you should be careful to document what was decided and the commitments that were made to you. Send a memorandum back to the decision maker summarizing what you understood to be the results of the meeting and asking for a response to any portions of the memorandum that may not be accurate. Then keep a copy of the memorandum that you sent and any responses in your files. It is amazing how often commitments are "forgotten," but they are much more difficult to forget if there is a written record.

Second, take whatever actions are required of you personally and carefully document all of your activities. Ideally you should write progress reports to your supervisors keeping them posted on your activities and demonstrating that you are making progress toward whatever goals you may have set.

Third, schedule any required follow-up meetings as quickly as possible to demonstrate your commitment to this new project or proposal and to keep it fresh in people's minds. Don't let it fall between the cracks, or people will likely remember that they agreed to do something but it did not work—not that it failed due to lack of effort on their part.

Summary

Arguing in an organization is in many respects similar to arguing in any other context. People still evaluate arguments in narrative form, arguments need to be supported by evidence and analysis, careful preparation pays dividends, and decision makers typically act out of a sense of self-interest. The key difference in the organizational context is that the person you are trying to convince may also be the person who signs your paychecks. Consequently, in this context more than in almost any other, it is important that arguers not allow personal antagonisms to develop. A clear track record of thoughtful, polished, and professional argumentative presentations will be most helpful in convincing your superiors that you are indispensable to the organization and deserving of promotions.

Key Terms

coalitions	organizational cultures	resistance
compromise	power	visual aids
jargon		

Activities

1. Interview someone who holds a position in the profession you hope to enter when you have completed your education. How does he or she assess the organization's culture? What is this assessment based on? How does the organization's culture affect his or her daily life? Be sure to keep the answers confidential unless otherwise instructed.

2. Ask your instructors to reveal how they were taught the culture of their academic institution. Are there stories told that teach new faculty the organization's culture? Are there rituals that identify the institution's values?

3. Construct a hypothetical memorandum in which you present arguments to your boss for more resources. Be sure to consider the advice we presented in the "Preparing Your Arguments" and "Shaping the Message" sections of this chapter.

4. Have a friend or classmate engage in a role-playing exercise with you. Assume the roles of a subordinate and a superior. Have the subordinate orally present arguments for resources, or for a raise, and have the superior provide resistance to these arguments. Then reverse the roles.

Recommended Readings

Bennis, Warren. *On Becoming a Leader*. Reading, MA: Addison-Wesley, 1989.

Fisher, Roger, William Ury, and Bruce Patton. *Getting to Yes*. 2d ed. New York: Penguin Books, 1991.

Frost, Peter. "Power, Politics, and Influence." In Fred Jablin, Linda Putnam, Karleen Roberts and Lyman Porter, eds. *Handbook of Organizational Communication*. Newbury Park, CA: Sage, 1987. p. 518.

Graber, Doris A. *Public Sector Communication.* Washington, D.C.: Congressional Quarterly, 1992.

Hamilton, Cheryl. *Communicating for Results.* 4th ed. Belmont, CA: Wadsworth, 1993.

Neher, William W. and David H. Waite. *The Business and Professional Communicator.* Boston: Allyn and Bacon, 1993.

O'Hair, Dan and Gustav W. Friedrich. *Strategic Communication in Business and the Professions.* New York: Houghton Mifflin, 1992.

Pfeffer, Jeffrey. *Managing with Power: Politics and Influence in Organizations.* Boston: Harvard Business School Press, 1992.

Notes _____

1. Terrence Deal and Anthony Kennedy, *Corporate Cultures* (Reading, MA: Addison-Wesley, 1982), pp. 1–19.
2. Charles Perrow, *Complex Organizations: A Critical Essay,* 3d ed. (New York: Random House, 1986).
3. Gerald Goldhaber, *Organizational Communication,* 5th ed. (Dubuque, IA: W. C. Brown, 1990), pp. 255–256.
4. James Thompson, *Organizations in Action* (New York: McGraw-Hill, 1967).
5. Paul Krivonos, "Distortion of Subordinate to Superior Communication in Organizational Settings," *Central States Speech Journal* 33 (1982): 345–352.
6. John Gabarro and John Kotter, "Managing Your Boss," *Harvard Business Review* 58 (1980): 92–100.
7. Samuel B. Bacharach and Edward J. Lawler, *Power and Politics in Organizations* (San Francisco: Jossey-Bass, 1980), especially Chapter 4.
8. Gary L. Kreps, *Organizational Communication* (New York: Longman, 1986), pp. 43–44.
9. Patricia Andrews and John Baird, Jr. *Communication for Business and the Professions,* 5th ed. (Dubuque, IA: W. C. Brown, 1992), pp. 380–416.
10. Increased participation in organizational decision making also results in increased employee satisfaction, and decreased levels of job stress. See Eric M. Eisenberg and H.L. Goodall, Jr., *Organizational Communication: Balancing Creativity and Constraint* (New York: St. Martin's Press, 1993), p. 210.
11. Andrews and Baird, p. 408.

15

Argumentation in Interpersonal Relations

Disagreements are common in human interactions. The better we get to know someone, the easier it is to disagree with them. Upon just meeting someone, most of us are too polite to engage in open disagreement. As we come to know people better, however, we become more comfortable interacting with them, and our disagreements become easier to express.[1]

Many of us were taught to try to get along with others and avoid disagreements whenever possible. While it is sometimes necessary for us to express our disagreements, we do not wish to be seen as disagreeable. But not all disagreements should be perceived negatively; they are inevitable and many are important in the development of our relationships. Almost all healthy relationships will at some time or another experience conflict. Learning techniques for **conflict resolution** can actually lead to improved interpersonal relationships.[2]

This chapter will focus on how arguments develop and shape interpersonal communication interactions. Our focus is primarily on the process of arguing, and how this process can be conducted in such a way as to enhance and enrich our relationships with others. The chapter will discuss: the impact of arguing and conflict mediation on relationships, a conversational theory of argument, the relationship of argumentation style to self-esteem, and the importance of empathic listening.

In interpersonal relationships, as in other argumentation contexts, people engage in storytelling. They test the quality of claims by evaluating them as stories. One dimension of becoming an effective arguer in interpersonal conversation is learning to forcefully construct and share the stories that you believe to be true. Another dimension, however, is the ability to listen carefully and appreciatively to the stories that are told by others. Those with whom you differ are probably just as convinced that their stories are correct as you are that yours are correct. The world is filled with opposing stories, and with people who adhere to these different stories. Awareness of the theory of storytelling should help you to better understand how it is that people come to adhere to rival stories, and why not all people you meet agree with you.

Disagreements are typically expressed through arguments, and people argue to achieve at least three things in interpersonal interactions. First, people argue to reach decisions. When people have different opinions about what actions they should take, what values are most important, or even about factual statements, they usually attempt to resolve these differences through argumentation.

Second, arguments provide a means to manage interpersonal conflict and preserve the possibility of future social interactions. The alternative to resolving conflict through arguments is the use of coercion or force. Certainly having too many arguments can damage interpersonal relationships, but not nearly as much as having fistfights can undermine them.

Third, arguments are often about **power** in human relationships. Kenneth Burke wrote that people are "goaded by the spirit of hierarchy."[3] By this Burke meant that there is a certain hierarchical imperative that guides human symbolic action. All of us aim, in some way or another, to advance in the hierarchy, and consequently, all of us seek to be affirmed. We want to be perceived as knowledgeable, intelligent, and experienced, and we communicate these needs through the positions that we take and defend. While this hierarchical urge is certainly stronger in some persons than in others, and thus influences our symbolic choices differently, it is always a factor in human interactions.

Our goal should be to argue well, not just in the strategic sense of making strong and effective arguments, but also to conduct our arguments in a socially positive manner. Truly successful arguers have learned how to manage their disagreements so that they do not destroy friendships, prevent them from working with their colleagues, or result in marital separation and/or divorce. This chapter is intended to help you to understand the role that your **argument style** plays in shaping effective social interactions. We hope that by making you more aware of the ways in which arguments function in interpersonal interactions you will become more sensitive and self-monitoring in your own argument style and strategies, and more tolerant of the styles and strategies employed by others. In short, we wish to help you create and preserve positive social relationships.

In Chapter 1 we discussed Wayne Brockriede's theory of arguers as lovers, and the importance of avoiding coercive or exploitive argument styles. It is appropriate to begin this chapter by reemphasizing Brockriede's belief in the importance of creating positive and mutually reinforcing argument techniques:

> One does not pursue the art of being human by coercing others through superior power or by manipulating them by charm or deceit to gain adherence to propositions from powerless or naïve individuals. Instead, one seeks a dialogic acceptance of others as persons and develops a bilateral relationship by equalizing opportunities to express attitudes and intentions and by enhancing everyone's capacity for arguing.[4]

Just as some people may be more skilled than others in the strategic dimensions of arguing, likewise some people are also more skilled than others in the interpersonal and social dimensions of argumentation. Some individuals are so shy and reticent about expressing their opinions, and so eager to avoid conflict, that they are unable or unwilling to assert themselves or to stand up for their beliefs. These individuals may become like sheep, meekly going wherever they are led, simply because they lack the ability to effectively argue for their positions. Often these individuals have good ideas, but their reluctance to argue for them undermines their effectiveness and prevents them from having the influence that they should have in a group's decision making.

Other people are very forceful and dynamic, perhaps even overbearing, in stating their opinions and achieving their desired outcomes, but they leave many bruised egos, damaged self-concepts, and embittered enemies in their wake, because they do not use positive argument techniques. Sometimes these arguers also fail to influence decisions because people are so turned off by their argument style that they do not give the arguments themselves a fair hearing.

Effective interpersonal arguers realize that some arguments are not worth waging either because they are not winnable, or because any win would incur too high a cost. People should learn how to differ with others without destroying their friendships or work relationships with them. It is entirely possible to disagree in a socially acceptable fashion. It means focusing on issues and not the person, avoiding charged language, such as terms that are demeaning or designed to provoke; and by remaining calm and open to alternative ideas.

A Conversational Theory of Argument

Despite the fact that disagreements are inevitable in human social interactions, researchers who have studied everyday human conversations have generally found that most people seek to avoid disagreements. In fact, Sally Jackson and Scott Jacobs have suggested that the very nature of our language system discourages disagreements. Their research has demonstrated that arguments in everyday social conversations occur when one conversant or another violates an unstated but generally understood rule or convention in language. Specifically, Jackson and Jacobs introduced the notion of **adjacency pairs** to argumentation theory. These are linkages between types of statements that define their relationship to each other.[5] An adjacency pair might be said to exist when a first statement specifies, or calls for, a particular type of response. For example:

First paired-part	Second paired-part
REQUEST	GRANT/REFUSAL
QUESTION	ANSWER/REFUSAL TO ANSWER
BOAST	APPRECIATION/DERISION

In such adjacency pairs, the first paired-part (or statement) establishes a "next turn" position in the conversation because it solicits or expects a particular second paired-part response. Conversational disagreement, or arguments, occur when a first statement is comprehensible, but a *preferred* second paired-part (or response) is withheld.[6]

If, for example, a man asks the woman seated next to him for a date, he prefers to have his request met with an acceptance. If, on the other hand, the woman responds that she has other plans, and therefore signals her refusal with a *dispreferred* (undesired) response, then he can choose to ask for another evening, or mumble his regrets and slink away with as much of his pride intact as possible. On some occasions, hopefully rare, the woman may respond with an even more overtly dispreferred response. For example, she might say: "How can you even think to ask me out when you know that I have been seeing your best friend?" This response is not merely a refusal to the request, it is also an attack upon the man's character, his loyalty, and his commitment to his friend. Her conversational turn is directly confrontational, and it almost necessitates that he respond with a defense of some sort.

To further illustrate this process of conversational turn-taking, consider the following example:

Bob: The National League has always been tougher than the American League.

Steve: No way. The American League has better hitting; look at how much higher the batting averages are.

Bob: Their hitting is better because they feast on all that American League pitching. Look at how many home runs they give up in the American League.

Steve: Well those home runs are because American League pitchers have to face designated hitters who can hit the long ball rather than pitchers who can't even make contact with it.

Bob: Still, the National League has historically done better in the All-Star Game.

Steve: You're nuts! They got blown out this year, and they lost last year too.

Bob: Oh, yeah. I guess lately the American League is getting more respectable.

Steve: Wow, I can't believe you admitted even that much!

The above argument is typical of the kind of bantering that friends might engage in. Most conversations like this one are good-natured and even enjoyable to the participants The conversants were in disagreement as evidenced by the fact that they responded at several turns with dispreferred responses rather than with preferred responses, but in the end Bob acknowledges the superiority of Steve's position, and Steve acknowledges a sense of satisfaction with his win and with his continued good relationship with Bob. The conversation could, of course, proceed differently:

Steve: You're nuts! They got blown out this year, and they lost last year too.

Bob: Well that doesn't change my mind. I still think the National League is better.

Steve: Well, you certainly are entitled to your opinion. No one expects Giants' fans to be rational.

Bob: Well, Giants fans are every bit as rational as Brewers' fans.

In this example Bob refuses to acknowledge that Steve's arguments are powerful, and says that despite the facts and the quality of the arguments, he will not change his mind. Nonetheless, Steve decides that he is too fond of Bob to permit this refusal to stand in the way of their friendship. Rather than escalating the disagreement he avoids continued conflict and defuses the situation.

This conversation might, of course, have taken still a different turn:

Bob: Well you won't change my mind. I still think the National League is better.

Steve: Well, surprise, surprise, you're too bullheaded to listen to reason.

Bob: Oh sure, and you are always the reasonable one aren't you? You think you know everything.

Steve: Well at least I read the papers now and then, and know who wins and loses All-Star Games.

Bob: Well I am glad that you at least read the sports pages. I am sure the news features are too difficult for you to comprehend.

Steve: You're a jerk.

Bob: And you're an idiot.

This last conversation is, of course, far less pleasant than the two that preceded it. Neither speaker is willing to acknowledge the worth of the other's arguments, and neither views maintaining their friendship as sufficiently important, in the heat of the disagreement, that he is willing to modify his argument strategy. Consequently, a friendly and pleasant social interaction is permitted to become a hostile and quite unpleasant interaction. Such interactions are, of course, far too common, especially when the conversants are tired, insecure, angry, depressed, or developing their arguments through an alcohol-induced haze which diminishes their sense of judgment.

Jacobs and Jackson see conversational argument as a method for organizing our conversational activity and for managing these interactions.[7] In their research on conversational arguments, Pamela Benoit and William Benoit suggest that arguments will be enacted when people realize that two conversational pairs are in opposition to each other, and when they see the potential argument as worth the investment. They also say arguments are terminated when someone capitulates, when consensus or compromise is reached, or when escapes are enacted (someone departs, someone remains silent, or someone shifts the topic).[8]

Arguments occur, or do not occur, because individual advocates decide whether or not to pursue their differences. Some people are very reluctant to engage in arguments. Even when they sense that they disagree with someone they may decide that an argument is not worth the investment or the risk. This may be because they dislike conflict, it might be that they lack confidence in their own position or their argumentative ability, or perhaps because they do not wish to jeopardize their relationship with the other person. They may not wish to argue with a superior who might find ways to punish them. Other people may be very argumentative. These individuals are very willing, sometimes too willing, to engage in arguments, and may pursue these arguments with great intensity. Such people may lack the effective social judgment that is part of the self-monitoring process necessary for the maintenance of positive and rewarding social interactions.

Robert Trapp, in his discussion of arguments in interpersonal relations declares:

> Argument episodes begin when one or both participants perceive some kind of incompatibility. Sources of incompatibility range from attitudes to values, to behaviors. . . . Once arguers perceive an incompatibility of significant magnitude, they must decide whether or not to confront their partners. As long as the cost of confrontation appears to outweigh the costs of continued incompatibility, arguing is avoided. . . . Once arguers decide to confront each other, they need to develop the content of the arguments they will make and the strategies they will use. They must invent and edit the arguments and strategies they think will be most effective and appropriate in the situation. Since people can develop their arguments and strategies without conscious reflection, this process is frequently unconscious or mindless.[9]

Effective social arguers learn that the argumentative requirements and norms differ from situation to situation. One might employ very different argumentative strategies in an argument with one's lover than with a coworker or with one's superior. Regardless of the context for the argument, however, arguers need to avoid being hostile and demeaning in their interactions.

Dominic Infante has introduced the notion of **verbal aggression** to describe people who rely on character attacks, competence attacks, personal appearance attacks, insults, brutal teasing, ridicule, profanity, and threats in their argumentative interactions.[10] Infante believes that people rely on such aggressive and counterproductive argument techniques because of their psychopathology, their disdain for other people who hold different opinions, their social learning—the argument style practiced in their families when they were growing up, and because they lack the skills for effective argumentation.[11]

While awareness of argumentation techniques and strategies will not change people's personalities, cause them to be more understanding and loving, or make up for communication style characteristics shaped by their family upbringing, we can hope to achieve some improvement in interpersonal argumentation by teaching people better argumentation strategies.

Strategic Dimensions of Conversational Argument

One of the primary ways an arguer can avoid having disagreements disintegrate into episodes of verbal aggression is to focus on the issues and not the personalities or attributes of their opponents. Arguers should approach an argument in a conversation strategically, just as they should an argument in a more formal setting.

First, arguers should consider the likelihood that an argumentative resolution will be achievable. Is this an argument that I can win? Does a victory require that I change the other person's mind? What might be the repercussions if the conversation disintegrates into an argument episode? How might this affect our relationship? Is this issue sufficiently important that it is worth arguing over? Arguers should consider the fact that in unlike formal debate situations or courtroom settings, where winning means everything, in interpersonal arguments one can "win" and still lose. What good is securing a victory in an argument, if the person you have argued with sees you as a bully, refuses to be a friend, or comes to distrust or dislike you?

Effective interpersonal arguers should find ways to reach compromise and accommodation with their opponents and not merely to crush them in an outright victory. Are there ways in which the rival stories that are competing for acceptance can be made compatible, or at least can coexist with each other? Can my story be expanded to include alternative or rival stories? Can multiple stories coexist? Trying to adopt a win-win philosophy rather than a win-lose philosophy may help arguers to improve the quality of the decisions they reach. A decision reached through consensus is far more likely to be embraced, accepted, enacted, and even defended from attack by others, than is one that people feel has been forced upon them. Obviously it is not always possible to reach compromise and consensus. Some disputes (such as an argument between an abortion rights advocate and a pro-life advocate) are so intractable that people are not willing to surrender any ground, and rival stories cannot coexist. Nonetheless, in many circumstances the pursuit of inclusive stories and compromises preserves positive social relationships, and fosters a respect for the worth of alternative perspectives.

Second, once an arguer declares an argument to be worth waging, she or he should consider the source of the disagreement that has led to the conflict. Is the disagreement one that centers on differences in fundamental values? If so, this may limit the chances of your reaching a resolution. It will also influence your strategies in shaping your claim, and in responding to the claims advanced by the other person. Is the difference one of experience? If so, how can you help others to understand your experiences and how they influenced your opinions, especially if their experiences have been different? Likewise, how can you become sensitive to others' experiences? Is there appropriate evidence that you can muster to support your arguments? What evidence might be seen as credible and compelling? What stories do you share, and how can these shared stories be used as a resource? If you can figure out the essential causes for the differences being expressed, you might be in a better position to find a way to accommodate your story so that it is no longer incompatible with the opposing story.

Third, successful arguers must learn how to control their temper. When we are angry, or have decided that we do not care for someone, it is difficult for us to separate these feelings from our consideration of the issues in dispute. This is not to say that being angry is not sometimes an understandable, legitimate, or even a strategically useful device; it can be. But to be effective our anger should be controlled. Someone who is angry all of the time gets little if any strategic benefit from that anger, for it no longer serves to punctuate extremely important situations. On the other hand, an individual who very rarely exhibits anger will have a dramatic impact on a conversation through a carefully controlled and highly unusual display of temper. Such a display of anger might be noteworthy precisely because it seems to be out of character.

Argumentation and Self-Esteem

How people conduct themselves in interpersonal arguments says a great deal about how they conceive of themselves and of others. As we have already mentioned, our argument style may have been shaped by our formative interactions with our parents. For example, a child who grows up in a family in which conflict is expressed through very hostile and aggressive interactions, such as name calling and demeaning personal attacks, might be more likely to continue behaving in this way as an adult. Lacking role models to demonstrate more positive argument characteristics, he or she mirror the negative models that were provided.

People who have been demeaned and devalued by others' negative and verbally aggressive argument techniques may already suffer from diminished **self-esteem.** They may have been bruised and battered for so long that they have come to believe all of the disparaging things that have been said about them, and they now may lack confidence in their own worth. It is in such repetitive interactions—abuse decreases self-esteem, which leads to more abuse, which further reduces self-esteem—that problems like the battered spouse syndrome can develop.[12]

As Trapp has observed: "The way people argue carries important messages about their self-concepts, how they see each other, and how they see their relationship. Every argument episode is about some content, but in its shadow is a larger relational issue."[13]

Some of these relational issues are revealed in how the argument patterns of our loving relationships may change over time. All of us probably know couples, and some of you might have been in a relationship yourself, where there was a careful monitoring of communication behavior during the early formative stages of the relationship. Both people eagerly sought to please each other. They carefully monitored what they said, and they attempted not to anger, provoke, or hurt the feelings of the partner. Yet as the relationship developed, perhaps not until after they were engaged or married, their interest or willingness to monitor their communication diminished. Now they are far more willing to say what they really think, even at the risk of hurting the partner's feelings. To an extent this new honesty might be a desirable characteristic. They feel more comfortable in the relationship and as a result are more willing to be themselves. Yet it may also, if taken to an extreme, signal a serious deterioration of the loving relationship. People find that they monitor their comments less because they are becoming disinterested in the relationship and they are not willing to work as hard to preserve it.

In relationships such as the one which we have just described, we might see a quick deterioration. Every negative argumentative interaction may signal a willingness to be even more nasty and aggressive in the next interaction. If relationships continue to progress in this fashion people will probably eventually discover that they have fallen out of love and no longer even have the will or the energy to try to patch things up.

Arguers need to learn to express their feelings in such a way as to achieve their objectives in an argument. Do they want to change someone's opinion or behavior? Do they want to punish someone and hurt their feelings? Do they want to sabotage and help terminate a relationship? Often arguers will maintain that they only want to change someone's opinion, when in a subconscious way they may in fact be seeking to undermine their relationship. Arguers also need to consider how their relational partners are hearing and reacting to their arguments. We know that communication is a process, and that although we intend to say one thing, our listeners understand us to say something else. Many dysfunctional relationships develop because people become careless in framing their arguments and they are misunderstood as a result.

The Importance of Empathic Listening

Effective interpersonal arguers also need to develop their listening skills, and especially their capacity for **empathic listening.** It is often difficult in an argumentative situation, when our aggressive instincts are at work, when our energy level is high, and when our creative strategic senses are agitated, for us to listen at all, let alone to engage in empathic listening. Yet the most effective interpersonal arguers are those who have precisely this capability. Instead of listening to others with an eye toward refuting them, empathic listeners seek to genuinely understand where their fellow storytellers are coming from and why they are developing the arguments they are presenting. Empathic listeners are tolerant and patient, and they allow others the opportunity to develop their positions, and they give these positions careful consideration before forming their response to them.

Effective listeners are more likely to find ways to compromise, because they are less likely to speak without thinking, and to say things that they later regret. Empathic listeners communicate by their interest in hearing the alternative story that they are open to persuasion, that they respect their fellow arguers, and that they are reasonable people. Empathic listeners allow themselves more time to carefully and strategically weigh their responses to arguments, because they carefully consider the arguments made by others in the context of a search for a larger narrative.

Summary

There are no secrets to becoming an effective interpersonal arguer. The most important concepts have to do with understanding the larger narratives that characterize an individual's sense of self, of key values, and of his or her style of argumentation. Also important are the interpersonal skills of being polite, respectful of others, and tolerant of alternative perspectives and worldviews. For most of us this means working on developing good communication habits in all of our interactions. Some conversations will certainly go better than others, but by working to improve our interpersonal skills we can hopefully resolve our own argumentative deficiencies.

Our ability to argue effectively in interpersonal interactions is a measure of our ability to analyze the circumstances, avoid destructive interactions, and determine what techniques will lead to productive ones. The husband who knows how to communicate love and respect for his wife while also expressing his disagreements with her makes a better marriage partner. The boss who knows how to argue with a subordinate while demonstrating respect for his or her opinions is a better employer. The son who knows how to argue with his parents without communicating disrespect for them will continue to nurture a caring relationship. Our ability to reason—to use symbols to create and to evaluate the choices that are available to us—is our most important human capacity. It is a capacity that we should always be trying to develop and enhance, as we strive to create the good life that we all seek.

Key Terms

adjacency pairs	empathic listening	self-esteem
argument style	power	verbal aggression
conflict resolution		

Activities

1. An old but still effective means for improving your listening skills in interpersonal argument situations is to practice in the following manner: Have a friend or classmate enter a conversation with you on a subject where there is disagreement. After your friend speaks, you cannot respond with your own ideas until after you have paraphrased what your friend said. This paraphrase must be acceptable to your friend. Only then may you proceed with your comment. Similarly, before your friend may respond, your friend must paraphrase what you have said, to your satisfaction. While this process is arduous and cumbersome, it is effective at forcing us to listen empathically to one another.

2. A similar exercise calls upon interactants to label utterances and identify the preferred response before continuing the conversation. Thus, if one interactant

asks a question, the respondent would first identify the utterance as a question, then state that the preferred paired-part is an answer. The respondent could then answer as they wish. There is no requirement that the respondent provide the preferred paired-part because the purpose of the exercise is merely to reinforce the informal preferences which govern interpersonal argumentation, not to control the conversation.

3. Form three student interpersonal argument interaction triads. Two students participate in an interpersonal argument on a topic of their choice. The third student acts as an evaluator of the argument process. If the third student observes argumentative behavior that violates the norms of interpersonal argument, for example, an individual exhibits verbal aggressiveness, the student evaluator interrupts the conversation and indicates the norm which has been violated. The two student discussants cannot challenge the student evaluator, but must repair the conversation and proceed. After a predetermined time the role of student evaluator is rotated. The process continues until everyone has had a chance to participate as evaluator. The concluding segment of the exercise is to have all three students discuss the norms which were violated.

4. Have a classmate or friend engage in an argumentative interaction with you. Select a topic on which the two of you disagree. After about five minutes of argument, switch sides. In other words, if you were pro, you must now be con. Try your best to present as reasonable arguments as possible. After another five minutes, conclude your discussion by trying to reach a mutually agreeable resolution to the controversy. Does one side possess probable truth? Or does the other? Or is truth somewhere in between? Hopefully, you will learn to be less dogmatic in your views.

Recommended Readings _____

Benoit, Pamela J. "Orientation to Face in Everyday Argument." In Frans H. van Eemeren, Rob Grootendorst, J. Anthony Blair, and Charles Arthur Willard, eds. *Argumentation: Perspectives and Approaches.* Dordrecht, Holland: Foris, 1987. 144–152.

Benoit, Pamela J. and William L. Benoit. "To Argue or Not to Argue." In Robert Trapp and Janice Schuetz, eds. *Perspectives on Argumentation: Essays in Honor of Wayne Brockriede.* Prospect Heights, IL: Waveland, 1990. 55–72.

Canary, Daniel J. "Marital Arguments." In Robert Trapp and Janice Schuetz, eds. *Perspectives on Argumentation: Essays in Honor of Wayne Brockriede.* Prospect Heights, IL: Waveland, 1990. 73–85.

Jackson, Sally. "The Arguer in Interpersonal Argument: Pros and Cons of Individual Level Analysis." In David Zarefsky, Malcolm O. Sillars, and Jack Rhodes, eds. *Argument in Transition.* Annandale, VA: Speech Communication Association, 1983. 631–637.

Jacobs, Scott and Sally Jackson. "Conversational Argument: A Discourse Analytic Approach." In J. Robert Cox and Charles Arthur Willard, eds. *Advances in Argumentation Theory and Research.* Carbondale: Southern Illinois University Press, 1982. 205–237.

Jacobs, Scott and Sally Jackson. "Strategy and Structure in Conversational Influence Attempts." *Communication Monographs* 50 (1983): 285–304.

O'Keefe, Barbara J. and Pamela J. Benoit. "Children's Arguments." In J. Robert Cox and Charles Arthur Willard, eds. *Advances in Argumentation Theory and Research.* Carbondale: Southern Illinois University Press, 1982. 154–183.

Trapp, Robert. "The Role of Disagreement in Interactional Argument." *Journal of the American Forensic Association* 23 (1986): 23–41.

Notes

1. Joyce Hocker Frost and William W. Wilmot, *Interpersonal Conflict* (Dubuque, IA: W.C. Brown, 1978), especially Chapter 6.
2. Raymond Zeuschner, *Communicating Today* (Boston: Allyn and Bacon, 1992), p. 156.
3. Kenneth Burke, *Language as Symbolic Action* (Berkeley: University of California Press, 1966), p. 15.
4. Wayne Brockriede, cited in Robert Trapp and Janice Schuetz, eds., *Perspectives on Argumentation. Essays in Honor of Wayne Brockriede* (Prospect Heights, IL: Waveland, 1990), p. 41.
5. Sally Jackson and Scott Jacobs, "Structure of Conversational Argument: Pragmatic Bases for the Enthymeme," *Quarterly Journal of Speech* 66 (1980): 251–65.
6. Jackson and Jacobs, p. 253.
7. Sally Jackson and Scott Jacobs, p. 255.
8. William L. Benoit and Pamela J. Benoit, "Everyday Argument Practices of Naïve Social Actors," in Joseph W. Wenzel, ed., *Argument and Critical Practices* (Annandale, VA: Speech Communication Association, 1987), pp. 465–74.
9. Robert Trapp, "Arguments in Interpersonal Relations," in Robert Trapp and Janice Schuetz, eds., *Perspectives on Argumentation: Essays in Honor of Wayne Brockriede* (Prospect Heights, IL: Waveland, 1990), pp. 46–47.
10. Dominic Infante, *Arguing Constructively* (Prospect Heights, IL: Waveland Press, 1988), pp. 24–27.
11. Infante, p. 21.
12. For an excellent discussion of the development of self-concept see Ronald B. Levy, "Relationships Within the Self," in Joseph DeVito, ed., *Communication: Concepts and Processes* (Englewood Cliffs, NJ: Prentice-Hall, 1976): 227–237.
13. Trapp, p. 54.

Epilogue

As you have no doubt already recognized, this book about argumentation is itself an argument for a particular view of the argumentative process. Through reading this book you have learned something about us—the authors—our biases, our ideology, and our values, as well as about the subject matter we discussed. First, you have discovered that unlike many people, we are not averse to arguing. In fact, we are a couple of old debaters who enjoy the stimulation and challenge, indeed the sport, of a good argument. We believe that people can disagree yet nonetheless continue to like and respect each other, and to enjoy each other's company. Consequently, arguers need not approach arguments with a take-no-prisoners, win-at-all-costs attitude. Such an attitude will undermine the quality of the argumentative outcomes and needlessly destroy your relationships with others. Instead of trying to vanquish opponents, you should argue to try to achieve shared understanding.

Second, we are convinced that people are capable of making and evaluating well reasoned arguments. We are committed to the narrative or storytelling view of argumentation, and we believe that all people have the capacity to judge the quality of stories. We have confidence in the intellectual abilities and the goodwill of our fellow human decision makers. We see the creation and evaluation of arguments as an essential dimension of human social activity. People argue to reach decisions, to resolve problems, to influence others, and to improve the quality of their lives. These are worthwhile goals, and they could not be achieved without arguments.

Third, we believe that argumentation training can improve the quality of the public dialogue. While all of us are capable of evaluating narrative arguments and participating in public issues, many of us lack confidence in our argumentative abilities and in our opinions. We hope that exposure to the principles discussed in this book will enhance your confidence, empower you, and help you to find your voice so that you can more fully participate in public life. We want you to speak out about those issues that most concern you.

Fourth, while it is rewarding to succeed when we argue—all of us are gratified by victory—it is important that we define our successes with a long-term view. A short-term view focuses our attention on our immediate interests and gratifications. A long-term view reveals that it is sometimes not in our interest to pursue an argument; the personal and interpersonal costs might be too high. A long-term view helps us to understand that we are sometimes better off to lose an

233

argument rather than win one, and that we are often judged more by the way in which we conduct ourselves in argument than by our effectiveness in pleading our case.

In closing, we would remind you of Aristotle's declaration in Book I of the *Rhetoric:* "It is not true, as some writers assume in their treatises on rhetoric, that the personal goodness revealed by the speaker contributes nothing to the power of his [sic] persuasion; on the contrary, his character may almost be called the most effective means of persuasion he possesses."[1] As an advocate, your most precious asset is your reputation and your good name. Consequently, there can be no greater imperative for you to consider in forming your arguments than their ethical character.

Best wishes for your future arguments!

Note

1. *Rhetoric and Poetics of, Aristotle,* trans. W. Rhys Roberts. (New York: The Modern Library, 1954), p. 25.

Appendix A

Two Political Speeches

Bill Clinton,
Acceptance Speech for the Democratic Presidential Nomination,
New York City, July 16, 1992.

Tonight I want to talk with you about my hope for the future, my faith in the American people and my vision of the kind of country we can build together.

I salute the good men who were my companions on the campaign trail: Tom Harkin, Bob Kerrey, Doug Wilder, Jerry Brown and Paul Tsongas. One sentence in the platform we built says it all: "The most important family policy, urban policy, labor policy, minority policy and foreign policy America can have is an expanding, entrepreneurial economy of high-skill, high-wage jobs."

And so, in the name of all the people who do the work, pay the taxes, raise the kids and play by the rules—the hard-working Americans who make up our forgotten middle class, I accept your nomination for the presidency of the United States of America.

I am a product of America's middle class. And when I am your President you will be forgotten no more.

We meet at a special moment in history, you and I. The Cold War is over; Soviet Communism has collapsed, and our values—freedom, individual rights and free enterprise—have triumphed. And yet just as we have won the Cold War abroad, we are losing the battles for economic opportunity and social justice here at home. Now that we've changed the world, it's time to change America.

I have news for the forces of greed and the defenders of the status quo: your time has come . . . and gone. It's time for a change.

Tonight 10 million Americans are out of work. Tens of millions more work harder for less pay. The incumbent President says unemployment always goes up a little before we start a recovery. But unemployment only has to go up by one more person before we can start a real recovery—and, Mr. President, you are that man.

This election is about putting power back in your hands and putting government back on your side. It's about putting our people first.

You know, I've shared these thoughts with people all across America. But always someone comes back at me, as a young man did this week at the Henry Street Settlement on the Lower East Side of Manhattan: "That sounds good, Bill. But you're a politician. Why should I trust you?"

Tonight, I want to tell you, as plainly as I can, who I am, what I believe in and where I want to lead America.

I never met my father.

He was killed in a car wreck on a rainy road three months before I was born, driving home from Chicago to Arkansas to be with my mother.

After that, my mother had to support us. So I lived with my grandparents while she went away to study nursing in Louisiana.

I can still see her through the eyes of a 3-year-old: kneeling at the train station in New Orleans, waving goodby and crying as she put me on the train with my grandmother to go back home. She endured her pain because she knew her sacrifice was the only way she could support me and give me a better life.

My mother taught me. She taught me about family, hard work and sacrifice. She held steady through tragedy after tragedy. And she held our family, my brother and me, together through tough times. As a child, I watched her go off to work each day at a time when it wasn't very easy to be a working mother.

As an adult, I watched her fight off breast cancer. And again she taught me a lesson in courage. And always, always she taught me to fight.

That's why I'll fight to create high-paying jobs so that parents can raise their children in dignity. That's why I'm so committed to making sure every American gets the health care that saved my mother's life. And that's why I fight to make sure women in this country receive respect and dignity—whether they work in the home, out of the home, or both. You want to know where I get my fighting spirit? It all started with my mother.

When I think about opportunity for all Americans, I think of my grandfather.

He ran a country store in our little town of Hope. There were no food stamps back then, so when his customers—whether white or black—who worked hard and did the best they could came in with no money, he'd give them food anyway. Just made a note of it. So did I. Before I was big enough to see over the counter, I learned from him to look up to people other folks looked down on.

My grandfather had a grade-school education. But in that country store he taught me more about equality in the eyes of the Lord than all my professors at Georgetown; more about the intrinsic worth of every individual than all the philosophers at Oxford, and he taught me more about the need for equal justice than all the jurists at Yale Law School.

You want to know where I get my commitment to bringing people together without regard to race? It all started with my grandfather.

I learned a lot from another person, too. A person who for more than 20 years has worked hard to help our children. Paying the price of time to make sure our schools don't fail them. Who traveled our state—without a salary—for a year. Studying, learning, listening. Going to PTA meetings, school board meetings, town hall meetings. Putting together a package of school reforms recognized around the nation. Doing it all while building her own distinguished legal career and being a devoted and loving mother.

That person is my wife.

Hillary taught me. She taught me that all children can learn, and that every one of us has a duty to help them do it. You want to know why I'm so committed to children and their futures? It all started with my wife.

I'm fed up with politicians in Washington lecturing Americans about "family values." Our families have values. Our government doesn't.

I want an America where "family values" live in our actions, not just in our speeches. An America that includes every family. Every traditional family and every extended family. Every two-income family and every single-parent family, and every foster family.

I do want to say something to those parents who have chosen to abandon their children by neglecting their child support: Take responsibility for your children or we will force you to do it. Because governments don't raise children; parents do.

And I want to say something to every child who is trying to grow up without a father or a mother: I know how you feel. You're special, too. You matter. And don't let anyone ever tell you you can't become whatever you want to be. If the politicians who are lecturing you don't want you to be a part of their families, you can be a part of ours.

The thing that makes me angriest about what went wrong these last 12 years is that this government has lost touch with our values, while politicians continue to shout about them.

I was raised to believe that the American dream was built on rewarding hard work. But the folks in Washington have turned that American ethic on its head. For too long, those who play by the rules and keep the faith have gotten the shaft. And those who cut corners and cut deals have been rewarded. People are working harder than ever, spending nights and weekends on the job instead of at the Little League or the Scouts or the PTA. But their incomes are still going down, their taxes are going up and the costs of housing, health care and education are going through the roof. Meanwhile, more and more people are falling into poverty—even when they're working full-time.

People want change, but government is in the way. It has been hijacked by privileged, private interests. It has forgotten who really pays the bills around here—it's taking more of your money and giving you less in service.

We have got to go beyond the brain-dead politics in Washington, and give our people the kind of government they deserve: a government that works for them.

A President ought to be a powerful force for progress. But right now I know how President Lincoln felt when General McClellan wouldn't attack in the Civil War. He asked him: "If you're not going to use your army, may I borrow it?" George Bush: If you won't use your power to help people, step aside. I will.

Our country is falling behind. The President is caught in the grip of a failed economic theory. We've gone from first to 13th in the world in workers' wages. Four years ago, candidate Bush said America is a special place, not just "another pleasant country on the U.N. roll call, somewhere between Albania and Zimbabwe." Now, under President Bush, America has [become] an unpleasant economy stuck somewhere between Germany and Sri Lanka. And for most Americans, life's a lot less kind and a lot less gentle.

We've fallen so far, so fast that the prime minister of Japan actually said he felt "sympathy" for America. When I am your President, the rest of the world won't look down on us with pity. They'll look up to us with respect.

What is George Bush doing about America's economic problems? Well, he promised us 15 million new jobs by now. And he's over 14 million jobs short. We can do better.

He has raised taxes on the people who drive pickup trucks, and lowered taxes on people who ride in limousines. We can do better.

He promised to balance the budget, but he didn't even try. In fact, the budgets he submitted have nearly doubled the debt. Even worse, he wasted the money and reduced our investments in education and jobs. We can do better.

So if you're sick and tired of a government that doesn't work to create new jobs; if you're sick and tired of a tax system that's stacked against you; if you're sick and tired of exploding debt and reduced investments in our future—if, like the late civil rights pioneer Fannie Lou Hamer said, you're just plain sick and tired of being sick and tired—then join with us, work with us, win with us. Together, we can make the country we love, the country it was meant to be.

The choice you face is clear.

George Bush talks a good game. But he has no game plan to compete and win in the world economy. I do.

He won't take on the big insurance companies to lower costs and provide health care to all Americans. I will.

He won't streamline the federal government, and change the way it works; cut 100,000 bureaucrats, and put 100,000 more police on your streets. I will.

He never balanced a budget. I have. Eleven times.

He won't break the stranglehold special interests have on our elections and lobbyists have on our government. I will.

He won't give mothers and fathers a chance to take some time off from work when a baby's born or a parent is sick. I will.

He doesn't have a commitment to keep family farms in the family. I do.

He hasn't fought a real war on crime and drugs. I will.

He won't crack down on polluters, clean up the environment and take the lead on creating jobs in environmental technologies. I will.

He doesn't have Al Gore. I do.

And he won't guarantee a woman's right to choose. I will. Hear me now: I am not pro-abortion. I am pro-choice. I believe this difficult and painful decision should be left to the women of America. I do not want to go back to the time when we made criminals out of women and their doctors.

Jobs. Health care. Education. These commitments aren't just promises from my lips. They are the work of my life.

Our priorities must be clear: we will put our people first. But priorities without a clear plan of action are empty words. To turn our rhetoric into reality we have to change the way government does business—fundamentally. Until we do, we'll still be pouring billions of tax dollars right down the drain.

The Republicans have campaigned against big government for a generation. But they've run big government for a generation, and they haven't changed a thing—except from bad to worse. They don't want to clean out the bureaucracy; they just want to run against it.

But we Democrats have some changing to do too. It is time for us to realize that there is not a government program for every problem. And if we really want to use government to help people, we've got to make it work.

Because we are making those changes, we are, in the words of Ross Perot, a revitalized Democratic Party. I am well aware that those who rallied to his cause wanted to enlist in an army of patriots for change. We say to them: join us—together we will revitalize America.

I don't have all the answers. But I do know the old ways won't work. Trickle-down economics has failed. And big bureaucracies—public and private—have failed.

That is why we need a new approach to government. A government that offers more empowerment and less entitlement; more choices for young people in public schools and more choices for older people in long-term care. A government that is leaner, not meaner; that expands opportunity, not bureaucracy; that understands that jobs must come from growth in a vibrant and vital system of free enterprise. I call it a New Covenant—a solemn commitment between the people and their government—based not simply on what each of us can take but on what all of us must give to make America work again.

We offer our people a new choice based on old values. We offer opportunity. And we demand responsibility. The choice we offer is not conservative or liberal; Democratic or Republican. It is different. It is new. And it will work.

It will work because it is based on the vision and the values of the American people. Of all the things George Bush has done that I disagree with, perhaps the thing that bothers me most has been how he derides and degrades the American tradition of seeing—and seeking—a better future. He mocks it as "the vision thing." But remember what the Scripture says: "Where there is no vision, the people perish."

I hope you don't have to begin tomorrow without a vision. I hope you don't have to raise a child in this world without a vision. I hope you don't have to start a new business or plant a new crop without a vision. For where there is no vision, the people perish.

One of the reasons we have so many children in so much trouble in so many cities is because they have seen so little opportunity, so little responsibility and so little community that they literally cannot imagine the kind of life we are calling them to lead. Where there is no vision, the people perish.

What is the vision of our New Covenant?

An America with millions of new jobs in dozens of new industries moving confidently into the 21st Century. An America that says to entrepreneurs and business people: We will give you more incentives, more opportunity than ever before to develop the skills of your workers and create American jobs and wealth in the new global economy. But you must do your part; you must be responsible. American companies must act like American companies again—and export products, not jobs. That is what the New Covenant is all about.

An America in which the doors of college are thrown open once again to the sons and daughters of stenographers and steelworkers. We'll say: Everybody can borrow the money to go to college. But you must do your part. You must pay it back—from your paychecks, or, better yet, by going back home and serving your communities. We'll have millions of energetic young men and women serving their country, policing the streets, teaching the kids, caring for the sick, helping young people stay off drugs and out of gangs, giving us all a sense of new hope and limitless possibilities. That's what the New Covenant is all about.

An America in which health care is a right, not a privilege. In which we tell all our people: Your government will have the courage—finally—to take on the health care profiteers and make health care affordable for every family. But you must do your part: Preventive care and prenatal care and child immunization; saving lives and saving money and saving families from heartbreak. That's what the New Covenant is all about.

An America in which middle class families' incomes—not their taxes—are going up. And, yes, an America in which the wealthiest—those making over $200,000 a year—are asked to pay their fair share. An America in which the rich are not soaked—but the middle class is not drowning, either. Responsibility starts at the top; that's what the New Covenant is all about.

An America with the world's strongest defense; ready and willing to use force, when necessary. An America at the front of the new global effort to preserve and protect our natural environment—and promoting global growth. An America that will never coddle tyrants, from Baghdad to Beijing. An America that champions the cause of freedom and democracy, from Eastern Europe to Southern Africa, and in our own hemisphere in Haiti and Cuba.

The end of the Cold War requires us to reduce our defense spending. And we will plow those savings back into jobs right here at home. The world needs a strong America, and a strong America begins at home. That's what the New Covenant is all about.

An America where we end welfare as we know it. We will say to those on welfare: you have the opportunity through training and education, health care and child care, to liberate yourself. But then you have a responsibility to go to work. Welfare must be a second chance, not a way of life. That's what the New Covenant is all about.

It's time to heal our country.

So we will say to every American: Look beyond the stereotypes that blind us. We need each other. For too long politicians told most of us that what's wrong with America is the rest of us. Them. Them the minorities. Them the liberals. Them, them, them. But there is no them; there's only us. One nation, under God, indivisible, with liberty, and justice, for all.

How do I know we can come together to make change happen? Because I have seen it in my own state. In Arkansas we're working together and making progress. There is no Arkansas miracle. But there are a lot of miraculous people. Good people, pulling together. Because of them, our schools are better, our wages are higher, our factories are busier, our water is cleaner and our budget is balanced. We're moving ahead.

I wish I could say the same thing about America under the incumbent President. He took the richest country in the world and brought it down. We took one of the poorest states in America and lifted it up.

And so I say to those who would criticize Arkansas: come on down. Especially if you're from Washington—come to Arkansas. You'll see us struggling against some problems we haven't solved yet. But you'll also see a lot of great people doing amazing things. And you might even learn a thing or two.

In the end, the New Covenant simply asks us all to be Americans again. Old-fashioned Americans for a new time. Opportunity. Responsibility. Community. When we pull together, America will pull ahead. Throughout the whole history of this country, we have seen time and again that when we are united, we are unstoppable. We can seize this moment, we can make it exciting and energizing and heroic to be an American again. We can renew our faith in ourselves and each other, and restore our sense of unity and community. Scripture says, our eyes have not yet seen, nor our ears heard nor our minds imagined what we can build.

But I cannot do it alone. No President can. We must do it together. It won't be easy and it won't be quick. We didn't get into this mess overnight, and we won't get out of it overnight. But we can do it. With our commitment and our creativity and our diversity and our strength. I want every person in this hall and every citizen in this land to reach out and join us in a great new adventure to chart a bold new future.

As a teenager I heard John Kennedy's summons to citizenship. And then, as a student at Georgetown, I heard that call clarified by a professor I had, named Carroll Quigley, who said America was the greatest country in the history of the world because our people have always believed in two great ideas: first, that tomorrow can be better than today, and, second, that each of us has a personal, moral responsibility to make it so.

That future entered my life the night our daughter, Chelsea, was born. As I stood in that delivery room, I was overcome with the thought that God had given me a blessing my own father never knew: the chance to hold my child in my arms.

Somewhere at this very moment, another child is born in America. Let it be our cause to give that child a happy home, a healthy family, a hopeful future. Let it be our cause to see that child reach the fullest of her God-given abilities. Let it be our cause that she grow up strong and secure, braced by her challenges, but never, never struggling alone; with family and friends and a faith that in America, no one is left out; no one is left behind.

Let it be our cause that when she is able, she gives something back to her children, her community and her country. And let it be our cause to give her a country that's coming together, and moving ahead—a country of boundless hopes and endless dreams; a country that once again lifts up its people, and inspires the world.

Let that be our cause and our commitment and our New Covenant.

I end tonight where it all began for me: I still believe in a place called Hope.

George Bush,
Acceptance Speech for the Republican Presidential Nomination,
Houston, August 20, 1992.

Thank you. Thank you, thank you very much. I am proud to receive, and I am honored to accept your nomination for President of the United States.

My job has been made easier by a leader who has taken a lot of unfair criticism, with grace and humor—Vice President Dan Quayle. I want to talk tonight about the sharp choice I intend to offer Americans this fall—a choice between different agendas, different directions, and, yes, a choice about the character of the man you want to lead this nation.

I know that Americans have many questions—about our economy, about our country's future, even questions about me. I will answer them tonight.

First, I feel great and I am heartened by the polls—the ones that say that I look better in my jogging shorts than the governor of Arkansas.

Four years ago, I spoke about missions—for my life and for our country. I spoke of one urgent mission—defending our security and promoting the American ideal abroad.

Just pause for a moment to reflect on what we've done.

Germany has united—and a slab of the Berlin Wall sits right outside this Astrodome.

Arabs and Israelis now sit face to face and talk peace.

Every hostage held in Lebanon is free.

The conflict in El Salvador is over, and free elections brought democracy to Nicaragua.

Black and white South Africans cheered each other at the Olympics.

The Soviet Union can only be found in history books.

The captive nations of Eastern Europe and the Baltics are captive no more.

And today on the rural streets of Poland, merchants sell cans of air labeled: The last breath of communism.

If I had stood before you four years ago and described this as the world we would help to build, you would have said: "George Bush, you must be smoking something, and you must have inhaled."

This convention is the first at which an American President can say the Cold War is over, and freedom finished first.

Some want to rewrite history, want to skip over the struggle, claim the outcome was inevitable. And while the U.S. post-war strategy was largely bipartisan, the fact remains that the liberal, McGovern wing of the other party—including my opponent—consistently made the wrong choice.

In the '70s, they wanted a hollow army—we wanted a strong fighting force.

From Angola to Central America they said, "Let's negotiate, deliberate, procrastinate." We said, "Just stand up for freedom."

Now the Cold War is over and they claim, "Hey, we were with you all the way." Their behavior reminds me of the old con man's advice to the new kid. He said, "Son, if you're being run out of town, just get out in front and make it look like a parade."

Make no mistake, the demise of communism wasn't a sure thing. It took the strong leadership of presidents from both parties, including Republicans like Richard Nixon, Gerald Ford and Ronald Reagan. Without their vision and the support of the American people, the Soviet Union would be a strong superpower today and we'd be facing a nuclear threat tonight.

My opponents say I spend too much time on foreign policy.

As if it didn't matter that schoolchildren once hid under their desks in drills to prepare for nuclear war. I saw the chance to rid our children's dreams of the nuclear nightmare, and I did. Over the past four years, more people have breathed the fresh air of freedom than in all of human history. I saw a chance to help, and I did. These were the two defining opportunities—not of a year, not of a decade, but of an entire span of human history.

I seized those opportunities for our kids and our grandkids, and I make no apologies for that.

Now, the Soviet bear may be gone, but there are still wolves in the woods.

We say that when Saddam Hussein invaded Kuwait. The Mideast might have become a nuclear powder keg, our emergency supplies held hostage. So we did what was right and what was necessary. We destroyed a threat, freed a people and locked a tyrant in the prison of his own country.

What about the leader of the Arkansas National Guard, the man who hopes to be commander-in-chief? Well, while I bit the bullet, he bit his nails.

Two days after Congress voted to follow my lead, my opponent said this, and I quote: "I guess I would have voted with the majority if it was a close vote. But I agree with the arguments the minority made."

Sounds to me like his policy can be summed up by a road sign he's probably seen on his bus tour, "Slippery When Wet."

But this is serious business. Think about the impact of our foreign policy failures the last time the Democrats controlled both ends of Pennsylvania Avenue. Gas lines. Grain embargoes. American hostages blindfolded.

There will be more foreign policy challenges like Kuwait in the next four years. Terrorists and aggressors to stand up to; dangerous weapons to be controlled and destroyed. And freedom's fight is not finished. I look forward to being the first President to visit a free, democratic Cuba.

Who will lead the world in the face of these challenges? Not my opponent. In his acceptance speech he devoted just 65 seconds to telling us about the world.

Then he said that America was, and I quote, being "ridiculed" everywhere. Tell that to the people around the world for whom America is still a dream. Tell that to leaders around the world from whom America commands respect. "Ridiculed?" Tell that to the men and women of Desert Storm.

Let me make an aside. This is a political year, but there's a lot of danger in the world. You can be sure, I will never let politics interfere with a foreign policy decision. Forget the election: I will do what's right for our national security.

Fifty years ago this summer, I was 18 years of age. I believed deeply in this country, and we were faced with a world war. So I made a decision, to go off and fight a battle much different from political battles.

I was scared, but I was willing. I was young, but I was ready. I had barely lived when I began to watch men die. I began to see the special place of America in the world, and I began to see, even then, that the world would become a much smaller place, and faraway places could become more and more like America.

Fifty years later, after change of almost biblical proportions, we know that when freedom grows, America grows. Just as a strong America means a safer world, we have learned that a safer world means a stronger America.

This election is about change. But that's not unusual, because the American revolution is never ending. Today, the pace of change is accelerating. We face new opportunities and new challenges. The question is—who do you trust to make change work for you?

My opponent says America is a nation in decline. Of our economy he says, we are somewhere on the list beneath Germany, heading south toward Sri Lanka.

Well, don't let anyone tell you that America is second-rate, especially somebody running for President.

Maybe he hasn't heard that we are still the world's largest economy. No other nation sells more outside its borders. The Germans, the British, the Japanese—can't touch the productivity of you—the American worker and the American farmer.

My opponent won't mention that. He won't remind you that interest rates are the lowest they've been in 20 years, and millions of Americans have refinanced their homes. And you just won't hear that inflation—the thief of the middle class—has been locked in a maximum security prison.

You don't hear much about this good news, because the media also tends to focus only on the bad. When the Berlin Wall fell, I half expected to see a headline: "Wall Falls, Three Border Guards Lose Jobs." And underneath it probably says: "Clinton Blames Bush."

You don't hear a lot about progress in America. So let me tell you about some good things we've done together.

Just two weeks ago, all three nations of North America agreed to trade freely from Manitoba to Mexico. This will bring good jobs to Main Street, U.S.A.

We passed the Americans with Disabilities Act—bringing 43 million people into the economic mainstream. I must say, it is about time.

Our children will breath easier because of our new Clean Air Act.

We are rebuilding our roads, providing jobs for more than half a million Americans.

We passed a child care law, and we took a stand for family values by saying that when it comes to raising children, government doesn't know best, parents know best.

I've fought against prejudice and anti-Semitism all my life. And I am proud that we strengthened our civil rights laws—and we did it without resorting to quotas.

One more thing. Today, cocaine use has fallen by 60% among young people. To the teen-agers, the parents and the volunteers who are helping us battle the scourge of drugs in America: We thank you.

Do I want to do more? You bet. Nothing hurts me more than to meet with soldiers home from the Persian Gulf who can't find a job. Or workers who have a job, but worry that the next day will bring a pink slip. And what about parents who scrape and struggle to send their kids to college, only to find them back living at home because they can't get work.

The world is in transition, and we are feeling that transition in our homes.

The defining challenge of the '90s is to win the economic competition—to win the peace.

We must be a military superpower, an economic superpower, and an export superpower.

In this election, you'll hear two visions of how to do this. Theirs is to look inward and protect what we already have. Ours is to look forward, to open new markets, prepare our people to compete, to restore our social fabric—to save and invest—so we can win.

We believe that now that the world looks more like America, it is time for America to look more like herself.

And so we offer a philosophy that puts faith in the individual, not the bureaucracy. A philosophy that empowers people to be their best, so America can be at its best. In a world that is safer and freer, this is how we will build an America that is stronger, safer and more secure.

We start with a simple fact: Government is too big and spends too much.

I've asked Congress to put a lid on mandatory spending except Social Security. And I've proposed doing away with over 200 programs and 4,000 wasteful projects and to freeze all other spending.

The gridlocked Democrat Congress has said, "No."

So, beginning tonight, I will enforce the spending freeze on my own. If Congress sends me a bill spending more than I asked for in my budget, I will veto it fast—faster than copies of Millie's book sold.

Congress won't cut spending, but refused to give the President the power to eliminate pork barrel projects that waste your money. Forty-three governors have that power. So I ask you, the American people: Give me a Congress that will give me the line-item veto.

Let me tell you about a recent battle I fought with Congress. This spring, I worked day and night to get two-thirds of its members to approve a balanced budget amendment to the Constitution.

We almost had it, but we lost by just nine votes. Listen how. Just before the vote, the liberal leaders of Congress convinced 12 members who co-sponsored the bill to switch sides and vote no. Keep in mind, they voted against a bill they had already put their names on.

Something fishy going on? Well, look at my opponent on this issue. He says he's for balanced budgets. But he came out against the amendment. He's like that on a lot of issues, first one side, then the other. He's been spotted in more places than Elvis Presley.

After all these years, Congress has become pretty creative at finding ways to waste your money. So we need to be just as creative at finding ways to stop them. I have a brand new idea.

Taxpayers should be given the right to check a box on their tax returns, so that up to 10% of their payments can go for one purpose alone: To reduce the national debt.

But we also need to make sure that Congress doesn't just turn around and borrow more money, to spend more money. So I will require that, for every tax dollar set aside to cut the debt, the ceilings on spending will be cut by an equal amount. That way, we'll cut both debt and spending, and take a whack out of the budget deficit.

My feelings about big government come from my experience; I spent half my adult life in the private sector. My opponent has a different experience—he's been in government nearly all his life. His passion to expand government knows no bounds.

He's already proposed $220 billion in new spending, along with the biggest tax increase in history—$150 billion—that's just to start.

He says he wants to tax the rich but, folks, he defines rich as anyone who has a job.

You've heard of the separation of powers. My opponent practices a different theory: "The power of separation." Government has the power to separate you from your wallet.

When it comes to taxes, I've learned the hard way.

There's an old saying: Good judgment comes from experience, and experience comes from bad judgment."

Two years ago, I made a bad call on the Democrats' tax increase. I underestimated Congress' addiction to taxes. With my back against the wall, I agreed to a hard bargain: One tax increase one time, in return for the toughest spending limits ever.

Well, it was a mistake to go along with the Democratic tax increase. But here's my question for the American people. Who do you trust in this election? The candidate who raised taxes one time and regrets it, or the other candidate who raised taxes and fees 128 times, and enjoyed it every time?

When the new Congress convenes, I will propose to further reduce taxes across the board—provided we pay for these cuts with specific spending reductions that I consider appropriate, so that we do not increase the deficit. I will also continue to fight to increase the personal exemption and to create jobs by winning a cut in capital gains taxes.

That will especially help small businesses. They create two-thirds of the new jobs in America. But my opponent's plan for small business is clear, present—and dangerous. Besides new income taxes, his plan will lead to a new payroll tax to pay for a government takeover of health care, and another new tax to pay for training. That's just the beginning.

If he gets his way, hardware stores across America will have a new sign up: "Closed for despair." I guess you'd say his plan really is "Elvis economics." America will be checking into the "Heartbreak Hotel."

I believe small business needs relief—from taxation, regulation and litigation.

I will extend for one year the freeze on paperwork and unnecessary federal regulation that I imposed last winter. There is no reason that federal regulations should live longer than my friend George Burns. I will issue an order—to get rid of any rule whose time has come—and gone.

I see something happening in our towns and in our neighborhoods. Sharp lawyers are running wild. Doctors are afraid to practice medicine. And some moms and dads won't even coach Little League anymore. We must sue each other less—and care for each other more. I'm fighting to reform our legal system, to put an end to crazy lawsuits. If that means climbing into the ring with the trial lawyers, well, let me just say, Round 1 starts tonight.

After all, my opponent's campaign is being backed by practically every trial lawyer who ever wore a tasseled loafer. He's not in the ring with them, he's in the tank.

There are other things we need to do to get our economy up to speed—and prepare our kids for the next century.

We must have new incentives for research, and new training for workers. Small businesses need capital and credit, and defense workers need new jobs.

And I have a plan to provide affordable health care for every American, controlling costs by cutting paperwork and lawsuits, and expanding coverage to the poorest of the poor.

We don't need my opponent's plan for a massive government takeover of health care, which would ration care and deny you the right to choose your doctor. Who wants a health care system with the efficiency of the House post office, and the compassion of the KGB?

What about our schools? My opponent and I both want to change the way our kids learn. He wants to change our schools a little bit—and I want to change them a lot.

Take the issue of whether parents should be able to choose the best school for their kids. My opponent says that's OK—as long as the school is run by government. I say every parent and child should have a real choice of schools—public, private or religious.

So we have a clear choice to fix our problems. Do we turn to the tattered blanket of bureaucracy that other nations are tossing away? Or do we give our people the freedom and incentives to build security for themselves?

Here is what I'm fighting for:

—Open markets for American products.

—Lower government spending.

—Tax relief.

—Opportunities for small business.

—Legal and health reform.

—Job training.

—And new schools built on competition, ready for the 21st Century.

Why are these proposals not in effect today?

Only one reason—the gridlock Democratic Congress.

Now, I know Americans are tired of the blame game, tired of people in Washington acting like they are candidates for the next episode of American Gladiators.

I don't like it, either. Neither should you. But the truth is the truth. Our policies haven't failed—they haven't been tried.

Americans want jobs. On January 28, I put before Congress a plan to create jobs. If it had been passed back then, 500,000 more Americans would be at work right now. But in a nation that demands action, Congress has become the master of inaction.

It wasn't always this way. I served in Congress 22 years ago. Back then, we cooperated; we didn't get personal. We put the people above everything else.

At my first inauguration I said that people didn't send us to bicker. I extended my hand to the Democratic leaders—and they bit it.

The House leadership has not changed in 38 years. It is a body caught in a hopelessly tangled web of PACs, perks, privileges, partisanship and paralysis. Every day, Congress puts politics ahead of principle and above progress.

Let me give you just one example. February 20, 1991. It was the height of the Gulf War. On that very same day, I asked American pilots to risk their lives to fly missions over Baghdad. I also wanted to strengthen our economic security for the future. So that same day, I introduced a new domestic energy strategy which would cut our dependence on foreign oil by 7 million barrels a day.

How many days did it take to win the Gulf War? Forty-three. How many days has it taken Congress to pass a national energy strategy? Five hundred and thirty-two—and still counting.

Where does my opponent stand with Congress? Well, up in New York at their convention, they kept the congressional leaders away from the podium, hid them away.

They didn't want America to hear from the people who really make the decisions.

They hid them for a very good reason—because the American people would recognize a dangerous combination: A rubber check Congress—and a rubber stamp President.

Governor Clinton and Congress know that you've caught on to their lingo. They know when they say "spending" you say "oh, oh." So now they have a new word, "investment." They want to "invest" $220 billion more of your money—but I want you to keep it.

Governor Clinton and Congress want to put through the largest tax increase in history, but I won't let it happen.

Governor Clinton and Congress don't want kids to have the option of praying in school, but I do. Clinton and Congress don't want to close legal loopholes and keep criminals behind bars, but I will. Clinton and Congress will stock the judiciary with liberal judges who write laws they can't get approved by the voters.

Governor Clinton even says that Mario Cuomo belongs on the Supreme Court. If you believe in judicial restraint, you probably ought to be happy. After all, the good governor of New York can't make up his mind between chocolate and vanilla at Baskin Robbins. We won't have another court decision for 35 years.

Are my opponent and Congress really in cahoots? Look at one important question: Should we limit the terms of Congress? Governor Clinton says: "No." Congress says no. I say: "Yes."

We tried this once before, combining the Democratic governor of a small Southern state with a very liberal vice president and a Democratic Congress. America doesn't need: "Carter II."

We don't want to take America back to those days of malaise. But Americans want to know—where's the proof that we will have better days in Washington?

I'll give you 150 reasons. That's how many members of Congress are expected to leave this year. Some are tainted by scandal—the voters have bounced them the way they bounced their own checks. But others are good members. Republican and Democrat. They agree with me. The place just doesn't work any more.

One hundred fifty new members—from both parties—will be coming to Washington this fall. Every one will have a fresh view of America's future.

I pledge today to the American people, immediately after this election, I will meet with every one of these new members, before they get attacked by the PACs, overwhelmed by their staffs and cornered by a camera crew. And I will lay out my case, our case, for change. Change that matters, real change that makes a difference. Change that is right for America.

You see, there is a yearning in America, a feeling that maybe it's time to get back to our roots.

Sure we must change, but some values are timeless. I believe in families that stick together, and fathers who stick around. I happen to believe very deeply in the worth of each individual human being, born or unborn. I believe in teaching our kids the difference between what's wrong and what's right, teaching them respect for hard work and to love their neighbors. And I believe that America will always have a special place in God's heart, as long as He has a special place in ours. And maybe that's why I've always believed that patriotism is not just another point of view.

There are times in every young person's life when God introduces you to yourself. I remember such a time. It was back many years ago, when I stood watch at 4 a.m., up on the bridge of the USS Finback. I would stand there and look out on the blackness of the sky, broken only by the sparkling stars above. I would think about friends I lost, a country I loved and about a girl named Barbara. I remember those nights as clearly as any in my life.

You know, you can see things from up there that other people don't see. You can see storm clouds rise and then disappear. The first hint of the sun over the horizon and the first outline of the shore faraway.

Now, I know Americans are uneasy today. There is anxious talk around our kitchen tables. But from where I stand, I see not America's sunset, but a sunrise.

The world changes for which we've sacrificed for a generation have finally come to pass—and with them a rare and unprecedented opportunity—to pass the sweet cup of prosperity around our American table.

Are we up to it? I know we are. As I travel our land, I meet veterans who once worked on the turrets of a tank and can now master the keyboards of a high-tech economy. I see teachers, blessed with the incredible American capacity for innovation, who are teaching our children a new way to learn for a new century. I meet parents, some working two jobs with hectic schedules, who still find new ways to teach old values to steady their kids in a turbulent world.

I take heart from what is happening in America, not from those who profess a new passion for government, but from those with an old and enduring faith in human potential. Those who understand that the genius of America is our capacity for rebirth and renewal. America is the land where the sun is always peeking over the horizon.

Tonight I appeal to the unyielding, undying, undeniable American spirit. I ask you to consider, now that the entire world is moving our way, why would we want to go back their way? I ask not just for your support for my agenda, but for your commitment to renew and rebuild our nation—by shaking up the one institution that has withstood change for over four decades.

Join me in rolling away the roadblock at the other end of Pennsylvania Avenue, so that in the next four years, we will match our accomplishments outside by building a stronger, safer, more secure America inside.

Forty-four years ago—in another age of uncertainty—a different President embarked on a similar mission. His name was Harry S. Truman.

As he stood before his party to accept their nomination, Harry Truman knew the freedom I know this evening, the freedom to talk about what's right for America and let the chips fall where they may.

Harry Truman said: "This is more than a political call to arms. Give me your help, not to win voters alone, but to win this new crusade and keep America safe and secure for its own people."

Tonight I say to you—join me in our crusade to reap the rewards of our global victory, to win the peace, so that we may make America safer and stronger for all our people.

Appendix B

Value Debate Transcript

Final Round of the 1993 Cross Examination Debate Association*

This transcript of an academic debate is included so that you may gain a greater understanding of the process of arguing in this specialized context. The resolution is one of value. The outcome of the debate determined the championship team in CEDA debate for the 1992–1993 academic year.

What you will read is the verbatim transcript as it was spoken by the debaters. Although the participants in this debate are experienced speakers, the extemporaneous format, the specialized training of the audience, and the intense pressures of competing for the national championship result in some errors in evidence citation and presentation. Bracketed material was not presented by the speakers. Obvious errors of redundancy were deleted. Full source citations are presented at the end of the transcription.

The Teams

Affirmative: Kansas State University (K. J. Wall and Jill Baisinger)
Negative: Emporia State University (Greg Achten and Jim Haefele)

The Resolution

Resolved: That United Nations implementation of its Universal Declaration of Human Rights is more important than preserving state sovereignty.

First Affirmative Constructive: K. J. Wall

Now. Let's begin. Jill and I support case. Observation One is our definitions. Initially, implementation is defined by Vincent in 1986:

> What is called implementation of international human rights instruments is not the kind of process that one associates with a civil service carrying out the will

*Transcribed and verified by Patrick M. Jablonski, University of Alabama.

of an elected government. What is most commonly meant by implementation, in the United Nations context, is a system whereby states' parties to conventions report on their fidelity to their engagements, and then a peer group reviews the reports according to procedures varying with the instruments. Finally, recommendations to the states' parties will follow, and, international conciliation to resolve a particular problem. (1AC#1)

Thus, promoting a climate that allows the realizations of some of the rights in the declaration constitutes implementation. We think these violations are quite explicit with the torture, et cetera, occurring in El Salvador.

Now, sovereignty is defined as total independence of the state, as Raymond explains in 1992:

> Sovereignty is total and unreserved independence of a state; or a state able to make its decisions without outside influence. (1AC#2)

Finally, the resolutional context requires that investigation occur on a case by case and consensual basis.

Alvoro DeSoto, a UN mediator and negotiator explained in the *Is There a Transition to Democracy in El Salvador?* 1992:

> For the United Nations to get involved in an internal conflict there would have to be agreement on the part of the government of the country concerned to invite the United Nations to become involved in one way or another. And it would have to be on a case by case basis. (1AC#3)

Observation Two describes the conflict in El Salvador. For almost a decade, El Salvador has been ravaged by a brutal civil war which has left the nation embattled. Roberto Meza, writing in the book *Is There a Transition to Democracy in El Salvador?* explains in 1992:

> The cost of the war has been extremely high: More than 75,000 lives have been lost; hundreds of thousands have been injured and maimed; half a million people have been displaced from their homes in El Salvador; about one million people have been forced to flee the country and live as refugees. For those remaining in El Salvador, damage from the war has resulted in a substantially lower quality of life. (1AC#4)

Now, the terrible cost of the war created conditions that ultimately forced a negotiated settlement. UN negotiator DeSoto states in 1992:

> Both sides have come to the recognition that military victory is not possible [and] if it is possible, that it is only possible at an unbearable cost. This realization has been an important factor in making the negotiations possible. (1AC#5)

Now, independently, at the request of both sides, the consensual arrangement, the United Nations . . . has stepped in to mediate the dispute. The United Press International documented this fact in December of 1992:

> The UN was called in to help end the conflict 32 months ago after 10 years of fighting between the FMLN and the US-backed Salvadoran army failed to give either side a decisive military advantage. (1AC#6)

In July of 1990, the government and the FMLN signed an accord which submitted all phases of the peace process to UN verification. Joseph Tulchin, director of Latin American Program, explains in 1992:

By July 26 of 1990, in San Jose, Costa Rica, the FMLN and the Cristiani government completed in a landmark accord for the protection of human rights that provided for a United Nations mission to verify not only respect for human rights but also all other agreements reached. (1AC#7)

Now, what's at issue now is not the original UN involvement. The real question is whether the United Nations should remain in El Salvador to implement and fully implement the peace accords. Latin American scholar Gary Bland explains in 1992:

The series of agreements reached by the Cristiani government and the FMLN touch on all areas of society, including human rights protections, reforms in the judicial and electoral system, reduction of armed forces, creation of a new national civilian police force, economic and social policy changes, and the disarmament of the FMLN. The full implementation of these measures is critical to the country's future. The importance of the political and financial commitments of the United Nations and the international parties to ensuring that they are respected cannot be underestimated. (1AC#8)

Finally, in this observation, we note that this oversight, like several other operations currently in process, involves United Nations intrusion in El Salvador's internal conduct, thus violating at face value a sovereignty violation. *Los Angeles Times* reporter Stan Meisler explains in November 17 of 1992:

The operation in El Salvador, like a similar arrangement in Cambodia, involves an unprecedented level of UN involvement in a country's internal affairs. (1AC#9)

Contention One: Implementation of the peace accords is crucial for El Salvador. Initially, we note the decade of terror is not yet over, as a November human rights report by the United Nations suggests that abuses are continuing. The InterPress Service reports in November 1992:

The document notes that death squad activities have not ceased, as evidenced by the numerous summary executions that have taken place this year. According to the report, the government has "not complied" with the norms of international law which require the state to prevent, investigate and sanction human rights violations. (1AC#10)

Now, in addition, the current, the most significant current threat to peace is not a military coup but an upswing in human rights abuses. *Toronto Star* reporter Tracy Wilkinson writes last year:

The biggest danger now is not a coup d'état because that makes no sense. The danger is that they unleash a dirty war. Zamora and others are demanding that Cristiani eventually turn the commission's report over to independent leaders so that they can monitor the government's compliance. (1AC#11)

Now, actual implementation of the agreement is crucial to human rights advancement in El Salvador. Former Assistant Secretary of State Chester Crocker explains in December of 1992:

It will not do to organize high-level meetings [in] which stern measures are adopted—and then not enforced. It is not enough to arrange negotiated settlements of this conflict and not insist upon its implementation. It is time for candor about the law and order deficit we have helped to create in El Salvador. (1AC#12)

Now, in short, the only way to prevent a resurgence of serious human rights violations is to fully implement the peace accords. The InterPress Service reports in 1992:

> While the overall situation of civil and political rights shows improvement, failure to address the issue in the short term could lead to a resurgence of serious human rights violations. There is one known formula to prevent such an outcome—that is, full compliance with the peace accords. Economic, social and cultural rights are also largely dependent upon implementing the agreements reached on the economic and social issues in the course of the negotiations. (1AC#13)

Contention Two: Continued UN presence is necessary for full implementation.

Initially, we note that several aspects of the accords have not been fully carried out. The United Nations must ensure compliance. NPR commentator Tom Gibbs reports on December 15th:

> [When] Boutros-Ghali arrived last night, he emphasized the need for a continued UN presence until after new presidential elections in 1994. In addition to the delays in the Army purge, [the] new civilian police force is behind in the [its] training, and thousands of ex-fighters from both sides still have to be given land. The rebels will have to rely on the United Nations now to make sure that the government complies. (1AC#14)

Now, at this point, the withdrawal of the United Nations would allow the abuses to continue. *Los Angeles Times* reporter Stan Meisler writes in November 1992:

> The danger is that the United Nations human rights programs, if cut short before [they have] a chance to become effective, will serve as no more than a smoke screen satisfying the consciences of outsiders while human rights abuses remain at home. (1AC#15)

Fortunately, the worst case scenarios for El Salvador are not probable. While there may still be some threats that there may be some minimal threat of destabilization, it is unlikely that the right wing will stage any coup. *Current History* correspondent Pamela Constable writes in March of this year:

> Despite the accumulated mistrust and inequities of Salvadoran society, virtually all leaders across the political spectrum seem determined to put the civil war behind them and inaugurate a new era for the country. While [there are] some extremists on the fringes who continue to paint apocalyptic scenario, there are the mainstream actors of national life [who] appear increasingly committed to working with their former adversaries. (1AC#16)

Now, the UN is the only organization that has any hope of guaranteeing implementation. *The Central American Update* reports in 1992:

> The FMLN has banked on the reformation of the military, electoral, social, agrarian and judicial infrastructure. The peace agreement depended on their finally having found some effective levers. In calling upon the UN and the international community to oversee compliance with the peace agreement the FMLN has recourse to a verification structure that will guarantee implementation of the peace agreement. (1AC#17)

Now, in short, the UN verification mission is the best way to achieve human rights in El Salvador. *America's Watch* discovered in 1992:

> Taken together, the judicial reforms, the Ad-Hoc Commission, the Truth Commission, and the Ombudsman's office have the potential for helping to overcome impunity and providing for the structural basis for a more lasting respect of human rights in El Salvador. Just as important, however, is the full implementation of these reforms to the police and military: the abolition of the treasury police and the national guard, the creation of a new National Civilian Police, the abolition of rapid-reaction army battalions associated with numerous atrocities and the dissolutionment of the civil defense. UNOSAL, in one way or another is the observer, participant, or guarantor of nearly all of these processes. It thus operates within, and provides a context for, major reforms in observance of human rights in El Salvador. (1AC#18)

Finally, we note that the United Nations is the best hope for human rights advancement in El Salvador. They must fully implement these accords. Gary Bland concludes in 1992:

> The accords, of course, must fully be implemented, and their success today will directly influence the quality of democracy in the years ahead. Fortunately, it appears that most Salvadorans desperately want to live in peace and they will go to surprising lengths to work together in a spirit of compromise in an effort to secure it. (1AC#19)

Cross Examination of the 1AC

Jim Haefele, Emporia State University
K. J. Wall, Kansas State University

Haefele: What is the UN doing in El Salvador?
Wall: Currently they're doing a lot of things. They're trying to reform the civilian police force.
Haefele: How are they doing that is my question—they're purging the military, so what, they're forcing the military officers to resign, right?
Wall: That is the essence.
Haefele: The essence.
Wall: Yes.
Haefele: OK.
Wall: New courts there, et cetera.
Haefele: What's been the reaction—now recently there was a truth commission in El Salvador, right, publishing reports talking about what is happening. What's the military's reaction to that?
Wall: Well, it depends on who you ask, a lot of them retired because of it. Some of them were angry about it.
Haefele: OK, what's Cristiani's reaction to that?
Wall: It's been a little shifty. At first he condemned the report but now he says he'll comply with it.

Haefele: What's generally Cristiani's position on the UN? Initially, he was very, I mean, he really liked the UN. What's his position now?

Wall: He's a little shifty. I don't know, what do you mean?

Haefele: Is he implementing the peace accords? Is he the President of El Salvador following the UN or not?

Wall: On most of the issues, yes. There are some issues where he has showed some lack . . .

Haefele: Like what?

Wall: . . . of cooperation. Like a long time ago, the purges, they didn't comply with that. Now that the truth commission . . .

Haefele: Well, OK, now, recently the most significant purge that happened, was the major, the the ah, the ah, head, the head guy, one of the head guys, yeah, he resigned, yeah, a big guy, he resigned. What was Cristiani—you know what I'm talking about? He resigned. What was Cristiani—what was Cristiani's response to that?

Wall: Well, he didn't

Haefele: He didn't like it much then, yeah.

Wall: You have to keep in mind that that's just one element of the peace accords. There are several other reforms that are ongoing. And that there is cooperation.

Haefele: Yeah, that's true. Do you think Cristiani is crucial to the peace accords or would you say he is irrelevant?

Wall: The President of El Salvador is not irrelevant.

Haefele: So he is probably pretty important to have his reactions . . .

Wall: Yes, his reactions to some of the issues are important.

Haefele: OK, let's see, is there any reason why this is an implementation of the declaration?

Wall: Yeah, I've, yeah, because of all the implementation that we say, our definition indicates that an observer or anybody that observes is . . .

Haefele: Is there any evidence in here that are words that are not in the universal declaration <TIME> of human rights in case?

Wall: No, there are not.

First Negative Constructive: Greg Achten

Are you guys ready? Judges? The last thing in the world you want to do is maintain a United Nations presence in El Salvador. Our argument will be that when the United Nations acts in El Salvador it will only cause instability. The first off-case position is India. The A-subpoint is: India is at a national crossroads a crossroads. Malik explains in '93:

> The loss of Soviet support has created grave problems for India's military, shifts in strategic tectonic plates are offering India an opportunity to reassess its international orientation and to maneuver itself into a dominant regional position. (1NC#1)

The B-subpoint is: India perceives state sovereignty as vital to security. France Press Agency in December 8, 1992:

> The main sticking point is the idea of state sovereignty and the need for the agreement of the parties in the conflict before any international intervention. Following the example of India the developing countries are adhering firmly to these principles. The government in New Delhi is particularly supportive of these points because of the Moslem situation in Kashmir. (1NC#2)

The C-subpoint is that if India perceives a threat it will backlash militarily. Malik '93:

> Despite the constraints created by India's current economic crisis and lack of a reliable superpower ally, New Delhi remains committed to a military buildup. If India's unity or security interests are perceived as under threat in South Asia, New Delhi will not shy from using its military to protect national interests. (1NC#3)

The second off-case: Self-determination. The A-subpoint is the link. Global acceptance of human rights and democracy fuels separatism and ethnic self-determination. Fuller, who's a RAND policy analyst and Jim's girlfriend's father explains in 1991:

> We had better be clear about it: democracy will produce both the desire for greater cultural and ethnic self-expression and the electoral vehicles by which to express separatist ambitions. Increasing worldwide acceptance of human rights will make repression and suppression of these aspirations all the more unconscionable. (1NC#4)

The B-subpoint is: Ethnic separatism snowballs globally. Etzioni, who is a professor at George Washington University claims in '93:

> It is impossible to sustain the notion that every ethnic group can find its expression in a full blown nation-state, fly its flag at the United Nations, and have its ambassadors accredited by other nation-states; the process of ethnic separation and the breakdown of existing states will then never be exhausted. Many countries in the world continue to contain numerous ethnic enclaves. Even within those enclaves, further ethnic splinters exist. Moreover, new ethnic "selves" can be generated quite readily, drawing on fracture lines now barely noticeable. Subtle differences in geography, religion, culture, and loyalty can be fanned into new separatist movements, each seeking their own symbols and powers of statehood. (1NC#5)

The C-subpoint is: snowball to Central Asia causes disastrous instability. Rumer of Harvard University explains in '93:

> These prospects for destabilization are very real indeed, given the unstable nature of the core Central Asian region. Although often lumped together by outsiders as a single entity, the five Central Asian states are anything but homogeneous. Borders cut across ethnic enclaves, making Central Asia a patchwork quilt rent by ethnic, regional, and tribal disputes over land and natural resources which threaten to undermine both the existing regimes and the equilibrium in the region. The consequence of such an unfortunate but likely turn of events would be felt throughout Asia and, [inevitably], would have a significant impact even on the remote powers of the North Atlantic. (1NC#6)

The case debate, Observation Two:

The first card says the war left the nation embattled. However, the second card denies it. The second card, if you look at it now, says that there's been a forced negotiated settlement. However, what the card says is both sides have agreed to the settlement. They think this settlement which I think helps their solvency because it says that inevitably it's going to settle the conflict as both sides want. The last thing I want is—skip down to the last card—they say that oversight equals UN violation of sovereignty. This thing is our specific link to India because it says they have violated sovereignty and given the UN tons of power.

Contention One: They say that the terror is not yet over. First argument is: if this is true, it proves the United Nations is not solving. If that's why we're still there, why the UN is still there, I think it denies solvency to the case. The next thing: there's no threat of a military coup. The first argument is, the card, the slug of this card is that there's no risk of <FIVE> the coup. But if we prove there is a risk of a coup it would outweigh human rights. The second argument is: the purge of the military may incite a coup. Tom Gibbs and Linda Robinson, on November 23, 1992:

> The crisis peaked when Defense Minister General Rene Emilio Ponce and his vice minister, General Juan Orlando Zepeda, criticized the planned officer purge as a "leftist conspiracy," reigniting fears of a coup. Both are said to be on the purge list. (1NC#7)

Also, the purge will create a military coup. Pilsbury explains in 1993:

> Salvador's President Alfredo Cristiani has admitted that he is not going to purge the military of the top generals and colonels because to do so would jeopardize the stability of the country, which is a way of saying the military would attempt a coup. (1NC#8)

Additionally, purges cause military backlash. Wilkinson explains in '93:

> To counter the criticism, Cristiani has been meeting with diplomats, business leaders, politicians and others. In Thursday's interview with three American newspapers, Cristiani said flaws in the way the purge list was drawn up made it difficult to implement and would have led to a backlash. (1NC#9)

Also, the purge will cause military instability, the *New York Times* explains on February 12, 1993:

> Last month, the President decided to ignore the purge deadline by keeping eight military officials, including Defense Minister General Rene Emilio Ponce, in their jobs until next year and moving seven others to diplomatic posts abroad. He told United Nations officials <FOUR> that main elements of the purge, drawn up by a civilian commission created by the peace accords, had to be delayed in the interest of military stability. (1NC#10)

Now, additionally, they say the agreement is crucial and the peace accords increase human rights. The first argument is that official officers who are being purged say that this is violating their due process because they are not getting a chance to defend themselves. Shirley Christian explains in 1993:

> But the purge has been a point of great dissatisfaction among army officers. While saying they supported the peace process and the transformation of the army to a peacetime force, many officers asserted that the selection by three civilian lawyers of those to be purged had been carried out without thorough investigations and without due process for those affected. (1NC#11)

The second argument is: the purge will cause legal challenges by officers because their due process is violated. This will derail the entire peace process which means the United Nations can't solve. Wilkinson explains on January 8th, '93:

> After he began meeting with officers, Cristiani said he became convinced that many men who were to be fired would have been able to mount successful legal challenges to their dismissal, throwing the entire purge—and the peace process—

into disarray. They would have had legal grounds, he said, because the commission assigned to review the armed forces and recommend dismissals did not give the accused a chance to defend themselves. (1NC#12)

Additionally, the UN Truth Commission report which is the part of the United Nations is a flawed report **<THREE>,** which *Newsday* explains on March 17th:

> El Salvador's deputy president yesterday said a UN report that found army chiefs and rightist political leaders guilty of massive human rights atrocities was deeply flawed and "absolutely insulting." "The UN-appointed commissioners list a mass of names without being able to conclude what proofs they base their report on," Deputy President Francisco Merino told reporters in San Salvador. (1NC#13)

Additionally, the UN Truth Commission report will destabilize El Salvador. Constable explains in 1993:

> Some U.S. analysts and Salvadorans have warned that the report could have a destabilizing effect on the country, which is trying to heal the wounds of long, bitter conflict. (1NC#14)

Also, the UN Truth Commission report is destabilizing and risks a military backlash. Constable in 1993:

> "If this report names [names and] places responsibility for most killings on the army, the short-term effect could be very destabilizing," William Leogrande, a Central America specialist at American University, said. "Most officers have never taken the idea of democracy to heart. . . . It could open up a Pandora's box and put our entire new political system to the test." (1NC#15)

Additionally, Cristiani is refusing to comply with the purges. He will not allow the purges to continue. Sheppard explains on March 16th:

> The Ad-Hoc Commission recommended last September that more than 100 officers be purged, 15 immediately, for serious human rights violations. Cristiani said then that he would dismiss the 15 worst offenders by December, but he still has not done so. (1NC#16)

Also, **<TWO>** in order for the peace process to work, there must be a purge of the military. Without doing so they cannot solve. Christian explains on January 12, '93:

> The purge of army officers believed responsible, directly or indirectly, for the most serious abuses of civilians throughout the 12-year war was a pivotal point in the accords that led to a cease-fire a year ago and the formal end to the civil war. (1NC#17)

Finally, the government's resisting reform and this means that democracy is impossible in El Salvador. From NPR on March 25th:

> The government appears to be resisting fundamental reforms. Without it, government critics say there is no guarantee of genuine democracy or any real safeguard against a resurgence of officially sanctioned political violence. (1NC#18)

One more card: Cristiani will not negotiate purges with the United Nations. Wilkinson explains in 1993, excellent evidence:

In an interview, Cristiani said his formula for conducting the purge—a plan that would delay the departure of some high-ranking officers and spare others—is final and not negotiable, even if the United Nations determines it violates peace accords. "I've made my decision, and I am happy with it," he said in a rare discussion of his thinking on the purge. (1NC#19)

Contention Two, at the top; Jim and I offer the following conditional counterplan: The United Nations will withdraw from El Salvador. Pull the troops out and allow the Salvadoran government to proceed with a general amnesty to those <ONE> named in the UN Commission Truth report. Observation One: It's not topical. It is not enforcing human rights. The United Nations does not take any action, except for pulling out. Observation Two: Mutually, it is competition. The A-subpoint: It's mutually exclusive. We pull them out and they leave them there. Additionally, it's net beneficial. It avoids the two disads while it solves the case. The first argument is: the time is right for amnesty. French explains in '93:

President Alfredo Cristiani said tonight that he would seek an immediate amnesty for those implicated in abuses. . . . He said, "The moment for us to forgive each other has arrived." (1NC#20)

Also, amnesty is needed for national reconciliation. French on March 16th:

Cristiani called today for a sweeping amnesy and former guerrilla leaders <HALF> called for punishment. Mr. Cristiani immediately began urging the passage of a total and general amnesty, which he said was essential if the country were to consummate a national reconciliation. (1NC#21)

Finally, amnesty solves for military reprisals. Constable on March 15th:

After receiving a copy of the findings late yesterday, El Salvador's president, Alfredo Cristiani, called on television for a "general and absolute" amnesty to "close the door to all temptation of revenge and reprisals." (1NC#22)

Now, off their card that says UN withdrawal equals abuses. This is old evidence. Nineteen—it's November. Also, the UN is bad, we should withdraw. Group the rest of the cards. They say that the risk of the coup is outweighed. However, the cards I'm reading above deny it. Also, if the UN is bad, then <TIME> we solve the problem. They are reading no evidence to indicate otherwise.

Cross Examination of the First Negative

K. J. Wall, Kansas State University
Greg Achten, Emporia State University

Wall: The counterplan controls the bulk of the programs, then, maybe even if it is true that you would appease some of the military leaders, then you also don't get the reform of the judiciary, you don't get the land reforms, you don't get all of the other reforms that the UN's doing right now.
Achten: I don't think that's necessarily true. The cards I'm, well,
Wall: If the UN is not there, there's nobody else to continue to . . .
Achten: That's not true, the government . . .

Wall: . . . do the reforms.

Achten: They could do them on their own. Also, the ultimate impact . . .

Wall: Is there any evidence that indicates the government would follow . . .

Achten: No, you haven't made that argument yet.

Wall: Right, that's why I asked the question.

Achten: OK, but the cards you read say that there will be a national reconciliation, and that it says the two sides will come together and the nation will finally be able to reconcile their problems.

Wall: That, that was Cristiani, right?

Achten: That's what Cristiani says, yes.

Wall: That's what Cristiani says. OK, now, the India disadvantage. They're there right now, the action, the violation of sovereignty has already occurred.

Achten: Right.

Wall: **<TWO>** How's the disad unique?

Achten: It's happening. India's happening.

Wall: Why did it happen because of El Salvador? Your cards seem to assume that.

Achten: It says, It says . . .

Wall: But even if it heightened their fears, it's not the impact. It put them on the brink but that's not an impact.

Achten: No, it's the cards we are reading. The last card specifically says that India's increasing their military spending.

Wall: Well, that's not an impact, but . . .

Achten: It's not, it hasn't happened yet there's certainly time for such—still a very good impact.

Wall: It's like when the fears maybe, but it's already . . .

Achten: You're right, K. J. there is an issue. There's been a disadvantage to all UN [unintelligible]. The counterplan subsumes the case. We solve the case absolutely.

Wall: How do you get absolute solvency though without any piece of evidence that you continue all the other necessary reforms like the civilian police force?

Achten: You don't need to have impacts for that. The only impact cards that you read are human rights abuses which assume some sort of conflict between the government and the FMLN and rebred the war which we solve with the national reconciliation.

Wall: Contention Two cards say that the reforms of all these are very important.

Achten: All right.

Wall: Land reforms, et cetera.

Achten: But the reason those reform authors would solve the human rights abuses . . .

Wall: It's not only that, but it's also true that the power of the public to empower the peasants that are in the nation.

Achten: Which I think we would do with amnesty.

Wall: How?

Achten: I think we would do that by **<ONE>** causing national reconciliation and when you read those cards we'll read our turns.

Wall: Now self-determination. What about every other ethnic conflict going on right now?

Achten: Such as?

Wall: Such as Yugoslavia.

Achten: Our argument will be that when the UN takes action in El Salvador and sets up a democracy in El Salvador that is a unique model for other countries to act instead of the **<HALF>**.

Wall: So, it's bad for others to strive for democracy? What is distinct about El Salvador?
Do we create the same model or is it a different model that eases tension?

Achten: Our argument see our argument would be that my guess you would make—

Wall: Let me change my question.

Achten: OK.

Wall: If our solvency gets a stabilized government and they model that, then why do we
get the impacts?

Achten: The problems is they model democracy, right, and when you do that that allows
separatist groups to express their rights.

Wall: Right, right, but they model the current programs of the United Nations, right?

Achten: They model what happened in El Salvador, which is the spread of democracy.
Our argument <TIME> is democracy elsewhere would be a bad idea.

Second Affirmative Constructive: Jill Baisinger

Same order. Ready? They don't just have to read you a disadvantage, and give you some
unique reason why withdrawing from El Salvador now would reverse perceptions in India.
If they are correct, the perception has already been set. You might as well solve the people
in El Salvador. They do not have solvency for the counterplan which I think gives us net
benefits. Now on down. Now on the India disadvantage: they tell you they're at a crossroad.
First response: we are post-brink as much as we're risking if we pulled out right now would
reverse the perception I don't think that they can do that. There is if there is a perception
it has already been set, there is no way to solve, you might as well help people in El
Salvador. Next response: non-unique Somalia equals unprecedented humanitarian intervention. Crigler in '93:

> The Administration seems to be buying into the bolder option, one that would
> give the Secretary General and UN commanders unprecedented authority to
> impose order and enforce Security Council resolutions in Somalia, notwithstand-
> ing doubts about whether such authority squares with principles of non-
> intervention enshrined in the UN Charter. (2AC#1)

Next response: this is a more specific example. It says abuses—it'll be violating what
is going on the UN charter. They don't have these cards for El Salvador. Next response is:
non-unique. Nicaragua set election monitoring precedent. *America's Watch* in '92:

> As a first step, the United Nations was called upon to monitor the elections in
> Nicaragua, scheduled for February 1990. The United Nations Observer Mission
> for the Verification of the Elections in Nicaragua began operations in August 1989,
> marking the first time that the UN had overseen an electoral process in a sovereign
> state, and the first major UN operation in the Western hemisphere. (2AC#2)

Next response: their cards assuming non-essential intervention, which we are certainly
not doing that—that is <SEVEN> below. Now, on subpoint B: they say they perceive
sovereignty as vital. First response: not the case in El Salvador. Latin America's pretty much
irrelevant to everybody. Cavarozzi in '92:

> The carving of new niches in the more industrialized order has become an
> increasingly difficult task. The international financial and trade mechanisms
> created after the second world war have been partially disarticulated. The com-

bined effect of these trends is that Latin American economies have been partially de-linked from the international system, and the importance of Latin America within both world trade and the international capital markets has been reduced. (2AC#3)

Next response: there's no link from El Salvador. No one perceives them. Yugoslavia, Bosnia look to be more important. Now on subpoint C: they say independence will lead to military backlash. First of all, risk comparison is flawed. They ask you to hose El Salvador but possibly, not maybe, affecting India. The perception has already been set. Next response: India supports consensual peacekeeping. Yinhua [Xinhua] in September 1992:

> India will press for a stricter control on the peace keeping role at the United Nations . . . he said that no country should be allowed to move into another country on the basis of a claim that it enjoyed the UN mandate. He said that there ought to be a request from the country concerned and a precise mandate from the United Nations. (2AC#4)

Next response: this is a more specific answer than their scenario. They want consensual action. Next response: India supports strengthened peacekeeping operations. BBC '92:

> The spokesman stated that Foreign Secretary J. N. Dixit had a meeting with the UN Secretary-General, Dr. Boutros-Ghali. The Foreign Secretary assured the UN Secretary-General that India would be fully supportive of any efforts to strengthen the role of the Secretary-General, especially in matters relating to peacekeeping operations. (2AC#5)

There are more specific answers than they are reading. Now, on self-determination <SIX>: There is no ethnic group in El Salvador that is agitating for change or separatism. I would think you get worse risk if you keep oppressing people and keep talking risk. Now on subpoint A: they say global acceptance fuels separatism and they read you a Fuller card. First of all, this is not El Salvador-specific. There's no reason why El Salvador would cause this link. Next response: cross-apply the perception uniqueness evidence. There's no indication anyone would perceive Latin America. Next response: Fuller is not a good source. Wolfe 1992:

> *The Democracy Trap* is anything but a tightly argued, well-researched and historically grounded effort to predict the future by studying the past. It is, rather, an odd mixture of whatever is on Graham Fuller's mind, some of it interesting, some trivial. (2AC#6)

<APPLAUSE> They say any separatism snowballs. First response: there's not a group in El Salvador. This does not talk about El Salvador. Next response is a turn: their authors assume that we should make society more responsive. Etzioni in 1993:

> Structurally, democracy depends on more than regular elections. Elections were conducted frequently by an authoritarian Egypt and the communist USSR. A true democratic structure requires that nonviolent change of those in power can be made in response to the people's changing preferences. Such changes ensure that the government can continue to respond to the needs and desires of the people, and that if the government becomes unresponsive it will be replaced without undue difficulties. (2AC#7)

Next response, we get a net turn to the position by making them more responsive. We solve for the risk of people fueling separatism and everything else. Next response: there is no specific impact. If they read more cards, K.J. will get new answers in the 1AR. Now on case.

Observation One: Please extend the—they have a case-by-case analysis which gives us credibility on the non-specific links. They don't give you specific links to El Salvador. There's no reason why you would want to overstate it. Independently, extend the fact that only is consensual, there's no indication that anybody would perceive this badly. Now, on Observation Two: They say that both sides agree to the cease-fire and inevitably solvency. First response: that is not correct, still up to the UN to verify it. 1994 is a key test of the process. From Robinson in 1992 [1987]:

> If faithfully implemented, El Salvador will become much more democratic, and its 1994 presidential election will be the first in which all Salvadorans can participate in fair, peaceful conditions. It will be the true test of the peace accord's implementation and a defining moment for the country's political future. (2AC#8)

Next response: negotiating through the UN better. Now on the bottom he says it's a link to India, but it's not specific. We give you more specific link turns, link answers than they are providing for links. Now off Contention One: he says on the top that we are proving the United Nations doesn't solve for the abuses occurring. First response: they would be worse without the United Nations and that'll be our story throughout this round. They would be worse after the UN. If they can read you a card that says things will be better without the UN that would be one thing, but they can't do it. Next response: the UN is the only thing decreasing human rights abuses, from *America's Watch* '92:

> It is rare to find agreement on anything in El Salvador. But observers across the political spectrum concur that ONUSAL's presence in the country, both before and after the cease-fire, has dramatically improved the observance of human rights. This appears to be related to several factors: the prestige and moral authority of the United Nations **<FOUR>,** which made both sides in the conflict wary of incurring criticism. (2AC#9)

Next response: there's no alternative. There's nothing else that's going to promote any sort of pressure to equal change. If the United Nations is there, there is no other mechanism. Now on the next cards, they say that there will be an uprising, a purge, and a coup. Group these cards together. First response: they're talking about Ponce, this is the man that resigned because of the Truth Commission report. Next response: there's lots of resignations from the commission. They're not gonna coup; they're gonna resign. From Notimex News Service in '93:

> The report sponsored by the United Nations and released on March 15 named 40 military men as guilty of war crimes. Resignations and possible dismissals also reflect the changes registered in the army because of the peace accord signed by the government and the guerrilla in January 1992. (2AC#10)

Next response: There's no coup. It's just the last kick of a drowning man. Wilkinson in '93:

> Cristiani's political—this is March 25th, incidentally, Cristiani's political party, the right wing Nationalist Republican Alliance already has attacked the Commission on Truth. "It was the last kick of a drowning man," one Latin American

diplomat said of the army's response. "They are on their way out, and are trying to save face." (2AC#11)

. Next response: the middle-ranking officers won't allow coup to occur. From Reuters in 1993:

> While the army's campaign has worried diplomats and rebel leaders, few believe middle-ranking officers would back any open military challenge. "They couldn't do it. Not long ago, they would have simply carried out a coup but now they are coming out to do politics," (2AC#12)

Next response: there's no scenario for a coup. Who is going to do the couping? What or how are they going to do it? They don't give you any scenario for why this is to occur. There's no motivation to do this. Now, off the next, off their fourth, where they say purges equal military backlash and equals instability. First response: again there is no scenario. Who is going to do this and what's going <THREE> to be the scenario? Next response: how could it be worse than what's already happened? There is no risk comparison being made here. The United Nations presence is still superior and how does this occur? Next response: they're post-brink. This is all premised on the Truth Commission's report which was released two weeks ago and they are correct in all these cards are justification for keeping the United Nations there. Next response, here, is that 87 officers have already been purged, their card is non-unique. From Wilkinson in 1993:

> In a letter to the UN Security Council, Secretary-General Boutros-Ghali said Cristiani has successfully purged 87 officers from the armed forces, following the recommendations of a three-member civilian commission assigned to review the military as part of the peace accords. (2AC#13)

It should have already occurred. Now go to the next one; group this. Officers incur violations of due process, a purge equals legal challenges, means no solvency. First response: there's no scenario off this. The cards are as good as their tags [unintelligible]. Next response: they're post-brink, they've already issued the Truth Commission report. If there's going to be a coup it should already have occurred. There's no way they can take back the Truth Commission report. They have—there is nothing that says that things would be better without the United Nations there. They're the ones who can guarantee anything. Now, group the next three cards. The UN Commission is bad and won't stabilize and this is destabilizing. First response: the cards say better only the military, there's no reason to give these cards any credibility. Next response: the Truth Commission shifts the balance of power to democratic forces. Reuters, March 15th of '93:

> A UN report on war crimes will lift the veil on El Salvador's ugly past Monday; naming the military chiefs, rebel leaders and rich businessmen behind the atrocities <TWO> committed during twelve years of civil war. The report is expected to push several top army officers into resigning and could tilt the balance of power as El Salvador approaches key democratic elections after years of political violence. (2AC#14)

Next response: empirically true, the defense minister's [unintelligible] this isn't the defense minister, which empirically true that there is some sort of solvency. Next response, last response here: there is no scenario for destabilization. Who—what's going to happen? They don't have any clear answer. The last response—, I lied, there is one more response— that we still need the UN to do their reforms, that is the cards below. Now, on the next: Cristiani won't comply and there must be a purge. First response: this means that there is a reason for the UN not to want to withdraw. This is the main reason the UN shouldn't withdraw. They're only feeding our cards. Next response: every card they read is justification for the United Nations. The only hope of getting a purge is by keeping the military there. Last response is: you don't need a purge if people are resigning. The two cards that the government is resisting reform and democracy, they won't negotiate the purges. First response: they'll resign, is the cards I'm reading above. Additional response: other parts of the reforms can still be carried out, therefore the judiciary, the police which they're conceding below. Now off of Contention Two on the conditional counterplan: He says withdraw and grant amnesty. First response would be: a perm or a test. We could do both of them. Maintain the UN presence in El Salvador and continue the amnesty. That'll be the assumption. I'll read the cards below. Now, Observation Three: They say the time is right for amnesty they [unintelligible]. First response: these cards <ONE> are only quoting Cristiani. There's no reason why these cards have any credibility. Next response: unconditional amnesty will lead to a worse situation. The *L.A. Times* in '93:

> Amnesties can serve a purpose. Even this one—if it specifically declined to protect persons named in the commission's report—could help heal Salvador's nightmarish wounds. As it stands, the amnesty is ripping them wide open. (2AC#15)

Next response, the amnesty means international pressure is necessary. These are the cards—responses—cards that support my perm. From French in '93:

> Many in El Salvador's political class who opposed the amnesty if it was not matched with compliance with United Nations-recommended reforms said the consolidation of the country's peace agreements would now depend on international pressure to bring about the changes in the armed forces and judiciary that the government has so far resisted. (2AC#16)

Next response: this is just another net benefit for keeping the United Nations there. If they are <HALF> correct and people are going to be unhappy that's just another reason why we have to keep the United Nations in there to get some sort of solvency. Now, he says it solves for reprisals but that assumes that he wins the purge. There's no scenario for purge. Also, extend the fact that this is the only hope. There's no alternative, leave the UN in if you want to stop the abuses. Now he says that withdrawal's an old card and the UN should withdraw, the UN is bad. [Unintelligible] why the fact that this is a '92 card is relevant. We get worse the harms without the United Nations there because that allows the abuses to continue without anyone watching. Extend the three, four and five cards. The UN's the only hope of guaranteeing solvency and the UN's the only hope to get change. There's no comparison of risk being made here. I think our cards are just <TIME> better.

Cross Examination of the Second Affirmative

Greg Achten, Emporia State University
Jill Baisinger, Kansas State University

Achten: Alright, let's talk about self-determination.
Baisinger: OK.
Achten: What, you, you . . .

Baisinger: Alright.

Achten: You are. I'm sorry, the United Nations sets up a democracy in El Salvador, right?

Baisinger: I don't think that's an accurate characterization. They were asked to help the keepers of the democracy.

Achten: Right, the effect of what's going on is that the people are setting up a democracy, right?

Baisinger: Om, yeah, they're setting up a democratic nation.

Achten: OK now, assuming, and, this is not happening, but assuming we win, the world would model the situation.

Baisinger: Sure.

Achten: Because it's a snowball effect. Even if the government in El Salvador becomes more responsive, what effect would the cards <TWO> that talk about the effect of democracy worldwide, specifically, Central Asia, which is our scenario?

Baisinger: Well, the cards you're reading assume fragmentation. There's some—they assume fragmentation and ethnic groups wanting separatism.

Achten: Our, our . . .

Baisinger: But if you get a more responsive government that stops the need for separatism . . .

Achten: But our . . .

Baisinger: . . . it stops your impact.

Achten: Our link cards say that democracy supplies the fuel for separatism. Maybe it doesn't in El Salvador but why wouldn't it in Central Asia?

Baisinger: The Fuller card assumes, I believe, that the ethnic groups' agitation for separatism and the use of democratic rhetoric is what causes the problem. He's not indicting democracy, he's indicting ethnic separatism as a way of getting democracy.

Achten: Isn't he indicting democracy as a way of getting ethnic separatism?

Baisinger: I don't think so. That's not how I read your link card.

Achten: Alright, where's the link, where's our shell? Alright. OK. Aw, forget it. Alright, this card.

Baisinger: OK.

Achten: Says increasing worldwide human rights. This card says democracy will produce <ONE> both modern greater cultural and ethnic self-expression and the electoral vehicles by which to express separatist ambitions. So it says . . .

Baisinger: That's why one of my answers is there's no group in El Salvador.

Achten: But that's irrelevant, right, but the . . .

Baisinger: No, I think it's relevant.

Achten: The model is—the model is democracy.

Baisinger: No, the model is separatism.

Achten: No, the model is democracy. The card says that democracy produce[s] the desire and the ambition . . .

Baisinger: He's not indicting all democracy, he's assuming . . .

Achten: He's not? Democracy will produce both the desire to act separately and the vehicles by which people express these—he's not saying it's bad? What's he saying?

Baisinger: He's not assuming all democracy is bad. He just [says] ethnic separatism is a bad thing. We don't have . . .

Achten: Right, but in [if] a democracy which, Fuller's dad says, causes ethnic separatism is bad, why isn't he indicting democracy?

Baisinger: Well, then you're non-unique and that's—I mean . . .

Achten: Which is irrelevant to the link question, right?

Baisinger: No, because we've got a lot of democracy . . .

Achten: That's irrelevant to the link question, right?

Baisinger: No, I don't . . .

Achten: The UN increases democracy which Fuller says causes ethnic separatism.

Baisinger: I'm not sure why it's unique at that level then.

Achten: But that's not the link. It might be—that's the uniqueness question, it's not the link question, right?

Baisinger: No, I think it is.

Achten: Oh, so, link and unique is same. No.

Baisinger: No, that's not what I am saying, Greg. **<TIME>**

Achten: Alright.

Second Negative Constructive: Jim Haefele

I'm going to do self—India and self-determination. I think they have tremendous problems on the top of the India position. We are reading specific links which suggest they are wrong by maybe not fearing consensual arrangements. The problem is that India perceives that a consensual arrangement would be bad because Pakistan wants involvement in Kashmir, which means that action there would be consensual. India doesn't want that at all, which means that, I think, they have a pretty compelling link as to why India would backlash. Their first argument is that we are post-brink. The first answer is: we haven't solved yet. According to their case claim, the UN has to be there, which means that there's no reason why we wouldn't have some level of uniqueness. Also, El Salvador serves as a model for future actions. Constable explains in March of this year:

> Determined to reduce the chance that violence or other complications would undermine the cease-fire, Boutros-Ghali announced immediately after assuming his post that 1,000 UN peacekeeping troops and police would be sent to El Salvador to monitor the peace process. As during the negotiations themselves, the role of the UN monitoring mission, known as UNOSAL, proved a critical guarantee; observers have suggested that El Salvador could become a role model for future UN involvement in conflict resolution. (2NC#1)

Also, El Salvador is a model for action. Posner argues on February 18: **<SEVEN>**

> If Washington is serious about multilateralism, it must be willing to work with other nations to strengthen the UN human rights program. The Clinton administration needs to encourage the UN secretary-general to become more closely involved in human rights protection, following the models in El Salvador, where significant UN human rights initiatives are in place. (2NC#2)

The next argument: the counterplan would make it unique, that to pull the UN out which means we'd solve any risk the disad would have. If we solve case I think even a tiny, tiny risk would be enough to outweigh. Her next argument is: Somalia makes it non-unique—sets a precedent. The first answer is: not for India. India's supported small intervention which also assumes the cards she's reading. Zorroli explains November 28 of last year:

> In fact, there is great willingness among diplomats right now to overhaul the UN's operation in Somalia and to consider tougher action against the Somali

warlords. Even countries that traditionally oppose UN intervention in internal affairs, such as India, are backing the move. At least in theory, the US offer this week has found a receptive audience in the international community. (2NC#3)

The next argument is: Somalia will not set the precedent. *Newsday* in '92:

> But if the presence of US troops turns out to have saved millions of lives and pressured local warring factions to make peace, then the intervention is certainly justified. Can it apply to other cases? That is a decision to make case by case, not on the basis of a precedent. (2NC#4)

Now, her next argument says it's more specific, but I'm answering that above. Remember, we're reading specific links **<SIX>** now. Her next claim is: non-unique because of Nicaragua. The first argument is: the card doesn't say it set a model, it only says it was the first thing, the first country to act, it doesn't say it set a model for other actions, which is our link now. The second argument is: doesn't say it violates sovereignty. There's no clarification of why it's important. The third argument is: it's empirically denied. Remember, as far as uniqueness turn goes, uniqueness answer goes because that was happening in 1990, our brink evidence postdates by a lot. Her next argument says it's non-consensual. The first answer is that Pakistan wants action in Kashmir but India does not. *Japan Economic Newswire* '93:

> Militants in India-ruled Kashmir, fighting for independence or merger with Pakistan, have demanded implementation of an early UN resolution demanding a plebiscite among Kashmiris. Pakistan has sought UN intervention, particularly on the question of holding a plebiscite, [but] India insists that a 1971 agreement ending the third war between India and Pakistan clearly states that the issue of Kashmir must be settled bilaterally. (2NC#5)

Now, this is not a claim—we are not claiming directly that they will cause an intervention in Kashmir but it proves that India fears consensual intervention because that's what Pakistan wants. Which means that it's possible India could backlash against that [unintelligible]. It's only in three and four scenario stories **<FIVE>** that independent link. Her next argument though, is that it's, that El Salvador is irrelevant, all of Latin America is irrelevant. The first argument: so is the case! If El Salvador and Latin America are irrelevant then why are they a thing of consideration? I don't understand that. The next argument is: the model is sufficient. If we group it serves the model then it demonstrates it's not relevant. The third argument is that the fact that the international community pays attention to it at all would demonstrate that she's wrong [unintelligible] national theory. She says there's no El Salvador link but that's above. The C-subpoint: She says risk comparison but I think we would solve the case too. Her next argument is: India supports consensual agreements. The first answer is: but the model could be a pain in India's necks which means that India could backlash. That is the arguments we're making. Second argument: the counterplan solves any risk of this. Also, the card doesn't say that. It assumes action against claim there's no reason why. Also, it's only the rhetoric. The third argument is: they say it's more specific, but I'm reading links above. The last argument is: India supports increased peacekeeping. The first argument is that India has adopted and the first argument is [sic]: India rejects UN violations of sovereignty. UPI, October 24th last year:

> He cautioned that reforms should not curtail the national sovereignty **<FOUR>** of member-states or dilute the UN's social and economic mandate. India

has argued that since the organization was formed at a time when most developing countries were still colonized, its power structure needs to be overhauled. India itself won independence only two years after the UN was established in 1945. (2NC#6)

Also, India will oppose international human rights actions to promote sovereignty. Ganguly argues in the fall of 1992:

> Again in 1991, during the Security Council debate on the creation of a security zone for the Kurdish minority in northern Iraq, India made common cause with the PRC, opposing the creation of such a zone because it infringed on Iraqi sovereignty. President Ramaswamy Venkataraman of India suggested that his country and the PRC should stand united to oppose the pressures of the Western world on a range of issues from trade liberalization to human rights. (2NC#7)

Extend the impact that says India will backlash momentarily. Independently, a future war between India and Pakistan could go to nuclear war. Warnke argues in '92:

> Take the Indian subcontinent, and look at what the Hindu has done to Muslim and vice versa over the years. It would seem to me that if you had a Pakistani bomb—which they may have—and an Indian bomb—which we know they have— and some kind of a conflict that aroused passions to a particularly high point of intensity, I can conceive of a nuclear war. (2NC#8)

The next argument is that India threatens the entire—I'm sorry, the next argument is: India threatens the whole subcontinent. The Middle East News Network on March 3rd:

> There is no country in the Indian Subcontinent or the entire Asian **<THREE>** Continent, which does not face the threat of Indian nuclear weapons or which has not been the victim of Indian aggression. Pakistan, Sri Lanka, and the Maidires have already faced direct Indian military aggression. (2NC#9)

The next argument is that it could spur Indian Ocean conflicts. *The Asian Bulletin* in '91:

> India is a strategically unique state, more than a regional power but something less than a multiregional or global power. Not only will India dominate the rest of South Asia, it could challenge China and other large powers in the Indian Ocean and nearby regions if it feels its economic, political and strategic interests are threatened. (2NC#10)

The last argument is: Indian Ocean instability could escalate. Gurgel argues in 1992:

> The interruption of access to the Indian Ocean that might result from a major conflict would seriously damage the international trade of not only nations in the area of the dispute but also those countries economically tied to them. The preservation of peace in the Indian Ocean is thus in the general interest of the international community. (2NC#11)

Self-determination; Her first answer is: there's no specific link to El Salvador. The first answer is: if we win the model stuff though all our cards I'm reading above it is specific link. The second argument is: the risk is sufficient. We can solve the case too, which means that any focus on human rights would be enough. We don't do that. We focus on amnesty. Her next argument is a perception, also even if we solve human rights, it doesn't contradict focus on human rights, only a side effect. Her next argument is perceptions **<TWO>** a source of uniqueness but we're reading but the risk is sufficient also the perception evidence I read below will be enough. Her next argument is: Fuller's a bad source. The first argument is: this is a terrible card. It says the book isn't organized; it doesn't say he's not qualified. The second answer is: he *is* qualified. He's a senior policy analyst at the RAND Corporation and a former executive in the CIA, which I think makes him qualified. The third argument is: how dare they? I have to get on my moral post here and say that's just not fair. Also I think that the A-subpoint evidence explains very cogently why it is they're wrong. The B-subpoint. Her first argument is there's no ethnic splintering—there's not an increase in El Salvador. But that's irrelevant, it's the model that becomes the link. Her second argument <ONE AND A HALF> is: they make the government more responsive—it becomes a turn. The first argument is: all cards from Etzioni are not talking about self-determination. His article encompasses a lot of things and this card is not focusing on that. The next argument is: insistence on human rights exacerbates separatism. From Fuller in '91:

> The collapse of totalitarian rule and new aspirations toward democracy will unleash profound forces of both neo-nationalist and radical religious movements that will destabilize large regions of the world. American values—such as the principle of national self-determination and our insistence on human rights—will serve to exacerbate these forces. (2NC#12)

Her next argument is that net-turn they become more responsible. Why? She's not explaining this. She reads no evidence. Her last argument is: there's no impact. That would be below and there's no reason why K.J. gets new answers except to the impacts. The first argument is: Central Asian instability equals prolif[eration] and international instability. Barowiec explains in 1992:

> Ethnic tensions and post-communist difficulties in the former Soviet republics of Central Asia are likely to cause nuclear proliferation and far-reaching international instability. (2NC#13)

The next argument is that destabilization in Central Asia sucks in China, India, and Russia and escalates the war. This is ex—this is excellent evidence from Rumer in 1993:

> Such geopolitical <HALF> domino theories can easily suggest a scenario of explosive instability. The destabilization of Central Asia could come to include China, whose Western provinces are still at times called "East Turkestan"; after all, the latter area is home to a significant Turkic minority of Uygurs, Kazakhs, and Kyrgyzes, who have a long history of resistance to Beijing. No less vulnerable is Afghanistan, whose northern regions are populated by millions of Tajiks and Uzbeks, all contesting the dominance of Afghanistan by the Pushtuns. The Pushtun population of Pakistan, in turn, would hardly remain indifferent to a Tajik-Pushtun conflict in Afghanistan. India, given its fragile relations with both Pakistan and China, could also become embroiled. And of course destabilization in Central Asia would inevitably involve Russia, <TIME> given its long-standing involvement in the region. (2NC#14)

Cross Examination of the Second Negative

Jill Baisinger, Kansas State University
Jim Haefele, Emporia State University

Baisinger: I think I don't understand why isn't India going to react to the operation in El Salvador now?

Haefele: They may not. I mean, they may not react to the operation in El Salvador but if the operation in El Salvador ultimately solves, then that sets a precedent for future reactions that you . . .

Baisinger: But who owns Kashmir now? It's an Indian province, right?

Haefele: Well, that's up for debate, that's the whole question.

Baisinger: But that's technically under India's jurisdiction right now.

Haefele: Ah.

Baisinger: If there's going to be a post . . .

Haefele: No, I I mean . . .

Baisinger: . . . plebiscite saying that Kashmir belongs to India or Pakistan. Right now,

Haefele: Yeah, there's debate over, there's a debate between the two about who it is that wants to—you know there's again there's a question.

Baisinger: But India, it is technically theirs, right?

Haefele: But there's two. But, Jill, there's two parties involved there.

Baisinger: I understand that.

Haefele: Which they in order to meet the definition of consensual arrangements—both would have to agree to . . .

Baisinger: In El Salvador, both have agreed to it, right?

Haefele: Yes, it is consensual not [unintelligible].

Baisinger: Why? Why would India be consensual when India's not supporting it?

Haefele: Because Pakistan wants it which means they fear their necks right. They fear that the fact that **<TWO>** other people, especially . . .

Baisinger: Let me see the cards. I don't mean to interrupt you.

Haefele: No, that's alright. Yeah, that, it's just one card that says unusual checks and it says you're free to check factual claim Pakistan wants India. **<ONE AND A HALF>**

Baisinger: I, this doesn't—I mean this doesn't say anything about this. It's just your analysis. It doesn't say anything about consensuality.

Haefele: No, it demonstrates Pakistan wants it which makes it in a sense a consensual agreement because Pak—your card though that says India wants consensual thanks to the state that's involved, i.e. Pakistan is asking . . .

Baisinger: But India's also involved.

Haefele: Yeah, but the fact that Pakistan's asking for it would none the less demonstrate that India has a fear.

Baisinger: But this is the only card you read. The

Haefele: That is **<ONE>** That card is exclusively a demonstration of India's consensual action.

Baisinger: But this is the only card you read making the connection . . .

Haefele: Yeah.

Baisinger: . . . to consensual action.

Haefele: You're right.

Baisinger: All it says is "militants in India-ruled Pak"—it does say India-ruled Kashmir— "fighting for independence, have demanded implementation of an early UN resolution demanding a plebiscite among Kashmiris." Now, why doesn't that take out your uniqueness on press—they've already asked for UN implementation.

Haefele: The fact that, that it hasn't happened. There's a lot of wonderful new stuff—it doesn't mean it's happened.

Baisinger: Why wouldn't this be enough to trigger the risk if they're already . . .

Haefele: There's no sovereignty violation. Nothing has happened to violate Pakistan's or India's or anybody's sovereignty. The in Pakistan just says please violate our sovereignty—they have guns.

Baisinger: When is it going to happen?

Haefele: I don't know. **<HALF>**

Baisinger: I mean we have solvency, you say it comes off solvency which is 1994. When does this scenario occur, 1995?

Haefele: Well, there's a risk that it could happen in 1995, I guess.

Baisinger: OK.

Haefele: I mean if we are right on case. If our claim—case claim is correct we need this much risk. And I think that's [unintelligible].

Baisinger: OK.

First Negative Rebuttal: Greg Achten

Straight through case. You guys ready? UN cannot solve in El Salvador, our argument will be twofold. The first thing is that Cristiani will not complete the purges. Our argument is that he's not going to throw the military out of power. If this is true, it is impossible for the UN to solve because the military will still be in control of the government. However, if Cristiani does strike the purges, they are conceding that the due process of those being purged was violated. Which means there'll be a legal battle and throw the entire peace process in disarray. It means the UN can't solve. They are conceding those cards. The debate is easy. The Observation Two: We say solvency is inevitable. Our second card, she says not correct, which means they should stay there. However, the card in 1AC denies this, it says that both sides want peace. They think it's the only inevitable result, which means you do not need the United Nations. It's OK to pull them out and that's a good thing because the purge is a bad thing. Contention One: Off the top, extend they prove that their first card proves the UN can't solve. She said it'd be worse without the UN but it's terrible now. There are death squads, how much worse could it get? Our argument will be that if it's terrible now what is it going to do to if UN pulls out. There are death squads; it's not going to be any worse in the future. She says **<FOUR>** you will violate human rights abuses. It's a '92 card. Their card in the 1AC postdates it. It says there's still terror now even if the UN is doing something which means there is an alternative. She says there isn't an alternative but that's not true. The counterplan allows amnesty which creates national reconciliation and solves the problems which they are flat out conceding. Now, our group of good cards. She says it assumes Ponce. However, our argument is: Cristiani rejected Ponce's resignation; he will not comply with the purges. Sheppard, March 16th:

> "We received the Truth Commission report this morning . . . ," Cristiani said. He also had rejected the resignation of the defense minister, General Rene Emilio Ponce, a key figure in the UN commission's accusations. "We don't take decisions to comply with the purge of the army because of pressure from anyone," Cristiani said. (1NR#1)

Which means that Ponce resigned, [but] Cristiani is not going to let him sit down. Which means that they haven't resolution. She says there's no officers' recognition for the coup besides Ponce. Also, it's not the people are being purged. The people being purged are still in power. Now, her 3rd card says there's no coup, the military will not allow a coup.

The first argument is that the entire military has backlashed against UN action. The *Times,*
March 25th:

> In a challenge to both President Alfredo Cristiani and the United Nations, El
> Salvador's top military commanders angrily denounced an international investi-
> gation that blamed **<THREE>** them for widespread wartime atrocities. The bitter
> military response to the UN-appointed Commission on Truth sent tremors
> through political and diplomatic circles Wednesday and threatened to deepen the
> hatreds that continue to divide the country after a brutal civil war. (1NR#2)

Also, military defiance is increasing. The *Times,* March 25th:

> Using the most defiant and bellicose language since peace negotiations to end
> the war began more than two years ago, the army's high command and more than
> a dozen other top commanders took the rare step of appearing on national
> television to attack the UN report on human rights abuses. "We consider the
> report to be unjust, incomplete, illegal, unethical, partial and insolent," Defense
> Minister General Rene Emilio Ponce said in the broadcast, which aired simulta-
> neously on all television stations. "(It) defrauds the hope and faith of all Salva-
> dorans, who were expecting a serious and impartial document that might
> contribute to peace." (1NR#3)

She says, fifth, there's no scenario for a coup. But that's not true, the people who'll
commit the coup are people who aren't that important. Initially, the purge will cause
instability and backlash. Christian explains in '93:

> When he finally sent to Mr. Boutros-Ghali last week the list of actions to be
> taken for each individual on the list, Mr. Cristiani acknowledged that he had
> altered somewhat the agreement on conducting the purge and delayed the
> schedule. He said that was done to assure stability in the country and avoid
> individual acts of violence by affected officers. (1NR#4)

Also, extend the cards I read. It says the purges cause a coup, it'll cause a military
backlash and would cause instability. She says there's no scenario for a coup but I want you
to think about the people who are indicted. She says **<TWO>** how could he be forced out?
However, if they take Cristiani's place, with the coup the military will be in complete
control. She says now things are post-brink, however, the instability is increasing, these are
the cards we are reading above [unintelligible]. She says 87 officers already purged.
However, the purge has been delayed. Those are the cards we're reading below. Additionally, our argument is that when we purge the top leaders, that is when the coup will
occur. Now, off the turns I read that says it violated due process. She says there's no
scenario, but what does that mean? Our cards line up a purging scenario. It says they will
try to create a legal challenge, throw the entire process in disarray. A complete scenario.
She has no cards, no answers **<ONE AND A HALF>,** which means there's no solvency.
She's not answering. Her only other argument is it's post-brink because there's no coup.
But this is not a coup argument. Even if the military does not backlash through a coup
they will backlash daily which will throw the peace process into disarray.

Now, the next arguments we make are about the Truth Commission. Extend that it is
bad. She says only military, however, our cards aren't military, which means they're the
ones who would backlash. She says shift the balance of power to democratic forces.
However, that's not true. The Truth Commission causes instability and military unrest.
Constable on March 15:

But analysts said they feared that the commission report—far from providing a formal conclusion to the country's saga of political strife—could open a new chapter of recriminations, <ONE> military unrest and instability. (1NR#5)

She says empirically it's true [unintelligible]. However, that's not true, extend the Truth Commission causes the instability and backlash. Now, off where we say there's no purge now. She just reads the UN does not withdraw. It's justification for the UN. However, that's not true, it says the UN can't solve now. She says you need a purge for peace. Extend that it is some card. Additionally, it is a reason for the UN to pull out, because the purge is unnecessary. She says not need purge, if you have purge necessary for the peace process. Remember, if the UN is going to stay there they have to purge. Otherwise, they cannot solve. Now extend the cards which say the government which is in reform and Cristiani long ago. She says withdrawing and other reforms <HALF> no cards on the [unintelligible]. Counterplan. She says perm. Now, the first argument is: the counterplan would deny the propensity. The UN would, we would withdraw the UN. Also, the perm is counter-UN action because the UN forces would leave first. Not answering, also the perms not testing competition, it just doesn't mean it could be done. On the amnesty cards, she says only reason to leave them in, it'd be a worse situation of power. Extend the cards that say you cause national reconciliation. She says amnesty needs the support, however this doesn't mean it has to be the UN. The US can still pressure. She says it is a net benefit for the UN but that's not true, it's a reason why the UN should withdraw because then they can give them amnesty. Remember, the perm is not just accomplished, she's assuming they would win the purge. We say the amnesty solves the <TIME> but that's not true. We are meeting constitutionally which now the impact to the case the counterplan solves. We get national reconciliation.

First Affirmative Rebuttal: K. J. Wall

Off-case in order; Case in order. They dropped the turn on the counterplan which means they don't solve for the case advantage. Independently, there is zero risk of the disads. Off-case: Now, on the India position on the one: Indicates that there's no solvency evidence is unique, however, Meisler evidence on case indicating that sovereignty's already been violated. Which also which would take out the uniqueness to the disad. Also, independently, evidence on case that withdrawal equals a guarantee of backlash indicates they would satisfy the consciousness of outsiders which means the model has already been set. The disad should should be post-brink. Extend also Jill's ans—first answer that it is post-brink. He says creates a model, however the evidence doesn't say you increase the amount of the intervention. Only indicate that you would change the type of intervention, once you agree you already do it in the first place. Now, off number four: he says the counterplan equals uniqueness. However, the withdrawal evidence indicates it's already satisfied the consciousness of outsiders, which means the model has already been established once the sovereignty violation has occurred. Now, off number two: the uniqueness argument that we apply. He says India's supporting, et cetera. First response: that only proves that they have worked a consensual arrangement. It takes out his link to the disad. Independently, it postdates. No, our evidence postdates, indicates the Somalian after operation after the United States which are which setting a unique new precedent. Please extend the evidence. Now, please drop down to the number five: <FOUR> assumes a consensual arrangement. He says Pakistan wants it. First response: the evidence also says India rejects and then controls Kashmir which proves this would not be a consensual arrangement. If this is truly a model then it would stop the intervention. It becomes a net-turn to the disad. Now, off of his next: he says who is [unintelligible] of model for international community. However, our argument is just: the perception of the world has no influence on El Salvador. However, it does become a model pre-India. It is a non-consensual one. His own evidence indicates that there would be intrusive. Now, please drop down to Jill's number two off the C-subpoint: Indicates the model equals India. However, there's no internal link. No evidence indicates we'll go to India next; however, if it is a model we go consensual. This evidence indicates that we get some possible turn on the disad. Now on number four: indicates rejection of violation of sovereignty will oppose. First response: the evidence in here assumes that the consensual arrangement subsumes. Please extend Jill's argument that you're not rejecting the consensual arrangement. That it may reject human rights then is opposed over there, but they don't reject the consensual arrangement. Now, self-determinism. Now at the top: Indicates it establishes a model, however, that's not the model that they [unintelligible] Central Asia. There's no internal link to his impact. Independently, it's post-brink that's our arguments cross-applied from the <THREE> other disad. Now, please drop down to number ten: he says below, however, we don't increase the amount of intervention, right, it only becomes a different model which is our argument on the other disad. Off the B-subpoint specifically. Please go to the turn: he says not self-determinism, however, this article was specifically—the evidence is certainly isolating it. Then he says, he reads one more card that says it exacerbates the conflict, however, extend the evidence indicates it solves the core reason for the self-determinist movement which means they may delay self-determinism but we're the only ones that get solvency which means I get a bigger turn. I will extend, you have to reform the governments to stop the transformation to self-determinism. Etzioni in 1993:

> The need to tilt in favor of fuller representation, responsiveness, and democratization—and against self-determination by fragmentation—is most evident in those countries that are already basically democratic but within which one subgroup is, or feels that it is, under-represented or isolated. (1AR#1)

Now, off the impact stuff, there's just no internal link. On case. At the top: extend the case-by-case focus which takes out the link to the off-case disads. On Observation Two: he says the 1AC cannot solve, however, all the evidence indicates that withdrawal would be bad which gives you a comparative advantage. Independently the evidence in Contention One indicates that there is some improvement they just have to maintain. Contention One at the top: They say it is terrible there and the 1AC postdates. However, it indicates in Contention One that it's improving now, but they have to stay there until '94. Please extend the evidence that was on Observation Two Jill read in 2AC. Now off the coup stuff. Indicates Cristiani reject not comply. In the cards, please group <TWO> he makes four arguments, but please group. First response: we still get a comparative advantage because the withdrawal would take this out. Our evidence also is postdating which becomes the most recent trend in El Salvador. Extend Jill's number three that it's the last kick of a drowning man. Even if they make the claims, they don't act upon it. More importantly, extend number four, even if the leaders want a purge, the middle-level officers will not allow it. I will extend, the officers are resigning now. They are not going to purge; they are not going to backlash. *The Independent* explains on March 26 of 1993:

Juan [Orlando Zepeda], El Salvador's Vice-Minister, [of] defense officer [sic] recommended for dismissal for human rights abuses, said he would resign at the end of the month, AP reports from San Salvador. (1AR#2)

Also, **<ONE AND A HALF>** the Truth Commission forced the resignation of Zepeda. The Truth Commission is promoting Army resignations. Notimex News Service in 1993:

The resignation of Ponce, Zepeda and other military leaders accused of systematic human rights violations during the country's civil war was brought on by the Truth Commission. (1AR#3)

Also, if they are resigning, there's no need for a purge. [Unintelligible] doesn't take out our solvency. Now, please drop down to the next argumentation. It says that equals institutional backlash and controls increasing now. However, you're extending there's no risk comparison. UN withdrawal would guarantee resurgence. Now, down below: indicates that the legal challenge, however, this is non-unique and we're arguing that 87 have already been purged, which takes out uniqueness. **<ONE>** Also, there's no propensity, right, the Truth Commission's already out. Please extend Jill's number two and number three which indicates the shift of balance of power to democracy. Which is post-dating his argumentation and, also, extend at the very bottom, that's the counterplan. Contention Two: He says the perm, the counterplan's denies et cetera the UN supports. However, all this assumes that amnesty has to be backed with the United Nations. That's the third argument Jill is making. Now also he says UN supports it but there's no indication of solvency. He's dropping the second argument on the counterplan, amnesty exacerbates the conflict, which means when he's saying that they solve for case on the disad that is untrue—they don't get the same **<HALF>** solvency. Now off specifically that the Observation Two competition stuff he says equals reconciliation. However, extend Jill's argument if this is an indict it's only Cristiani. Cristiani which certainly is a biased source. Extend number two also that only exacerbates the conflict. He does not get to these two things, he does not trust us, I will extend. Amnesty only increases the problem. *L.A. Times* explains in 1993:

Amnesties can serve a purpose. Even this one—if it specifically declined to protect persons named in the commission's report—could help heal Salvador's nightmarish wounds. As it stands, the amnesty is ripping them wide open. (1AR#4)

Which is a net-turn on the counterplan, which means he doesn't get this risk analysis **<TIME>** that he said. Extend that there's no alternatives.

Second Negative Rebuttal: Jim Haefele

Our last round ever. We will win it on the case debate. There are two things that are certain: the first thing is for certain, because he flat concedes it, that Cristiani will not complete the purges. K.J. does not go there and he also concedes the purges are absolutely crucial to the peace process. Which means that there is no way they can solve. He does not answer it in the 1AR. The second thing you know is they will at least make some attempts to move towards due process to invoke their due process rights to move towards legal recourse which will disrupt the pro-peace process. Consequently, their argument, their plan, their UN implementation is far worse than the alternative, which I think is the counterplan. The Indian debate. On the top, extend their first answer which is the evidence is the sovereignty violation takes out the uniqueness which means that it's empirically denied. Also, he skips—claims it's a turn but, it's not unique because they would have to demonstrate some reason why they would go. Now, he skips down off the B-2 subpoint and says there's no internal link because they're not going to go to India next. Which I will concede. That proves that there's no turn to the position anymore because they're not going to go to India which means there's no reason why India would possibly perceive it. Now, self-determination: He can have his first answer which is true there is no internal link to the impact anymore. He says that there is no way El Salvador would spiral <FOUR> to Central Asia. Now, he reads a turn below that says they would stop responsiveness, but I'm not reading any generally self-determination impacts, only in Central Asia, which means that his last thing he says in the disads is there no snowball to Central Asia. Ultimately, there's no internal link from El Salvador, which means even if they solve self-determination there they don't solve it in Central Asia so there's no turns. The case. On the top: He—on the top of Observation Two—I will not deal with Observation One—the top of Observation Two he claims that withdrawal worse but, the counterplan would solve, will be debated—well, also I don't think that's true if we prove that not only but two things: first, if the UN can't solve because they won't complete the purges and second of all that the UN would make things worse by invoking the Truth Commission would cause military problems that would necessarily prove that the UN is a bad thing their implementation is not good. Now, on the Contention One debate, he says that there would be a lot worse and the UN has smoothed things. But remember they're not solving now—if they were right then their more recent evidence would not say that the UN's not doing anything that they're just not working which demonstrates that they're wrong about the claims that the UN is right. He says that there is still a comparative advantage but that's not true. Remember if they would increase the problem, that debate's happening below. He says he extends across <THREE> cards in 2AC that says it is the last kick of a dying man, but our evidence suggests that they're causing instability right now. It is critiquing what is exactly happening. Extend the two cards from March 25th that are read in 1AR alright the 1NR. I think we'll win the round on these two cards, the top two, they're awesome. The second one explains the military events decreasing. He says they're resigning now but the card says the people who are resigning aren't the ones who are being forced to resign. The people who are bad—the people who are resigning wanted to resign, the ones that backlash are not the ones who chose to—it's a different sector. The next thing is the military will resist UN efforts. From The *Times,* March 25th:

> Ponce offered his resignation March 12, three days before the commission report was released, and Zepeda was to have retired this month. But so far, Cristiani has not accepted the resignation of either man. In Tuesday night's broadcast, the military officers made clear that despite Cristiani's pledge to the United Nations, they would resist the commission's recommendations. (2NR#1)

Now read these two cards and the one that I just read at the end of the round. He says the resignation means there's no purge and the Truth Commission [unintelligible] we'll debate that below. He says resignation means there's no purge we don't need the purge anymore but that's not true. The evidence that we read says we do need a purge in order to have any solvency of the peace plan. He says there's no risk because withdrawal would equal <TWO> the purge. There's no ultimate impact, but remember the purge only creates a military backlash and causes more instability in the country. If you vote affirmative, your vote is supposedly creating stability in El Salvador. The problem is that the UN's only making it worse there's no reason to think they're effective. Now the next way that we will win the debate happens on the two cards about legal challenges. He says it's non-unique because 87 have been purged. The first answer is that they haven't solved completely. Remember, some people have been purged, but there's no explanation. Off the second answer, **<ONE AND A HALF>** our cards say the completion of the purge which means if that happens and it has to happen in order for them to solve then they can't win. The third argument is that they could be in the process. Remember, our evidence explains that eventually they will do it even if true the time frame is somewhat slow, eventually, they will derail the peace process. Which means there's ultimately no hope. Extend the Truth Commission is flawed. His last answer on the contention is to say that it will the Truth Commission will actually help democracy but extend it equals destabilization equals destabilization both from the 1NC and also the card that's read in the 1NR says it only equals more instability. Now, draw a line because everything else on Contention One is conceded, including all of the evidence that says Cristiani **<ONE>** will not allow the purges. No purge equals no peace. The government is ready to go, but will not have reform and Cristiani's not negotiating. K.J. flat concedes them I don't want to hear Jill talking about them. Remember this evidence says that the government, in order to have any peace if you want peace in El Salvador you must have the purge. But they concede the purge won't happen. They can't win. Contention Two: He says withdrawal of the UN is much worse and UN action is bad. First answer: remember we get we have oh, I'm sorry the first answer is gonna be amnesty would be [unintelligible] there's no evidence. Remember, we withdraw. He says that it would increase conflict we will debate that below. On the Observation Two, **<HALF>** he says that also remember the perm will not compete, that's the evidence we're making—the argument Greg's making. He says Cristiani—it's from Cristiani, but I think he's in the know he knows what the best thing for this country. Above and down, though, our evidence is not all Cristiani, it's assuming what's happening. He answers says that it makes the problem worse but extend equals national reconciliation. Also, it would stop unrest. Wilkinson in '93:

> "The hour to ask for mutual forgiveness, for whatever damage caused, has arrived," . . . a general amnesty will allow the report to produce "the fruits of reunification for which it was conceived." "An immediate, general and absolute amnesty . . . closes all the temptations of revenge and reprisal." (2NR#2)

He says that the UN ultimately is necessary to solve. Extend the last card that says it solves the reprisals **<TIME>** which means that it can solve any risk of the coup. Why vote for the UN? It just makes things worse.

Second Affirmative Rebuttal: Jill Baisinger

It'll go the same order. Jim wants you to vote on the assumption that somehow withdrawing the United Nations would be worse, but he doesn't have a single card that would indicate that fact. There is no card that makes the necessary internal link between the fact that while there may be destabilization in El Salvador now—he maybe absolutely correct—there is nothing that says things will be better, absent the UN there. There's not a single card that makes the internal link that he has to have to win this round. As it stands now, either the officers are resigning because of the Truth Commission which would, is the divining rod to get this the destabilization evidence you know the UN is the only hope and you know that the amnesty without the United Nations presence will only cause continued abuse. There are no answers to these arguments and he never tells you a compelling story on this stuff, I don't think. Now, he tells you three reasons to vote and I suppose I'd address those. He says Cristiani won't purge and that is his cards. First response, and most importantly: the resignation means that they don't have to have the purge—that is K.J.'s argument. The officers are resigning Ponce the officers they're talking about so upset is that he will resign. They are also [unintelligible] that other officers are resigning as well. Then he says due process will cause the risk but he is conceding that there's not going to be a coup; he is also conceding that there is not a risk to destabilization. He is also conceding that, I'll point this out, our card that the UN peace would be the best <FOUR> chance for solvency. Now, finally, he says the counterplan gets solvency, but he's not answering the fact that before you have workable amnesty you have to have UN pressure. There's no answer. I think we win the counterplan cold. I'm not sure what they're winning on case. Observation Two: He says the counterplan solve and that is not true withdrawal's not bad. Extend the Meisler evidence, that is really good evidence. It says that withdrawal before the programs are completed would only allow us to feel better while abuse continued in El Salvador. He is conceding this evidence. He says it's bad evidence, but there's no analysis why. There is no comparative card once again. This is the best comparative card in this round. It says withdrawal will be worse. Now he next says the United Nations can't solve, we shouldn't have them there. That's the incorrect analysis, it's not that they aren't solving completely you should throw them out. It's that we should allow them to stay there until they have a chance to complete their program. That is the evidence I read on top of Contention Two one and it says you must give them until 1994 in order to implement—this is also comparative evidence which he is not answering. Now, he says the Truth Commission is important. It's not a reason for you to vote, but that's not true. If the Truth Commission is actually destabilizing things, after it has been released by two weeks, that is a reason for the United Nations to be there. If every card they read is true, if you give them every single card, then it already is justification for the United Nations to remain there and make sure the abuses don't escalate or at least the outside world knows. There is no comparative advantage to removing the United Nations. Now, on top of Contention One. Again, same story. The United Nations is better than withdrawing. He says they're not solving now. First response, they are decreasing. Extend the *America's Watch* '92 card that I read in the 2AC and K.J.'s also extending. It says that they are the only force decreasing human rights abuses. That is the only chance you have to get solvency in El Salvador. This has been conceded. Now, on the next group, this is where he's arguing destabilization. Remember, the report is post-brink. It has already been issued. That is the reason why you want the United Nations to stay there. If these officers are really so upset and if they are really going to cause a coup, that is the reason why you want the United Nations in there in order to at least decrease the propensity of this happening. Now, he says that we increase problems, but his cards don't say that. That is the evidence that says things are worse because of the UN, which is what he has to have to win this round. Please extend K.J.'s number two. We postdate. We are reading March 26th and March 27th cards that say there's not going to be a coup. Now on the next, he says the instability now on March 25th. First response: read the cards—they're not that good. I think we are reading better analysis. But, independently, I will extend. There will not be a coup, the government will become more responsive. <TWO> From Tomlinson in '93, March 25th:

The government appears to be resisting fundamental reform. Without it, government critics say there is no guarantee of genuine democracy or any real safeguard against a resurgence of officially sanctioned political violence. The Communications Minister believes such fears are unfounded, because the far right has reformed its violently intolerant attitude to political opposition. (2AR#1)

Next response: the resignations are proof, they're not going to pur—have a coup, they're going to resign. Now, please extend K.J.'s number four. It says the middle officers won't allow the coup which takes out the propensity for his scenario. Now, he next says, off the Truth Commission, that they are different people and they will resist efforts, but they are the same people. **<ONE AND A HALF>** So Ponce, the Defense Minister resigned because the Truth Commission takes out the propensity for his coup. Now, he says read my cards. Fine, read mine, I think they're better. Now, he next says the resignation means he says it's not true, the resignation's irrelevant. Extend there's no need for purge there's a resignation. Independently, if there is instability, in either case you'll be going for the UN presence. Now, on the legal stuff. Group this together. He says they haven't solved completely, they can't do it and that the Truth Commission is flawed. All of this is post-brink, they've already issued it. None of this is a reason to pull the United Nations out. Because in the description of the status quo, not a reason to pull the UN out. Also extend K.J.'s last analysis, that they are shifting the balance of power to democracy. This is non-unique **<ONE>** they've already purged 87 officers. This should have occurred by now if there was going to be a risk. And they're conceding the card that says we can get the shift to democracy. Now on Contention Two. All he's going for is the counterplan. He says that the perm doesn't compete, but it certainly does, they're reading a card of evidence that says that we should have amnesty with the United Nations there. This is more truth than any of the evidence he is reading. Independently, his counterplan assumes the status quo. His cards say amnesty is good, not UN withdrawal. Now specifically, on the counterplan: He says Cristiani's a good source. But there's no reason to believe that. This man has a vested interest in maintaining the status quo. **<HALF>** But independently, please extend the original cards. That amnesty without pressure only exacerbates it, only exacerbates the problem. He says it causes national reconciliation, but extend it only increases the problem. It's just specific cards that they're not answering. If you have amnesty without forcing the United without allowing the United Nations in there to allow some sort of change you get a bigger risk of instability. Extend K.J.'s last argument, which they are conceding, that requires the United Nations to get solvency. Look, if they're right there is a risk to destabilization—that is only justification for the United Nations to stay in there. Their cards describe the status quo. You want the UN if you want to have any hope of solvency. **<TIME>**

Decision

Kansas State (Affirmative) won the debate on a 6-1 decision.

Evidence Used During the 1993 CEDA Final Round

1AC#1 Vincent, (1986). *Human Rights and International Relations.* New York: Cambridge University Press, p. 94.

1AC#2 Raymond (1992). [Unverified.]

1AC#3 DeSoto, A. (1992). *Is There a Transition to Democracy in El Salvador?* Boulder, CO: L. Rienner Publishers, p. 154.

1AC#4 Meza, R. M. (1992). *Is There a Transition to Democracy in El Salvador?* Boulder, CO: L. Rienner Publishers, p. 105.

1AC#5 DeSoto, A. (1992). *Is There a Transition to Democracy in El Salvador?* Boulder, CO: L. Rienner Publishers, p. 149.

1AC#6 Alder, D. (December 15, 1992). "El Salvador Celebrates Formal End to Civil War." The United Press International—BC Cycle.

1AC#7 Tulchin, J. & Bland, G. (1992). *Is There a Transition to Democracy in El Salvador?* Boulder, CO: L. Rienner Publishers, p. 5.

1AC#8 Bland, G. (1992). "Assessing the Transition to Democracy in El Salvador." In J. Tulchin & G. Bland, (Eds.), *Is There a Transition To Democracy in El Salvador?* Boulder, CO: L. Rienner Publishers, p. 163.

1AC#9 Meisler, S. (November 17, 1992). "UN Peacekeepers Face a Crisis of High Expectations." The *Los Angeles Times,* p. A1.

1AC#10 InterPress Service (November 24, 1992). "El Salvador: Human Rights Violations Continue, Says UN Report."

1AC#11 Wilkinson, T. (1992). "Salvador Military Awaits Probe." *Toronto Star,* p. A19.

1AC#12 Crocker, C.A. (December 20, 1992). "The Global Law and Order Deficit; Is the West Ready to Police the World's Bad Neighborhoods?" The *Washington Post,* p. C1.

1AC#13 InterPress Service (November 24, 1992). "El Salvador: Human Rights Violations Continue, Says UN Report."

1AC#14 Gibbs, T. (December 15, 1992). National Public Radio Transcript: "Morning Edition."

1AC#15 Meisler, S. (November 17, 1992). "UN Peacekeepers Face a Crisis of High Expectations." The *Los Angeles Times,* p. A1.

1AC#16 Constable, P. (March, 1993). "At War's End in El Salvador." *Current History* 92, p. 108.

1AC#17 *The Central American Update* (January 21, 1992). [Unverified.]

1AC#18 *America's Watch* (September 2, 1992). p. 5. [Unverified.]

1AC#19 Bland, G. (1992). "Assessing the Transition to Democracy in El Salvador." In J. Tulchin & G. Bland, (Eds.), *Is There a Transition to Democracy in El Salvador?* Boulder, CO: L. Rienner Publishers, p. 195.

1NC#1 Malik, J.M. (Winter, 1993). "India Copes with the Kremlin's Fall." *ORBIS* 37 (1), p. 69.

1NC#2 France Press Agency/Agence Presse France (December 8, 1992). "Restore Hope—Unified Facade on Right to Intervene."

1NC#3 Malik, J.M. (Winter, 1993). "India Copes with the Kremlin's Fall." *ORBIS* 37 (1), p. 82.

1NC#4 Fuller, G. (1991). *The Democracy Trap: The Perils of the Post-Cold War World.* New York: Dutton, p. 100.

1NC#5 Etzioni, A. (Winter, 1993). "The Evils of Self-Determination." *Foreign Policy,* p. 27.

1NC#6   Rumer, B. Z. (Winter, 1993). "The Gathering Storm in Central Asia." *ORBIS*, p. 90.

1NC#7   Gibbs, T. & Robinson, L. (November 23, 1992). "Saluting a New Day in El Salvador." *U.S. News & World Report* 113, p. 66.

1NC#8   Pilsbury (January 22, 1993). "The Future of El Salvador." (A Letter to the Editor.) *Christian Science Monitor*, p. 20.

1NC#9   Wilkinson (January 8, 1993). The *Los Angeles Times*.

1NC#10   *New York Times* (February 12, 1993). "El Salvador's Chief Dismisses Demand He Speed Army Purge." p. A6.

1NC#11   Christian, S. (January 12, 1993). "El Salvador Army Purge Violates UN Peace Accords, UN Chief Says." The *New York Times*, p. A6.

1NC#12   Wilkinson, T. (January 8, 1993). "Delayed Purge to Prevent Unrest, Salvador Chief Says." The *Los Angeles Times*, p. A6.

1NC#13   *Newsday* (March 17, 1993). "Salvador Report Hit." p. 14.

1NC#14   Constable, P. (March 16, 1993). "Salvadoran Report Raises Hopes of Reconciliation." The *Houston Chronicle*, p. A7.

1NC#15   Constable, P. (March 15, 1993). "UN Report Names Six Top Officers in Killing of Priests in Salvador." The *Boston Globe*, p. 1.

1NC#16   Sheppard, N. (March 16, 1993). "Salvadoran Leader Dismisses Report." The *Chicago Tribune*, p. N10.

1NC#17   Christian, S. (January 12, 1993). "El Salvador Army Purge Violates UN Peace Accords, UN Chief Says." The *New York Times*, p. A6.

1NC#18   Tomlinson, A. (March 25, 1993). "Amnesty in El Salvador Fails to Heal Wounds of War." National Public Radio Transcript: "All Things Considered." [Note that this card is identical to 2AR#1]

1NC#19   Wilkinson, T. (January 8, 1993). "Delayed Purge to Prevent Unrest, Salvador Chief Says." The *Los Angeles Times*, p. A6.

1NC#20   French, H. W. (March 15, 1993). "Salvadoran Leader Will Seek Amnesty in UN Human Rights Cases." The *New York Times*, p. A9.

1NC#21   French, H. W. (March 16, 1993). "In Salvador, Amnesty v. Punishment." The *New York Times*, p. A12.

1NC#22   Constable, P. (March 15, 1993). "UN Report Names Six Top Officers in Killing of Priests in Salvador." The *Boston Globe*, p. 1.

2AC#1   Crigler, F. (March 8, 1993). "Peacekeeping Task Demands Strong Hand." *Christian Science Monitor*, p. 19.

2AC#2   *America's Watch* (September 2, 1992). [Unverified.]

2AC#3   Cavarozzi, M. (October, 1992). "Beyond Transitions to Democracy in Latin America." *Journal of Latin American Studies* 24 (3), pp. 665–684.

2AC#4   *Xinhua General Overseas News Service* (September 17, 1992). "India Minister Talks on UN Peace Keeping Role."

2AC#5   BBC (April 27, 1992). "UN Secretary-General Meets Indian Foreign Secretary."

2AC#6   Wolfe, A. (June 7, 1992). "Superpower Blues." The *New York Times*, Sec. 7, p. 20.

2AC#7   Etzioni, A. (Winter, 1993). "The Evils of Self-Determination." *Foreign Policy,* pp. 31–2.

2AC#8   Robinson, L. (Fall, 1987). *SAIS Review.* [Unverified.]

2AC#9   *America's Watch* (September, 2, 1992). [Unverified.]

2AC#10   *Notimex Mexican News Service* (March 26, 1993). "Deputy Defense Minister Announces Resignation."

2AC#11   Wilkinson, T. (March 25, 1993). "Salvadoran Military Assails UN Report." The *Los Angeles Times,* p. A6.

2AC#12   Murray, K. (March 26, 1993). "Salvadoran Army Chiefs Pressure Cristiani on Purge." *Reuters.*

2AC#13   Wilkinson, T. (January 12, 1993). "Purge of Salvadoran Officers Fails to Punish 15, UN Says." The *Los Angeles Times,* p. A10.

2AC#14   *Reuters* (March 15, 1993). "El Salvador Awaits Crucial UN Report on Massacres."

2AC#15   The *Los Angeles Times* (March 22, 1993). "Avoiding the Road Back to Bloodshed." p. B6. [Note that this card is the exact same as 1AR#4.]

2AC#16   French, H. (March 22, 1993). "Amnesty in Salvador Denounced as Against Spirit of Peace Pact." The *New York Times,* p. A2.

2NC#1   Constable, P. (March, 1993). "At War's End in El Salvador." *Current History* 92, p. 108.

2NC#2   Posner, M. (February 18, 1993). "Here and There: Human Rights Should Be a Common Concern." *International Herald Tribune.*

2NC#3   Zorroli, J. (November 28, 1992). "Somalia: UN Examines US Offer of Troops." National Public Radio Transcript: "Weekend Edition."

2NC#4   Stasi, A. (December 24, 1992). "Charity in Somalia." *Newsday,* p. 48.

2NC#5   *Japan Economic Newswire* (January 2, 1993). "Kashmir Situation Improves, Says Indian Army Officer."

2NC#6   UPI (October 24, 1992). "India Calls for Major Reforms."

2NC#7   Ganguly, S. (October, 1992). "South Asia after the Cold War." *The Washington Quarterly* 15, p. 173.

2NC#8   Warnke (June 17, 1992). "As Bush, Yeltsin Meet, Do Nuclear Treaties Still Matter?" *USA Today,* p. 13A.

2NC#9   *The Middle East News Network* (March 3, 1993). "Comments on CIA Chief Remarks on Nuclear Issue."

2NC#10   *The Asian Bulletin* in '91: [Unverified.]

2NC#11   Gurgel (Winter 91-92). *Harvard International Review.*

2NC#12   Fuller, G. (1991). *The Democracy Trap: The Perils of the Post-Cold War World.* New York: Dutton, p. 3.

2NC#13   Barowiec, A. (October 21, 1992). "Central Asia Republics Ripe for Nuclear Expansion." *Washington Times,* p. A7.

2NC#14   Rumer, B. Z. (Winter, 1993). "The Gathering Storm in Central Asia." *ORBIS,* p. 90.

1NR#1   Sheppard, N. (March 16, 1993). "Salvadoran Leader Dismisses Report." The *Chicago Tribune,* p. N10.

1NR#2   Wilkinson, T. (March 25, 1993). "Salvadoran Military Assails UN Report." The *Los Angeles Times,* p. A6. [Card identified in round and on brief as being from The *Times.*]

1NR#3   Wilkinson, T. (March 25, 1993). "Salvadoran Military Assails UN Report." The *Los Angeles Times,* p. A6. [Card identified in round and on brief as being from The *Times.*]

1NR#4   Christian, S. (January 12, 1993). "El Salvador Army Purge Violates UN Peace Accords, UN Chief Says." The *New York Times,* p. A6.

1NR#5   Constable, P. (March 15, 1993). "UN Report Names Six Top Officers in Killing of Priests in Salvador." The *Boston Globe,* p. 1.

1AR#1   Etzioni, A. (Winter, 1993). "The Evils of Self-Determination." *Foreign Policy,* p. 25.

1AR#2   *The Independent* (March 26, 1993). "In Brief: Officer to Quit Over War Crimes." p. 12.

1AR#3   *Notimex Mexican News Service* (March 26, 1993). "Deputy Defense Minister Announces Resignation."

1AR#4   The *Los Angeles Times* (March 22, 1993). "Avoiding the Road Back to Bloodshed." p. B6.

2NR#1   Wilkinson, T. (March 25, 1993). "Salvadoran Military Assails UN Report." The *Los Angeles Times,* p. A6. [Card identified in round and on brief as being from The *Times.*]

2NR#2   Meisler, S. & Wilkinson, T. (March 15, 1993). "UN Report Condemns Prominent Salvadorans." The *Los Angeles Times,* p. A1.

2AR#1   Tomlinson, A. (March 25, 1993). "Amnesty in El Salvador Fails to Heal Wounds of War." National Public Radio Transcript: "All Things Considered."

Glossary

abstraction The notion that as one's language becomes more general (less concrete) there is greater opportunity for confusion and obfuscation. For example, "writing implement" is more abstract than "pen."

ad hominem A false attack on an advocate rather than the advocate's argument. This is a fallacy of reasoning in which an individual offers criticism of an advocate as the grounds for rejecting the arguments of the advocate. It is considered a fallacy because the attacks on the advocate may have nothing to do with the wisdom of the arguments.

adjacency pairs Two statements that occur one right after the other and that are defined by their relationship to each other.

ad populum A false appeal to the people. This is a fallacy of reasoning in which an advocate offers the agreement of most people as the grounds for a claim. It is considered a fallacy because the majority may be wrong.

adversarial A system of interactions that pits advocates against each other as opponents in order to test the quality and credibility of their claims.

affirmative The side in an academic debate that advocates support for the resolution.

ambiguity The deliberate use of overly broad or unclear language to confuse or conceal an advocate's real thoughts.

analysis The separation of a claim into its constituent parts for individual study.

appeal to fear A false appeal to the need for safety. This is a fallacy of reasoning in which an advocate offers a threat as the grounds for compliance with a demand. It is considered a fallacy because the threat of force denies the audience any real choice.

appeal to pity A false appeal for sympathy. This is a fallacy of reasoning in which an advocate offers a request for sympathy as the grounds for a claim. It is considered a fallacy because the request for pity may have nothing to do with the wisdom of a claim.

appeal to tradition A false appeal to the way things have historically been done. This is a fallacy of reasoning in which the advocate offers a history of behavior as the grounds for continuing to act in a particular manner. It is considered a fallacy because previous ways of doing things may not justify doing things the same way in the future.

arguing The process of resolving differences of opinion through communication.

argumentative metaphor The epistemic function of metaphor. A linguistic device in which an advocate contends that phenomenon "A" should be seen as phenomenon "B."

argument by analogy A form of inference suggesting that if two things are alike in some respects they will also be alike in other respects.

argument by example A claim that examines one or more specific cases and then generalizes to other like or similar cases.

argument from causal correlation An argument that examines specific cases to identify a pattern of relationships between them that will permit a more general inference to be drawn.

argument from causal generalization A claim that reasons deductively from a general claim that is presumed to be true to a specific case that is unknown.

argument from sign   A claim that identifies a substance and attribute relationship between a generalization and a specific case.

arguments   The claims that people make when they are asserting their opinions and/or supporting their beliefs.

argument style   The manner in which one conducts himself or herself in an argument. Some arguers are passive and some are active.

artistic proof   Support or grounds for a claim that originates with the advocate.

audience   The readers, bearers, or viewers reached by a speaker, a book, a broadcast, or some other form of communication.

backing   The support for an argumentative warrant.

begging the question   A fallacy of reasoning in which the advocate offers a restatement of the claim as the grounds for the claim. It is considered a fallacy because the advocate has not offered new information that constitutes support for the claim.

better definition standard   A means used in academic debate to determine which definition, when there are competing definitions, should be used to interpret the resolution.

blame   The reason or cause for the existence of an ill; sometimes referred to as the inherent need.

brink   An element of a disadvantage. The argument that the present system is on a precipice and that the proposed action will push the system over the edge and into an undesirable consequence.

breadth standard   An argument in academic debate concerning the means used to determine the better definition of terms in the resolution. For example, debaters may argue that broader resolutions are preferable and thus, the better definition is the one that provides the broadest interpretation.

burden of proof   The understanding that whoever advances an argumentative claim has the responsibility to provide evidentiary support for it. In academic debate, this refers to the expectation that the affirmative has the obligation to prove the resolution true.

case flow   That part of the systematic note-taking process in academic debate in which the arguments dealing with the affirmative case are recorded.

character   The ethical integrity and personal qualities of a speaker or an actor in a story. A social actor in a story.

characterological coherence   The ability of an actor in a story to act out his or her role in accordance with the audience's expectations for that role.

character type   The function the actor plays in an argument, for example, hero, villain, or victim.

circumvention   An argument claiming that a proposal will not work because there exists a motive and a means for individuals to get around the intent of the proposal.

civil   Pertains to the rights of individuals and to legal proceedings concerning those rights.

claim   A conclusion of an argument.

coalitions   Alliances of factions.

comparative advantage case   A set of arguments through which an advocate demonstrates that there is an advantage to the adoption of the advocated policy when that policy is compared to the present system.

competence   A component of credibility. An audience's assessment of the capability and ability of a source to make a specific observation or judgment.

competitiveness   A standard in academic debate for whether or not a counterplan should be accepted instead of the affirmative plan, whether or not the counterplan constitutes a reason to reject the resolution.

compromise A settlement of differences. An accommodation reached between competing interests.

conclusion The claim advanced in a syllogism.

conflict resolution Tactics or strategies introduced to resolve problems and reduce tensions.

connotative meaning The unique meaning given a symbol or word by an individual. The emotional or attitudinal meaning evoked in an individual by a symbol or word.

constructive speech The speeches in an academic debate in which the debaters present the major arguments they will pursue in the debate.

context standard An argument in academic debate concerning the means used to determine the better definition of terms in the resolution. The view that the better definition takes into consideration the other words in the resolution.

cost The burdens or disadvantages that will be incurred if the proposed cure is enacted.

counterplan A plan advanced in academic debate by the negative as a replacement for the plan offered by the affirmative. It must be competitive and non-topical.

credibility The audience's assessment of the competence and trustworthiness of a source.

criminal Pertains to the administration of penal law as distinct from civil law.

criteria The method in a value debate for determining the value judgment contained in the value resolution.

criteria case A set of arguments through which an advocate demonstrates that the advocated policy is superior to alternatives because it better achieves a specified standard or standards.

cross-examination Close questioning in order to compare the answers given to previous answers. Used to refute or discredit an adversary's case in the courtroom and to resolve questions and clarify information in academic debates.

cultural knowledge Those things we know to be true because we have been taught they are true by our culture. The shared values and truths codified in the rules, principles, laws, or practices adhered to by a culture. The values and truths contained in the stories shared by the members of a culture.

cure The proposed solution for resolving an ill or harm.

debate format The nature of speeches. The speaking order and the time limits of each speech in the specialized argumentative field of academic debate.

deductive reasoning Claims that entail moving from the general to the specific.

denotative meaning The explicitly shared understanding of a symbol or word such as that found in a dictionary.

descriptive statistics Numeric representations that describe an entire population.

descriptive testimony Grounds for a claim that relate the observation of supposedly factual (verifiable) information.

direct examination Close questioning in order to solicit answers that will be helpful to support the development of your own case.

disadvantage An argument advanced in an academic debate in which the advocate claims that undesirable consequences will result from a particular course of action.

discovery That part of the investigation of a legal case that focuses on finding the "facts" that are relevant to the claim being advanced.

doublespeak A pernicious use of euphemistic language to confuse or conceal an advocate's views.

empathic listening The capacity for listening sympathetically. Trying to understand or experience by relating to the problems of others.

epistemic function of language The concept that the language we learn and employ shapes and constrains our understanding of what constitutes reality.

equivocation The use of language with multiple meanings to conceal an advocate's actual views.

ethics A set of moral principles or values. The moral quality of conduct and discourse.

euphemism The use of mild or inoffensive language in the place of language that might offend or suggest something that is unpleasant.

events The actions engaged in by the characters in a story.

examples Specific instances or occurrences of a given phenomenon used as the grounds for a claim.

external consistency A test of the grounds for a claim. Is the testimony offered in support of a claim in agreement with the testimony of others?

fallacy of composition A fallacy of reasoning in which an advocate argues that what is true of a part is true of the whole. It is considered a fallacy because a whole may or may not possess the qualities of the individual parts.

fallacy of division A fallacy of reasoning in which an advocate argues that what is true of the whole is true of the component parts. It is considered a fallacy because a component may or may not possess the qualities of the whole.

false dichotomy A fallacy of reasoning in which an advocate falsely divides the situation into only two alternatives. It is considered a fallacy because there may be other alternatives in addition to the two indicated by the advocate.

fiat The assumption in academic debate that an affirmative need only demonstrate that a proposal ought to be adopted, not that it would be adopted. The assumption that the plan in an academic debate would be adopted by normal means if it is proven desirable and that, therefore, the focus of the debate should be on the desirability of the proposal, not on whether the proposal would actually be adopted.

field definitions An argument in academic debate concerning the means used to determine the better definition of terms in the resolution. The view that the better definition is the one used by members of the appropriate field.

fields Areas of human activity or interest. Topics or specializations of study.

flowing The systematic process of note-taking in academic debate.

future narratives Scenarios, hopes, dreams, or expectations for tomorrow.

general sources References that provide a broad understanding of a controversy. References that require little prior knowledge of a controversy.

generative capability of metaphor The ability of an audience to infer additional similarities between the two phenomena linked in an argumentative metaphor.

goals case A set of arguments through which an advocate demonstrates that the advocated policy has a better chance of achieving a present system goal than do the policies of the present system.

grounds The foundation or basis for a claim.

historical narratives Scenarios, plot-lines, and accounts of events that have already occurred.

hypothesis-testing paradigm The academic debate judging perspective in which the judge views the resolution as a hypothesis for testing in the debate context.

ill The harm or problems identified in the present system.

image A concept or mental picture of someone that is held by the public.

impact The consequence of any given argument on the resolution of the dispute. In academic debate, the effect of the argument on the outcome of the debate.

inartistic proof   Support or grounds for a claim that originates with someone other than the advocate.

inductive reasoning   Claims that entail moving from a specific case to more general conclusions.

inferential statistics   Numeric representations that describe a sample of a population and infer that what is true of the sample is true of the population.

internal consistency   A test of the grounds for a claim. Is the testimony offered as grounds for a claim free from self-contradiction?

interpretive testimony   Grounds for a claim that relate the judgments of the advocate or a source provided by the advocate.

interval sampling   A technique used by researchers to ensure each member of a population has an equal and independent probability of being selected. The selection of members of a population at a given interval.

intrinsicness   An argument in academic debate that the value object possesses inherent qualities that are causally related to the value judgment.

jargon   The specialized or technical language of a profession, trade, or class.

judging paradigm   The lens through which a judge views an academic debate. The judge's perspective of the debate experience that guides what burdens the judge considers important.

justification   A procedural argument in academic debate similar to topicality. A negative argument that the affirmative has not provided sufficient rationale to believe that the resolution, in its entirety, is true.

language   A shared symbol system.

limiting standard   An argument in academic debate concerning the means used to determine the better definition of terms in the resolution. The view that the better definition is the one that narrows the focus of the resolution.

Lincoln-Douglas debate   A debate format in which two individuals debate each other.

linear   An element of a disadvantage. The argument that the proposed action will move the present system some distance down a path, and that each step in that direction is undesirable.

link   An element of a disadvantage. The requirement that there must be a causal relationship between the proposed action and the resulting disadvantageous consequence.

loaded question   A question that indicates to a witness how he or she should answer the question.

major premise   The first statement provided in a syllogism. Typically, the major premise asserts a generalization that prescribes the category.

margin of error   The acknowledgment by opinion poll researchers that their statistics are not precise, but occur within a range of plus or minus the specified error from the indicated statistic.

minor premise   The second statement that is asserted in a syllogism. Typically, the minor premise relates a specific case or class.

modality   The degree of certainty that an advocate has for a claim.

multistage sampling   A technique whereby researchers randomly select a group or subset of the population and then randomly select from the members of the subset.

mutual exclusivity   One of the two tests of counterplan competitiveness in academic debate. To be a reason to reject the resolution, the counterplan must be unable to coexist with the plan.

myths   Real or fictional stories that appeal to the consciousness of a people by appealing to their cultural ideals.

narrative Having the characteristics of a story. Accounts that contain elements of a developing plot-line.

narrative fidelity The degree to which a story "rings true" with experiences or with other stories that are believed or known to be true.

narrative perspective An academic debate judging perspective in which the judge views the debate as competing stories.

narrative probability How believable a story is; how coherent it seems to be.

needs case A set of arguments through which an advocate demonstrates there is a problem in the present system that justifies the adoption of the advocated policy.

negative The side in an academic debate that advocates rejection of the resolution.

net benefits standard One of the two tests of counterplan competitiveness in academic debate. To be a reason to reject the resolution, the counterplan must be more advantageous than the affirmative plan or both the affirmative plan and the counterplan.

non sequitur Any claim that "does not follow" from the grounds offered in support of the claim.

obfuscation A deliberate attempt by an advocate to conceal his or her real argument.

objective facts Facts that are knowable and uncontested.

obvious truths Generalizations that are commonly shared and understood.

off-case flow That part of the systematic note-taking process in academic debate in which the procedural arguments and the disadvantages are recorded.

operational definitions Methods of defining terms in academic debate in which terms are not explicitly defined but can be derived from the totality of the arguments advanced.

organizational culture The values, norms, and practices that characterize an institution.

ornamental metaphor A figure of speech in which the advocate asks an audience to see that phenomenon "A" has some characteristic of phenomenon "B."

overreporting A problem in the statistical description of a phenomenon caused by incentives to report the specific instances of the phenomenon.

parametrics An aspect of procedural arguments in academic debate. The argument claims that an affirmative case does not need to prove the whole resolution is true: rather, the resolution merely serves to set the boundaries for what is or is not topical.

parliamentary debate A debate format that is modeled after debate in the British Houses of Parliament.

permutation A tactic in academic debate used by an affirmative to show that a counterplan is only artificially competitive.

personal knowledge That which we know to be true because we have had firsthand experience with it.

plan spikes Elements in an academic debate of an affirmative plan that are incorporated to preclude disadvantages of counterplans.

policy debate A type of academic debate in which the resolution calls for a plan of action that changes the present system.

policy-making paradigm An academic debate judging perspective predicated on general systems theory in which the judge compares competing policy systems.

power The ability or capacity to act. The influence or control that one has over others.

precedent A judicial decision that may be used as a standard in deciding other similar cases.

precision standard An argument in academic debate concerning the means used to determine the better definition of terms in the resolution. The view that the better definition is the one more specific or concrete.

premise   Grounds for a claim that makes use of points of agreement between advocates and audiences.

presence   The strategy of making an argument or a claim seem especially noteworthy or important so that it is clearly understood and deemed significant by the audience.

presumption   The belief that most people, most of the time, are comfortable with the way things are. The belief that current positions and/or policies should continue until a good reason is presented for change.

prima facie case   The obligation in academic debate of the advocate affirming the resolution to present a story which, on its first hearing, would meet the burdens necessary to persuade a reasonable audience that the resolution is true. A set of arguments that are sufficient to overcome presumption.

procedural arguments   The arguments in an academic debate that must be resolved by the judge prior to consideration of the substantive issues. The arguments that determine the process by which the truth of the resolution will be determined.

proposition   A statement that expresses the subject and defines the grounds for dispute.

proposition of fact   A statement that asserts a claim known as a certainty.

proposition of policy   A statement that outlines a specific course of action.

proposition of value   A statement that asserts a principle, standard, or moral claim.

random sample   A subset of a population where each member of the population has an equal and independent probability of being selected.

reasonable doubt   Rational uncertainty.

rebuttal   The exceptions that might be offered to a claim. The opportunity to refute arguments previously offered by one's opponent in a debate.

recency   A test of the grounds for a claim. Has anything happened between the date of the testimony and the time the testimony is used by an advocate that would make the testimony invalid?

reducing to absurdity   One of the strategies of refutation by additional consideration in which the reasoning behind the argument to be refuted is taken to its logical and undesirable conclusion. Known by its Latin name *reductio ad absurdum*.

refutation by additional consideration   The strategy of refutation in which the advocate argues that the arguments of another do not take into consideration the complete picture. The process in which an argument is rebutted by showing that the outcome of accepting the argument is not desirable.

refutation by denial   The strategy of refutation in which the advocate attempts to prove that the claims offered by another are erroneous. The process in which an argument is rebutted by denying the validity of the argument.

refutation by mitigation   The strategy of refutation in which the advocate attempts to minimize the importance of another's arguments. The process in which the strength of an argument is reduced by counterarguments.

refutation process   A series of actions that culminate in the denial of the arguments advanced by another advocate.

reluctant testimony   Observations or judgment given grudgingly by a source because the testimony is contrary to the best interests of the source.

research   The supplementation of one's own knowledge with the facts and opinions of others.

research plan   A strategy for determining what additional information is needed and the best way to obtain it.

resistance   That force exerted to oppose or retard movement or change.

resolution   Another name for the proposition. The proposition used in academic debate.

reverse voting issue An argument presented by an affirmative in response to a topicality argument, claiming that the issue of topicality should be a voting issue for the negative as well as the affirmative in order to discourage frivolous topicality arguments.

rituals Behaviors that have been repeated so often that the participants come to know and expect the performance of these behaviors.

role Sets of assumptions about how individuals or characters should act based on perceptions of an individual's position, occupation, behavior, and/or status.

scene The images constructed by an advocate that describe the context in which the characters act.

self-esteem One's sense of self, self-concept, and sense of personal worth.

shifting the burden of proof A fallacy of reasoning in which the advocate challenges another to refute his or her argument rather than offer grounds in support of the claim. It is considered a fallacy because each advocate has the burden of proving his or her own claim.

should/would argument To dispute in academic debate whether the plan would be adopted, rather than whether it should be adopted. This is considered an illegitimate argument in academic debate because of fiat power.

simple random sampling A technique used by researchers to ensure each member of a population has an equal and independent probability of being selected. The use of a random numbers table to generate a statistical sample.

slippery slope A false appeal to the inevitability of an undesirable outcome if a first step is taken. This is a fallacy of reasoning in which the advocate argues that an action should not be taken because it will eventually lead to some unwanted end. It is considered a fallacy because one action does not necessarily lead to subsequent actions.

solvency The affirmative burden in academic debate to demonstrate that the proposed course of action will actually accrue the advantages claimed. The stock issue of cure.

specialized sources References that give a detailed understanding of an aspect of, or a particular side of, a controversy. References targeting audiences that generally already possess background information on a controversy.

standards The method to be used in academic debate for determining how an issue should be evaluated. Criteria for determining the issue of topicality.

stasis The issue or point where one chooses to clash with or challenge a claim.

statistics Grounds for a claim in which descriptions are expressed in numeric terms.

stock issues Arguments that naturally recur in disputes over propositions of policy. Topicality, ill, blame, cure, and cost are stock issues.

stock issues paradigm The judging perspective in academic debate where the judge expects the affirmative and negative to clash over the stock issues.

stories Accounts of events; the plot; an allegation of the facts.

storytelling The process of sharing accounts or stories.

stratified sampling A technique used by researchers to generate a sample in which the researchers divide the population into groups or strata that they want to sample. A random sample is then generated for each strata.

straw man fallacy A fallacy of reasoning in which an advocate presents a weak argument of an opponent and, in refuting it, characterizes all of the opposing arguments as equally spurious. It is considered a fallacy because the advocate may perniciously select a particularly inadequate argument to refute.

substantive arguments The arguments in an academic debate that deal with the truth of the resolution.

syllogism   A form of deductive reasoning that consists of a major premise, a minor premise, and a conclusion.

symbols   Special types of signs that represent something by association. The building blocks of a language system.

systems analysis   The evaluation of a group of interacting, interrelated and interdependent elements. A consideration of how these elements function together to achieve an outcome.

tabula rasa paradigm   The academic debate judging perspective in which the judge attempts to approach the debate as a blank slate enabling the debaters to determine how the judge should evaluate the debate.

take out   An argument of refutation in academic debate that breaks, or takes out, a link in the chain of reasoning.

testimony   Grounds for a claim that makes use of the observations and/or judgments made by the advocate or a source cited by the advocate.

theory of the case   A view of the dispute that accounts for the evidence and offers an explanation for the events that occurred.

time frame   A test of statistics that considers the time period described by the statistics. An element of a disadvantage concerning when the adverse consequences of a course of action will occur.

topicality   An obligation in an academic debate that the affirmative's arguments prove the specific resolution true. A negative debater who believed the affirmative was proving a different resolution true would challenge the affirmative's topicality.

Toulmin model   An argument diagram developed by Stephen Toulmin. This model dissects an argument into its constituent parts to reveal the reasoning process.

trustworthiness   A component of credibility. An audience's assessment of the integrity of a source.

tu quoque   Literally "you're another." The fallacy of reasoning in which an advocate defends his or her actions by pointing out that others acted in a similar fashion. It is considered a fallacy because the actions of others are frequently irrelevant to whether or not one's actions are responsible.

turnaround   An argument in academic debate in which a debater argues that a disadvantage is actually an advantage, or vice versa. Also known in non-debate contexts as turning the tables.

turning the tables   One of the strategies of refutation by additional consideration in which the advocate argues that the undesirable consequences identified by another advocate are actually desirable.

underreporting   A problem in the statistical description of a phenomenon caused by disincentives to reporting or announcing the specific instances of the phenomenon.

unique meaning standard   An argument in academic debate concerning the means used to determine the better definition of terms in the resolution. The view that the better definition is the one that does not render a word in the resolution meaningless.

uniqueness   An element of a disadvantage. The requirement that the proposed action must be the sole cause of the identified disadvantageous consequence.

universal audience   An abstract audience created by an arguer as a reference point for testing one's argumentative claims. Arguments appealing to a universal audience would be compelling, self-evident, timeless, and independent of local or historical contingencies.

value debate   A type of academic debate in which the resolution calls for a change in the value structure of the status quo.

value objection An argument in a value debate claiming that the value or value hierarchy presented should be rejected because it is an undesirable value or value hierarchy.

values Principles, standards, or qualities that are considered to be important.

verbal aggression The tendency to attack one's opponent in an argument by using very confrontational and personal arguments.

verifiability A test of grounds for a claim. Is the source offered as the grounds for a claim properly identified and available to all?

violation A component of a topicality argument. This argument identifies the specific term in the resolution that the negative believes the affirmative has misinterpreted.

visual aids Charts, graphs, photos, and other material that helps to pictorially communicate information.

warrant The reasoning that authorizes the inferential leap from the grounds to the claim.

whole resolution An argument in academic debate that the affirmative must prove the truth of the entire resolution, not just an example or examples of the resolution.

Index

295